THE SAFEST SHIELD

This selection of lectures, essays and speeches by Lord Judge, nearly all written when he was Lord Chief Justice of England and Wales, brings together his analysis of a wide range of topics which underpin the administration of justice and the rule of law. Apart from a few personal reflections, the discussion ranges from the development of our constitutional arrangements to matters of continuing constitutional uncertainty, with observations about different aspects of the court process and the discharge of judicial responsibilities. Based on Lord Judge's experience in the law and deep interest in history, this selection offers sometimes uncomfortable, sometimes amusing, but always stimulating reading, and will provoke thoughtful reflection on and better understanding of the arrangements by which we are governed and the practical application of the rule of law.

The Safest Shield

Lectures, Speeches and Essays

Lord Judge

·HART·
PUBLISHING
OXFORD AND PORTLAND, OREGON
2015

Published in the United Kingdom by Hart Publishing Ltd
16C Worcester Place, Oxford, OX1 2JW
Telephone: +44 (0)1865 517530
Fax: +44 (0)1865 510710
E-mail: mail@hartpub.co.uk
Website: http://www.hartpub.co.uk

Published in North America (US and Canada) by
Hart Publishing
c/o International Specialized Book Services
920 NE 58th Avenue, Suite 300
Portland, OR 97213-3786
USA
Tel: +1 503 287 3093 or toll-free: (1) 800 944 6190
Fax: +1 503 280 8832
E-mail: orders@isbs.com
Website: http://www.isbs.com

© Lord Judge 2015

Reprinted in 2016

Hart Publishing is an imprint of Bloomsbury Publishing plc.

British Library Cataloguing in Publication Data
Data Available

Library of Congress Cataloging-in-Publication Data

Judge, Igor, 1941–   author.
[Essays. Selections]
The safest shield: lectures, speeches and essays / Lord Judge.
pages cm
ISBN 978-1-5099-0189-0 (hardback : alk. paper)
1. Law—England. 2. Law—England—History.   I. Title.
KD358.J83J83 2015   349.42—dc23
2015035225

ISBN: 978-1-50990-189-0

Typeset by Compuscript Ltd, Shannon
Printed and bound in Great Britain by
TJ International Ltd, Padstow, Cornwall

To Judith
Sine Amore Nihil

Preface

Sir Edward Coke was the Chief Justice who was dismissed and ended up in the Tower of London as a result of his obstinate refusal to see his responsibilities in quite the same way as King James I.

On the day of his appointment as Chief Justice of the Common Pleas in 1606, in accordance with tradition, he was first admitted as a Serjeant-at-Law. Rings inscribed with the words '*Lex est tutissima cassis*' were distributed as part of the celebrations, but there was insufficient space for the saying to be inscribed in full. It continues, '*sub clypeo legis nemo decipitur*'. Translated, the full text reads, 'The law is the safest helmet; under the shield of the law no one is deceived.' Not a man always able to resist the temptation to use ten words when five would do, perhaps as an amplification, perhaps simply by way of emphasis, Coke later wrote in the Second Part of his *Institutes of the Laws of England*, 'the law is the safest sanctuary that a man can take, and the strongest fortress to protect the weakest of all; *lex est tutissima cassis; sub clypeo legis nemo decipitur*'. In summary, therefore, 'the law is the safest shield'. Many commentators describe this brief phrase as Coke's motto.

In the early seventeenth century the term 'rule of law' was understood to identify a defined legal principle—what we should call a rule. As far as I can discover, the concept of the rule of law in its more important, modern sense made its first appearance a few years after Coke's appointment as Chief Justice. It is found in the text of the Petition of Grievances of the House of Commons. From everything we know about Coke's life after he became a judge, reinforced by his removal from office, what he wrote in his *Institutes* about the law as a sanctuary and a fortress was intended to convey this newly developing meaning and what we now recognise as a defining hallmark of our unwritten constitution.

The rule of law is indeed our safest shield.

Acknowledgements

It would be invidious and utterly impossible for me to attempt to recall the innumerable people with whom I had conversations or the writings which have influenced my thinking and led me to the opinions expressed in this collection. That said, I should like to highlight the phenomenal advantage of a childhood cocooned in love and familial security. At home my parents relished the exchange and discussion of ideas and knowledge and events (without always agreeing with each other) and instilled in me the importance of acknowledging the value of different opinions, and evaluating them by thinking for myself.

Beyond that crucial early influence I simply acknowledge that throughout all our lives what we read and hear from others inevitably impacts on our thinking, and the way in which our thinking develops and changes.

The idea behind the publication of this book, together with much encouragement, was given to me by Bill Asquith, the Commissioning Editor of Hart Publishing, who were good enough to publish *Magna Carta Uncovered*, which I co-authored with Anthony Arlidge QC. The Managing Editor, Mel Hamill, leads a remarkable team in Hart's quiet office in Worcester Place, Oxford. Help, guidance and humour have been the hallmarks of all their dealings with me.

My last word of grateful acknowledgement goes to Glenys McDonald MBE, my clerk during my last years as Lord Chief Justice. Without her constant patience, loyal support and commitment, this book would have remained forever in the process of preparation.

* * *

The author and publishers thank the British Library Board for permission to reproduce the image of a section of the Dering Roll on the jacket.

While every care has been taken to establish and acknowledge copyright, and to contact copyright owners, the publishers apologise for any accidental infringement of copyright.

Contents

The Judiciary

Personal Reflections

Introduction

IF, ENJOYING THE happy treat of browsing in a bookshop, you should happen to pick up this book, you will soon discover that although from time to time it includes references to events during my life, this is not an autobiography. Equally, it does not contain any devastating accounts of any confidential discussions with ministers and officials that took place when I held judicial office.

Everything you read here has been spoken publicly or published on an earlier occasion. There is virtually nothing new. 'Virtually' is written deliberately. The lectures and speeches were delivered to live audiences. Therefore the texts were never read out, nor repeated verbatim. The reaction of my audiences determined the extent to which I would depart from the written text. On occasion humour would be introduced, or an aside or two, or an anecdote inserted to add emphasis, and sections or sentences (sometimes, if time became pressing, even paragraphs) would be omitted. Unless a transcript was being made, the new words did not insert themselves into the text, and words which were omitted did not remove themselves from it. As suggested in 'The Art of Advocacy',[1] my objective was to maintain the interest of my audience. These were not judgments. The delivery of lectures, even on legal and historic topics, requires an element of passion and energy—if you like, oratory. These elements, necessary for the spoken word, do not leap from the printed page.

The content was always entirely my own. I never used a scriptwriter, and none of these lectures started out with the preparation of a preliminary text by an assistant. When a lecture or speech was imminent I would allow ideas to bubble about in my head, but I very rarely got down to the actual preparation until a day or two beforehand—most frequently indeed, until the evening before delivery. This approach partly reflected the pressures of time, but it also had the advantage that the very process of writing at the last minute embedded my thoughts in my head for long enough for me to address the audience rather than read aloud to it. I particularly recall the anxiety of those running the Commonwealth Law

---

[1] This volume, p 183.

Conferences in Hong Kong and Cape Town where I was to give the final keynote addresses.[2] There was much consternation at the absence of any texts at the beginning of the conferences, and—even worse—the night before the lectures were delivered. The assurances of my wife, Judith, that there was no need for anyone to be worried were greeted with polite scepticism.

These lectures were delivered on specific occasions to particular audiences. The publication of a selection of them was never envisaged. To provide me with at least one supporter in the audience, Judith came to every lecture, and as time went by, she spoke of her hope that they would be collected together. We did nothing about it ourselves until Bill Asquith raised the idea. Thereafter, in making the selection of works to be included in the book, I sought to provide a level of coherence which would certainly not have been apparent at the time the individual lectures were given.

I have largely omitted many talks designed to improve the efficiency of the administration of justice which either led to improvements or have since been overtaken. I have instead focused on broader issues which seem to me to affect the community as a whole. The problems that face trial by jury,[3] the difficulties encountered by child witnesses,[4] and the social impact of the sentencing decision[5] are not confined to legal practitioners or the operation of the court system. The historic development of our constitutional arrangements—beginning with Magna Carta[6] and continuing to current questions about the sovereignty of Parliament, and the relationship between the United Kingdom and Europe[7] and the constitutional imperatives of an independent judiciary and an independent press[8]—have, and will continue to have, a societal impact. The true extent of what are usually compendiously summarised as human rights,[9] and their ambit in relation, for example, to the possible decriminalisation of assisted suicide[10] concern us all.

---

[2] Respectively in this volume 'Judicial Independence and Responsibilities' (p 273) and 'Equality before the Law' (p 123).

[3] See 'Trial by Jury', this volume, p 198.

[4] See 'Half a Century of Change: The Evidence of Child Victims', this volume, p 211.

[5] See 'The Sentencing Decision', this volume, p 257.

[6] See 'Magna Carta: Luck or Judgement', this volume, p 7.

[7] See 'Constitutional Change: Unfinished Business' and 'Sovereignty: A View from London', this volume pp 73 and 89 respectively.

[8] See 'The Judiciary and the Media', 'Press Regulation' and 'Judicial Independence and Responsibilities', this volume pp 141, 158 and 273 respectively.

[9] See 'Human Rights: Today and Tomorrow', this volume p 132.

[10] See 'Assisted Suicide: Moral and Constitutional Issues', this volume p 107.

Our constitution has evolved over many centuries, and we are entering a period of great controversy and uncertainty. As a judge I could never express any 'political' opinions—that is to say, state anything which might have appeared to support or disagree with the position taken or which might be taken by one or other of our major political parties. By strictly confining myself to constitutional and legal questions, I hope I was able to avoid any breach of this important constitutional convention. Since leaving office I have become less inhibited in the expression of my views, although I have been determined not to say anything which might enable anyone to suggest or even imply that I may have been in breach of confidences.

I have also tried to avoid repetition, but a number of recurring themes, expressed in the same way, are relevant in different contexts. I do also have some favourite quotations. It seemed preferable to leave the lectures as members of the individual audiences would have heard them, or at any rate close to the texts prepared for those audiences, rather than omit a paragraph or two here and there and break the continuity of the thought processes, or to rewrite passages which the reader might regard as repetition, simply using different words to express the same meaning. I have resisted the temptation to improve the text, or update my thoughts after the lectures were delivered. When necessary to reduce any lack of clarity or to correct what when I was at school were described as grammatical 'howlers', I have allowed myself a minor degree of light revision.

None of these lectures reflect any deep personal scholarship or fresh research. During the course of delivering them I drew attention to the books which had provided me with material, and checked the accuracy of any quotations attributed to those books, but they were delivered without footnotes. In preparing this publication I added some footnotes, but, contrary to the modern fashion, they remain sparse, and I hope I may be forgiven for avoiding, or at any rate seeking to avoid, any anxious parade of knowledge.

Towards a Constitution

Magna Carta: Luck or Judgement

This lecture, given in Middle Temple Hall on 19 February 2015, was one of a very large number of lectures, to virtually identical effect, about Magna Carta given during 2015. The next lecture, on William Marshal,[1] develops my thinking about the extraordinary part he played in the history of these convoluted events.

W E ARE GATHERED at a place where history was being made 800 years ago. The Temple Church, the round part of the Temple Church, had recently been consecrated. The area was then known as the New Temple, and in late 1214 and early 1215 it became one of King John's two bases in London. The first was the Tower, the second the then New Temple. From either site he could keep a watchful eye on the City, already a powerful institution. And when he was in the New Temple he was in a place of sanctuary, reinforcing the protection from violent attack which had been one of his prizes for promising to go on crusade. The fact that he had sought protection twice over tells you something about the febrile tensions of those days.

It was from here that the first negotiations which culminated in Magna Carta took place, and from which in November 1214 and January 1215 he issued charters to the Church which became the first clauses of Magna Carta. And which when inserted into Magna Carta were, by contrast with the concessions to the rebel barons, expressly stated by John to have been granted freely, and with his full consent.

Now, of course, the Temple is the home of barristers and judges. It is a strange but remarkable inheritance that we, the lawyers, with our current responsibility for maintaining the rule of law, and equality before the law, should be doing so 800 years later in the very area of London where Magna Carta began its long journey into history and the fabric of the nation.

I have chosen the title to this lecture quite deliberately. By definition history is only studied with the benefit of hindsight. It seeks to answer the questions 'what happened?' and 'why did what

[1] This volume, p 24.

happened, happen?'. And as each generation that studies the past gets further from the crucial events, so we become more remote from what contemporaries were thinking. And those contemporaries cannot even for a nano-second have begun to imagine that here we would all be, besuited in an Elizabethan Hall built 350 years after they had been so heavily engaged in negotiations, speaking what to them would have been this very strange language that we now speak, discussing whether the outcomes which they could not have foreseen were the result of luck or accident.

I shall tell the story, or something of the story, and you can make up your own minds whether this was luck or judgement, accident or destiny, inevitable or fortuitous, or even, as some of us might arrogantly assume, the inevitable cause for our rousing tribute on the Last Night of the Proms to the determination of Britons never, never, never to be slaves. Except that whatever else they were, these people were not British; British did not exist, they were hardly English at all. The king and the barons were, at best, Anglo Norman and the bigwigs in the City of London were largely Anglo Saxon. They spoke different languages, and they certainly did not speak ours.

We must also remember that this was a generation of charters. On the continent equivalent charters were being issued by other monarchs. The Golden Bull of Hungary of 1222 and 1231, charter concessions made by the Holy Roman Emperor in 1220 and 1231 and Grants by the king of Aragon in 1283 and 1287 were all typical. Yet although we know about them, none of them had the long-term impact of Magna Carta. To confirm that we are looking at an age when charters were dished out like confetti, we have simply to remember that what we describe as Magna Carta was in fact four charters: the charter sealed by John in 1215, two—one in 1216 and the next in 1217—both sealed by the Regent, William Marshal, and the papal legate, and the 1225 charter when the infant king Henry III had reached an age where he could assume some regal powers and, importantly, traded his seal on the fourth charter in this series for the grant of tax by the counsel of the realm. But that is four charters in a decade, not one in 800 years. Indeed, by contrast with the charters on the continent, Magna Carta was confirmed over 50 times by English kings, until well into the fifteenth century. At each confirmation its evolved meaning became embedded. Each new iteration confirmed what had become its current meaning. As the continental charters withered and decayed, Magna Carta emerged as the first, and still, to my way of thinking, the most important, of all legal codes meriting the description 'living instrument'.

For convenience I shall refer to Magna Carta as a single document, with particular focus on the 1215 edition. The document that we celebrate was never signed by King John. It was sealed on his behalf at Runnymede. Even the date is controversial. Leading scholars of the history of these turbulent years have argued that the correct date is 19th June, although the document itself actually carries the date 15th June. With the classical education I see gathered all around me, I know that you would all be able to read the Latin, if the script was fractionally more manageable, and if you did you would note that the word 'parliament' cannot be found. Nor can the word 'democracy'. Nor can the words 'trial by jury'. Indeed, perhaps most surprising of all, the two words 'Magna Carta' themselves do not appear.

So perhaps the writers of the charming spoof history *1066 And All That*[2] have a point when they say that King John was compelled to sign the Charter (although as we have seen he didn't) which provided, among other conditions, that:

— 'No one should be put to death, save for some reason (except the Common People)'
— 'Everyone should be free (except the Common People)' and
— 'The barons should not be tried except by a special jury of other barons—(that would be because only the barons would understand each other)'.

But for all that, there are other crucial words—constitutional words—political words—to be found in the 1215 Charter. They include 'liberties' and 'customs' and 'rights' and 'justice' and 'lawful judgment' and 'the law of the land' (which became due process) and 'the common counsel of the realm' (which very shortly afterwards came to be known as 'parliament') and 'security', the crucial guarantee clause 61 (which was the 'rule of law' in gestation). The constant reissuing of the charter itself demonstrates its gradual evolution. As examples of the living instrument, the title *Magna Carta des Libertatibus Angliae* was first used in a statute in 1297, and thus formally linked Magna Carta to what we would now describe as fundamental freedoms. By 1331, whatever the controversy may have been earlier, the justice and safety provisions were attached to every man in the land, whether a freeman or a villein or indeed a serf. The words 'due process of law', an essential foundation for our rights and liberties, emerged in 1354. Gradually, in social conditions and societies which are remote from our own, Magna Carta and what

---

[2] WC Sellar and RJ Yeatman, *1066 and All That* (London, 1930).

Magna Carta was believed to stand for became part of the fabric of our political thinking. And as the centuries unfolded it came to be exported to places which none of those assembled at Runnymede had ever heard of, like the future United States of America, and its ideas of constitutional legal freedoms came to be encapsulated in the Universal Declaration of Human Rights, which was described by Eleanor Roosevelt, one of its architects, as 'a Magna Carta for the modern world'.

This is portentous stuff. But the crucial fact to be grasped is that Magna Carta was sealed at the outbreak of a civil war, as a step to avoid its horrors. The apparently inevitable destiny was the scrap heap, not worth the vellum it was written on. Conceivably it would have provided an opportunity for a PhD for an excessively bright and geekish young man or woman on the way to an illustrious academic career. After all, how many of us have heard of the Charter of Liberties of Henry I? That is its title. It contains aspirations of firm peace and the restoration of good old law. How many remember the Oxford Charter of King Stephen in 1136? There too there is a general clause promising peace and justice, and the king will get rid of all unjust practices and once again revert to the observation of good ancient and old customs. Medieval monarchs and monarchs all over the continent swore to be good kings, to uphold the law and to do justice. But the Coronation Oath was made by the new monarch to God in heaven, and it was to God, not his subjects, that he was answerable. So when he died, he came before the judgment seat, and if he had not been true to his oath, heavenly damnation to hell fire would follow. But the sentence, however appalling for the dead monarch's immortal soul, would have had absolutely no alleviating impact for the suffering of his subjects left behind on this earth.

These were years of crisis and civil war. The anointed king against a group of rebel barons. The rights and wrongs do not really matter for today's purposes, although it can fairly be said that no one was fighting for the democratic right of each subject to vote in an election. Civil war is poisonous. And there were people still alive who had memories of the wars between Stephen and Matilda, King John's grandmother, and the murder of Thomas à Becket, all as recent to them as Winston Churchill is to us. Perhaps the final contemporary ingredient is that unlike our present secular age, we are reflecting on a time when life was short and cheap, and the immortal soul and the heavenly judgment which would follow death was vividly in mind. So Magna Carta did not emerge like a bright apparition, with reverberating violins playing ascending chords, from the muddy, misty field at Runnymede. It was set, as all historic events are set, within its own context.

Religion and politics were enmeshed. Dealing with it on a purely political front, although this impacted on the exercise of religious belief, England was placed under papal interdict by Innocent III just 10 years before the charter was sealed. That meant that most of the holy sacraments, which mattered so much to medieval people, were not available. By January 1209 John himself was excommunicated. When neither the interdict on the country nor the personal excommunication served to change his conduct, in January 1213 Innocent III pronounced sentence of deposition on him, and again, using a phrase with which we are sadly familiar, authorised the king of France, Philip Augustus, to wage Holy War against him. More bothered by the impact of the papal order on the exercise of his power on earth than he had been by the potential consequences to his own immortal soul, John submitted to the Pope in May 1213. The political consequence of this submission was that John accepted the Pope not only as his spiritual lord, but as his feudal lord. His kingdom was surrendered and John became the Pope's vassal. In other words, quite apart from the Pope's spiritual authority, this was unadulterated political authority over John's kingdom. In feudal law John could not make any agreement which could bind his feudal lord without reference to his feudal lord.

Pope Innocent III was never someone who knowingly undersold himself. He was generous enough to acknowledge that he was lower in status than God, but he was 'greater than man, judge of all men and judged by none'. The Euro-sceptics of the day would have rent their garments, and when later the Pope directed the rebel barons how they were to pay taxes required by the king irrespective of their consent, which, to the Pope, was irrelevant, nowadays they would have donned sackcloth and ashes and gone on *Newsnight*. Instead they donned weapons and armour. And then, into this turbulent mix came the catastrophic defeat of John's allies in France in the summer of 1214 at the Battle of Bouvines. When John returned to England in autumn 1214 his treasury was empty and he had been utterly humiliated. Wars then as now involved huge expenditure. And John needed to replenish his funds, and there was no quantitative easing available for the purpose. Instead, John wanted to raise taxes, including scutage.

Scutage was shield money, an old form of taxation. When a feudal lord went on campaign he could summon you to join him, bringing an appropriate number of men to fight with you and for him.

It became pretty obvious that you had a better chance of victory in the forthcoming battle if you paid armed mercenaries rather than untrained yokels armed with bill hooks to fight. So instead of sending yourself, or your villeins, you paid for their equivalent in scutage or shield money so that the king could buy men at arms. If the king was entitled to claim scutage from you whenever he decided to do so, it was and was certainly seen as a form of taxation. So scutage, to pay for wars outside the country, was resisted.

And so the toing and froing towards civil war began. Attempts were made to achieve a negotiated peace. As I said at the beginning, many of those stages took place in the Temple. John issued a charter to the Church in England in November 1214, and then another one in January 1215. He had not suddenly become holy. He was there seeking to get the Church—the most powerful institution—on his side. The next most powerful organisation locally was the City of London and he tried to do a deal with it, in May 1215, with another charter issued from the Temple, granting the City power to have its own Lord Mayor; by contrast with the application by the city 15 years earlier, costing the City nothing at all. In another modern word, it was appeasing the City, and like appeasement in our world, it did the king no good. The city gates were opened to the rebel barons. And those of you who are here in London next November can have a grandstand view of the Lord Mayor's Show, as the new Lord Mayor is sworn in before the Lord Chief Justice. That is a direct consequence of this 1215 City charter.

And so the parties met at Runnymede. Armed forces on each side. The barons had their terms and conditions ready in the Articles of the Barons. The Church looked after itself, and the first clause of the charter simply reproduced the two charters already granted a few months earlier to the Church. There are a couple of features to be noticed here. First, the Articles of the Barons made no reference to the Church, but nevertheless they were somehow persuaded to agree that the Church's interests should come first. What is more, this clause was expressly said in the charter to be granted 'by our free and spontaneous will'. It is noticeable that no such expression of voluntariness was attached to the grants to the barons.

What this should bring home to us is that this was a tough negotiation over a four-day period. You have to imagine the toing and froing. The conversations. The private discussions. The whispers. Every lawyer has been party to a negotiated settlement. That's what this was.

John was in a hopeless position. His opponents had the largest forces, and London just up the road supported them. His own supporters among the nobility were simply being true to their obligation of fealty. Apart from his supporters from abroad, there was no personal loyalty. The throne of England had been offered by the rebel barons to Louis of France. Basically John had no cards to play. And so his seal was attached to the charter.

Let me identify four crucial areas addressed in the charter. First, our now well-known 'justice' provisions. Justice will not be delayed or denied or sold. The consequence of this provision, still with us, is that you were entitled to justice. You could not be locked up on the whim of a king, or, as we shall see, a baron. You were entitled to 'due process', and before long the great writ of 'Habeas Corpus' evolved from it. What is more, it was provided that the punishment should fit the crime, a first step to our Sentencing Guidelines Council and that those responsible for enforcing any judgments, like the sheriff or the coroner, or bailiffs, were not to be judges (embryonic separation of powers), and that injustices would be put right.

Then, there was to be no scutage or aid without the consent of the counsel of the realm, with provisions about how the counsel was to be summoned. If the king could live off his own estates and traditional sources, fine, but if he wanted anything extra, he could not take it without consent. That was a direct answer to the order of Pope Innocent. And during the regency for the boy king Henry, this principle was applied, and people became used to it.

The third crucial paragraph is the king's agreement that he was required to rectify any failures to abide by the new agreement, and that if he did not, his subjects were absolved from their obligations of fealty and obedience to him. In other words the subjects of the king did not owe him absolute and unconditional fealty. The right of resistance to the king was expressly authorised, an authorisation which extended to the 'whole community of the land'. On the continent John was derided for agreeing to what were described as 'over kings'. And Professor David Carpenter's recent researches have revealed a contemporary poem copied into the *Melrose Chronicle*.[3] (For those of you who don't know it, Melrose is in Scotland.) It reads:

England has ratified a perverse order;
who has heard such an astonishing event
For the body aspired to be on top of the head;
The people sought to rule the king.

[3] David Carpenter, *Magna Carta* (Harmondsworth, 2015).

There is a fourth crucial provision, which I have not sufficiently emphasised on earlier occasions. It is the answer to the criticism in *1066 And All That* that the Common People were excluded from the benefits of the charter. Clause 60 required everyone, whether cleric or civilian, to ensure that they extended the rights granted by the charter to them, to 'their men', that is their own vassals, villeins and serfs. Someone, somewhere, probably in view of his political thought, Archbishop Langton, but possibly William Marshal, had a vision which was years ahead of its time. And, by now, at Runnymede, probably everyone else was too tired to spot what was going into the draft and certainly much more attention would have been given to the structure of Clause 61, the security or enforcement clause.

Taken on their own, and more importantly together, these were critical provisions in this medieval document.

So scribes wrote out copies of the charter, and the king and rebel barons and royal barons and archbishops and bishops all stood around and took an oath to keep the terms of the Charter in good faith and without evil intent. As these oaths were being taken, a number of immortal souls were in a state of mortal sin. John had not the slightest intention of abiding by the charter forced out of him.

In law the charter was unenforceable as a contract, sealed as it was under compulsion or duress. But to coin a modern phrase, 'Peace in our time' was secured. For just a short time, even shorter than the Munich Agreement. As soon as the Pope heard of it, just a few weeks later, he immediately annulled it. And he did not use language which might have left any misunderstanding. The Bull described John's wickedness, and the consequent surrender of the crowns of England and Ireland to the Pope, and then, having rubbed John's nose in it, his promises in the charter were annulled.

> We utterly reprobate and condemn any agreement of this kind, forbidding, under ban of our anathema, the fore said king to presume to observe it.

It was declared void. The charter itself and the obligations and safeguards made in it were 'entirely' abolished. They should have 'no validity at anytime whatsoever'.

From the Pope's point of view, we should be utterly ashamed of ourselves for celebrating the survival of Magna Carta. But it was gone. The originator of all our liberties. Not worth the vellum it was written on. You would never have bet on it having any future at all. And worse was to come.

Civil war broke out in earnest. So did a French invasion, which everyone seems to forget. It is simply not true that the last invasion of England was in 1066 and resulted in the Norman Conquest. At the invitation of the rebel barons to become king of England, Louis, then prince, but later king of France, arrived in England in May 1216 and the Lord Mayor and the City opened the gates and rendered homage to him. In military terms the rebel barons, supported by 7,000 French troops, were in a very strong position. We were in danger of a Capetan king replacing the Plantagenets. It is reasonable to assume that that would have been the end of the common law, crushed before it had really begun; and however the English language might have developed, it is most unlikely that it would have developed as it did.

Then two deaths occurred. First Innocent III, and then in October 1216 John himself. To describe John's death as very fortunate is a privilege based on looking back at it; that is, the historians' privilege. At the time, to contemporaries, it was a catastrophe. His heir was a child, Henry III, a boy of nine. He had no uncles, born legitimately, to act as his Regent. In medieval times this was a desperate moment. Child kings with no uncles had no future. Even with uncles they were murdered. John had after all disposed of his nephew Arthur, the son of an older brother, and we all know what happened to the Princes in the Tower some 260 years later.

So there we have it. The charter was annulled by the spiritual head of Christendom and the feudal lord of England. French soldiers and armed men loyal to Louis' cause were in a strong military position. And the king was a little boy of 9. Luck or judgement, destiny or accident?

Yet it survived. The loyal barons, led by William Marshal, Earl of Pembroke, arranged for the boy's coronation. But not at Westminster Abbey, because London was occupied by the rebels and the French, so the little boy was crowned at Gloucester Abbey as Henry III. Within 10 days of John's death William Marshal, now approaching 70 years of age, was elected as Regent. He had come up the ladder to advancement from virtually nowhere. At Runnymede he had been the main non-clerical negotiator for John. His great quality was that he was trusted on all sides, not least for his remarkable commitment to his personal oaths of fealty to successive vile-tempered Plantagenets, and for his land in France, to the French king. But apart from these qualities, the situation was novel. Notice, Marshal was *elected* into this office. So he could be deselected. And his regency represented— as it had to—a serious first attempt at true conciliar government.

With the Papal Legate, Marshal reissued a new, different charter—Magna Carta—in November 1216 using his own seal. My own assessment is that this was issued from his position of weakness in the hope of persuading the rebel barons back to the negotiating table. That indeed was the idea expressly referred to in the 1216 Charter. In modern language, it meant 'let's sort this out'. But, given the military strength of the opposition, this reissue did not bring peace. In passing, we should notice that Marshal issued the charter in Dublin, on the basis that those in Ireland were entitled to the same rights as those who lived in England. Well, it did not work out quite so well there, did it? Luck or judgement? But it enabled Edmund Burke to argue that the rebellious colonists in the future United States of America were entitled to rely on Magna Carta. Its blessings were not confined to England.

In 1217 Marshal himself led loyal forces into battle at Lincoln. I mean, literally. He was in such a hurry to lead a charge when the strategic opportunity arose that he forgot his helmet. Luckily one of the squires reminded him to wear it, and just as well. After the battle it was heavily dented. A very heavy defeat was inflicted on French forces and the rebel barons. The French invasion floundered. Shortly afterwards in a sea battle French reinforcements were beaten off and peace was achieved.

So again Marshal reissued the charter, in yet different terms, in 1217—this time, importantly, not under compulsion as John was when he sealed it at Runnymede, and not out of a position of weakness, as Marshal was when he issued the 1216 Charter. Now he was in a position of strength based on victory in battle. Showing much magnanimity in victory, and indeed paying Louis to leave the country and abjure his claim to the throne of England, the rebel barons were brought back into unity with the Crown. It was a remarkable achievement. Shortly afterwards, in 1219, he died. He is one of the great heroes of our history, and we largely ignore him. In the three short years from 1216 until his death, if he had not stood by the boy king, and accepted the responsibilities which went with a regency, and reissued, and again reissued Magna Carta, and, by success in battle driving out the invading French, ruling by consensus and achieving a peaceful end to civil war, our history, and that of a future United States of America, and all the countries where the common law has taken root, would have been very different. He was given the equivalent of a state funeral, and described by the Archbishop of Canterbury as 'the greatest Knight that ever lived'.

And where luck came into it was this. The disaster of a boy king was rescued by the right man happening to be in the right place at the right time.

Henry III came, first, to partial majority, and then full majority. He needed money, and turned to a device employed by John much earlier, a tax on movables, that is to say personal property and rents. It was also a tax used to raise the sums to ransom Richard the Lionheart. At a council at Christmas 1224 a fifteenth of the value of all movables was sought for the king. The Great Council insisted that before it would be given the king should issue the charter himself. And in 1225 he did so. There are some important features to notice. This charter was granted freely of the king's spontaneous goodwill to a whole class of the nobility and 'all our realm'. The significance is that in the liberties and concessions granted by John in 1215, it was only those relating to the Church which expressly said that he was acting voluntarily. As we have seen, in relation to the other concessions, the assertion that he was acting voluntarily was omitted. Henry III, advised by Archbishop Langton, was not under any compulsion of force of arms. This charter could not be said to be void for duress. It simply was a trading deal. You can have your tax provided you reissue the charter, and, by implication, abide by it. And that pattern developed through the reign. There were occasions when the council refused the financial support sought by the king, no less than three times in the 1240s. *Tallagio non concedendo* (we shall not concede taxation) led Edward I to agree that this required the common assent of all the kingdom. By now the word 'parliamentum' was being used to describe assemblies of the council. And it was just a few years later that further civil war broke out, Simon de Montfort taking on the now aging Henry III. There is poetic justice here. Henry had never ceased to criticise William Marshal for his generosity to the defeated barons and French. He never understood the value of a peace settlement, particularly of a civil war. The precious peace dividend.

And this feature of our medieval constitutional arrangements, the link between tax and consent first of the council, and then of Parliament, provided the basis for our constitutional struggle in the seventeenth century and the eventual establishment of the King-in-Parliament as the ruling authority, and the battle cry 'No taxation without representation' adopted by the American colonists in the following century. Withholding of tax demanded by the king until the grievances of the council, and ultimately Parliament, were addressed, represents one of the major reasons why we ended up with parliamentary government while the Estates General in France and the Cortez in Spain, together with all the other promises in all the charters issued in the twelfth and thirteenth centuries, disappeared under absolute monarchies.

It is very easy for us eight centuries on to sneer at the Charter as no more than the barons looking after themselves, or to suggest that there are only three clauses of the charter currently in force, so what's the fuss about it all. But, with respect to them, they are wrong. The charter made an immediate impact. By a way of example, we know from the records that by 1220 a baron from Northumberland defended his right to maintain his castle and sought judgment 'in the court of the Lord King by the judgment of my peers'. By 1226 a huge dispute arose in Lincolnshire between the sheriff and four knights (notice they were not barons, nor members of the body responsible for enforcing the 'security' clause). The argument against the sheriff was that his actions were 'contrary to the liberty which they ought to have by the charter of the Lord King'. No printing press. No iPad. No email. No newspapers. No *Newsnight*. Yet, as we have seen, there is that vivid poem recorded in the *Chronicle* being written North of the Border. By 1234 the Great Council had decided a case against the king, who admitted that he had dispossessed Gilbert Basset without 'lawful judgment of his peers and by the law of the land', a direct lift from Magna Carta, and the Council ordered that the land should be returned to Basset. And at this time in a treatise attributed to the judge Henry Bracton, we find the statement that the king is 'under God and under the law, because the law makes the king'. These were the very words used by Edward Coke when he tried to give the newly crowned James I a lesson in English constitutional history. It cost Coke his job as Chief Justice, and a spell in the Tower.

Now Parliament became increasingly influential. Thus, and it is one example only, when Richard II was deposed by the future Henry IV, the victorious new king went to Parliament sitting at Westminster, justifying his assumption of the crown, where Articles of Deposition were promulgated. The Articles justifying Richard's removal included his refusal to do justice according to law, his assertion that 'the laws were in his mouth, or sometimes in his breast', and that 'he alone could alter and create the laws of his realm', and perhaps even more obviously related to Magna Carta, that the king had 'wilfully contravened the statute of his realm' which provided that 'no free man shall be arrested etc or in any way destroyed, nor should the King proceed, or order any process against him, unless by lawful judgment of his peers, or by the law of the land'. The new king, according to his spokesman the Archbishop of Canterbury, was determined 'to be advised and ruled by the honourable, wise and prudent people of his realm' and by their 'common advice, counsel and consent'. In short, the endorsement of Parliament was regarded as an essential element in the legitimacy of the new reign. And so indeed it was, for example, when Henry VII succeeded Richard III. And those of you who have read *Wolf Hall*[4] will, I am sure, have begun to appreciate the political mastery of Thomas Cromwell who made Parliament a party to the dramatic changes in the relationship between Church and State, between England and Rome, between the lands of the monasteries and the new gentry which had acquired them, with all the unintended consequences arising from Parliament's new strength less than one hundred years later.

Parliamentary sovereignty, of course, was still a long way off. But it was becoming increasingly central in our arrangements. And although the Tudors managed the institution, the early Stuarts simply did not. The plain simple fact was that when James I succeeded to the throne he had a deep conviction that regal authority was bestowed by God on the monarch, and that it was to God that the king was answerable. That was, on examination, precisely the problem which had to be faced in the early thirteenth century. If the king was answerable to God when he died, and would be judged accordingly, his subjects on earth would simply be left hoping that he would be succeeded by a better, fairer, more just king. That was when Chief Justice Coke quoted Bracton to the king, and the king responded that it was treason to affirm that the king was 'under the law'. Coke was dismissed and sent to the Tower. He then entered Parliament. The Commons. And there, with a forensic technique which made the blunderbuss seem an instrument of exquisite delicacy, he led the advance of what parliamentarians regarded as 'rights' under the banner of Magna Carta. He had many supporters. This was not a one-man show. But, for example, Coke challenged the use of the word 'sovereign' in relation to royal power. It was no parliamentary word.

Magna Carta is such a fellow that he will have no sovereign.

On another occasion he said:

If my sovereign would not allow me my inheritance ['inheritance' in the sense of 'birthrights'], I must fly to Magna Carta ... when the king says he

---

[4] Hilary Mantel (London, 2010).

cannot allow our liberties of right, this strikes at the root. We serve here for thousands and ten thousands.

Even now it was not democracy as we know it, with a universal franchise. But Magna Carta was the banner—if you like the trumpet call—for the privileges of Parliament and its authority. It was seen by seventeenth-century lawyers as the foundation for the rights and liberties of the nation represented in Parliament.

There were too many occasions of detention without trial. And, for example, when Edwin Sandys of the Middle Temple was detained, this was challenged as contrary to the 'privileges of this Land by Magna Carta and many laws since'. So Magna Carta was now in use both to protect the liberty of individual citizens from unlawful arrest, and as the foundation for the constitutional position of Parliament. It all ended in civil war. At the risk of appearing facile, the issue can be summarised by simply considering the old-fashioned punctuation we were taught when I was young. Who ruled? 'The King, in Parliament' or 'The King-in-Parliament'? It all turns on a comma or a couple of hyphens.[5]

We all know how the war between Parliament and the king ended. The finest moment of Charles I's life came in the last few hours before it ended on the scaffold in Whitehall. And those who judged him and condemned him to death were later to suffer the most agonising deaths as traitors: hanged, drawn and quartered.

By the end of the century, his son James had abdicated. We had new rulers. They were chosen by Parliament. Our constitution was irrevocably based on the sovereignty of Parliament. The ideas for which Magna Carta was the inspiration had triumphed here. It is just worth remembering, however, that although we know the outcome of the Civil War, that outcome would not have been predicted in advance; and as to why James II simply fled the country without fighting for his crown, well, it is an example of how dependent history is on the workings of an individual's mind.

In the meantime the Eastern seaboard of the future United States of America was being colonised. Something like 350,000 men and women left England for the colonies between 1616 and 1700. All the colonists treated Magna Carta as the foundation for their constitutional ideas. It was not an accident that the first charter granted to Virginia in 1616 created by Edwin Sandys, of the Middle Temple,

---

[5] The distinction between 'King, in Parliament' and 'King-in-Parliament' was made by Jeffrey Goldsworthy in *The Sovereignty of Parliament: History and Philosophy* (Oxford, 1999).

was called the Great Charter. The colonists had the same rights as if they had been born in England. The assembly in Maryland legislated that all the inhabitants should have their rights and liberties 'according to the Great Charter of England'. In Massachusetts a body of 'grounds of law in resemblance to a Magna Carta' was framed. In 1680, an indication of trouble lying ahead, there was resistance to taxation by New York, only just recently a British colony, against taxation which was 'contrary to Magna Carta and the Petition of Right'. The complaint did not realise that it was looking forward; at the time it was looking back.

Then our sovereign Parliament here exercised its authority over the colonies in one of the most foolish statutes ever enacted, the Stamp Act of 1765, and then the Declaratory Act the next year. Between them they sought to deprive the colonists of their right to trial by jury for breaches of the Stamp Act, and then declared that they were, in effect, mere colonials, who would have to do what they were told, without being represented in Parliament. And so the citizens of the future United States of America rebelled, relying, again, on Magna Carta as embodying principles of their birthright as Englishmen. And so to another war, the War of Independence—although my American friends do not like it—in truth another civil war.

Parliamentary sovereignty was established here on the basis of Magna Carta. But it was parliamentary sovereignty that had produced the abhorrent Stamp Act and the Declaratory Act in the American colonies. If it was being said that they were entitled to be ruled without being represented, they relied on what they believed were their Magna Carta rights. They rejected the principle of parliamentary sovereignty, but just to make sure that parliamentary sovereignty did not prevail, by evoking John Locke and natural law, they turned not to rights which had been created by parchments and seals, but to rights 'founded on immutable maxims of reason and justice'. They produced a constitutional arrangement which limited parliamentary sovereignty while simultaneously asserting the rights encompassed in and developed from Magna Carta. The constitution itself was supreme, and virtually immutable. It is a strange paradox that, inspired by the same source, two great democracies, one of which used to be the most powerful nation on earth, and the second of which is probably even now still the most powerful nation on earth, ended with fundamentally different constitutional arrangements. Yet both have Magna Carta as their foundation stones. Or, putting it another way, Magna Carta is bred into the bones of their constitutional arrangements.

The short answer to this paradox is that both constitutions were creatures of their times, in just the same way as Magna Carta itself in the decade 1215 to 1225 was itself, by its very terms, a product of its times. None of these great events simply emerged from a cloud of vapourless gas. For me, they have never dissipated into the air.

Nevertheless, even with 800 years of history behind it, I venture to suggest that this very condensed account of Magna Carta and its creation demonstrate the dangers of studying history, without remembering that what is history to us, was simply the future to those who were involved at the time. And by definition, as Shakespeare reminded us in *Twelfth Night*, first performed here in this hall, 'What's to come is still unsure'. We know that D-Day was successful. On 1st June 1944 there would have been an endless stream of those with power and authority, and ultimate responsibility, exercised about what in truth was a great gamble, no less than an armed invasion across the channel against a fortress. And those founding fathers of the United States of America, so many of them Middle Templars, did not *know* that they would prevail. As Tom Paine argued in *Common Sense*,[6] whatever may have been inevitable in the long run, did not seem inevitable to them. They were committing treason, and the consequences to them of failure would have undoubtedly been death. And going back to Magna Carta itself, our history would have been very different if John had lived, or Innocent had lived, or William Marshal had not lived into what by medieval standards was old age, and still had the energy to take on the burdens of the Regent to a boy king. Or indeed, if someone else had been elected instead of him. History is not made by events, but by the particular people at particular times and their responses to them.

One last word.

We have every reason to be proud of Magna Carta. For me it remains a living document. It is the banner, the symbol, of our liberties. In the United States it has an even more direct impact. Just because it is 800 years old, we can adopt, and I suspect we have all noticed occasions when we have adopted, a somewhat arrogant attitude to what I shall describe as the newer democracies, countries seeking to establish democracy, espousing the cause, and then, for one reason or another, being overtaken by authoritarianism and militarism and dictatorship. Where we are sometimes arrogant, can we be humble. Where we might be a little patronising,

---

[6] Pamphlet published 1776.

can we remember that the democracy which is now established in this country took hundreds of years to establish. And involved the shedding of much blood. And, perhaps most important of all, that even now, here in this country today, we should be careful never to assume that the liberties and 'right' and 'justice' and 'consent' can be taken for granted. There is a warning direct from the first publication of Magna Carta in the United States in 1687 by William Penn, yes our William Penn, Old Bailey William Penn and the jury, their William Penn, in Pennsylvania:

> It is easier to part with or give away great privileges, but hard to be gained if once lost.[7]

What William Penn called 'privileges' we now call 'rights'. There are still many countries in the world where what we happily call our 'rights' remain 'privileges' waiting to be won and entrenched. And those of us who are blessed with them must guard them. If Magna Carta, and everything that it has meant to us, and continues to mean to us, is to survive, it is no longer a question of luck. It is our responsibility to make it so.

---

[7] William Penn, *The Excellent Privilege of Liberty and Property* (1687).

William Marshal, Earl of Pembroke

First published in Magna Carta: Muse and Mentor *(New York, 2014).*[1]

WILLIAM MARSHAL, EARL of Pembroke (c 1146–1219) is the hero of the convoluted events which culminated in the creation and survival of Magna Carta. None of his contemporaries played such a pivotal role. Without him the Charter of 1215 (not entitled Magna Carta) would have been the only charter, rather than the first of four in a single decade, and would have been relegated to a minor note in history; one more charter in an age of charters, annulled by the Pope almost as soon as it was sealed by King John, and revoked by King John at the first available opportunity. Yet, apart from professional historians of the period, William Marshal is virtually unknown today.

Few recognise Marshal's contribution to the protracted negotiations which culminated in the sealing of the Charter. Yet the Charter itself acknowledges his importance by listing him as the first of the non-clerical individuals who advised the king to agree the Charter. Perhaps more significant, few remember that after the annulment of the Charter by the Pope and its revocation by the king, and in the middle of the subsequent civil war, the king died leaving an infant son to succeed him. Marshal was elected regent of the infant king Henry III, and then rapidly reissued and distributed a new version of the Charter in 1216 in his own name and under his own seal, and again reissued it in 1217. Finally, few remember that in that same year, by then 70 or so years old, he returned once more to the battlefield and defeated an invading French army at the Battle of Lincoln, bringing to an end the serious prospect of a Capetan dynasty replacing the Plantagenet dynasty in England. The potential consequences were not merely dynastic: the political and constitutional

---

[1] Generally I relied on the chapter devoted to William Marshal in *Magna Carta Uncovered*, which I co-authored with Anthony Arlidge QC (Oxford, 2014), for which the main sources were David Crouch, *William Marshal: Court, Career and Chivalry in the Angevin Empire 1147–1219* (London, 1990); Sidney Painter, *William Marshal: Knight Errant, Baron, and Regent of England* (Baltimore, MD 1933); David Carpenter, *The Struggle for Mastery: Britain, 1066–1284* (London, 2003); and JC Holt, *Magna Carta* (Cambridge, 1992).

developments that occurred over succeeding centuries may well have been significantly different.

Marshal is indeed one of the forgotten men of history. Yet his immediate contemporaries appreciated his life far more than we do. On his death in 1219 he was given the equivalent of a modern state funeral. In his funeral oration the Archbishop of Canterbury described Marshal as 'the greatest knight that ever lived'. It was an apt summary of the admiration and respect in which his contemporaries held him.

Within a very short time the story of Marshal's life was being told in *Le Histoire de Guillaume le Mareschal*, the first, ignoring the exception of a self-laudatory autobiographical effort, the only known or surviving 'lay' or story of the life of an individual who was not a monarch or, in our language, Head of State. Discounting the risk of hagiography and the danger of over-romanticising the life of the hero of the story, by checking the assertions in the *Histoire* against facts which can be established independently of it, a remarkable story of a towering figure of medieval history emerges.

Yet his start in life was hardly propitious. William was the fourth of his father's sons, and although his father John enjoyed the hereditary office of 'Mareschal' (from which his sons drew their surnames), he was not and would not have been regarded as a grandee. William had to make his own way in the world. One way to advancement from humble origins was through the Church. Another was to make an impact as a warrior. William's talents in this direction were unsurpassed. As his reputation burgeoned, he had the good fortune to encounter and impress Eleanor of Aquitaine, the wife of Henry II. Through her influence he entered the hazardous service of the royal Plantagenet family. The level of dysfunction in that family is notorious. Henry II imprisoned his wife for well over a decade. At different times, each and sometimes more than one of his sons was in open rebellion against him. They warred against each other. John was almost certainly complicit in the murder of his older brother Geoffrey's son Arthur, then a teenager with, on primogeniture grounds, a better claim to the throne. In this venomous atmosphere contemporaries gradually came to be struck by the unswerving loyalty of Marshal to his oath of fealty, not least at times when others saw that over-enthusiastic adherence to this principle might create an obstruction to advancement.

Taking it very briefly, backed by Eleanor, at the request of Henry II, Marshal assumed responsibility for their oldest son, Henry, who although crowned as the Young King, predeceased his father. When he died, it was Marshal who fulfilled the Young King's vow to go on crusade to the Holy Land. On his return he re-entered the service of Henry II. We can see evidence of his gradual assimilation into the group of close advisers of the king in some of the records towards the end of this reign. For example, in 1186 Marshal's name is included as a witness to the termination of a dispute between the Bishops of Hereford and Worcester. Among the list of witnesses, plain, untitled William Marshal comes a very long way behind the Archbishop of Canterbury, and a variety of named bishops and earls, at that time the highest rank of the nobility in England. Less than 20 years later, now vested with the dignity and title of Earl of Pembroke, he appeared as the first great noble man of the realm witnessing Magna Carta. That, however, was for the undecided future.

In the war which erupted between Richard and his dying father, Marshal remained loyal to Henry II until the very end. Indeed shortly before his death, Marshal encountered Richard, who he had trained in the skills of war in the field, reconnoitring Henry's defences. Marshal spared Richard's life, but humiliatingly for Richard, he killed his horse under him.

When Henry II was dying, Marshal remained with him to the end. His career prospects thereafter cannot have seemed very bright. Nevertheless when he offered his fealty to Richard, no doubt bearing in mind that as well as his loyalty to his father, Marshal had also demonstrated conspicuous loyalty to his first patron, his mother, Eleanor, Richard accepted it. Moreover when he went on his own crusade, Richard appointed Marshal to be the first of the co-justiciars to William Longchamps, the Archbishop of Canterbury. Among the burdens falling on Marshal and his co-justiciars was a siege of the troublesome John at Windsor Castle. A burden of a different kind which fell on the illiterate Marshal was to sit as one of the judges in Westminster Hall. Perhaps he was happier on the battlefield. His standing with Richard on his return from captivity would have been undiminished by his stupendous folly in leading the way up the scaling ladder and knocking out the constable of Beauvais Castle when it was under siege by Richard in 1197. As a public acknowledgement of Marshal's increasing standing, he was allowed to marry the heiress, Isabel of Striguil (Chepstow), a notable heiress, with vast interests in Wales and Ireland. In stark terms of career progress, this represented significant public recognition.

In 1197 Richard died, without issue, naming John as his heir. It is an indication of how Marshal had arrived in the inner circle of power that he was immediately consulted about the succession by the Archbishop of Canterbury. William recommended that in accordance with Richard's last wishes, John, rather than Arthur, should become king. Shortly after John's coronation, William was invested as the Earl of Pembroke in his own right.

At the outset of the new reign Marshal's fortunes continued to flourish. Perhaps inevitably in any working relationship with John, things changed, and in 1205 Marshal left the court in England and went into political exile in Ireland. The main area of dispute was relevant to the issues which came to be resolved in 1215. John was determined to recover land in Poitou. Marshal refused to join the expedition as this would contravene the fealty he owed in France to Philip Augustus. John alleged that this was treasonous, but when William elected trial by battle, his reputation as a warrior meant that no one took up his challenge to fight. Perhaps more important, whether or not Marshal's refusal was a form of special pleading, or a principled adherence to his oath of fealty, the issue was very public, and a few years later, rebel barons would have recollected Marshal's refusal to serve the king abroad, and this would have provided the basis for their contentions that they should have no liability for 'scutage'[2] to replace service to the king outside England. Clauses 12 and 14 of the 1215 Charter may have had many progenitors, but as Marshal conducted negotiations on John's behalf in those turbulent months, he may well have had some sympathy for the determination of the rebel barons that the consent of the Council should be a pre-requisite of liability for scutage. This is a very long way from 'No taxation without representation', but it is not too fanciful to discern the link between the requirement of formal consent to the raising of royal revenue which became the foundation for the constitutional struggle in seventeenth-century England, and the assured defiance of London by the colonists in eighteenth-century North America.

His time in Ireland, whereby by virtue of his wife's descent from King Dermott of Leinster Marshal and his wife had many interests and responsibilities and troubles, proved to be a training ground for the future Regent. 'In his Irish policies we can at last see the Marshal as ruler rather than courtier and soldier.'[3] Ireland was not overlooked when the Charter later came to be reissued by Marshal in 1216 and again in 1217, when he required that it should be distributed in Ireland on the basis that Irish subjects should enjoy the

---

[2] See above, p 11ff for a description of scutage.
[3] Crouch, ibid.

same liberties as those of England (a promise which was not ful-filled, but which supplied Edmund Burke with his powerful reasoning in support of the proposition that the American colonists were entitled to the same rights as the king's subjects in England).

John's reign became increasingly turbulent. In 1207 England was placed under a papal interdict, with all ecclesiastical offices save for baptism and deathbed confession banned. In 1209 John was excommunicated. By 1212 two senior barons had been accused of conspiracy to murder the king, and fled the realm. In January 1213 the Pope pronounced a sentence of deposition on John, and authorised Holy War against him. Unsurprisingly, John was virtually bereft of any allies. By a process of reconciliation which began in 1212, Marshal responded to the king's summons to return to England in May 1213. There were now almost exactly two years to go to the meeting at Runnymede.

With others, Marshal advised John to reach an accommodation with the Pope, which John eventually did in sufficiently sycophantic terms for the Pope to embrace him as the returning prodigal son. John then embarked on the disastrous expedition to France which culminated in the Battle of Bouvines, which constituted not simply a defeat but utter humiliation for John, whose treasury was empty. After Bouvines Marshal organised the mustering of loyal troops (wherever they could be found) and the preparation of defensive royal positions. Although John was the anointed king, and the vassal of the Pope who would stand behind him, and had the support of a formidable and tried military campaigner in Marshal, his vulnerability could not be disguised. And so negotiations began with Marshal as John's key envoy. The narrative of the negotiations which began at the Temple in the autumn of 1214 need not be repeated here. What matters is that Marshal was the only civilian (as opposed to clerical) guarantor of John's good faith during these meetings. At the risk of stating the obvious, it follows that he must have been a very close, if not the closest, advisor of the king—not a comfortable role for an individual of marked integrity who was as well aware as anyone of the unpredictable nature of the royal personality. Nevertheless he was sufficiently influential to give dispassionate and unpalatable advice. Indeed it has been suggested that he was the joint author of the terms of the Charter—a suggestion which modern historians regard as improbable, but which does serve to underline how very close to the heart of the negotiations he must have been when the Charter was eventually sealed at Runnymede in June 1215. As already noted, it is certain that the first 'illustrious' (that is, non-clerical) magnate from the baronial class to be named in this Charter was Marshal. After it was sealed he was given the responsibility of informing London, still hostile to the king, of its terms.

To no avail: the 1215 Charter was buried under the turmoil of civil war. John appealed to the Pope for its annulment, which duly followed, and the rebel barons, despite the 'security' clause, could not enforce its terms. Forces from France invaded England. The rebel barons offered the throne to the future king of France, Louis VIII. Military action continued. Marshal himself was first committed to action in Wales, and then sent as an emissary to France to seek, without success, to dissuade Philip Augustus from supporting his son's claim to the throne of England. As 1216 was drawing to a close, the outcome of the civil war and the French invasion was uncertain.

Marshal was at Gloucester when John died in October 1216. That was a most fortunate accident for the history of Magna Carta. Some contemporary material suggests that on his deathbed John nominated Marshal as the guardian for his infant heir, Henry III. The evidence to support this suggestion is problematic. What mattered was that Marshal took urgent action to secure the Plantagenet succession by summoning the barons loyal to the king to Gloucester Abbey and arranging for the Young King to be conveyed there. Westminster Abbey itself was unavailable for the coronation as it was under the control of French forces. Marshal knighted the boy, who was then crowned king in the presence of the Papal Legate, Guala. After obtaining the consent of the Earl of Chester, the most senior nobleman in England, Marshal accepted the office of Regent (*Rector noster et Regni nostri*), a new title and office. In effect and in practice he became Regent or Protector, and the Ruler of the Country.

> All those in the abbey's vast crowd would have realised that this was a dreadful way to start a reign. The most uncertain transfer of power seen for nearly a century was placing the crown on the head of a child ... Henry III was fortunate to have around him a group of supporters committed to not seizing power for themselves, but to maintain the fragile office of kingship as his predecessors had created it ... It was not just to the solemn 9-year-old Henry's advantage that (Marshal's) attitude prevailed among a few good men in England. The future of the dynasty depended on it.[4]

The undoubted leader of this small loyal group was William Marshal.

Armed with Marshal's new authority, within less than a month of John's death, and notwithstanding John's repudiation and the

---

[4] D Jones, *The Plantagenets: The Kings who Made England* (London, 2012).

Pope's annulment of the Charter, it was reissued in the name of the Young King, but under Marshal's personal seal and that of the Papal Legate. By contemporary standards this was a remarkably rapid response. The reissue included a number of revisions, no doubt reflecting the reality that civil war was continuing and French invaders were still present in England. The objective seems clear. It was a gesture towards reconciliation with the rebel barons. The omission of clauses restricting the authority of the king may have reflected the exigencies of the civil war and the need to secure the throne, and perhaps, just because the monarch was a boy, a belief that he should not suffer in the event of misconduct by the Regent. Significantly however, in the final clause, reference was made to the resolution of outstanding issues when fuller council would be possible, so as to do what was best for the common good and the peace of the kingdom. By way of further encouragement, this reissue was accompanied by a threat of excommunication for those who rejected its terms. This effort to achieve peace failed.

The war continued. The next year, the rebel army, backed by Louis of France, besieged loyalist troops at Lincoln Castle. Marshal was now 70 or so years old. Nevertheless he was at the forefront of both the battlefield tactics and the very fighting itself. Anxious to take advantage of the unfolding military situation, he forgot to wear his helmet. His supporters reminded him to wear it. During the hand-to-hand fighting it was dented in more than one place. The end result was a great victory, in which 46 of the rebel barons were captured. The French invasion nevertheless continued until Louis was defeated shortly afterwards in a sea battle off Sandwich.

That brought the civil war to an end and culminated in the departure of the defeated French. In the peace treaties, Louis abandoned his claim to the throne of England, the rebel barons renewed their homage and were absolved from excommunication, and Marshal, together with the Papal Legate, undertook that the liberties demanded by the rebel barons would be restored. And so as part of what today we would describe as the peace process, after a meeting of the Council, an undated Charter was reissued in November 1217, again in the name of the king, but again under the seal of Marshal and the Papal Legate. Significantly, this Charter was sealed not under the pressure of military weakness which led John to seal the 1215 Charter, nor in the desperate need to secure the succession of the Infant King, as in 1216, but this time with the confidence of victory in battle. Indeed in his endeavours to secure this peace and bring to an end a war which it is apparent from the *Histoire* that he loathed, Marshal made concessions which a later generation, led by Henry III himself, regarded as a virtual betrayal. Victory, they believed, should have been crowned in brighter garments. That was the perspective of hindsight, easily asserted by those contentedly basking in the peace which had been secured during Marshal's rule. Henry III was later to learn the bitter price to be paid for civil war. Perhaps, however, for this reason, and perhaps because notwithstanding his large family Marshal's immediate line died out very quickly, his name gradually faded into obscurity.

Yet in the few short years between his return from Ireland in 1213 and his death in 1219, at the very least, Marshal had been at the heart of all the negotiations which culminated in John's reluctant sealing of the first Charter in 1215; he had himself reissued new charters during 1216 and 1217, and thus countered the annulment and revocation of the 1215 Charter; he had saved the Plantagenet dynasty, driven out a powerful invading French army, and brought a civil war to an end; and his method of government, using councils and assemblies during his regency, produced a period of 'proto-parliamentary government, opening the way for the emergence of parliament'.[5] Many more famous names in history have achieved rather less.

---

[5] JR Maddicott, *Origins of the English Parliament* (Oxford, 2002).

1361 and All That

This lecture was given to the Anglo-Australasian Lawyers Society at Melbourne and Sydney in September 2011 and was first published in (2013) Australian Law Journal Reports. *In celebration of this important date I gave lectures in similar terms to magistracy associations in this country, but I have included this particular lecture rather than one of those given to magistrates to indicate the way in which the common law has spread around and to the other side of the world. In England and Wales, of course, the magistracy continues to play a crucial, invaluable role in the administration of justice, and it remains, to outsiders, one of the more astonishing features of our constitutional arrangements that we rely so much on non-lawyers to administer justice. Yet this involvement of citizens in administering justice, just like trial by jury, is an important, if underrated, indication of how the rule of law is embedded in the fabric of society.*

THE TITLE OF this talk has been unashamedly taken from the spoof History of England written in 1930, *1066 and All That*.[1] The history celebrates 103 Good Things, 5 Bad Kings, and 2 Genuine Dates. The last English king was Edward the Confessor. Actually that was a mistake. He was Harold of England, and from time to time a memorial notice appears to him, thanking him for dying for defending his country from the Normans. He was succeeded by waves of Norman kings who were French, Tudors who were Welsh, Stuarts who were Scottish, and Hanoverians who were German, as well as the memorable Dutch king—William and Mary. As to the Norman Conquest, that was a Good Thing.

As from this time onward England stopped being conquered and was thus able to become top nation.

The last line is:

America was thus clearly top nation, and History came to a.

Five noble reasons are given for all memorable historic events. They are:

— 'I want your wife—I'll start a war'
— 'I want your money—I'll start a war'

---

[1] WC Sellar and RJ Yeatman, *1066 and All That* (London, 1930).

— 'I want your things—I'll start a war'
— 'I see the world a bit different to you—I'll start a war'
— 'You look a bit different from me—So I'll start a war'

There is a drawing showing the men. The writers say: 'The absence of women in this drawing is intended to reflect who we should blame for history.' In the context of wars that is a somewhat chilling observation. With so many ladies here, they might perhaps think that the world story would have been different if instead of it being called history it was called herstory.

But the fundamental thesis is this:

History is not what you thought. It is what you can remember.

So I have picked on 1361, a date which no one really remembers, because it happens to be 650 years ago. So it is some sort of anniversary. But then I wonder how many remember 1787, the Charter of Justice, promulgated by George III shortly after the War of Independence by the colonists in what was to become the United States of America had been ignominiously lost. The Charter is directed to the transportation of offenders to the eastern coast of New South Wales or some one or other of the Islands adjacent, and establishing a system for the administration of justice, civil and criminal, and giving power to justices of the peace

to keep the peace, arrest, take bail, bind to good behaviour, suppress and punish riots, and to do all other Matters and Things ... as Justices of the Peace have within that part of the Great Britain called England.

Justices of the peace were incorporated into the law of Australia by the Australian Courts Act 1828. There is, of course, no longer any power in the Parliament in the United Kingdom to legislate for Australia, and it is a matter for each State to decide whether justices of the peace shall continue to exist, and if so what their responsibilities should be. But that really is for the future.

Beyond reflecting that whenever considering the future it is crucial, in days when we are offered instantaneous reaction to whatever the immediate headline may be on the television screen or in our newspapers, to remember that the future is long as well as short; that vision and strategy demand reflection on the potential long-term consequences of events, and proposed legislative change in particular.

So how do I come to 1361? Let us go back to the time of the Charter of Justice. It was followed, almost immediately, by the French Revolution, and the ascendency of Napoleon and a proposed invasion of

England. If the Battle of Trafalgar had been lost rather than won, you might all be speaking French. But whatever language you would have spoken, the common law concept of the Queen's Peace would have been eradicated, along with all the other aspects of the common law which we hold so precious.

But I want to go further back to moments of our common history. The Bill of Rights; the execution of the king, who claimed that because he was the law he was above the law; the great Petition of Right, which, with Magna Carta, inspired the foundation of what did become the United States of America; mighty Edward Coke, the Lord Chief Justice who spoke to the Monarch who wanted pliable judges who were to be lions under the throne in words which every judge and indeed every justice of the peace should always remember: 'the judges will do what it is appropriate for the judges to do', followed by the inevitable and fully appreciated consequence that, aged 70, he was thrown out of the office and into the Tower of London. But we are still in the 1600s. In this journey you have to go back beyond the Armada, another moment in your history as well as our history, where, if the forces of Phillip II of Spain had succeeded, you would probably all be speaking Spanish, and so would the inhabitants of the United States, and none of them would have had the common law to inspire them. And then back to the Reformation, the establishment of the Protestant faith, and you are still not there. America has yet to be discovered. There are many years to go before you are back to the days when our language, later to be the language of Shakespeare, and now indeed a universal language, was still a strange mixture of Latin, Norman French and Anglo Saxon, and the kings were the first two Plantagenets, Henry II and Richard the Lionheart.

Neither Plantagenet king was a man you would want to meet in a dark street on a Saturday night. Both were men of stupendous, irrational temper. And any pre-sentence report on them would describe them as members of a wholly dysfunctional family, and, if honest, would have said about each that there was no prospect of curing their tendency to be violent, but if their energy could be properly directed they might achieve something.

Now what is the purpose of going back to these kings? It is to show that there is one invisible but unbroken thread in the common law stretching from us in 2011, 800 years back to the concept of the King's Peace.

It was Henry II who made his judges travel out to the country, taking justice with them, owing no debts to any over mighty subjects.

A blow against a judge was like a blow against the king. It was treason. To this day we judges are not the Prime Minister's judges or Parliament's judges. We never shall be. We are Her Majesty's judges, independent of both, in exactly the same way as your judges are independent of executive and legislature, and—although this is not always fully appreciated—independent of each other. And just because we tend in our communities to take judicial independence for granted, we should not forget what a precious gift to our community this concept is. It is indeed one of the great foundations of living in a community which respects the rule of law. We common lawyers must be unceasing in our vigilance for its preservation.

It was Richard the Lionheart who created the first commission for local people to preserve the peace. That is the first written reference we have to the development of the story of justices of the peace. In 1285 the Statute of Westminster appointed keepers of the peace. In 1327 a statue provided that 'in every shire good and lawful men shall be assigned to keep the peace'. And so we come to the Justice of the Peace Act 1361.

I do not apologise for reminding ourselves of what it says. This is history as we should remember it.

> In every county in England there shall be assigned for the keeping of the peace ... 3 or 4 of the most worthy in the county, with some learned in the law *[it is important to underline the 'some']* and they shall have power to restrain the offender, rioter *[and you need no explanation from me about what a rioter is]* and other barators *[that is a medieval term for troublemaker]* ... and to cause them to be imprisoned and duly punished according to the law and customs of the realm and according to that which to them shall seem best to do by their good discretions and good advisement ... to the intent *[again, underline that]* that the people be not by such rioters or rebels troubled nor endamaged nor the peace blemished ... nor others passing by the highways of the realm disturbed nor put in the peril which may happen of such offenders.

This, ladies and gentlemen, is remarkable language, and notice at once that, like the jury system, it expressly links the decent citizen, but importantly, the non-lawyer citizen, and even more importantly the non-professional judge citizen, directly with the administration of criminal justice. 'Some', but not all, will be learned in the law. It was an extraordinary idea, but remarkable, and it has survived. It preceded trial by jury as we know it now, but was consistent with it. And thus we embodied in our cultures the principle of public participation in the administration of justice. This is your heritage as well as my heritage. It is indeed a common heritage for all of us, whether we live in England and Wales, or Australia or New Zealand, for in spite of all the ghastliness, so graphically described by Robert Hughes in *The Fatal Shore*,[2] these concepts came here too, and have thrived. And when young Thomas Wentworth, having with Blaxland crossed the Blue Mountains, went to England and joined the Middle Temple, and canvassed and advocated for trial by jury, for the right of ex-convicts to vote at elections, and for a free press, he, together with others, was directly linking himself to that history. And he understood that the success of the revolution in the United States would provide the catalyst for the way in which the colonies in Australia would one day be governed. He understood history. And so should we.

Back in England we have reminders of those dates of 1189 and 1361. The ruined castles, overtaken by gunpowder and shot and cannon, symbolising the mutability of earthly things. And there are the cathedrals, and the creation of mighty buildings—Lincoln and Winchester, Durham and Canterbury, and so many others—the response of men and women living in what nowadays would be described as abject poverty, inspired by their faiths. But these great edifices are rarely filled with worshippers expressing a common faith; they are nowadays the meeting places for awestruck visitors.

There is much to admire in this history of castles and cathedrals, but it is not unique to common law countries. France, Germany, Italy, Spain, all have phenomenal buildings from medieval times. What is unique to the common law is the concept of the King's Peace linked with the continuing living embodiment of community involvement in the rule of law and responsibility for keeping the peace. The responsibility for its preservation is not confined to judges and justices of the peace and magistrates, or lawyers. In truth it symbolises that we are all—every citizen—involved, and that is why we are all eligible to serve as jurors.

The changes in every conceivable aspect of life in the last 650 years are beyond description. In the context of the blemishing of the Peace I cannot, of course, comment on the riots which in London and other cities in England disfigured your television screens, for the simple reason that I shall in due course have to deal with some of the cases, but I can, without difficulty or controversy and without fear of contradiction, venture to suggest that one thing has never changed. If at any time since 1361, and indeed if at any time in the future, you were to go out into the streets, as you will be going out

---

[2] Robert Hughes, *The Fatal Shore* (London, 1987).

to work shortly, and ask yourselves, ask each other, ask the man and woman walking in the street in the same direction as you are, or, as you sit around the table at the weekend, ask, 'Apart from personal matters like health or anxieties about the children or grandchildren, what is it you want most from your community?', the most likely answer, in any age, would be the same.

> I want to be safe in my home. I want my family to be safe in their home. I want to be safe as I walk the streets. I want my family to be safe in the streets. I do not want to live under the fear and tension of possible violence, however slight it may be. I want to live my life in peace.

The value of the preservation of the peace is beyond price, and the message that comes down to us from the creation of the concept of justices of the peace with the deliberate purpose—there can be no more express statutory purpose than the words 'to the intent'—that the peace should not be 'blemished' and those using the streets should not be 'disturbed or put in peril'.

And so, I end where I began. If history is what we remember, then let us remember that one of the longest-standing bulwarks of the rule of law in our countries is the ancient concept which runs in an unbroken thread through hundreds of years of our history. That is why 1361 really matters. Probably we will not need to remember the date itself, but it would be catastrophic for all our communities if we were to forget exactly what it stands for.

Authorised Version of the Bible: 'Divine Right'

This lecture was given at Westminster Abbey in October 2011, as part of a series organised by the Dean, The Very Reverend John Hall, to celebrate the anniversary of the Authorised Version of the Bible. In the preparation of this lecture I drew on the material to be found in The Elizabethan House of Commons *by JE Neale (London, 1949),* The Lion and the Throne *by Catherine Drinker Bowen (London, 1957),* The Sovereignty of Parliament *by Jeffrey Goldsworthy (Oxford, 1999), and* Power and Glory *by Adam Nicolson (London, 2003). The original texts quoted in this lecture, many of which are familiar, can be found in one or more of those sources.*

THIS IS A wonderful anniversary. It is 400 years since the publication of the Authorised Version of the Bible. And before I come to address the ferment of legal and constitutional issues which were being played out here, in the heart of Westminster, contemporaneously with the preparation of the Authorised Version not only at Oxford and Cambridge, but here in the Jerusalem Chamber, perhaps I may be allowed to repeat a point that I have made before, and to do so at the beginning of the first of these lectures.

The men involved in the task of translating the Bible believed that they were translating the Word of God into English. The precise meaning of every word mattered. Without precision, as TS Eliot tells us, the words would decay, slip, slide, and perish.[1] For the Word of God that simply could not be. Precision of language always matters in any legal contract. But this was infinitely more important than that. It was about the immortal soul, and the destiny of the immortal soul. Ever since 1517, when Martin Luther had pinned his 95 theses to the door of the church at Wittenburg Castle, men and women had died horrible, agonising deaths because of endless disputes about whether in his letter to the Romans St Paul was saying that salvation could be achieved through faith, or through faith alone, exclusively through faith. But if faith alone, where stood

---

[1] TS Eliot, *Four Quartets* (London, 1943).

'charity', the greatest of the great trilogy, faith, hope and charity? And if we were pre-destined, and the destiny of our immortal souls was already fixed, did we have free will? In the discussion at Hampton Court on this very subject, it is recorded that the king himself wished that this doctrine should be handled 'tenderly'. And how many deaths followed the doctrinal dispute as to whether what happened in the sacrifice at the altar was consubstantiation or transubstantiation? Christendom is divided on this question to this day. Was it necessary for a priest or bishop or the Pope to intervene in any respect in the relationship between each immortal soul and his or her God? Men and women endured martyrdom over questions like these, not just here in London, but all over Christian Europe. To find the answers they sought inspiration from the Bible, the word of God. No wonder the precise meaning of each word in the Bible mattered. And if I may say so—and this is not my subject, so I say so with humility—unless we understand the religious context of the Authorised Version we have missed the real point that mattered to those who produced it. And no wonder it took seven years to produce.

At just the time when Lancelot Andrewes and his team were at work striving to make the Bible 'shine as gold more brightly, being rubbed and polished',[2] side by side, simultaneously, with this mammoth task another struggle was in the making. The results on our legal and constitutional affairs are with us to this day, and they have crossed the seas to continents which were then unexplored or undiscovered.

Between 1604 and 1611, and the years which followed, although this was not the sort of language used in those days, our constitutional arrangements were examined, discussed, argued, and eventually fought over. They culminated in the public trial of the king. We always think of Charles I and his dignity on that cold January day in 1649. Our image of him is cloaked in the story of his death, and the dignity with which he met it. We should not be grudging in our respect and admiration. At his trial the king argued that the court had no jurisdiction to try him. Legally, the point was seriously arguable. What was the lawful authority which permitted the anointed king to be put on trial? The answer was that the Commons of England assembled in Parliament had 'constituted this court'. Whatever the inaccuracies in this assertion, it encapsulated the issue that had divided the country for nearly half a century. After the king was

---

[2] Authorised Version of the Bible, 'The Translators to the Reader'.

convicted and sentenced, in his sentencing remarks (as we now call them) Bradshaw, the President, told him that at 'one blow you had confounded the liberties and the property of England'.[3] So the king was executed and some 40 years or so later, in 1688, his son James II was, in effect, removed from the throne.

None of this was even in remote contemplation when Elizabeth I died in 1603, after a reign of 44 years. She was a lonely, companionless old woman. Her glory had gone and her achievements had faded in the public memory. The preparation of the defences against a succession of Armadas (the Armada of 1588 is the only one which we remember now) together with an unsuccessful campaign in Ireland and some shocking harvests had left the country impoverished. Her great speech at Tilbury was for the ages. But the speech illustrates something of her ability to understand, and to convey to her subjects that she understood, their concerns. It is, I point out, also a remarkable piece of advocacy.[4] We all know it, or some of it. But I cannot resist a quotation. Consider the beginning:

> My loving people, we have been persuaded by some that are careful about our safety, to take heed how we commit ourselves to armed multitudes ...

Notice here, the royal, 'we', and 'ourselves'. This was an anointed monarch speaking to her subjects. The speech could have gone on in this same way, conveying the same message, but if it had it would have lacked the inspirational quality that arose when she personalised her leadership.

> ... and therefore I am come amongst you, as you see, at this time, not for my recreation and disport, but being resolved, in the midst and heat of the battle, to live or die amongst you all, to lay down for my God, and for my kingdom, and for my people, my honour and my blood, even in the dust.

This is sublime advocacy. The 'We' had become 'I', and 'Our' had become 'My'. Notice how her use of 'I' was a message of inclusivity, universality. In effect, they were all in it together. In this moment of national emergency, she was both the crowned Queen and a flesh and blood human being, like all her subjects, with a weak and feeble body, but the stomach of a king. I cannot help allowing myself to imagine that her shadow was hovering above Winston Churchill when he inspired the nation in the dark days of 1940.

---

[3] Quoted in Richard Lee Bradshaw, *God's Battleaxe: The Life of Lord President John Bradshawe* (California, 2010).

[4] *Book of Speeches* (Folio Society, 2007).

This knack, this instinctive grasp of the politically possible, never deserted her, even when her Parliaments became difficult, as they did, even when she imprisoned members for discussing the succession, or the role, if any, to be played by Bishops. She agreed to 'liberal but not licentious speech, liberty, but with due limitation'. Nowadays we would deride the concept of any limitations, but in sixteenth-century Europe this was an astonishing concession to be made by any monarch. This was the century of Thomas Hobbes. The Cortez in Spain and the Parlement in France were fast withering away. Parliament was, she said, 'the body of the realm'. And when after a heated debate in March 1593 a subsidy was voted, she addressed the Commons personally, saying:

> The subsidy you give me I accept thankfully, if you give me your goodwill with it ... if the necessity of the time of your preservations did not require it, I would refuse it.

It was now 1603. All that had gone. James I came to the throne of England, and he was greeted with jubilation. It is unfair to say that he was all things to all men, but all men believed that the arrival of the new king would give them something. Yet he had already written his *Trew Law of Free Monarchies*. His opinion was unequivocal. Kings were 'the authors and makers of the Laws, and not the Laws of the Kings'. There were kings before there was law. The king was created by God 'to sit on his throne and rule over other men'. Subjects must never rebel, and even when 'oppressed by Nero' should endure 'without resistance, but by sobs and tears to God'.

Obviously this was a very different king to Elizabeth, with a very different approach to the role of the monarch. Although he had declared his position, everyone was thrilled, everyone. Perhaps they did not understand what he had written, or appreciate how deeply he believed it. Perhaps however the very fact of a safe and peaceful succession had relieved the uncertainty in the minds of virtually everyone who was not involved in the careful preparation for the succession, and clouded judgement. And no one was later to remind the king that his Divine Right to rule meant that God had vested the arrangements for the succession to the throne of England in the hands of a somewhat surprising agent of the heavens, Robert Cecil.

The new king was generous. Immensely generous. It did not occur to anyone that he was generous with what nowadays would be described as the national assets. He spent money he did not have. Perhaps things do not change very much. And just as today, with a change of government, he was allowed a honeymoon period.

The previous regime was gone. The new regime was exciting and vibrant. For example, the new king created an endless stream of knights, so much so that it began to be said that it was better to be a gentleman than a knight because knights had become so common. Francis Bacon, who was happy enough to accept his knighthood at a mass investiture of some 300, recorded that the title of knighthood was 'almost prostituted'.[5] In the first year alone, 1,000 knights were created—more knights than Elizabeth had created in her entire 44-year reign. And later James I created a new title of Baronet. This was not a mark of distinction or honour. All that was needed to be granted the hereditary title was the simple ability to afford to pay.

In all this glamour and excitement, there was one incident which astounded even those observing events in the honeymoon period. On his way to London, at Newark, James I ordered that a thief should be hanged, without any trial or any hearing. John Harington, one of Elizabeth's many godsons, and the man who had the distinction of inventing the water closet system—he was a surprisingly handy man—made this well known observation:

> I hear our new King hath hanged one man before he was tried; 'tis strangely done: now if the wind bloweth thus, why may not a man be tried before he hath offended?

It is immensely pleasing to me, and I hope to you, that coming down the centuries to us, such a question was being raised in this country over 400 years ago. How can a man be sentenced without trial? The idea was preposterous. If the incident had happened after the honeymoon was over it would have been more widely condemned.

And so to the great conference at Hampton Court. In the course of the discussions the king learned what puritans thought of his responsibilities as the Supreme Governor in Causes Ecclesiastical.

> If you aim at a Scotch Presbytery, it agreeth as well with Monarchy as God with the Devil. Then Jack and Tom and Will and Dick shall meet and sensor me and my Council ... I know what would become of my Supremacy, for no bishop, no King.

As Adam Nicolson explains in his wonderful, readable *Power and Glory*:

> The beauty of the Church of England, with its full panoply of bishops and archbishops, was its explicit acceptance of the King at its head ...

---

[5] Quoted in Catherine Drinker Bowen, *The Lion and the Throne: The Life and Times of Sir Edward Coke, 1552–1634* (London, 1957).

but a king without bishops, subject to a presbytery, was always in danger of being removed.[6]

During the discussions an issue was raised as to whether the cross should be present in baptisms. This was followed by the further question,

> how far the ordinance of the church bindeth, without impeaching Christian liberty?

The response of the monarch to the suggestion that every man is to be left to his own liberty was stark:

> I will have none of that. I will have one doctrine, one discipline, one religion, in substance and in ceremony.

In other words, in accordance with the Peace of Augsburg some 50 years earlier, '*cujus regio, ejus religio*', which meant that the man who ruled the country could dictate its religion to his subjects—or as the French expressed it: '*un roi, une loi, une foi*'.

And so to his first Parliament of 1604. James I declared that a righteous king was ordained for his people, and not his people for him. But he was given a very simple message, and he never took notice of it. The Commons refused to rubber-stamp his argument that, now the two kings of Scotland and England were united, he was Emperor of Britain, and then that he should adopt the title of King of Great Britain by proclamation. In essence the argument was simple. On one view, allegiance to the king was a personal matter between the subject and his monarch. The contrary view, maintained in the Commons, was that allegiance was owed not to the person of the individual king, but to the Crown and the law. Probably on Robert Cecil's advice, the king did not pursue the point further at that stage. He did later partially succeed in the course of *Calvin's Case*,[7] when the court was persuaded that a man born in Scotland after his accession was a natural subject of the king, and thus could hold land in England of which James was the king.

The Divines went off to produce the Authorised Version, and then came the Gunpowder Plot, which demonstrated once and for all to the public mind that two religions could not live together. Of course the Plot represented a direct physical risk both to the king and to the members of both Houses, and for a while perhaps the fact

---

[6] Adam Nicolson, *Power and Glory: Jacobean England and the Making of the King James Bible* (London, 2003).

[7] *Calvin's Case* (1572–1616) Co Rep 1a.

that they had all been subject to the same risks obscured the potential for difficulty between them.

In 1606, Sir Edward Coke was appointed Chief Justice of the Common Pleas. It is worth emphasising that he had, among many different aspects to his life, been a Commons man, and indeed its Speaker. The motto displayed on his rings was significant. '*Lex est tutissima cassis*'—the law is the safest shield. Contrast this with James himself writing shortly afterwards in 1607 that 'before any parliaments were ... or laws made', there were kings. He was very rude about Parliament. Parliaments were a trial laid on by the Almighty as plagues were laid on by Pharaohs. He did not need to be rude about judges. Judges only held office for as long as they behaved themselves—that is, for as long as the king thought they were behaving themselves. In his judgment in *Calvin's Case*, his Lord Chancellor asserted that '*rex est lex loquens*'—the law is the king speaking. In the dispute in the Privy Council between the judges and the bishops, the Archbishop of Canterbury, Bancroft, asserted that 'judges are but delegates under the King'. There is not much room in this analysis for an independent judiciary.

Edward Coke, however, consistent with the motto on his rings, asserted that 'the King is under God and the law' and that the 'the common law hath admeasured the King's prerogative'. In their different ways these observations encapsulated the burning issue. Was the king above the law, or subject to it? James himself had no doubt. In 1609 he told Parliament that the monarchy 'is the supremest thing upon earth'. No room there for the supremacy of the law. Even God himself spoke of kings as Gods. Throughout the declamation he described the laws as 'my' laws, adding that 'never King was in all his time more careful to have laws duly observed ... than I'. I asked you to notice the way Elizabeth had personalised herself. So did James. But in his 'I' his claim was not all-embracing, all-encompassing: this was divisiveness, separation. And he asserted a claim that, just like God, kings had power to 'judge all, and to be judged or accountable to none'. Again, no doubt about that message.

Elizabeth would have appreciated how tactless and confrontational, and ultimately provocative, such sermonising from the royal throne in Parliament would have been. In her entire reign she had never sat in judgment nor claimed the right to do so. If she had done so, one wonders whether it would have been questioned. But to acquiesce in the idea that the king could sit as a judge in accordance with his claim, allowed legitimacy for his further observation that he was accountable to no one. The honeymoon was over. In the

Commons His Majesty's loving subjects perceived that their common and ancient right and liberty had much declined and been infringed 'in these late years ...'. This was not a trumpet sounding a charge to battle: it was not the full Verdi. That lay ahead with the Petition of Right in 1628, one of the great constitutional documents of our so-called unwritten constitution. Rather it was a delicate tune written perhaps by Haydn, utterly compelling to those with ears to hear. James was not listening.

So, while Lancelot Andrewes and his team were beavering away, an immensely serious issue arose between the common law courts and the Ecclesiastical High Commission. The Commission represented long-established principles that the Church should govern in matters spiritual and clerical. In one sense the problems were encapsulated in the name. The Commission was now calling itself the Court of High Commission. The question was whether it was a court at all. And although the issues were extremely complex, and this brief summary cannot do justice to the refinements of the arguments, what brought the dispute to a head was that personal inquiries about troublesome areas of conscience in questions of religion were no longer being directed at Catholics (who by virtue of any loyalty to the Pope were regarded as potential traitors in any event—the word 'Papist' was not intended as a compliment)—but to Protestants and Non-Conformists, whose loyalty to the king was not diminished by possible loyalty to any external authority. The court asserted that it was entitled to examine Non-Conformists on their oath about their beliefs. Parliament challenged this jurisdiction, and the Court of Common Pleas asserted that a man should not be examined on his private beliefs. We take that principle for granted now, but this was a new declaration. What is more, it added that the Ecclesiastical Court, if it was a court at all, was not entitled to exercise any jurisdiction in lay as opposed to ecclesiastical matters. And so, when the Court of High Commission exercised what it believed was its jurisdiction in circumstances which Common Pleas regarded as an improper exercise, orders of prohibition were issued. In our secular age it is difficult to comprehend the importance of these questions. If this dispute happened in the modern age, can you imagine the collection of reporters that would be standing outside the Royal Courts of Justice or for that matter the Supreme Court just over the road?

The situation was complicated, in the public eye at any rate, when a barrister, Nick Fuller, appearing on behalf of Puritans who were trying to avoid fines for not conforming, asserted in his submissions that bishops were 'popish'—an allegation which was close to treasonous, and one which would have had Lancelot Andrewes surging forward out of the Abbey straight into Westminster Hall in a volcanic explosion. Fuller went on that bishops were under the jurisdiction of 'anti-Christ' and that they embezzled the fines paid by Non-Conformists. So the court locked him up for contempt. Isn't it strange how counsel then, as now, did not always appreciate that there are occasions when the rapier is a much more powerful weapon than the bludgeon?

Common Pleas issued a prohibition on the basis that the barrister's conduct in any court was a lay matter, to be tried at common law. Bancroft asserted the contrary. Fuller was convicted in the Ecclesiastical Court and imprisoned. The case was discussed in Parliament. The Commons took Fuller's side. The Ecclesiastical Court did not have the power to imprison. This was seen by James as an attack on his Supremacy over the Church. In essence, if the authority of the Ecclesiastical Court was criticised, then by implication at any rate, the king as head of the Church was also being criticised. More importantly, his supremacy was being criticised. And this had what we would call political implications. If there was no equivocation about the king's supremacy in matters of religion, his supremacy on secular matters would follow ineluctably.

We must leave Nick Fuller. The upshot of the widespread use of prohibition by the common law courts to curb the powers of the Ecclesiastical Court, and the response of the Commons to its use, led to a meeting of the Privy Council to which the judges and bishops were summoned. The king sat to decide the argument. What on earth was he doing? It was not merely that Elizabeth had never sat in judgment; a great fifteenth-century Chief Justice, Fortescue, declared in *In Praise of the Laws of England* that it was not 'customary for the kings of England to sit in court or pronounce judgment themselves'.[8] Judges against bishops. The mind boggles. But the real issue was the position of the head of the Church of England. The meeting was tumultuous. The judges made a simple point. Ecclesiastical courts have jurisdiction over ecclesiastical but not temporal issues. When a temporal issue arose it must be transferred to the common law courts. The king interrupted. Patience was not one of his qualities, and he knew the answer anyway. It was contended

---

[8] John Fortescue, *In Praise of the Laws of England* (London, 1660).

that judges were 'but delegates of the King, and that the King may take what causes he shall please from the determination of the judges and may determine them himself'. Unsurprisingly, Bancroft agreed. 'This was clear in divinity that such authority belongs to the King by the word of God.' Louis XIV himself could not have put the matter more clearly. Coke asserted that

> the King in his own person cannot adjudge any case ... [Cases] ought to be determined and adjudged in some court of justice according to the law and custom of England.

It is difficult nowadays to appreciate the seriousness of the argument and what was at stake. The potential consequences for Coke when the king told the Chief Justice that he 'spoke foolishly' was insult enough, and potentially catastrophic—but worse was to come. Coke would not be silenced. He responded: 'The Laws and Customs of England protected His Majesty in safety and peace.' The king was even more offended. If this was right it would mean that the king was 'under the law—which it is treason to affirm'. Coke replied with a quotation from Bracton, a medieval legal philosopher who had written *Laws and Customs of England*, that the king should not be under any man, but '*sed sub Deo et Lege*'—under God and the laws. Contemporary records tell us that in his fury the king raised his fist and shook it at Coke. What a moment. There is some dispute as to whether Coke fell flat on his face or to his knees. But at the very least he knelt down. The Tower beckoned. No one knew better than Coke how little evidence was required to prove treason. Or how a traitor was executed. For now the debate—as a debate— was over. Coke was not deprived of his office. That came later. So did his period of imprisonment in the Tower. What is remarkable is the courage involved in the issue on the following day of a new prohibition out of the common law courts against the Court of High Commission.

The Commons were concerned about another matter: the use of a royal proclamation, issued after the assassination of Henry IV of France in May 1610, which required every subject to take the Oath of Allegiance. Look at it from the king's point of view. The assassination of his fellow king was what we would now describe as a terrorist situation, demanding to be addressed urgently by the exercise of the widest possible powers. At such times, as we know to this day, the argument is attractive. But even the tyrannical Henry VIII had not asserted the right to rule by proclamation, at any rate without the express sanction of Parliament which was given in

1539 in the notorious Act of Proclamation. This Act was repealed on his death and has never been renewed, although the tendency to govern by proclamation—or vesting powers in the government of the day to do so (that is, Henry VIII clauses)—has certainly come under consideration in our country in recent years. I discovered that during the parliamentary session up to 10 November 2009 'around 70 such powers' were contained within legislation. And between 10 November and the end of the parliamentary session 2008–09, there were an additional 53 such clauses. Thus in one very recent parliamentary session there were over 120 Henry VIII clauses.

Let me return to 1610. The Commons presented an address to the king. The language was courteous but unequivocal. Different forms of proclamation were identified. For us, perhaps the most interesting complaints were directed against proclamations made shortly after the session of Parliament in relation to 'matter directly rejected in the same session'. It is obvious, is it not, that if the king could by proclamation in effect set aside the decision of Parliament, parliamentary government would be at an end. The address turned to other forms of proclamation: 'appointing punishment to be inflicted before lawful trial and conviction' (perhaps a reference to the mindset of a king who was prepared to hang the thief at Newark), and other proclamations of which complaint was made '… referring punishment of offenders to courts of arbitrary discretion …' (a complaint against the absence of what we would call due process). James summoned the judges before him so that he could consult as to whether the power to issue such proclamations was vested in him. This was the moment when judges were supposed to do their duty. James knew what the answer should be. So did his Lord Chancellor. Without this power, James suggested that the king would be no better than the Duke of Venice. Coke asked for time for thought, expressing his preliminary view that without Parliament the king could not change any part of the common law or create any offence which had not been an offence before. After an adjournment the judges expressed the view that the king could not alter the law by proclamation. Such proclamations did not form part of the law of England. Then, more boldly, they added: 'The King hath no prerogative but that which the law of the land allows him.' This is mighty stuff, ladies and gentlemen. Judges supporting the Commons against the king. In other words the concerns expressed by the Commons were in the view of the judges entirely justified. Perhaps it was just as well that when this view was expressed, James himself was out hunting in the country.

There are perhaps two or three significant points to notice here. First, that the Commons and the judges led by Edward Coke were making common cause. The Commons was filled with lawyers, or those who had been trained in the Inns of Court. And the physical proximity of the Commons to the courts in Westminster Hall meant that there was ample time for gossip and discussion among them all. Coke in particular had been a Commons man. After he was deprived of office, he resumed his role as a Commons man. All the events I am describing happened in a very small, tight geographical area, say a mile radius from where we are today. Imagine in those years, even before the telephone, the gossip, the chat, the way in which what we now describe as 'public opinion' was being formed.

Second, Coke was extremely troubled, and together with the judges asked the king and Council that they should not constantly be summoned to express views about issues which might arise for decision in court. The point eventually struck home, but not before a different device was tried. After the Authorised Version was published, in 1615, poor old Mr Peacham was charged with treason after his house was broken into and his papers searched, and a draft sermon—never preached—was found which suggested that there were circumstances in which a subject would become entitled to resist his sovereign who sought to reduce his liberties. This did not look like a very strong case: unspoken words written on a piece of paper. So the papers were sent to Coke, in effect to obtain an opinion from him in advance of the proceedings. It was reported that Coke, using words 'more vehement' than the writer dared to repeat, thought that this taking of judicial opinions one by one was 'new and dangerous'. And so it was. And so it would be to this day.

Third, on behalf of my judicial colleagues, perhaps I am allowed to say that when James tried his hand as a judge he summarised how difficult the exercise of our responsibilities can be. The problem was that you had to listen to both sides, a fairly elementary part of the judicial function. He said:

> I could get on very well hearing one side only, but when both sides have been heard, by my soul I know not which is right.

In the absence of the king, the Privy Council accepted that the king could not by proclamation create an offence which had not been an offence before the proclamation, and that his proclamations formed no part of the law of England. The king himself did not raise the point again. It was a victory of the greatest possible importance to our constitutional developments. Without it, our Parliament would have gone the way of the Cortez and the Parlement.

I must now come to a piece of litigation. In 1610 the famous decision in *Bonham's Case* was reached.[9] Bonham was a doctor. He practised medicine without a certificate from the Royal College of Physicians. The College was entitled, by the Statute of Incorporation, to 'regulate all London physicians and punish infractions with fine and imprisonment'. So Bonham was arrested and put in prison. He brought an action for false imprisonment. It was all very simple. The College should win. But there was a problem. Half of any fine imposed by the College was paid to the College. Bonham won. The main reason for his victory was the common law maxim, derived from Roman Law, which continues to this date, that no man should be a judge in his own cause. The College was both the party to the case, and the judge of it, and the beneficiary of any conviction and fine. That was unacceptable. The statute, which was regulatory only, was insufficient to bypass this essential principle. So far, so good. And that should have been the end of the case.

The historic interest of *Bonham's Case* arose from an observation which was but a discarding comment by Coke that the common law was entitled to control an Act of Parliament if such Act was against 'common right and reason, or repugnant, or impossible to be performed'. For all the subsequent publicity and importance attached to this comment, at the time it attracted no particular interest. It was a throwaway line, obiter dictum, not relevant to the case—if you like a judicial whimsy, although judges should not indulge in whimsicalities. Certainly Coke thought nothing of it, nor did his contemporaries, nor—most important of all—did Parliament, and the observation was handed down in Westminster Hall adjacent to Parliament. Perhaps more important, Coke would never have imagined for one moment that Parliament was capable of passing an Act which was against common right and reason. From his point of view the concept was a contradiction in terms.

Nevertheless, notwithstanding years of scorn poured on the observation by subsequent Chief Justices, the time for this obiter dictum was to come. Go forward 150 years. The Stamp Act of 1765 was passed in Parliament. The Massachusetts Assembly declared that the Act was invalid because it was against Magna Carta and the natural rights of Englishmen, and therefore, according to Lord Coke, null and void. John Adams, the second President, and one

---

[9] (1610) 8 Co Rep 113b.

of the founding fathers of what we now call the United States of America, expressed himself determined to die of the opinion that Acts of Parliament could be null.

There is here a crucial point. In our constitutional arrangements, the sovereignty of Parliament remains the essential principle. It was through the parliamentary processes that our constitutional arrangements were discussed, argued and eventually established. The absolutism of a monarch was curbed by the authority and power vested in Parliament. For the colonists their problem was Parliament itself. In the Stamp Act it was enacting legislation that took away the liberties which had been successfully established by Parliament in the previous century.

May I emphasise that *Bonham's Case* was decided while the Authorised Version was being translated, and that while it was being translated, a year or two earlier in 1606, the charter for the new colony in Virginia was settled. It was effectively drafted by Edwin Sandys, a barrister and Commons man who, like Coke, and Eliot, and Valentine, and Holles, all Commons men to whom with many others we are indebted for our liberties, ended up in the Tower. But in 1618 he, in effect, wrote and was granted the 'Great Charter' for Virginia. And by this Charter the settlers and any of the children born in the new colony and plantations were to have 'and enjoy all liberties, franchises and immunities to all intents and purposes as if they had been abiding and born within this our realm of England'. The Charter provided guarantees of 'self-government, freedom of speech, equality before the law, and trial by jury'. These were all believed to be principles applicable in England; or at any rate, when Sandys declared them to be established, they were at least on the aspirational agenda. They were being transported across the Atlantic. The language of this Charter was later to be repeated, as colony after colony was established, from Maryland in 1632 all the way to Massachusetts Bay in 1691.

This is a moment of the greatest possible importance to the eventual widening of the common law world. When the colonists in the United States were arguing their case in 1776 for 'no taxation without representation', they were simply echoing what they believed were the constitutional rights which had been established in the mother country. For what it is worth, I believe that they were right. And that message was carried by young Thomas Wentworth, born in a convict ship on the way to Australia, the first man to describe himself as a native of Australia, who, from studying the way in which the colonies in the United States had established their independence, foresaw that one day the same common law principles would be established in Australia.

So Coke's dictum in *Bonham's Case* was much more influential in the United States than it ever was in this jurisdiction. Its significance was not appreciated while the Authorised Version was being translated, and the Charter of Virginia hardly merited any attention when that new colony was settled. But the constitutional arrangements for the new United States after the War of Independence was won gave to the Supreme Court authority over the constitution which our House of Lords, now Supreme Court, does not have. In this jurisdiction the sovereignty of Parliament remains the essential principle. I have digressed, but only in this limited sense. I have sought to highlight the tiny judicial acorn, discarded on apparently stony ground, while the Authorised Version was being translated, from which a mighty oak was to grow.

Let me briefly return to 1611. The Authorised Version was produced. It was to have its own glorious history. Others in this series of lectures will speak of all that. But while the work was being done by Lancelot Andrewes and the team, issues of the greatest importance to what we now call constitutional matters were in full flow. It is perhaps worth emphasising, because of the way in which history actually happened, that in 1611 the overwhelming majority of the Commons and the judges and the lawyers believed in the monarchy. One of the legal scholars, John Seldon, another man incarcerated in the Tower, made the simple point that 'a King is a thing men have made for their own sakes, for quietness' sake'. The wonderfully pugnacious John Eliot, made of more heroic clay than Seldon, and who was to die in the Tower, was to say later that if 'false glasses did not stand between us and the King, our privileges and his prerogative might both have been enjoyed'. As I have said before, James was not a great listener. This is symbolised in the Star Chamber in 1616 when before a large crowd of lawyers and parliamentarians James declared that:

> Kings are properly judges and judgment properly belongs to them from God: the Kings sit in the throne of God whence all judgment is derived ... it is presumption and high contempt in the subject to dispute what a King can do, or say that a King cannot do this or that ...

He ordered them not to meddle in things 'against the King's prerogative or honour', adding that 'if judges permitted these matters to be argued then those who argue it and the judges who allowed it to be argued would suffer'.

It was increasingly difficult to find an acceptable compromise, and the clash of views continued unabated. The king asserted that parliamentary privilege 'derived from the grace and commission of our ancestors and us, for most of them grow from precedence, which shows rather a toleration than inheritance'. On the other hand, in the Commons the counter contention was that

> the privileges of this House is the nurse and life of all our laws, the subject's best inheritance ... When the King says he cannot allow our liberties of right, this strikes at the root.

It is all in your history books, the Protestation, which the king tore out of the records. Then the accession of Charles I. If James was a poor listener, Charles I was utterly deaf, and—notwithstanding his dignity at the moment of his death—devious. Then came a series of issues, including the Petition of Right, the imprisonment of the five Knights and their release, the long period when there was no Parliament. And then the worst of all wars, the Civil War. Anyone who troubles to read about these events, and the way they unfolded, and pauses for a moment to remember that the history book which is being read is telling the story of real people, of real individuals, subject to all the frailties and concerns that people have today, will never believe that history is boring.

Once the monumental task of completing the Authorised Version was over and it was published, that was an end of it. But alongside the activities of Lancelot Andrewes to try, as accurately as possible, to translate the word of God into English, for the benefit of men's immortal souls, the struggle for the new constitutional arrangements, to govern our lives on this earth, had begun. Principles which we now take for granted were not established beyond argument during these seven years, and some of them had still to be fought over, but the ferment of ideas represented ideas whose time had come. Our constitution is not fixed. It retains an element of flexibility. But whenever we consider it, or consider changing it, we are—unconsciously at any rate—influenced by these early struggles. And so it is that, in the first few years of the reign of James I, we were blessed by the Authorised Version of the Bible. I believe we should simultaneously recognise that it was produced during a seminal period in the history of this country, which influences the way in which it is governed to this day, and the way in which we ourselves as a nation are content to be governed.

From start to finish the essential issue remained the same. Was the king above the law? The answer eventually forged in conflict is simple. In the words of Thomas Fuller, 'Be ye never so high, the law is above you'.[10] Constitutional monarchy was established. Kings were not little Gods. They played an important, indeed a crucial part of the constitutional arrangements. But not above the law.

[10] Quoted by Lord Denning in *Gouriet v Union of Post Office Workers* [1977] QB 729.

'No Taxation Without Representation': A British Perspective on Constitutional Arrangements

This lecture was given in Colorado Springs in August 2010 and was first published in (2011) 88 Denver University Law Review.

WHERE I TOUCH on the affairs of the USA I offer my thoughts with due humility, apologising in advance for the inevitable (but, I assure you, unintended) errors or insensitivities, and having listened to the entire conference so far for perhaps picking up the wrong end of a particular discussion. No offence is intended. What follows are my personal thoughts, as an outside observer—an admiring outside observer certainly, but no expert. I am profoundly aware that the true experts on your constitutional arrangements are here, among you.

I was called to the Bar of England and Wales at the Middle Temple in London. So was the man credited with coining one of the most historic and symbolic phrases ever coined: 'no taxation without representation', John Dickinson. He also wrote the Liberty Song in 1768:

> Then join hand in hand, brave Americans all,
> By uniting we stand, by dividing we fall.

Five American lawyers from the Middle Temple signed the Declaration of Independence.[1] The Americans were publicly supported, among many others, by Edmund Burke, a Middle Templar, and all were greatly influenced by William Blackstone, another. We know that the father of the great Chief Justice Marshall, to whom I shall come, subscribed to his own edition of Blackstone, and the Chief Justice referred to it in his seminal decision in *Marbury v Madison*.[2]

---

[1] See generally Eric Stockdale and Randy J Holland, *Middle Temple Lawyers and the American Revolution* (Minnesota, 2007).
[2] [1803] 1 Cranch 137.

Just to be clear that men of action as well as men of thought were involved, it was a Middle Templar, John Laurens, who fought at the battle of Yorktown and negotiated, as George Washington's representative, the surrender of the British forces. And when Washington was appointing his first justices to the Supreme Court, two were Middle Templars. Two of that hugely impressive line of Justices from their day to this happened to have been with us. And it is indeed a privilege that Justice Ginsberg and Justice Sottomayor have been here.

Mrs John Adams, the wife of the second President, would have approved. Her letters show how determined she was that the founding fathers should have recognised that half the human race was female. And what a tribute to John Adams himself that such a remarkable and wonderful woman should have loved him as she did. There must have been something very special about him, and indeed in my view there was.

Dickinson's first journey to England in 1753, in what was not much more than a wooden tub, took 59 days—2 months. And he wrote home to his mother that he had been seasick on 35 of them. My wife Judith and I arrived here after nine hours in an aeroplane. But Dickinson, and hundreds like him, braved the elements. A lot of them rather enjoyed their visit to London, although according to Charles Carroll, perhaps a rather toffee-nosed young man from Maryland, there were 'few young gentlemen ... to be found of sound morals'. Well no doubt, for young men then, as for young men always, wine, women and song did not lack their attractions. The President of the first Continental Congress, who preceded the first President of the United States as the titular head of the infant Republic, was a Middle Templar. This was Peyton Randolph. So were two of the following Presidents of the Congress, Thomas McKean and Cyrus Griffin. So were four drafters of the Articles of Federation; so were seven of those who signed the constitution.

I am not drawing your attention to these facts for the purposes of decoration. They matter to me personally because I believe that the rule of law which we all espouse comes from deep within the roots of our national histories. That is why they merit examination. The deeper the roots go, the more entrenched they become in the unconscious as well as the conscious soul of the nation. In our communities, the citizen does not merely hope for justice based on the rule of law, but expects and demands it. We live in happier lands just because these roots go so deep, and my thesis is that your roots did not begin in 1776, and you should not assume that they did.

One of the problems with history is that when we look back at what happened we assume that what happened would inevitably have happened. I mean no disrespect, but even if the American War of Independence was destined to succeed, those who took part in it had no particular reason to believe that it would. It took great courage to sign up to it. As a Middle Templar, I am proud of my forebears who had the courage to take their stand of principle at an uncertain time when, if they had been unsuccessful, they would undoubtedly have been hanged. That was a point, I believe, explained by John Adams at one of the early Congress meetings when the chubby, future President pointed out to one of his skinnier colleagues that it would take him longer to die because he did not weigh so much. Benjamin Franklin made the same point. If they did not hang together, they would be hanged separately. That is something we can laugh at now, but for them it was not a joke. The risks were huge.

Of course for the reasons given by Tom Paine in *Common Sense*,[3] that great seminal work, independence was bound to happen; but not necessarily then, not necessarily as an outcome of their particular struggle. Moreover, this particular war divided both nations. It was in truth a civil war. That is why William Pitt, who only a few years earlier had been the Prime Minister in London when the Colonists—that was what they were called then—fought side by side with British soldiers in the Seven Years War with France, was able, during the course of the conflict, in a speech in the House of Lords, to assert that America could not be conquered, and that he would seek to invoke what he described as the 'genius of the constitution'.[4] Edmund Burke, who was responsible for one of my favourite sayings, that the rule of law demanded the hearing of disputes before the 'cold neutrality of an impartial judge', confessed in *On Conciliation with America*[5] that he did not know 'the method of drawing up an indictment against a whole people'. These were great Englishmen, who understood and spoke out in favour of the justice of the Colonist position.

Here, as we have seen, Peyton Randolph was the first President of Congress, a Middle Templar, but his brother John took a different view of the struggle, and he went to live and eke out his days in sad exile in England. Yet his son, Edmund, became an

---

[3] Pamphlet published 1776.
[4] William Pitt, 18 November 1777.
[5] Speech, 1775.

aide to George Washington, and his first Attorney General. But
if you want to understand that this was indeed a civil war, look
no further than Benjamin Franklin himself. His achievements
were manifold. In view of the discussion here this week, perhaps
I should point out that he changed Jefferson's mellifluous style in
the first draft of the Declaration of Independence from 'we hold
these truths to be sacred and undeniable' to the much briefer, but
the inescapable and ultimately incontrovertible words which echo
to us down the ages: 'we hold these truths to be self-evident'. One
word, or perhaps two, is always better than three, and the one he
chose put the issue beyond argument. Returning to my theme, his
son took the opposite side to his father. They never fought in battle, but, except on one occasion to resolve the payment of a debt,
I believe that they never spoke again. His son's son, that is his
grandson, took the same view as Benjamin Franklin himself. Thus
are the tribulations of civil strife imposed as a burden on contemporaries who have to live through it. For you, of course, an even
greater civil war was to come. And by then we had already had our
own civil war.

These considerations enable me to suggest to you that some of the
documents of English history which matter greatly to me continue
to matter greatly to you, and should be seen as part of the foundation of your nation. They include Magna Carta in 1215, the Petition
of Right of 1626, the Grand Remonstrance of 1641, and the Bill of
Rights of 1689. Your constitutional roots include a civil war which
culminated in the execution in 1649 of a monarch who proclaimed
the Divine Right of Kings, and the removal of another in 1688 when
he sought to subvert the constitutional changes consequent on the
execution of his father. All these events influenced the thinking of
the Colonists, and the constitutional arrangements which they were
seeking to uphold. It was part of their history, as it is part of our
history. And that is why I respectfully suggest that it remains part
of your history. But notice for the future—our civil war was a war
brought about in a struggle about the rule of law. Could it possibly
be that, in the Latin, '*rex est lex*' or '*rex est lex loquens*'?. It was
lawyers; not exclusively lawyers, but many of the most influential
members of Parliament who challenged the concept of the Divine
Right were lawyers. By the end of the Civil War there was a public
trial of a monarch for waging war on his subjects. And we have the
record. The king argued that the court had no jurisdiction to try him.
In constitutional theory, it was an arguable point. In practical terms,
however, it was doomed to failure. And his execution demonstrated

the reality of the seventeenth-century observation, 'be ye never so high, the law is above you'.[6]

May I go back: Sir Walter Raleigh, a man who saw a great future in the potato as well as tobacco, was a Middle Templar. I am not here on behalf of the Middle Temple to receive a writ in a class action. He received a charter which enabled him to explore the east coast of America, which is now Virginia. Less important, his nickname was Swisser Swatter. You may wonder how that came about. We are told that he was engaging in very close social exchanges with a pretty young lady in court, who began by saying 'Oh sweet Sir Walter', but who, as her rapture increased, found herself confined to uttering 'Swisser Swatter'. And to think that we thought that the joys of sex had only been discovered in the last century.

One of the ships that explored Virginia and settled a small number on Roanoke Island was captained by Phillip Amadas, another Middle Templar. His efforts were met by a fine from the Benchers on the basis that he was absent for longer than he should have been without permission. They presumably failed to understand that in those days timetables across the Atlantic were not very efficient.

Another link is Sir Francis Drake, who sailed the *Golden Hind* around the world, and in his circumnavigation explored the west coast of America, now California. Our records show that his 'happy return' was greeted with much joy and acclamation at the Middle Temple.[7] Francis Drake is famous in English history for his determination, when the news of the great Spanish Armada was approaching the coast of England in 1588, to finish his game of bowls before returning to what became the great sea battle. If the Armada of 1588 had prevailed, the history of the USA would have been very different. There would have been no license to the Pilgrim Fathers. The common law, and its principles, would have been extinguished before they ever left the shores of England. Francis Drake did make one observation, which I offer to you as still encapsulating a principle of life:

There must be a beginning of any great matter, but the continuing unto the end until it be thoroughly finished, yields the true glory.[8]

---

[6] John Fuller, quoted by Lord Denning in *Gouriet v Union of Post Office Workers* [1977] QB 729.

[7] 'Drake's Happy Return', *Minutes of the Parliament of Middle Temple*, 4 August 1586.

[8] Drake's *Despatch to Francis Walsingham*, 17 May 1587, in *Navy Record Society*, vol 11, 1898.

When you are called to the Bar at the Middle Temple you sign the book, and I did, and so many of your forebears did, on a table made from a gun hatch of the *Golden Hind* itself.

Interesting as these considerations all are, one of the great heroes for us all, and that includes you, is Sir Edwin Sandys, who drafted the first Royal Charter granted to the Virginia Company in April 1606. Sandys was no supporter of the Divine Right of Kings. He was one of those who questioned and opposed it. He found himself in the Tower for his beliefs. But in 1618 he succeeded in obtaining the 'Great Charter' for Virginia. This charter established the right of settlers and any of their children born in the new colonies and plantations to 'have and enjoy all liberties, franchises and immunities to all intents and purposes as if they had been abiding and born within this our realm of England'. This language was later to be repeated as other colonies were established, including Maryland (1632), Maine (1639), Connecticut (1662), Carolina (1663 and 1665), Rhode Island (1663) and Massachusetts Bay (1691). And these words, hardly surprisingly, led those with trained legal minds to question the constitutionality or the legality of the efforts of Parliament in London in the eighteenth century to curtail or diminish what they believed were their now longstanding rights. And the Virginia Charter similarly provided guarantees for the Colonists of 'self government, freedom of speech, equality before the law, and trial by jury'. Thus it is that 1776 was not about abstract rights. It was about the preservation of what were believed to be existing rights.

One of the major complaints against the Stamp Act of 1765 was the deprivation of those charged with contravening its provisions of trial by jury. Another Middle Templar, Robert Goldsborough of Maryland, spoke of 'acts and legislative aggression by the mother country'. And here was the context in which Dickinson's great phrase 'No taxation without representation' was coined. And, echoing the dictum of Sir Edward Coke, one of my great predecessors, who in 1616 was deprived of his office and hurled into the Tower because he responded to the king's belief that judges should be lions *under* the throne, that the judges would do what it was appropriate for the judges to do, and who had suggested in *Bonham's Case* that statute was not always supreme, James Otis of Massachusetts urged that 'an act against natural equity was void'. And John Adams himself told a judge who was doubtful about the possible nullity of an Act of Parliament, 'tell the jury the nullity of acts of Parliament ... I am determined to die of that opinion.'[9]

[9] Quoted in Catherine Drinker Bowen, *The Lion and the Throne: The Life and Times of Sir Edward Coke, 1552–1634* (London, 1957).

Am I the only person here who is moved by the thought that as long ago as 1618 a tiny band of individuals believed that concepts like freedom of speech and trial by jury actually mattered, at a time when such concepts would have been beyond the comprehension of any other contemporary society of which I am aware? And we all still believe it. Your constitutional arrangements, and ours, seek above all to ensure equality before the law, and in particular the concept that no one is above the law or may break it with impunity, which was established by our civil war; self-government, what is now called democracy, should always be at work in our constitutional arrangements; freedom of speech as a matter of right, what President Roosevelt identified as 'the first freedom'; and trial by jury, that no one should be liable to imprisonment for a serious crime unless he or she has publicly admitted it, or sufficient evidence has been produced to enable 12 of his fellow citizens to be convinced of his guilt. As Lord Devlin once memorably put it, trial by jury is the 'lamp by which we know that freedom lives'.[10] These venerable and venerated concepts are an ineradicable part of the fabric of both our societies, and our constitutional arrangements are there to preserve and uphold the rule of law. Not, of course, rule by lawyers or by judges, but the rule of law itself.

In the United States you have a written constitution. Contrary to popular myth, we in Britain also have a constitution that is written. The main difference is this: your constitution is embodied in a single document to which, as needs must, amendments or additions have been made over the years. Our constitution is not. It is largely, but not exclusively (but that would take a lecture of its own), to be found in statute, in legislation enacted in Parliament. In our system, Parliament is sovereign. In relation to all the great nations that were once part of the British Empire, like Canada, Australia, New Zealand and India, it ceded its theoretical sovereignty to another body; recently it ceded some sovereignty to the European Court of Justice in relation to affairs arising in the European Economic Community. But ultimately in the United Kingdom it is sovereign. Our recent constitutional changes were produced by the Constitutional Reform Act of 2005. It had many facets, but notice the first, and most significant, is that it is an Act of Parliament. That process could not have happened in the USA. Your constitution would have forbidden it.

The process for change began with an announcement by the Prime Minister that the Lord Chancellor's office would be abolished. In other words, 1,300 or 800 years (whichever it was, a very, very

---

[10] Lord Devlin, *Trial by Jury* (London, 1956).

long time) of history would be wiped out. The initial proposal was met with severe opposition in the House of Lords. The fact was that you could not abolish the office. No fewer than 400 statutes provided for the existence of this office. In the result the office of Lord Chancellor survived, but with radically altered powers. He is no longer the Speaker of the House of Lords, nor President of the Courts of England and Wales, nor the Head of the Judiciary, nor able to sit as a judge. Many of the responsibilities of the Lord Chancellor were devolved to the Lord Chief Justice. Thus the Lord Chief Justice is the Head of the Judiciary of England and Wales and President of its courts. He (and she is always included, but will not always be repeated) is responsible for representing the views of the judiciary to Parliament, to the Lord Chancellor, and to Ministers of the Crown as and when necessary. He is required to maintain appropriate arrangements for discipline, welfare, training and guidance of judges, within the resources made available by the Lord Chancellor, as well as maintaining arrangements for the deployment of judicial office holders throughout the courts of England and Wales. He must negotiate with the Lord Chancellor a budget for the efficient administration of justice. But, above all, and I speak entirely personally, he must sit as a judge. For me that remains his primary responsibility.

All that may lead you to understand why I spoke with the passion that I did the other day about the need to manage time. I asked Judith's permission to refer you to Andrew Marvell's poem 'To his Coy Mistress'. When I was a teenager I knew all the naughty bits, but now I cannot remember how long he intended to adore each of her breasts. I only remember that all around him he could hear 'time's wingèd chariot hurrying near'.

This leads me on to a point about which there was much discussion at the conference. Another major change in our new constitutional arrangements was the creation of an independent Judicial Appointments Commission (JAC). Effectively the Lord Chancellor and the executive are deprived of involvement in judicial appointments. The Lord Chancellor is not a member, nor is he represented among the members of the JAC. In constitutional theory every judge at every level is appointed by the Queen. So the Commission recommends the appointment to her. Perhaps I can tell you of the system for my appointment as Lord Chief Justice. The selection was made by a Commission consisting of two senior judges, the senior Law Lord and the Master of the Rolls, together with the Chairman of the JAC and her nominee, who could not be a judge. They did not present a slate of candidates from which the Lord Chancellor or Prime Minister could choose one. They put forward one name. The Prime Minister is entitled to decline to recommend that name to the Queen, provided he gives public reasons for doing so. If he had done so, that would have been a veto on the appointment. But the nuclear option could only be fired once: if fired, the Commission would then have met again, and the Prime Minister would then have had no option but to put that name forward to the Queen for appointment. Similar processes follow for all the senior Heads of Division and the members of the Supreme Court, although for appointment to the Supreme Court, which is the final court for Scotland and Northern Ireland as well as England and Wales, the head of the Judicial Appointments Commission for each of those countries forms part of the selection panel.

I like to think that the selection of our judges and in particular the senior judiciary is now as immune from the political process as it is possible to be in a democratic society.

Another change related to the removal of Lords of Appeal in Ordinary from the House of Lords, and the creation of the new Supreme Court of the United Kingdom. The previous members of the Appellate Committee of the House of Lords became the first members of the Supreme Court, and the Senior Law Lord became its first President. This provision consolidated in constitutional theory the separation of the judiciary from the legislature at the highest level. I hasten to add that it did not turn a group of 12 lambs into lions: for years there have been government complaints about the way in which, putting it shortly, the Law Lords have failed to implement government policy, and frustrated exclamation by politicians about judges frustrating the will of Parliament. The old Law Lords were lions alright. And they did not change when they moved premises. Nevertheless the new Supreme Court has not been vested with any additional power to the jurisdiction and authority enjoyed by the Appellate Committee of the House of Lords; and there has been no diminution in its powers either.

The result is that the final court in Britain, the Supreme Court, does not enjoy the constitutional authority of the Supreme Court of the USA. It cannot strike down, and has never yet sought to strike down, legislation properly enacted. There is a developing theory that any legislation which can properly be said to be 'unconstitutional' may be open to question, but this is being tentatively explored in judgments. It has nothing to do with the Constitutional Reform Act itself.

Be all that as it may, as things stand, the role of your Supreme Court in what in truth are social questions is, to British eyes, quite remarkable. Let me offer three examples: the question of termination of pregnancy, issues of life and death, and the dignity and autonomy of women. The attitude of the law to these questions tells us much of what sort of a country we are. For us, the issue of abortion was resolved by an Act of Parliament, the Abortion Act 1967. For you, the issue has been resolved by the Supreme Court.[11] Am I wrong to understand that a 5–4 vote of unelected judges represents the law which governs 'we, the people'? This is not a criticism. I am merely identifying an important difference. And I shall offer my own theory for the difference in a moment.

This question of judicial voting in your Supreme Court led to an element of the discussion at the conference which troubled me. I hate the word 'ideology' to be applied to any judge. Surely every judge applies the law as he or she conscientiously analyses it.

Any politicisation of the process is fraught with danger. Judges are not politicians. They are independent of the political process. And the appointment of judges should not give anyone the opportunity for political posturing, let alone political preference. I recognise that within your constitution the functions of the Supreme Court are fundamental, whereas if our Supreme Court reaches a decision of which Parliament does not approve, Parliament can enact whatever amending provision it likes. Nevertheless if the process of appointment to your Supreme Court were the process in England and Wales I should be immensely troubled, and for this reason. The more we allow the appointment of judges to become part of the political process, the quicker the judiciary will become subsumed into it. And what price then, judicial independence?

But how has all this come about? In my view, but I do not claim any scholarship, the differences are a consequence of the circumstances which obtained in the 1770s, and the very early days when the new republic was working out its own destiny. My thesis is that in England we granted ultimate sovereignty to Parliament because it was through Parliament that we sought to curb the divine right of kings, first in consequence of the ancient arrangements which prohibited the imposition of taxation without parliamentary consent—'no taxation without representation' indeed—and then, as the claim for privileges and protection grew when Parliament refused to endorse

---

[11] *Roe v Wade*, 410 US 113 (1973).

the king's request for additional taxation without some concession from him, and ultimately by going to war. In other words, in our arrangements the potential for tyranny was gradually removed by insisting on the parliamentary legislative process, and victory in battle. In your situation, many years later, as we have seen from Goldsborough, and Otis, and Adams, and perhaps most important of all, from Jefferson's first draft of the Declaration, which directly attacked Parliament, Parliament was undoubtedly perceived to be integral to the problem. Central to your grievances was the Stamp Act—an Act of Parliament, not simply the diktat of a monarch, like the demand for ship money was. Your ancestors were claiming the same right not to be taxed unless they were represented which had been established, as they believed, in their constitutional affairs for years: now it was being taken away. And if that was being taken away, so could all the other immunities and privileges and principle, such as trial by jury, and so on. In the 1760s and 1770s Parliament in London appeared to be unwilling or unable to see that the position of the Americans was entirely consistent with established constitutional principles. For you a sovereign Parliament was the problem. It could therefore not be the solution.

Consciously or unconsciously, the founders of the constitution decided on a method of limiting or controlling not only the executive, but the legislature. For these purposes the principle of separation of powers, formulated at any rate in the sense of expressed constitutional theory by John Locke at the end of the seventeenth century, when we in England were enmeshed in the development of a constitution based on our own Bill of Rights, provided the answer. The celebrated French philosopher Montesquieu examined the English constitutional system in the eighteenth century in the context of contemporary France, where the king was untrammelled by the equivalent of parliament, and enjoyed dictatorial powers, perhaps best encapsulated in the (to our eyes) repugnant *lettres de cachet*. Like Voltaire, he believed that the solution to the dangers of an absolute monarch had been achieved in England and attributed them to a concept of a separation of powers which did not exist—and never had, and indeed never has, existed—in England. All this shows that you should never doubt the value to lawyers of a legal or political theory which perfectly appears to address what their instincts tell them is needed. But so it was that the separation of powers assumed such crucial importance in your arrangements.

The world does not love lawyers. It never has and it never will. Sometimes the world is right, of course, but sometimes it is wrong.

In his early years, William Shakespeare wrote the history of the reign of King Henry VI in three parts. These are blood-infused offerings: that is what his audiences wanted. In the whole of these three plays there is but one joke. A rebellion led by Jack Cade comes into London, intent on trouble. And when the rebels are mingling among themselves and asking how they should begin, Shakespeare offers the immortal line 'the first thing we do, let's kill all the lawyers'. And indeed in historical fact they did attack and destroy much of what is now the Temple, where the lawyers were already congregating. In the theatre everyone laughs. And it is a good joke, but that rebellion is followed by the most terrible bloodshed. I shall come back to it.

But what I suggest is striking about your revolution and ours is this. Of course it was war. Men died and were maimed. There was much suffering and much heroism. But when it was over, it was over. After the execution of the king in 1649, I do not for a moment suggest that life was comfortable for his supporters, but when the fighting was ended, they were not rounded up and killed after a series of ritual trials. After your War of Independence, those who supported the defeated king and Parliament were allowed to leave if they wished. Again there was no rounding up and series of ritual trials. Contrast that with the French Revolution, which occurred less than 20 years later than your own, or the Russian Revolution and the pogroms which followed them and the slaughter of different classes of citizens. Is it too utterly fanciful to believe that these truly were wars intended to establish legal principles by which the country should be governed, and that many of the participants were genuinely not after power for its own sake, and certainly not after absolute power, but for power to be exercised within constitutional restraints? I think so, and both our communities are indebted to this focus on legality.

After your war was won, one critical constitutional issue and one critical social issue remained unresolved. The role of the judiciary did not require to be addressed in those very early days, when a war had to be fought and the peace properly secured. But when the issue did come to be resolved, what was at heart was the success or otherwise of Jefferson's campaign against the Federal judiciary. In England we have a saying, 'cometh the hour, cometh the man'. For you that hour was 1801, and the man was Chief Justice John Marshall. In the history of the common law, his is one of the greatest and most influential of names. Probably more than any other judge— or, to be fair to his brothers, any group of judges—and certainly probably more than any leader of a group of judges, in the decision in *Marbury v Madison* his judgment established the constitutional arrangements and defined the role of the judiciary within an infant democracy. It was in truth law creation. Even for the moment ignoring the lecture to the Jefferson administration about the rule of law, he in effect returned to Sir Edward Coke in *Bonham's Case* and, as you all know, asserted that it was for the court to interpret the constitution. It is just worth repeating my emphasis on the distinction between interpreting the law as expressed in statute or at common law and applying it (the role of the court in England and Wales), and the authority to interpret the very constitution itself (the role of your Supreme Court). It is this that brings into stark focus such issues as the right of a woman to terminate a pregnancy, not as a matter of legal right capable of alteration or amendment through Act of Parliament, but as a matter of constitutional entitlement in an arrangement in which amendments to the constitution are, and in reality can only be, events of extreme rarity.

Jean Edward Smith, in his biography of John Marshall,[12] summarised the distinction between the tradition established by John Marshall and our tradition in this way:

> The English tradition held that the great constitutional documents of British history were purely political statements that lay in the realm of Parliament to interpret, not the courts. Jefferson subscribed to that view; so did Jackson, and even Abraham Lincoln doubted the authority of the Supreme Court to resolve fundamental constitutional issues in the course of ordinary litigation ... Marshall took the opposite position ... he consistently held that the constitution was law.

But I want to highlight this remarkable feature. This was an infant republic, beset with problems, not bound to survive, fortunate that Britain was concentrating on the defeat of Napoleon who had subjugated the entire mainland of Europe. I am not perhaps wholly able to disguise that I do not share the view that Jefferson should be sanctified. Personally I prefer Adams. But, I cannot withhold my admiration for Jefferson's sense of constitutional propriety, that notwithstanding the public lecture on the rule of law, and his profound disagreement with Marshall's decision, after what I regard as a show of defiance, the decision itself was allowed to stand. In the long term that secured the rule of law in the USA. I hope that a modern politician, elected to power in our countries, would comprehend

---

[12] Jean Edward Smith, *John Marshall, Definer of a Nation* (New York, 1996).

why in similar circumstances it would be appropriate to do what Jefferson did.

There remained of course the social question. The issue of slavery was not resolved. It still rankles a little that in the first draft of the Declaration, a Virginian slave owner raged against slavery. It is even more ironic given that at the very time when there were those in Parliament who were supporting the American cause, there were others who were seeking to attack the slave trade. And indeed the great *Case of James Somersett* in 1772, heard before another of my predecessors, Lord Mansfield, following an earlier decision from the reign of Elizabeth I herself, finally and through a complicated process established that the ownership of a slave in England was incompatible with the laws of England, irrespective of any legal claim which might be valid elsewhere. There could be no property in another human being. But all that said, it is easy now for us to be critical of failure to address the slavery issue in the early constitutional arrangements. And we know that it all culminated less than 100 years later in the ghastly catastrophe of your civil war.

May I just return to Shakespeare's early *Henry VI* plays. They are far from his greatest plays. We all know about his portrayal of human fallibility and frailty in its many manifestations in *Macbeth*, *King Lear*, *Othello* and *Hamlet* and the rest. But I venture to suggest that nowhere in the entire canon of Shakespeare's plays is the condition of the common man better portrayed than in his description of civil war; none better than the haunting scenes where one soldier pulls a body on to the stage, and then, unmasking his enemy, discovers that he has killed his father, followed by another in which another soldier pulls a dead body on to the stage, and after congratulating his opponent on his toughness in the fight discovers that he has killed his son. These are haunting scenes, filled with pity. The son remembers that he will have to tell his mother what he has done, and the father that he will have to tell his wife that he has killed their boy. Although no mother or wife appears on the stage, Shakespeare is able to convey that each of these women is there, but invisible, not actually on the stage, weeping the bitter tears of the lifelong grief that lies ahead, truly part of the dreadful lamentable scene, symbols of the nameless but innumerable victims of the ghastliness of a civil war.

My respectful view is that the Founding Fathers had little choice. If the slavery issue had been addressed the cause about which they were united would have been paralysed; with such deep-seated divisions, we might never have had a 'United' States of America, but rather a continent of North America, fragmented into different states. Indeed the history of the world in the last century would almost certainly have been different, and not for the better.

With the greatest of deference I suggest that these appalling sacrifices of this civil war were not in vain, and that all who died must be honoured. Their sacrifices should be regarded as part of the price of your independence, your nationhood, your constitution, and the greatness of your country, exactly as forecast by John Adams, now carrying the immense burden that it does, as the most powerful nation on earth.

My country once performed this role. It was known as Pax Britannica. That is no longer our role. No one loved us very much for it. Everyone can find fault with it. And of course we made mistakes, but there were a great number of plusses in the ledger too. You too will now attract criticism, even when it is not deserved. If one of your young men or women behaves in a way which all of you would find unacceptable, the pictures flash around the world: there are no pictures of the brave young man or woman who, at great personal risk, steps in to save the life of a child in some foreign country. So your mistakes will be highlighted and magnified, and the blessings you provide will largely be ignored. To be the most powerful nation on earth is indeed a thankless task. Well, you do not and will not lack for thanks from me.

Continuing Constitutional Concerns

Constitutional Change: Unfinished Business

This lecture was delivered at University College London in December 2013, the first lecture I gave after my retirement. Strictly speaking, I was no longer constrained by the principle that serving judges do not discuss political questions. It would however have been a breach of this soundly based principle to have ignored it altogether. Nevertheless, I hope that this self-imposed reticence did not disguise my meaning.

THERE IS A broad title to this lecture, but as you all know it is linked to the project on the Politics of Judicial Independence in Britain's Changing Constitution. Of course, if I were to address all the challenges now facing our constitution, you would be here until midnight. Instead I shall examine some broad themes to put in context developing constitutional arrangements which impact directly or indirectly on the judiciary.

I have said before that in a democratic country, all power, however exercised in the community, and whatever the individual features of the electoral system, must be founded on law. Each and every stage of the system which bestows political power has to be accounted for to the electorate at the ballot box, as and when elections take place, but the exercise of these powers must at all times be answerable to the rule of law. Independent professions protect it. Independent press and media protect it. Independent police officers protect it. Ultimately, however, it is the judges who are the guardians of the rule of law. They have a particular responsibility to protect the constitutional rights of each citizen, as well as the integrity of the constitution by which those rights exist. Without judicial independence and without respect for judicial independence these elementary facets of our civilised community are threatened.

Let me, therefore, emphasise at the outset that although the rule of law must be an overarching principle of a civilised state, I am not asserting that the judiciary has any such overarching power. In this jurisdiction, Parliament is sovereign. No individual, or group of individuals, nor even any judge, nor any minister, nor Parliament itself, enjoys any suspending or dispensing power. On this question, the Bill of Rights of 1689, a constitutional document in our half written constitution, asserts an irrebuttable principle which extends to the fact that statute has bestowed authority on judicial bodies in Europe which effect the operation of our judicial system, and indeed judicial decision-making itself.

With that background, let me begin with a strong assertion. In my entire 25 years as a full-time judge, and some years before that as a part-time Recorder, no one—in particular, no politician or civil servant or special advisor—ever once sought to indicate to me what my decision should be, or that a particular outcome might be appropriate or advisable. No one has written to me as Lord Jowitt LC wrote to Lord Goddard CJ in 1947:[1]

> I do sincerely hope that the judges will not be lenient to these bandits [who] carry arms [to shoot at the police] ... you know I do take the view, which I think you share, that we have got rather soft and woolly when dealing with really serious crime.

If any other judge, from the most senior to the most junior, had been offered this kind of 'advice', I should have heard of it. I am confident that in my time it has never happened. In that sense judicial independence in the course of judicial decision-making is untarnished.

Such an event will not happen in my lifetime, not least because if it were to happen, the outcry would be shattering, and at least one ministerial career would be destroyed. The public may be very critical of judicial decisions, but there is a deep understanding in the community that the fact that the decision, right or wrong, is made by an independent judge, independent in particular of the government and ministers, is an asset of unquantifiable value to the community itself.

The independence of judicial decision-making is an integral structure of the constitution, but it takes life and authority and protection from the institutional independence of the judiciary. Without institutional independence the critical environment on which the independence of judicial decision-making depends would gradually wither. I must therefore go on to examine the constitutional context in which we embrace or purport to embrace the separation of powers—the executive, the legislature and the judiciary—and which indeed, following years of criticism of, taking one particular feature of our arrangements as an example, the role of the Lord Chancellor as a member of the judiciary, the executive and the legislature,

---

[1] Robert Stevens, *The Independence of the Judiciary: The View from the Lord Chancellor's Office*, quoted in Tom Bingham, *The Business of Judging: Selected Essays and Speeches, 1985–1999* (Oxford, 2000).

was the declared justification for the constitutional changes first promulgated in 2003, and enacted in the Constitutional Reform Act 2005. In passing, however, let us not fool ourselves. In our constitutional arrangements, we still do not have separation of powers, at any rate in the sense that it is understood elsewhere.

The executive and the legislature are not and never have been separate. Today every member of the Cabinet sits in our legislature; so do virtually all members of the Shadow Cabinet. So, with a very rare occasional exception, does every single minister outside the Cabinet. Queen Elizabeth I, for all her many qualities, was hardly enamoured of the democratic process, and the early Stuart kings, who believed in Divine Right, recognised the obvious good sense of having ministers in Parliament, and in this respect at least they would have been entirely at ease with the continuing influence of the legislature by the executive. It would have come as no surprise to them to be told that between 2001 and mid-2012, during some 2,500 divisions in the House of Commons, the government of the day was defeated on only six occasions. The fact that the legislature and the executive are effectively inseparable was brought home to me only a few days ago when last week, watching the television in the morning, I heard the BBC announcer say that 'the Government will amend the Banking Reform Bill', to control the cost of payday loans. I am not being critical of the BBC. We hear remarks like this every day by politicians. I have little doubt that this information was supplied to the media by special advisors. But can we be clear. In our constitutional arrangements the government neither creates nor amends the law. It proposes changes, but the only source of power is Parliament. The problem with the shorthand form of reporting is that it tacitly accepts the control of the executive over the legislature. In constitutional theory that is an absurdity. In constitutional practice, as the headline indicates, it has become very close to the reality—and, no less important, the perception of the reality. And that is very troublesome not only for the judiciary, but for all the different independencies which contribute to our free society.

I have lost count of the number of times I have given judgments in court or spoken in lectures about the sovereignty or supremacy of Parliament. But I have never, ever spoken about the supremacy of the government—only and exclusively about the sovereignty or supremacy of Parliament. This supremacy is confined to the legislative process which culminates in an Act of Parliament. Resolutions or motions before one House or the other, or even both, however heavily supported, have no legislative authority. They cannot create new law or amend old law. Today's Parliament cannot bind tomorrow's Parliament, even if the attempt to bind the later Parliament is enshrined in an Act of Parliament.

The House of Commons is elected, through our democratic processes. At present, the House of Lords is not, but, save as a revising or advisory part of the constitution, it has no power. If the House of Lords advises or makes suggestions with which the House of Commons disagrees, the House of Commons must win: so that imposes a huge responsibility on our elected representatives in the legislature.

On the rare, very rare indeed, occasions when the government loses a vote in the House of Commons, the media falls enthusiastically on it using the language of 'humiliation', and speaking of the dissentients as 'rebels', with its war-like connotations, with learned commentators identifying the dangers of a 'party split'. The media never minds reporting what it considers to be a confrontation. Perhaps because it is so very rare indeed for the government to lose a vote in the House of Commons, the occasion is truly newsworthy. I wish it were not so reported, but we have a free media, and they must report as they wish, and perhaps, as I have said, because it is so rare that such an occasion is newsworthy. But why?

An occasional vote against the government by members of its own party is a triumph—a manifestation—that we are living in a democracy. The executive is not always right. Neither the party of government nor the party of opposition enjoys a total monopoly of wisdom. The government should not always have its way. Our history is littered with examples of noble dissent. Without dissent, publicly expressed in the House of Commons itself by members of the governing party, led by Leo Amery, when defeat stared us in the face, and compromise and surrender were in the air, Winston Churchill would not have become Prime Minister in 1940: to inestimable consequences for our freedoms. And at a different level, judges give dissenting judgments, disagreeing with their colleagues, to the long-term health of our legal system. We do not accept the view of judges from a different tradition, that the authority of the court is weakened by dissent. To us it underlines the independence of each judge.

Currently the government loses more votes in the House of Lords than in the House of Commons, but that is as it should be. Dare I say it? That is healthy, not least because of the volume of legislation which has been badly drafted, and indeed on many occasions not even considered by the House of Commons. Membership reflecting party balance, related in some way to the proportion of votes cast in any particular general election, increases the influence of the government, and ultimately will serve to produce a controlling influence by the government over the House of Lords. Yet, as Baroness Hayman, speaking in the House of Lords on 24 October 2013 pointed out, the function of the House of Lords is to pressure test legislation and when appropriate 'to ask the Commons to think again'. With the authority of a former Lord Speaker she reminded us that 'democratic power, accountability and legitimacy lie with the Commons'. Of course: so does it really do any harm for the government of the day to lose a division? Whatever the reason for this proposal which will simultaneously add to the extraordinary bulk of the second legislative assembly, the effect, even if unintended, will be to increase the control of the legislature by the executive. Of course the executive is bound by the law and must obey it, but it is troublesome that it is gradually achieving an increasing stranglehold on the body responsible for making the law. And therefore, concerns are raised that our constitutional arrangements may be falling out of balanced kilter. The remedy must be for Parliament itself, pre-eminently the House of Commons.

For me to return to the 2003 announcement of the abolition of the office of the Lord Chancellor, and the changes eventually encompassed in the Constitutional Reform Act 2005, may appear to be old hat, looking at water that has already passed through the mill. The harsh unavoidable reality, not sufficiently noted, was that the institutional power of the judiciary, notwithstanding all the repeated assertions of the importance of its position as the third arm of the state, was inadequate to ensure that it was consulted about changes to the constitutional arrangements of direct application to it. The stealth—and I use the word deliberately—was explained by Jonathan Powell in his account of events in *The New Machiavelli*.[2] This broad account has been effectively confirmed in evidence to the House of Lords Select Committee on the Constitution from Lord Turnbull and Lord Irvine as well as the then Prime Minister, Mr Blair.

Mr Powell was, it will be remembered, Chief of Staff to Mr Blair at the time with which we are concerned. From his account of events it emerges that a decision was deliberately taken to hide the proposals from the judiciary. As he explains, in 2001 it was proposed 'to put the courts into the Home Office'. The absurdity of this idea

---

[2] Jonathan Powell, *The New Machiavelli—How to Wield Power in the Modern World* (London, 2011).

was perhaps too obvious for me to explain it now, but just in case anyone may be in doubt, a few words will suffice. If implemented, rather than being the fabled lions under the throne, the judiciary would have been relegated, in the unforgettable phrase used by Stable J in 1944 following the decision of the House of Lords in *Liversidge v Anderson*,[3] to the role of mice squeaking under the Home Secretary's chair.[4] When we heard about the proposal Lord Woolf, as Lord Chief Justice, asked to see the Prime Minister, and four of us were invited to attend 10 Downing Street where the Prime Minister, Mr Blair, was persuaded of the disadvantages of the proposals.

The 2005 Act was a major constitutional change, and in a constitution which provides for and is based on at least the theory of the separation of powers, how could this freeze-out be? This is not just a matter of courtesy to the Lord Chief Justice and the judiciary, although that is not unimportant. Nor is it a question of whether the changes were right or wrong, desirable or unwise. The real question which arises for consideration is whether we have a separation of powers at all. We have a separation of powers which manifests itself in a separation of decision-making responsibilities by the judiciary which is independent of the executive and the legislature, but it is hardly a manifestation of the institutional independence of the judiciary for it to be sidelined on matters of direct, immediate concern to them. In the end, as I accept, the final decision would have to be for Parliament, but the possibility that the Prime Minister and the government might change their mind about how to approach these issues after discussion with the judiciary was apparently obviated because of the earlier occasion on which the judiciary had successfully persuaded the government that it was a daft idea to put the courts into the Home Office: as indeed it was, and subsequent events undoubtedly proved.

The clamour for the separation of powers led the Law Lords, now transferred into the Supreme Court, and the Lord Chief Justice to be deprived of their longstanding right to speak in debates in the House of Lords. The single method of communication now available to the Lord Chief Justice is a letter to Parliament, but he cannot stand up and speak in our sovereign Parliament even on issues which directly affect the administration of justice. Although the change was based on lip service to the separation of powers, as I have already described, government ministers continue to

---

[3] [1942] AC 206.

[4] Quoted in RFV Houston, '*Liversidge v Anderson* in Retrospect' (1970) 86 *LQR* 33.

enjoy rights of audience in the House of Commons and the House of Lords—opportunities of which the Lord Chief Justice was and remains deprived.

In the Concordat subsequently published in early 2004, 'the overall aim of these reforms is to put the relationship between the executive, legislature and judiciary on a modern footing, respecting the separation of powers between the three'. Nevertheless, when the decision was taken to remove responsibilities from the prisons from the Home Office into the Ministry of Justice, I first read about this proposal, which was enacted in 2008, in a ministerial article written in a Sunday newspaper. I doubt if we shall ever know—and by the time we do know, if we do, it will not matter—whether this was part of the original plan put together in Downing Street in 2003, equally concealed, so that the project was implemented in two stages rather than one, or whether the second stage reflected some further thinking, equally concealed, quite unconnected with the original proposal to bring the areas of responsibility for the Home Office closer to the judicial system. At the time I was one of the Heads of Division, the Division most closely affected by the proposal, and was totally unaware of it until after the article had been published. The then Lord Chief Justice was equally left in the dark.

These proposals, both directly impacting on our constitutional arrangements and of immense importance to the judiciary and now implemented, have had their own combined effect on the position of the judiciary. Although its impact has been overlooked, the second change—that is the expansion of the responsibilities of the Lord Chancellor—has been detrimental to institutional independence. It is not a tidal wave, but rather the consistent steady drip. The entire change is symbolised in the notepaper. The once great office of Lord Chancellor has been relegated to second place behind the new ministerial office of the Secretary of State for Justice. That presumably was another deliberate decision. As a matter of symbolism, if nothing else, the Lord Chancellor has become an after-thought to the Secretary of State. What's in a name? Well, this particular rose does not smell as sweet as once it did. The judiciary is no longer represented at the Cabinet table by an individual holding an ancient office whose only personal ministerial responsibility—his specific role and sole focus—was to represent and protect the independence of the judiciary and to ensure that the needs of the administration of justice were clearly understood both by the government and by Parliament. I have heard from a number of different sources, former Cabinet ministers on both sides of the political spectrum, that this specific role was understood by the Lord Chancellor's colleagues to be distinct from their own. The additional responsibilities now attaching to the department mean that the judiciary, and the administration of justice, have ceased to be his weightiest responsibility. The role of the Lord Chancellor has been diminished.

As Lord Chief Justice for five years, I had dealings with three separate Lord Chancellors, one in the previous government and two in the present government. My observations are not critical of any of them personally. Perhaps indeed I should say that in my dealings with Jack Straw, Ken Clarke and now Chris Grayling, first, that we could agree or disagree, and that on occasions each of them was persuaded to the view that I was advocating. Second, that I believe that each sought to reflect the views of the judiciary to his Cabinet colleagues as I had relayed them, if and when any such questions arose. But however sympathetic and supportive the Lord Chancellor may be, in relation to his responsibility for supporting the judiciary, and judicial independence, his clout has been reduced. On these issues the office cannot carry the weight it once did.

Faced with this situation, I asked for—and I acknowledge that no difficulty was presented for arrangements to be made (and I imagine this too was a further step in our developing constitutional arrangements)—the Lord Chief Justice to see the Prime Minister on a more or less regular basis, about twice annually, to speak to him about matters of concern to the judiciary. The content of the meetings is confidential, but it would not be a breach of confidence to suggest that this was not without its value to his understanding of our position. But this is a substitution, and speaking for myself as the substitute, I can say a pretty poor substitute. The substitute must and cannot be a politician, and cannot and must not have a seat at the Cabinet table, and cannot perform the previous function of the Lord Chancellor. The Lord Chief Justice is therefore a very different Head of the Judiciary to the Lord Chancellor.

For many years now it has been the convention that judges do not comment on matters of political controversy. The principle is very sound. Even on the most superficial basis, judges have to make controversial decisions in the cases before them, which is probably quite enough controversy for anyone. But obviously the reasons go deeper, and are well understood. As Lord Chief Justice I adhered to that principle. I am no longer bound by it, although, obviously, I cannot breach confidences or discuss matters which were entrusted to me when I was in office. What my successor would do if faced with any repetition of the public announcement of major proposals for constitutional change affecting the administration of justice without any prior consultation with him will, of course, be a matter for the Lord Chief Justice. Those of you who have listened so far will recognise my hope, indeed my expectation, that there will be no repetition. Never again.

One of the major consequences of the constitutional changes related to the method for funding the court system. Its importance to the issue of independence was described by Lord Browne-Wilkinson during his *Francis Mann* lecture:[5]

> If Parliament and the minister between them control provision and allocation of funds, how can the administration of justice be independent of the legislature and executive? He who pays the piper calls the tune.

Writing when he did, he was speaking of a rich country without any 'real conflict as to the provision and allocation of funds'. That has changed. We have been going through the national financial crisis. The cost of the administration of justice is but one of a number of demands on public funding, and it is for Parliament and the government to identify the priorities, and then for the expenditure of public funds on the judicial system to be explained and accounted for to Parliament. There is now an annual budget exercise for Her Majesty's Courts and Tribunals Service (HMCTS). The Concordat arrangement, in very brief summary, left the Lord Chief Justice with three options when considering the proposed annual budget: to agree it; to neither agree nor dissent from it; or to reject it, explaining why in writing to Parliament. On every occasion bar one, after taking advice of my colleagues, I agreed the proposed budget. On one occasion I neither agreed nor disagreed, but as it turned out, my pessimism was misplaced and the funding proved adequate, just, but there is no fat or flab left, and when the national emergency is over, we must anticipate improved facilities.

In the meantime, I became increasingly dissatisfied with these new arrangements. They needed reconsideration. The proposed reforms of HMCTS attracted headlines which suggested that the court system was about to be privatised. The headline, as often the case with headlines, was inaccurate.

My concerns were varied, but they included the way in which the funding of the Prison Service—demand led, as it is—inevitably tends to take priority in the allocation of the financial resources of the Department, the equally inevitable overall reduction required of

---

[5] 'The Independence of the Judiciary in the 1980s' [1988] *PL* 44.

the Department by the Treasury, the consequent absence of capital investment at a time when both the estate and, perhaps more important to the modernisation project, IT required significant investment; all in an overall process which was worked on the basis of an annual assessment, and hoped-for agreement between the Lord Chancellor and the Lord Chief Justice of the day. These, and other flaws, needed closer examination, and reform.

No breach of confidence is involved in suggesting that in the context of a basic principle that it is for the state to provide the funding for an effective judicial system, accountable to Parliament, the proposed creation of a new funding system will inevitably give rise to a number of different points of view which will not necessarily be consistent. It would also be surprising if the views of different bodies with a justified interest in any new arrangements always coincided. There is the minister, and the government, his department, the Treasury, HMCTS itself, and, last but certainly not least, the judiciary.

We must all wish the discussions well. If, however, there is one absolute principle to be underlined in the context of the issues we are now addressing, changes should only take place with the concurrence of the Lord Chief Justice. It is not enough for him to be consulted. Consultation can sometimes be no more than a fig leaf, and this leads me to the further suggestion that stems from the new responsibility of the Lord Chief Justice as Head of the Judiciary of England and Wales. In short, although he is not in charge of a department of state, he is responsible for an arm of the state. And if the separation of powers is to mean anything at all, the concurrence of the Lord Chief Justice is required, and his concurrence to any change affecting the administration of justice should, from now on, automatically be built into any proposals for further change. This, it seems to me, is an essential minimum requirement and the logical response to the constitutional changes to which I have referred. The same would of course apply to the Heads of the Judiciary in Scotland and Northern Ireland.

So, for example, I was delighted when the Lord Chancellor accepted my strongly held view that in relation to televising of the court processes, concurrence not consultation with the Lord Chief Justice was required. With the expertise of the judiciary generally, the Lord Chief Justice is in a far better position to make an objective judgement about the impact of televising court trials on the administration of justice generally, and the witnesses and victims, and the process, than a minister, particularly given that the Lord Chancellor no longer has to be a lawyer, and that in any event, in his capacity as a minister, there will be political imperatives for him to consider. This underlines that the concurrence of the judiciary must now become a significant feature of our constitutional process.

To that I must just add one short, but nevertheless important footnote: of course in the unlikely event that the concurrence of the Lord Chief Justice to any measures requiring his (or her) concurrence is unreasonably withheld, as we all know, it would be open to the Minister to go to Parliament and seek the enactment of legislation to implement changes to which the Lord Chief Justice was opposed. But there would then, at least, be a full debate and argument on the issue. As I accept, the legislature will always win. Such a process, however, would ensure that the country at large would appreciate the full importance of the issues.

Would it, however, be totally inconsistent with out nebulous concept of the separation of powers for the Lord Chief Justice to be permitted to address the House of Lords in such an event? However much weight is attached to a paper or written submission, in our traditions the value attached to orality has not been diminished. And, in accordance with our traditions, we tend not to make judgments without giving an equal opportunity to both sides to be heard. How much better for these processes to take place within our existing constitutional arrangements rather than for the Lord Chief Justice of the day to, in effect, call a press conference in his court in the Law Courts, to argue his point of view? It takes very little imagination to envisage the potential dangers of using such a method of negotiation; rather than encouraging a solution, it would foster division.

In my view therefore the prohibition, at any rate as it affects the Lord Chief Justice, in relation to matters affecting the administration of justice, and in particular any issue which in his view affects the constitutional position and institutional independence of the judiciary, should be reconsidered. Notice, however, my continuing acceptance and underlining of the principle of ultimate parliamentary sovereignty.

Unlike the United States of America, our judiciary, even the judiciary in the Supreme Court of the United Kingdom, does not provide a check or balance against the supremacy of Parliament. The Founding Fathers of the United States made express provision for this form of check and balance just because they were deeply suspicious of Parliament. Properly enacted Acts of Parliament triggered off the events which culminated in the Declaration of Independence. Nowadays, in very brief summary, in the United States legislation must not contravene the constitution, the written constitution, and the Supreme Court of the United States has supreme authority over the interpretation of the constitution. This cannot simply be amended by the will of a bare majority of both Houses. The end result is that on an issue of profound moral, social and personal importance, like termination of pregnancy, the final decision was made by nine Justices, and indeed it was actually the final decision by five of them. In our constitution, an Act of Parliament was required. What is more, by contrast, if Parliament disagrees with the law as enunciated by our Supreme Court it can and sometimes does immediately overrule it by fresh legislation. That is one side of the coin. The other side is too frequently overlooked.

The consequence of the sovereignty of Parliament is that, whether they like it or not, judges are bound to apply an Act of Parliament even where that Act provides for the application of judicial authority from a foreign court. This was the result of the European Communities Act 1972. The position of the judiciary is frequently misunderstood. Judges have no choice. They are bound by British law to follow the rulings of the Court of Justice of the European Union in Luxembourg. Our judiciary cannot set aside the law enacted by Parliament, nor suspend it nor dispense with it. To do so would contravene the Bill of Rights. Exactly the same principle applies to the enactment of the Human Rights Act 1998. The courts are required by domestic legislation to implement the European Convention on Human Rights just because the Human Rights Act is legislation enacted by Parliament.

I suspect that I was not the only judge (and I suspect that it was not only judges) who was astounded to read the observation of the Home Secretary at the recent Conservative Party conference that 'some judges choose to ignore Parliament and go on putting the law on the side of foreign criminals instead of the public'.[6] With great respect it is no good in our parliamentary democracy for anyone to believe, or to suggest, that resolutions of one or other or both Houses of Parliament, or public declarations of the wishes of the Prime Minister and his ministers, can alter the constitutional obligation of the judiciary to apply the enacted Human Rights Act, and therefore the European Convention.

This was yet one more reaction by successive Home Secretaries which underlines how right the judges were, when they were

---

[6] Home Secretary speaking at the Conservative Party Conference, reported in *The Guardian*, 30 September 2013.

provided with the opportunity to do so, to fight the proposal in 2001 that the Home Secretary should become the Minister responsible for the administration of justice. It is, of course, for the other political parties who were said to 'value the rights of terrorists and criminals more than the rights of the rest of us' to make their own case. I confidently assert that there is not a single judge in the jurisdiction who would seek to put the interests of a foreign criminal ahead of those of a victim of crime, or the public generally. But, while a judge cannot ignore an Act of Parliament, a resolution of the House of Commons has no sufficient legal force to suspend or dispense with legislation. Judges must apply statute, no more, no less, and if the consequences of legislation properly enacted, as it worked out in practice, are unacceptable to Parliament, the remedy is in Parliament's hands.

What I have described as the statutory bestowal of judicial authority on Europe has been and remains highly problematic. Undoubtedly it represented constitutional change, and addressing the consequences will itself represent further constitutional change. The issues merit a lecture of their own, but there is no doubt that, whatever the political implications, the consequent constitutional issues will have to be addressed.

In the context of an economic community of nations, it seems clear that one court must interpret the relevant treaty and its consequences and effect. In simple terms, each nation joining the community has to accept that all the nations in the community are in it together. If each country decided that it could ignore the decisions of the Luxembourg court in relation to economic matters with which they disagreed, and adopt those which were regarded favourably, the community itself would disintegrate. But as I have emphasised, this is a court giving rulings about the workings of a common market.

My major concern arises from the impact on our domestic arrangements of the role of the European Court of Human Rights in Strasbourg. This is not a jurisdiction directed to the running of a common market. And unlike the USA, Europe is not a federal state. It is not a state at all. The court is a judicial body, in which a group of independent nations is each represented by one judge. Each nation is sovereign within its own territory, each has its own constitutional arrangements, and each enjoys its own traditions. There has been a considerable difference of views between judges in this jurisdiction, both in judgments and in public lectures, about the Human Rights Act and the particular wording of four words in section 2(1) of that Act. This provides that our courts 'must take into account' the decisions of the court in Strasbourg. The obligation is mandatory. But what does it actually mean?

The different arguments are superbly addressed by Sir John Laws in his very recent Hamlyn lecture,[7] and indeed when I read it, as I did on Monday, I reduced many of the things I was going to say on this issue. Personally, I have never doubted, and have spoken publicly to this effect, that the words mean what they say. To take account of the decisions of the European court does not mean that you are required to apply or follow them. If that was the statutory intention, that would be the language used in the statute. The language of the 1972 Act would simply have been repeated. However, the principle that superior courts bind inferior courts, principles which govern the way in which our domestic courts work, has been erroneously applied to the decisions of the Strasbourg court; in effect, with a few limited exceptions, the suggestion is that our courts, if not bound to do so, should follow the Strasbourg court on the principle of *stare decisis*.

In my view, the Strasbourg court is not superior to our Supreme Court. It is not, and it is important to emphasise, that it has never been granted the kind of authority granted to the Supreme Court in the United States of America—authority, let it be re-emphasised, which is well established in the constitutional arrangements of that country. Nevertheless, although not in any sense a Supreme Court of Europe, which, I repeat, does not consist of a federation of states as the United States of America does, by using the concept of a 'living instrument', the court appears to be assuming, or seeking to assume, the same mantle.

Thomas Jefferson would have forecast that this assertion of judicial power was inevitable. He wrote in 1820,[8] following the decision in *Marbury v Madison*,[9] 'it is a very dangerous doctrine to consider the judges as the ultimate arbiters of all constitutional questions'. He was worried that the constitution would become 'a mere thing of wax in the hands of the judiciary'. Addressing those issues in Europe today, he would have applied them to the Convention. This is not a lecture about the constitutional affairs of the USA, but it was this process that ultimately led to the supremacy of the Supreme Court on issues like abortion.

---

[7] *The Common Law Constitution* (Cambridge, 2014).
[8] Letter to William Jarvis, 1820, quoted in William J Quirk and R Randall Bridwell, *Judicial Dictatorship* (New Jersey, 1995).
[9] *Marbury v Madison*, 5 US 137 (1803).

Let us now consider a very recent decision, *Del Rio Prada v Spain*,[10] a decision of the Grand Chamber given on 21 October 2013, where the court referred to the 'progressive development of the criminal law through judicial law-making' as a well-entrenched and necessary part of the legal tradition in the Convention states in a way which suggested that the court itself was vested with the power progressively to develop the criminal law throughout Europe. Later in the judgment, addressing Article 46 of the Convention, the Grand Chamber unequivocally stated that its effect was that when the court finds a violation of the Convention, the state against whom the finding is made is under a 'legal obligation' not only to pay the sums awarded by way of just satisfaction, but to take individual or, if appropriate, 'general measures in its domestic legal order to put an end to the violation found by the Court and to redress its effects'. Notice, this is not a recommendation. Although the judgment then acknowledges the freedom of the state to choose the means by which the 'legal obligation' will be discharged, it is left with no alternative, and the court may order the particular measures required to remedy the violation. All this is said to arise from a Convention obligation. This is no longer a question of statutory construction of the Human Rights Act. If this observation of the Grand Chamber means what it says, the court in a foreign jurisdiction is asserting an unacceptable right to impose legal obligations with which this country, and ultimately every country in Europe, must comply.

Let us return to our constitutional position. Even in relation to the Convention, the Supreme Court cannot dispense with a clear statutory provision. At best, it can make a declaration that a statutory provision is inconsistent with it. That leaves the remedy to Parliament. The court cannot order 'general measures' to be taken, and if it did, Parliament could simply ignore the court, or immediately take legislative steps to disapply the ruling.

Where do we go from here? It would, I believe, make sense for section 2(1) of the 1998 Act to be amended, to express (a) that the obligation to take account of the decisions of the Strasbourg court did not mean that our Supreme Court was required to follow or apply those directions, and (b) that in this jurisdiction the Supreme Court is, at the very least, a court of equal standing with the Strasbourg court. Attention could then be directed to Article 46(1), that the parties to the Convention 'undertake to abide by the final judgment of the court in any case to which they are parties'. This was

---

[10] *Del Rio Prada v Spain* (2014) 58 EHRR 37.

not part of the Human Rights Act itself. In theory, it applies only to cases to which the United Kingdom is a party. But that merely means that the application of the legal obligation to remedy the fault found by Strasbourg would be delayed until a British case raising the same point reached the court. If Article 46 means what the Strasbourg court has said it means, the disputes about the meaning of 'must take account' will become increasingly academic.

My profound concern about the long-term impact of these issues on our constitutional affairs is the democratic deficit. As I emphasised at the outset, in our constitutional arrangements Parliament is sovereign. It can overrule, through the legislative process, any decision of our Supreme Court. In relation to the Strasbourg court, and the Convention, is this principle negated by our accession to the treaty obligation contained in Article 46? Do we, can we, accept the obligation recently announced in *Del Rio Prada* that when a UK case arises, our Parliament must take 'general measures in its domestic legal order to put an end' to the violations found by the European court? Can that possibly be required if Parliament disagrees? For me the answer is, of course not.

These issues are of huge importance not only to the citizens of this country, but to the sovereign states of Europe as a whole. They are not confined to the United Kingdom. Are we, are they, prepared to contemplate the gradual emergence of a court with the equivalent jurisdiction through Europe of that enjoyed by the Supreme Court in the United States of America? Thomas Jefferson would have strongly advised us against it.

This is not a pro or anti European stance. It is a constitutional issue which has never had to be faced in our jurisdiction, partly because the constitution is largely unwritten, and partly because we have always accepted that ultimate authority was vested in legislation enacted by Parliament—so much so, that again under the Bill of Rights the processes in Parliament cannot be questioned. You can argue for and against prisoner voting rights. You can argue for and against the whole-life tariff. Reasonable people will take different views. My personal belief is that parliamentary sovereignty on these issues should not be exported, and we should beware of the danger of even an indirect importation of the slightest obligation on Parliament to comply with the orders and directions of any court, let alone a foreign court. Ultimately, this is a political, not judicial, question. In the meantime, the House of Commons is answerable to the electorate, and our judiciary will continue to apply properly enacted legislation.

Sovereignty: A View from London

This lecture was a response to an article which appeared in Counsel *in February 2014. My response would have come as no surprise to anyone who has heard me speak on these issues, which were addressed in 'Constitutional Change: Unfinished Business'.[1] Nevertheless I decided to include this particular article because it sought to answer the specific constitutional question raised by the President of the European Court of Human Rights.*

THIS RESPONSE TO the recent article in *Counsel* by my respected friend Dean Spielmann, President of the European Court of Human Rights at Strasbourg, addressing what he identified as the two main criticisms of the court, is entirely personal.

My fundamental concern, and it is at the root of my disagreement with the President, is sovereignty. When I have written and spoken, as I frequently have in the past, about the rule of law, so long established in this country, I have always insisted that by rule of law I did not mean rule by lawyers or judges. In my view, in any country which embraces the principle of democracy, and certainly in the United Kingdom, ultimate authority over constitutional and societal questions is not vested in a body of judges, however wise and distinguished, and even if the system for their appointment is beyond criticism. This is true whether the democratic principle is enshrined in a modern or relatively modern written constitution, or in a constitution like our own, which has evolved over the centuries and, although not precisely written down as a modern constitutional document, is partly written, largely in statute, and partly based on convention.

In the United States of America, when the new republic was in its infancy, authority to interpret the constitution was vested in—or, more accurately, taken over by—the Supreme Court. To me it remains an irony that in a written constitution which proclaims the authority of 'we, the people', the decision about, for example, the lawfulness of a termination of pregnancy was left to nine—or, more accurately, five—judges. When that same question was decided here, Parliament enacted the Abortion Act 1967. Be that as it may,

---

[1] This volume, p 73.

the Supreme Court of the United States differs significantly from the Strasbourg court. The United States of America is a federal country, with a written constitution which applies to the entire sovereign state, where the authority of the Supreme Court reflects that constitution and has done so for 200 years. Moreover, although the process is subject to stringent conditions, in the United States the constitution itself may be and very occasionally is amended. By contrast, the Strasbourg court is an international court for a group of independent sovereign states, each with its own separate democratic constitution, given authority by Treaty to interpret the Convention. It has no authority to amend or override the constitutional arrangements in any country which is party to the Convention.

Our Parliament is vested with authority to defer its sovereignty and pass it to any body it may choose: hence the authority vested in the court in Luxembourg where the decisions are—and, for as long as Parliament does not repeal the European Communities Act 1972, will remain—binding. That legislative structure was not adopted when the Human Rights Act incorporated the Convention into domestic law, and did not vest the same authority in the Strasbourg court. Indeed the debates in Parliament show that the suggestion that legislative authority should be given to the Strasbourg court to 'bind' our courts here was expressly rejected. And if it could not bind our courts, it certainly could not bind Parliament.

This is not the time to analyse the difficulty our judiciary has had in interpreting the obligation imposed on the courts by the apparently simple words 'take into account' which defines and limits the extent of the obligation of our courts to follow the decisions of the Strasbourg court. Whatever those simple words may mean, they do not have the same meaning as the language which was used to create the relationship with the court in Luxembourg. In any event, however the relationship with Strasbourg may be defined, the Human Rights Act represented an exercise of sovereignty in this jurisdiction by a sovereign Parliament. That is our democratic process at work.

The President suggests that the 'rule of law' sometimes 'trumps' the democratic process. This proposition, however, begs the question, which is: where in a democracy does the power to make the law ultimately reside? That is the sovereignty issue.

In our constitution, as a result of the constitutional struggles in the seventeenth century, sovereignty was vested in Parliament, or, more precisely and pedantically, the King-in-Parliament. We have proceeded for centuries on the basis that the decisions of the highest court in the land can, if Parliament so decides, be subjected to parliamentary scrutiny and legislative amendment. A very good recent example was the enactment of the Criminal Evidence (Witness Anonymity) Act 2008, which overruled the decision of the House of Lords in *Davis*.[2] This principle has not undermined the rule of law in this country. On the contrary, it has stood the test of centuries. It represents a simple acknowledgement that in our constitution, ultimate sovereignty does not rest with the courts, but with Parliament. What is more, in our arrangements, although Parliament is expected to respect a Treaty obligation, it is not bound to do so, and legislative enactments are themselves of course subject to subsequent amendment or repeal by the same or later parliaments. For us this principle, embodied in a constitution which is partly written and partly unwritten, underpins the rule of law and represents the rule of law in operation.

If I may say so, I respectfully agree with the observations of Lord Sumption that the Supreme Court in the United Kingdom should seek to follow the decisions of the Strasbourg court and 'treat them as the authoritative expositions of the Convention'. A different and perhaps stronger emphasis may be found in Baroness Hale's identification of the 'mirror principle'. But I hasten to add that, as Baroness Hale herself appears to accept, the 'mirror principle' is not a new way of describing the old-fashioned rubber stamp. We should perhaps recognise that in this jurisdiction some aspects of the law are judge-made, but many more result from statute. Where the relevant law is judge-made the likelihood is that, applying the mirror principle, in the absence of any contrary enactment, the Supreme Court would follow the decision in Strasbourg, leaving it to Parliament to enact any amending legislation. In reality, because by definition any such enactment would be incompatible with the Convention, the chance of any subsequent contradictory legislation would be remote.

Where, however, any 'offending' provisions depends on statute, and comes under criticism from Strasbourg, different considerations apply. The President suggests that the government must ensure the passage of any necessary amending legislation. If he is right, whether or not Parliament agrees, Parliament is bound to enact laws which will bring the decisions of the Strasbourg court into effect.

Let me take prisoner voting as an example of the problems that arise. Many clear, absolutist, but contradictory positions can be

---

[2] *R v Davis* [2008] 1 AC 1128.

taken. I believe that there are respectable arguments on both sides. At present prisoners cannot vote. Universal suffrage is a fundamental principle of a democratic state, but exceptions to it have always been recognised. Many are younger than the minimum age, however that is defined. Some are disqualified from voting. If the Supreme Court were to decide that any of these disqualifications infringe the Convention, a declaration of incompatibility would follow. Parliament should then address the issue and, despite the declaration of incompatibility, is entitled to maintain the 'offending' disqualification. If Strasbourg concludes that the statutory disqualification constitutes an unjustified interference with any individual rights, the process by which this apparent flaw may be amended continues to be statutory enactment. In my view it would be a negation of the democratic process for Members of Parliament to be obliged to vote for a measure with which they disagree. The Treaty obligation does not 'trump' statute, and even if the government of the day supported the reform proposed by the Strasbourg court, it could not guarantee success in Parliament.

There can surely be no argument about many Convention principles, which are reflective of the common law. Torture and slavery are prohibited. Life is sacred. A fair, open trial of alleged criminal offences is axiomatic. There are, however, greater difficulties with provisions which refer to considerations which are 'necessary' in the democratic society found, for example, in Article 8(2). If the President is correct, what constitutes a necessity in a democratic society is left, in the ultimate analysis, exclusively, to a body of unelected judges, and has been removed from the legislative body elected through ordinary democratic processes. I recognise the importance attached by the Strasbourg court when considering Convention rights in this context to the principles of proportionality and margin of appreciation. As we know, and he underlines, they loom large in the approach of the Strasbourg court. The difficulty, however, is simply identified. As the court sees these principles, they are principles of self-denial. Indeed, in a very recent speech the President underlined 'that the margin of appreciation is something that is *allowed* to States by the *Court*' (his emphasis). On this basis, the court decides for itself whether and when these principles should apply. The President explains later in his article that the court should 'only exceptionally ... impose its view on that of national authorities', but this proposition underlines his opinion that it is entitled to do so when it thinks appropriate.

This brings us back to the issue of sovereignty. I profoundly disagree with the President's opinion. The force of Treaty obligations and the authority of the Strasbourg court on the correct interpretation of the Convention, and the rights established by it, are well understood. The adoption by our Supreme Court of the Convention principles identified by the Strasbourg court usually follows. The respect owed by Parliament to the views expressed by that court is embodied in the Human Rights Act itself. But, using the President's language, the imposition of those views on Parliament represents a dramatic and unconstitutional extension of judicial authority.

Parliamentary Self-Government

This was the Mansion House speech given in July 2009.

MY LORD MAYOR, you assumed your ancient office last autumn in the eye of a financial hurricane. Life must have seemed much easier for your famous predecessor, Dick Whittington, who on 23 November 1415 rode out to Blackheath, accompanied by 24 Aldermen, all fully and gloriously caparisoned, to greet Henry V after his famous victory at Agincourt and to lead him into the City. The celebrations were wonderful, the chroniclers made merry. They were the Venerable Joshua in *Troubadour Gazette* and the Blessed Frances in the *Merry England Times*. They were united in saying that the day was extremely convivial. What a lovely word. So evocative. I'll bet it was convivial. I don't think that on that day there was too much concern about ASBOs, Health and Safety issues, and it was a day when we can be sure that not a single human right was infringed.

It's easy to forget that Henry V's French campaign had been funded by loans from the City. If it had ended in the predicted disaster, the financial crisis that would have engulfed the City would have been shattering. As every child knows, or as I hope every child still does know, it was only courage and determination, inspired by the sound of blessed church bells, that converted Dick Whittington's poverty into plenitude. So, my Lord Mayor, this is not the first occasion on which the City that you lead has faced a crisis.

Some of your guests will remember an occasion when England had batted themselves into a crisis—indeed most of your guests will remember numerous such occasions, and it is perhaps just as well that we did not have as many financial crises as batting crises—but on this particular occasion a fast bowler, I think from Derbyshire, my wife's beloved county, picked up his bat and announced to his England team mates in the changing room, 'cometh the hour, cometh the man'. And with those words, my Lord Mayor, he was referring to you and the moment when you assumed your ancient office. The difference between you and the fast bowler in my story is that he was run out very quickly. You on the other hand are still there, not out—our very own Monty Panesar. May I be allowed to acknowledge the tireless and continuing efforts you are making to both address and alleviate the financial crisis with its alarming personal consequences for national prosperity which, whether we like it or not, will be with us for years to come.

As if the financial crisis was not enough, your mayoralty has coincided with a crisis of a different kind, and as with the financial crises, much depends on how it is addressed. We are, are we not, in the middle of, if not a constitutional crisis, then at the very least a constitutional problem, and that has arisen at a time when our constitutional landscape has recently undergone huge changes. In his recent book, Professor Vernon Bogdanor describes *The New British Constitution*.[1] Notice the '*New*'. He says how, in these last few years, a new British constitution is being created and the old constitutional order being replaced.

> This new constitution is as yet incomplete and its final outlines are at present only partially discernable. The description therefore, cannot be complete because the new constitution is not yet complete.

One possibly very minor consequence of the significant constitutional changes which govern the relationship of the judiciary with the executive and the legislature is that with effect from 1st October this year the Lord Chief Justice of the day will no longer have the opportunity to speak in the House of Lords.

My Lord Mayor, I hope you and the City will not mind if I treat this annual Banquet as an opportunity, where it is appropriate to do so, to say a few words publicly about what I shall no longer be able to say at greater length to Parliament itself on issues which affect our constitutional arrangements and the administration of justice.

We all understand the convention that Her Majesty's judges do not comment on political issues, or discuss legislation which we may have to interpret, or appear to support the views of one political party against those of another. But where our constitutional affairs are engaged, these are of direct importance to the judiciary, not least because any changes which have constitutional implications may affect the relationship between the citizen and the state. Even if we have not been consulted, we are entitled to speak. I believe that we are entitled to speak, and some indeed would think that we have a duty to speak.

And even as I do speak, the Parliamentary Standards Bill is currently being debated this very evening in the course of a rapid

---

[1] Vernon Bogdanor, *The New British Constitution* (Oxford, 2009).

legislative process. I comment with due deference because, as it seems to me, and the law for many years has been that Parliament alone must decide how it should be governed, and how it should govern itself.

The Bill has changed in numerous different ways during its passage through both Houses. The eventual Act will be significantly different from the original Bill. In other words the parliamentary process has been working. I am not commenting on what I have not seen. But I do suggest that in our constitutional arrangements it is imperative that ultimate responsibility for the governance of Parliament should remain with Parliament. Perhaps I may be allowed to offer my very personal view that on these issues members of both Houses should be able to vote in accordance with their consciences and their personal judgement.

I remain concerned at the possibility of any kind of judicial review of any aspect of the governance of Parliament. Such a process would have the potential to bring the judiciary into conflict with Parliament, and in particular with the House of Commons. This would be an unpalatable clash, and dangerous for our constitutional arrangements, and the understandings which enable them to work.

I am not being portentous; these dangers are not imminent, but it is sometimes easy to forget that the future is long as well as short. It is wholly unrealistic to believe that constitutional changes are fixed forever as at the date when change formally takes place, or that the constitution is then bound to ossify in the form intended by the successful proponents of change. I doubt whether the devolution arrangements for Scotland and Wales—different devolution arrangements be it noted—will stand forever where they now stand, and whether the West Lothian question is now resolved, never to be resuscitated.

As I have said, the judiciary should not be involved in the parliamentary process and that is underlined by this: the ordinary law of the country applies to members of Parliament as it does to everyone else. Responsibility for ensuring that our parliamentary arrangements are satisfactory is vested directly in the High Court of Parliament itself, and it is and should remain accountable, not to the judiciary but to the electorate which, in our democratic process, ultimately hires and fires both the executive and the major legislative body.

And by this time next year, my Lord Mayor, the process of hiring and firing will have been completed. The electorate will have spoken.

There are many requests I could make of the government and legislature which the electorate will give to the nation. Tonight, I identify two.

The major constitutional changes which affected the judiciary in June 2003 were proclaimed without so much as the courtesy of a letter or even a telephone call to the Lord Chief Justice. The equally important structural changes of 2007 were proclaimed by a Minister of the Crown in an article in a Sunday newspaper. My Lord Mayor, the Statute of Proclamations was enacted in the reign of King Henry VIII; it was repealed in 1547, after Henry's death.[2] In our new constitutional arrangements there should, I respectfully suggest, be an understanding that the judiciary should, at the very least, be consulted about proposed constitutional changes which may impact, directly or indirectly, on the role of the judiciary within the constitution. Anything which relates to the mechanics of government is likely to have such an impact.

My second request is one which has been frequently addressed, but so far without success. Can we possibly have less legislation, particularly in the field of criminal justice. The overwhelming bulk is suffocating.

May I take as an example the year 2003. In that year we had criminal statutes with the following titles:

— Crime (International Co-operation Act)
— Anti-Social Behaviour Act
— Courts Act
— Extradition Act
— Sexual Offences Act
— Criminal Justice Act.

The Crime (International Co-operation) Act had 96 sections and 6 schedules containing 124 paragraphs.

The Anti-Social Behaviour Act had no fewer than 97 sections and 3 schedules containing 8 paragraphs. 97 sections in an Act which is merely making provisions 'in connection with anti-social behaviour'.

The Courts Act contains 112 sections and 10 schedules with 547 paragraphs.

The Extradition Act has 227 sections and 4 schedules containing 82 paragraphs.

---

[2] See *Henry VIII Clauses*, this volume, p 99.

The Sexual Offences Act has 143 sections and 7 schedules with 338 paragraphs.

But finally, the great Daddy of them all, the Criminal Justice Act has 339 sections and 38 schedules with a total of 1169 paragraphs. This analysis excludes schedule 37, which sets out no fewer than 20 pages of statutory repeals—and that's not the end of it.

No fewer than 21 Commencement and Transitional Savings Orders have been made under this Act—the first in 2003, and the last in 2008. Plenty of provisions have not been brought into force. Many will not be, or so we are told. They will go into some sort of statutory limbo. But this year the Criminal Justice Act 2003 (Commencement No 8 and Transitional and Savings Provisions) (Amendment) Order of 2009/616 was made, amending the 8th Commencement Order. Each of these orders produced different starting dates for different statutory provisions. All for a single Act. This is the Criminal Justice Act 2003, one of six major pieces of legislation.[3] This on the other hand is the Criminal Justice Act 1972.

The only other piece of legislation affecting criminal justice in that year was the well-known Matrimonial Proceedings (Polygamous Marriages) Act, which ran to all of five sections and for some unaccountable reason lacked any schedule at all.[4]

In a rough and ready calculation, it seems to me that if every line of recent criminal justice legislation had been guaranteed by a payment to the Bank of England of £10,000 a line, the credit crisis would have been funded. We might have had a Dick Whittington moment and conviviality unbounded.

My Lord Mayor, thank you for allowing me the opportunity to speak about matters of consequence to the judiciary.

May I, through you, thank my colleagues who are here tonight, and indeed the men and women of the entire judicial family for their tireless commitment to the rule of law. As I come to the end of my first year in this office I want publicly to record the innumerable kindnesses and unswerving support that my colleagues throughout the country have offered me. Without them this job could not be done.

---

[3] The stack was alarmingly high.
[4] There was no stack at all.

Henry VIII Clauses

This speech was made at the Lord Mayor's Banquet in 2010.

AS AN HONORARY Liveryman of the Plaisterer's Company, My Lord Mayor, you know that for a while William Shakespeare lived in Silver Street close by the Company's Old Hall. I doubt whether a mere common actor, certainly not a Warwickshire country bumpkin—William Shakespeare and I have that in common—would have been invited to attend this sort of occasion at the old Plaisterers Hall. There is no doubt that as he wrote *Othello*, which was penned while he lived in Silver Street, he had in mind his experience of carousing Liverymen on their way back from a splendid evening in the Hall, when he gave that intriguing and feisty character Emelia the lines which read:

Men are ... all but stomachs ... and when they are full, they belch.

My Lord Mayor, none of us will belch tonight, but your hospitality has indeed been sumptuous.

Can I remind you: when your predecessor took office, I made a request of him. Between us, I said that he and I should win the Ashes in 2009. And we did. Although I do concede that Strauss and his team made their own individual contributions. But, my Lord Mayor, may I remind you that when you took office on the second Saturday of November—and I shall have to come back to that date—I made a very modest request. One William Shakespeare—our W S—is listed for failing to pay the tax on the 1596 subsidy rolls and the certificate dated 15 November 1597 is still in existence, and he is listed as a defaulter. I do hope that you are not holding Emelia's remarks about the carousing Plaisterers against him. If you are, you should read what she has to say about husbands and sex. Or maybe, on reflection, you shouldn't.

There are always times when we need our wives to speak up for us. This time last year the lawyers' cricket world cup took place in England. I received a letter inviting me to come and open it by opening the batting against Michael Holding. I wrote back saying that I would happily open the bowling against Michael Holding, but thought he might be a little too quick for me. But the organisers were adamant. Mike Holding wanted to bowl. What could I do? So Judith and I went up to Fenners for the great ordeal. At lunch the organisers sat me next to Mr Holding. And you who play cricket all know what it's like with really fast bowlers. You laugh uproariously at any joke they say. When he said 'hello' I was nearly hysterical. Then you try flattery. 'I didn't see it but I am told the over you bowled at Geoff Boycott in the West Indies was probably one of the best overs ever bowled.' The response: 'I just bowled fast.'

By now trembling, I ventured a further bit of flattery, speaking admiringly, and genuinely so, of the 14 wickets he had taken at the Oval in 1975, as I reminded him, on a batsman's wicket. The flattery did me no good. 'I just bowled faster.'

The verbal intimidation was too much for me, but Judith was listening in to this conversation. It still touches me now. 'Mr Holding'—notice none of this Mike or Mikey, 'Mr Holding, I have been married to my husband for 44 years, and I love him very much. If you kill him, I'll kill you.'

It wasn't Shakespeare, and she wasn't acting, and Michael Holding knew that she wasn't acting. So he said. 'That's all right.'

Mind you, I don't think he was trembling, but when I went out to bat, with Judith's intervention to help me, thanks to her advice to me not to 'present any threat to him' (*any* threat—I was flattered)— to this great man at all by wearing pads, gloves, helmet and a box (I wasn't bothered about the helmet but I was rather disappointed that she dismissed the box so peremptorily), Mike Holding bowled a ball to me that was so slow that he could have run and caught it before it bounced. I was through the shot before it got to me, and it hit me on the leg, and didn't even hurt. I am indebted to him. He was a delightful gentleman. And I say that knowing that I shall never have to face him again. Or laugh at his jokes. But no less, I am indebted to Judith for yet another occasion when she stood by and sustained me in the face of all the odds. Aren't we all judges indebted to our other halves and those we love?

My Lord Mayor, more seriously, at this Banquet last year some of you will remember my contention that we faced a financial crisis, which had alarming consequences for national prosperity, and that it needed to be addressed as an imperative necessity, and that whether we liked it or not, the effect would be with us for years to come. It was not a political speech, I was just facing the realities. What I knew then was that we have been as unwise as the Merchant of Venice, entering into a suicide bond on the basis that before too long his ships would come home, so that his debt would be paid off.

Well his ships didn't come home, and the debt wasn't paid off. And ours aren't paid off. We have had an election, and we now have a new government. The Chancellor of the Exchequer is no Portia; and the Lord Chancellor is no Nerissa. There is no Portia. There is no Nerissa. There would be no Legal Aid to come to Antonito's rescue: this was only, after all, a civil debt.

And we in the judiciary have to face practical realities. That is, after all, what we are trained to do, day by day—not in the ivory tower so beloved of our critics, but in court. We also recognise that in the current climate everyone can demonstrate why his or her particular resource from public funds should be left untouched, in other words that each and every one should receive the same treatment that the National Health Service receives. Save money, reduce expenditure.

Let me make it clear: when considering how best to respond to specific proposals which will save money and reduce expenditure, the judiciary cannot ignore the national fiscal realities. The question will however always be the same question. How will this proposal impact on the administration of justice? And for this purpose, too, we must be prepared to question—I emphasise question—all our own processes, including some very longstanding ones. I could give many examples. Let me choose a few.

Does our traditional, adversarial system continue to provide the best means of enabling judges to decide those desperately sensitive cases involving the future of children? In the Crown Court, time continues to be treated as an unlimited resource. This simply cannot continue. I do not understand why justice is less likely to be delivered in a criminal trial if a fair timetable is imposed, and the advocates are required to stick to the points that matter, instead of travelling over every bit of land without a stopping place. These and many other issues have been under consideration and are being addressed. We will have Criminal Procedure Rules shortly coming into force which will give judges express and wide powers to impose timetables in the Crown Court: I make it clear that I anticipate that these powers will be exercised. It will not be comfortable. In the Commercial Court, where the parties pay for their costs, the imposition of timetables was greeted with horror; now it works without a murmur and the quality of justice is not diminished. What I am saying is that we can no longer afford the luxury of allowing the parties in criminal and family cases, both sides of which are largely supported from public funds, to dictate the length of the case and take as long as they think they want. Although the judiciary has absolutely no control over Legal Aid and its implementation, can we at least ask the question whether these arrangements themselves are counter-efficient to the trial system, and observe that, as it seems to some of us, the best rewards are not necessarily received by the most efficient practitioners?

My Lord Mayor, this could be a very long list; but that is not what we are here for. In the end, the judiciary's concern for the doing of justice directly involves the speedy resolution of the dispute between parents about where the child or children should live, because if it is not speedily resolved the dispute has a corrosive effect on their relationship, and ultimately damages the children whose welfare is the paramount consideration of the process. Delayed trials mean that witnesses are called to give evidence about incidents which happened so long ago that inevitably their memories have faded, to the disadvantage of one side or the other in an individual trial, and to the damage of justice in that specific case. And how do we deal with victims of, say, sexual crimes unless we have an efficient process which will enable the boy or girl, man or woman, to receive the necessary treatment to help their recovery to the fullest possible extent from the ordeal they've undergone? We need to think on these things.

If the end result of our national financial crisis is that all these cases take much longer to be resolved, then justice will have been damaged. And in this context, could I remind us, that the demand for court services has steadily increased. Public law applications made in the Family Courts increased by 31 per cent between 2008 and 2009, and private law applications by 19 per cent. 2009 saw 98,095 receipts for trial in the Crown Court. That is the highest figure since 1992. So the fiscal realities will be hitting the system of justice at just the time when the demands on it are increasing. We will continue our longstanding commitment to achieving improvements in the processes.

My Lord Mayor, this time last year I spent some time addressing the problem of legislative plenitude—overload—and so I am not going to repeat it. I had to be circumspect, but I hope I did not use words which disguised my meaning. Since June we have been promised the Great Repeal Act ...

...

Which, I wonder, of the 2,492—yes, 2,492 laws—introduced during 2009 will still be in force 700 years from now? Presumably, whether there is a nuclear explosion or not, no one will have been charged with causing a nuclear explosion under the Nuclear Explosions (Prohibition and Inspections) Act 1998. But what if they had? After such an explosion it might be a little tricky to get a judge and jury together to try any defendant who might have survived the explosion, and been found and traced by any surviving member of the police force. That is what I call a really useful Act of Parliament!

I am, I suspect, not the only member of the judiciary who is troubled by the extent of the powers granted to so many council officials to enter people's homes without a warrant. Or the way in which apparently sensible powers—directed to the prevention of terrorism—appear on occasion to be used to control activities which, by no stretch of the imagination, have anything to do with terrorism. But my deepest concern at the moment is directed to the increased use of what are described as Henry VIII clauses. Last year, Lord Mayor, I said that I hoped to use this occasion to draw attention to matters of concern, and I propose to say something more on this topic.

Henry VIII was a dangerous tyrant. The Reformation Parliament made him Supreme Head of the Church, the representative of the Almighty on earth—hardly an encouragement to modesty and humility; that Parliament altered the succession at his will; it changed the religion backwards and forwards, at his will, depending on which religious book he had read most recently. They were a malleable, manageable lot. And there is a public belief that the Statute of Proclamations of 1539 was the ultimate in parliamentary supineness. The Act itself was repealed within less than 10 years, immediately on his death in 1547. But it had allowed the king's proclamations to have the same force as Acts of Parliament. That is a Henry VIII clause. It is perhaps worth emphasising that even this infamous Act, and even this supine Reformation Parliament, refused, or was not persuaded, to agree that proclamations alone could prejudice any inheritance, office, liberty, goods, chattels or life. The Act was subject to those limitations.

Do you remember the Legislative and Regulatory Reform Bill of 2006 which, under the guise of reducing red tape, sought to give ministers power to amend, repeal or replace any Act of Parliament simply by making an Order? It was eventually withdrawn when the House of Lords Constitution Committee alerted itself or was alerted to the implications of this provision. So we can sit back and relax. That's that then. But it is not.

Consider the Banking (Special Provisions) Act 2008, enacted in the hurricane of the banking crisis. It granted the Treasury, presumably the Prime Minister and First Lord of the Treasury, this power—to make:

(a) such supplementary, incidental or consequential provision, or
(b) such transitory, transitional or saving provision, as they consider appropriate for the general purposes, or any particular purposes, of this Act ...

But listen to this. It expressly provided that an order may

> disapply (to such extent as is specified) any specified statutory provision or rule of law

So, my Lord Mayor, we have an Act of Parliament which expressly grants to the Treasury power to disapply any other relevant statute bearing on the provisions of the 2008 Act or indeed any rule of law.

You can see the same process at work with section 51 of the Constitutional Reform and Governance Act 2010. This enables any Minister of the Crown, by order, to make such provision as he or she considers appropriate in relation to any provision of the Act. This is the Act which deals with our constitution. The order may:

(a) amend, repeal or revoke any existing statutory provision,
(b) include supplementary, incidental, transitional, transitory or saving provision.

So the new constitutional arrangements, and the old, can be revisited by ministerial order, directed not merely to amendment, repeal or revocation of any provisions in the Act, but directed at any of our existing statutory provisions which bear on our constitutional affairs.

I have tried to pursue this question, and recently read two letters from the Ministry of Justice on the topic. For me, it made alarming reading. First, it is clear that there is no routine method for collecting information about Henry VIII clauses. Doing the best the Ministry could, during the parliamentary session up to 10 November 2009, there were, I quote, 'around 70 such powers contained within the legislation enacted so far'. It is pointed out that at least 10 of them were not new, but were re-enactments, and 15 of them contained provisions allowing consequential amendments. But that was not the end of the session. Between 10 November and the end of the parliamentary session for 2008–09 there were some 53 additional such clauses, of which 10 were provisions allowing for consequential amendments, and 5 enabled the proper functioning of pilot schemes. So we are talking, in one parliamentary session, of over 120 Henry VIII clauses. It astonishes me.

It is said in the letters that they are only used when there is a substantial call for them, and no practical alternative for dealing with the issue in the original legislation, and that such powers are rarely used. Well, the two Acts of Parliament to which I have referred seem to me to be the opposite of narrow-ranging.

You can be sure that when these Henry VIII clauses are introduced they will always be said to be necessary. William Pitt warned us how to treat such a plea with disdain, but why are we allowing ourselves to get into the habit of Henry VIII clauses? Why should we? By allowing them to become a habit, we are already in great danger of becoming indifferent to them, and to the fact that they are being enacted on our behalf.

I do not regard the need for resolutions, affirmative or negative, as a sufficient protection against the increasingly apparent indifference with which this legislation comes into force. To the argument that a resolution is needed, my response is, wait until the need arises, and go to Parliament and get the legislation through, if you can. I continue to find the possibility, even the remote possibility, that the Treasury may by order disapply any rule of law to be extraordinary, or that a Minister may change our constitutional arrangements, to be deeply problematic. Of course I am not suggesting that any of the Ministers with whom we were dealing before June, or for that matter any of the Ministers we are dealing with now, are intent on subverting the constitution. I know that. You know that. But, and it is a very important but, the future is long as well as short. We should not just be thinking about 2015, but about 2025 and 2035, when our grandchildren will be responsible for running this country...

When the Great Repeal Act is under consideration, I do urge that somehow, somewhere, Henry VIII clauses, and indeed the modern Henry VIII Plus clauses, should be excluded from the lexicon, unless the Minister coming to the House says in express and unequivocal language that he or she is seeking the consent of the House to such a clause, so that, quite apart from the members of Parliament, the wider public may be informed of what is proposed on its behalf.

Half a moment's thought will demonstrate that proliferation of clauses like these will have the inevitable consequence of yet further damaging the sovereignty of Parliament, and increasing yet further the authority of the executive over the legislature. If I may adapt a phrase, if this is the way things are to go, the powers of the executive have indeed increased, and are indeed increasing, when many believe they ought to be diminished. Long before we get anywhere near the Great Repeal Act, Henry VIII clauses should be confined to the dustbin of history, along with the Act of Proclamations, itself repealed in 1547. We must break what I believe to be a pernicious habit and treat the plea to necessity as William Pitt treated it, with careful disdain, and we must do it now.

Assisted Suicide: Moral and Constitutional Issues

This lecture was given at King's College London in March 2015.

THIS MUST SEEM like a strange combination. Moral and constitutional issues are often perceived to dwell in separate and distinct compartments. The superficial wave of the hands says that the law and morals are distinct, and constitutional law must be yet further afield from morals. My thesis is that they are undoubtedly different, but certainly linked. In a democracy, the creation or amendment of the laws that govern us stem from and are ultimately dependent on the moral codes by which contemporary society expects to be governed. This present issue, assisted suicide or assisted dying, represents a huge moral and constitutional challenge.

Perhaps I should make it clear from the very outset that in this lecture I am not seeking to persuade anyone to any particular view about the possible decriminalisation of assisting those who wish to commit suicide to do so. I have listened to compelling arguments by men and women whose judgement I respect but whose views are diametrically opposed to each other. Ultimately this is a matter of conscience and judgement for each individual. The debate, the very limited parliamentary debate on the issues, about how to strike the correct balance between individual autonomy and the sanctity of life and its protection also impinges on our constitutional arrangements. The issues are fundamental. They involve the sovereignty of Parliament and the relationship between Parliament and the judiciary, and the exercise of prosecutorial and judicial functions in the criminal justice system. These are hardly trivial questions.

In Magna Carta year perhaps the starting point should be taken from one of the contemporary proverbs as it applied to the life and death of William the Marshal, the great hero of Magna Carta. It is very simple. It reads '*La bon fine va tout*'. Literally, the good end is worth everything. Marshal's death had indeed been a good death. After a life of epic achievement, but now comforted by the rites of extreme unction, and after taking some bread softened in milk, his body clock ticked its way to a peaceful and quiet end. One might say the end we all wish for—or in my grandmother's case, the one that she prayed for—and the one which we hope will bless all those whom we love, and, dare I say it? our own ends.

We have, however, to understand this proverb in its medieval context. It was referring only to bodily death. To the medieval mind life was a gift of God. How we lived our lives on this earth would be considered on the Day of Judgment, when the destiny of one's immortal soul and how it would spend the whole of eternity would be decided. For a man like Marshal, who spent much of his life in battle, and went forth on what we should describe as suicide missions, suffering in life, including suffering at life's end, was part of the testing ground, and therefore to be endured as part of life's journey. Dealing with it generally, one should not hasten into the presence of the Almighty before He called you to Him. If you were forced to undergo an agonising death of unrelieved pain, that was His Will, not to be challenged or complained of, but to be addressed and faced up to through the exercise of that enduring but nowadays underrated virtue, fortitude. St Thomas Aquinas regarded suicide as a mortal sin, not least because, if successful, the suicide had no room for remorse or repentance, or indeed forgiveness, and so burial in sanctified ground was prohibited. Indeed, of course, suicide was a crime. Self murder. A suicide *se murderavit* and the suicide died a felon with all his goods to be forfeited. The survivor of a suicide pact was a murderer, and someone who assisted another person to commit suicide was also guilty of murder. The sanctity of human life and the need to protect every life from a premature unnatural end pervaded European belief, and for very many centuries suicide was a crime, although not in Scotland. And, logically of course, it was equally a crime to be complicit in the suicide of another person, and it always has been in Scotland.

Yet from the earliest days this moral issue was contentious. Literally speaking, euthanasia comes from the Greek, and it means 'good death'. Let me immediately say that those who advocate the decriminalisation of assisted suicide are not speaking of euthanasia, and that whatever the original Greek may have meant, euthanasia has come to be associated in the modern mind not only with 'mercy killing', but also with the evils of Nazism and eugenics, and bringing an end to the lives of those whose lives were, for one reason or another, deemed to be deficient or incomplete, or simply incompatible with ideas current in any particular society about the ingredients of a sound body and mind, acceptable genes and a good life. In ancient

Greek thought, a doctor who provided a deadly drug to his dying patient, or suggested its use, would have contravened the ancient Hippocratic Oath. Plato and Aristotle rejected suicide, unless it was justified by incurable disease. St Thomas More, currently the anti-hero of *Wolf Hall*, in Utopia, rejected contemporary Christian thinking, and adopted the same Humanist approach.

There was much debate in medieval times as to whether suicide might be justified, for example where a woman facing rape and what would have been seen as the destruction of her chastity (not simply the physical horrors of rape) might kill herself first. And St Augustine would have thought it a sensible question to ask whether Thomas à Becket was truly to be regarded as a martyr in the light of the evidence that he appears to have welcomed, or perhaps acquiesced in, his own murder.

I have been name dropping.[1] Plato, Aristotle, St Augustine, St Thomas Aquinas and St Thomas More make a formidable quintet of philosophers who have had an enormous impact on the development of Western civilisation. My reason is simple. We must not begin to imagine that the moral issues have only become important in the last half-century or so. They have always mattered: for very many centuries. The nature of life and the end of life, in all its many constituent ingredients, have taxed human beings ever since the human race discovered its capacity to think.

Things change, as things always change. During my professional life, perhaps sparked by the horrors of genocide, perhaps sparked by the increasing secularisation of society, with the focus moving from the immortal soul in the hereafter to the life here on earth, individual autonomy, or the way in which the individual chooses to live his or her life, has moved significantly upwards in what I shall call the 'rights' hierarchy. Whatever the reasons, there were in the early 1960s a number of dramatic occasions when Parliament, that is the House of Commons and the House of Lords, then unreformed, acted as the conscience of the nation, decriminalising activity which had for centuries been stigmatised as crimes.

Homosexual activity between consenting adults in private ceased to be a crime. Until then the nature of the crime had not been theoretical. When I started at the Bar, I acted for a man who for committing buggery with a consenting adult in a garden shed was sent to prison for three years. Not long afterwards, by statute,

---

[1] See NDA Kemp, *Merciful Release: The History of the British Euthanasia Movement* (Manchester, 2002), which provided me with much valuable information.

not judicial decision, this conduct would not have been a crime at all.[2] Termination of pregnancy on therapeutic grounds ceased to be a crime. Abortion as such was not decriminalised, but abortion carried out in particular circumstances and under conditions expressly specified by statute, again not by the judiciary, fell outside the ambit of the criminal law.[3] The death penalty was suspended for a trial period of five years, and then abolished—again by statute, not judicial action.[4] And for present purposes, suicide, too, by parliamentary rather than judicial action was decriminalised.[5] From then onwards the pathetic, almost haunting spectacle of a man or woman standing in the dock charged with having tried unsuccessfully to kill himself or herself was removed. Nevertheless a person acting in pursuance of a suicide pact between himself and another who killed the other or was party to the other being killed by a third party was guilty of manslaughter. And anyone who aided, abetted, counselled or procured the suicide of another, or his attempt to commit suicide, was also guilty of a criminal offence, punishable with up to 14 years' imprisonment. Before proceedings for these continuing offences could be initiated, however, the consent of the Director of Public Prosecutions was required.

None of this legislation carried universal approval, and much of it was carried out in the face of serious, sustained criticism, by individuals who honestly believed that one or other of these forms of decriminalisation was wrong. The arguments were sometimes bitter and deep, and although the battle to accept sexual diversity is won, the abolition of the death penalty remains deeply controversial. The perceived abuses of the 'conditions' subject to which termination of pregnancy was decriminalised remain controversial. Euthanasia taking the form of eugenics practices remains abhorrent, but I do not detect any great continuing anxiety about the decriminalisation of suicide. Dealing with it very broadly, I suspect that there is a measure of sympathy for those who take their own lives, whatever it was that drove them to it. The controversy surrounds the next possible step, that is, whether assisting someone who wants to commit suicide to do so should, in carefully defined circumstances, be decriminalised.

The superficial response is that it is difficult to identify any significant difference between decriminalising the actions of the

---

[2] Sexual Offences Act 1967.
[3] Abortion Act 1967.
[4] Murder (Abolition of Death Penalty) Act 1965.
[5] Suicide Act 1961.

suicide while maintaining the sanctions of the criminal law against the individual who helps the intending suicide to achieve his purpose. But that is superficial. The first difference is fundamental. The assister is not exercising autonomy over his own body nor bringing his own life to its end. In this context the autonomy argument is diminished. At the same time, the alternative principle, the sanctity of human life and its protection, continues in full force. Indeed if the protective elements were diminished the lives of those who live with disabilities would be cheapened. In this context each life remains equally precious, and those with diminished ability to look after themselves require yet greater protection.

At this stage we have to be realistic about humanity. Not all of us are kind and generously motivated. Some of us are capable of being corrupted. Once we think that a life is valueless and wasteful it becomes harder to resist the thought process that the life we treat as valueless and wasteful should be ended ... and, thus motivated, to persuade the suffering individual that this is indeed so. You can create all sorts of legal safeguards to govern human affairs, but experience teaches us that the malicious can circumvent them. It is perhaps worth remembering that termination of pregnancy was decriminalised subject to certain stringent conditions. Between 2004 and 2013 official figures show that 1,898,719 terminations took place.[6] Hundreds of thousands of terminations during this period. Were there none which contravened the statutory provisions? Are we to believe that there was no over-generous interpretation of the statutory conditions to which each of them was, as a matter of law, subject? In this context the absence of effective enforcement provisions against the circumvention of statutory protections, as well as the slippery slope argument, have force, and I offer this thought: that every time we read of our aging population, and how endless numbers of the young among you are going to live past 100, and how the elderly are a huge drain on limited National Health resources, is it too utterly fanciful to imagine a time coming when lives which are deemed to be valueless and wasteful no longer attract the level of palliative care and protection which is embodied in the sanctity of life principle? The pressures then will not be from greedy or unsympathetic relatives: it will then be public policy. Is this all too portentous? With the world's population growing older at the pace that it is, I am not sure.

---

[6] Figures provided by the Operations Directorate, extrapolated from data held on the CPS Case Management System.

And yet, and yet ... As the law stands now the individual who, as a last act of devotion to a beloved, assists him or her to the death he desperately seeks, and which will leave the assister bereft and broken-hearted, is a criminal. In addition to the terrible price paid as a debt to love, the argument that it is inhumane to add all the paraphernalia of a criminal investigation as well as the risk of prosecution is compelling. If, after all, what is being done is to enable the intended suicide to achieve his own determined objective, the actions of the human agency which enables him to achieve that purpose should be seen as the actions of the intended suicide. If on this basis, and on these limited grounds, assisting suicide should be decriminalised, then it is nothing to the point that before a prosecution may take place, the Director of Public Prosecutions has to give her consent. Even if she refuses her consent, the assister has committed a crime.

Two further features need attention. If the DPP never prosecutes in cases like this—and she very rarely does—then in truth she has been vested with or acquired a power to dispense with or suspend a criminal statute. Constitutionally that is unacceptable. The Bill of Rights itself did away with any possibility of dispensation or suspension of the law. You can be pretty sure that the sight of a succession of individuals in the dock for assisting the suicide of someone they loved, just because of the debt to love, would quickly result in a public clamour for such obvious injustice to be alleviated. And it would be reinforced by an endless stream of judicial decisions making orders for absolute discharge, the clearest possible indication of the judicial mind that no true criminality had occurred. Yet, in reality, this would simply represent judicial second-guessing of the DPP's original decision. As it seems to me, to leave it to the 'system' is an idle way of addressing the issue of principle, which is whether, and if so in precisely which circumstances, assisting suicide should be decriminalised.

My journey through the history of the 60s and 70s of the last century was deliberate. I repeat my emphasis. All these changes resulted from parliamentary activity. They depended on statute. Parliament took on the responsibility of deciding whether or not to reduce or limit the ambit of the criminal law, and how, and with what measures to replace any decriminalisation. For years I have taken great pride in the fact that here in the United Kingdom, the decision to decriminalise termination of pregnancy subject to particular conditions, was made in Parliament, by our representatives, whereas in the United States of America, in a constitution which proudly proclaims how 'We, the People' govern the country, this question was left to be resolved by nine—indeed ultimately by five—human beings in the Supreme Court, in accordance with their constitutional arrangements.[7] Even if all nine of these human beings had been women, it would have been very hard to conceive of them as the 'conscience of the nation', rather than a body of individuals reflecting their own upbringing and background and education and prejudices, no doubt all honestly and faithfully held, but not on any view a cross-section of the nation. Here in the United Kingdom, the conscience of the nation is found in Parliament, and in particular in the House of Commons, where the nation is represented by the men and woman we have chosen to elect. At any one time there are something like 650 of them in sufficient health to attend the House of Commons. They produce legislation on topics of greater or lesser importance to the happiness of the nation. But on this issue, which can hardly be described as trivial, the House of Commons has largely been silent. The conscience of the nation—not I hasten to add the individual consciences of some individual members of the House, but the conscience of our sovereign democratic body—has been silent.

Not so, and by stark contrast, the unelected House of Lords. Bill after Bill, beginning with the Voluntary Euthanasia Bill in 1969 and continuing virtually to today in the Assisted Dying Bill, has produced debates of passion and compassion, forceful, persuasive, hallmarked with integrity and, in most of the debates, understanding and respect for opposing views. In the House of Commons there have been short debates, and oral questions designed to raise the issues. On the last occasion when a Bill was introduced, the Coroners and Justice Bill, which became the Coroners and Justice Act 2009, was plainly and explicitly not designed or appropriate to address these issues. And with the exception of one or two speakers, in the Commons it did not do so.

How much longer will this silence continue? In a few months' time we shall have a new House of Commons, newly elected. Will the new House ignore the issue?

I recognise, of course, that those who conscientiously support the maintenance of the present arrangements proceed on the basis that they are adequate, and that no change is needed. In today's lecture I repeat I am not advocating that the law should be changed. Nor am

---

[7] *Roe v Wade*, 410 US 113 (1973).

I advocating that it should stay as it is. What I am advocating is that it should be addressed by Parliament. There should be a free vote in both Houses. If after such a vote the law is changed, let us not forget that in theory Parliament can change it back. If the law remains as it is, let us also not forget that a future parliament can change it. The constitutional question arises from silence. The route to what the protagonists regard as a compassionate change in the law has become the litigation route—decision by judges. But in a country without a written constitution, and without its own charter of fundamental freedoms, and in which Parliament is sovereign as well as representative, this becomes a constitutional problem.

Let us look at where the litigation process has taken us. First, the case of Diane Pretty, a mentally alert woman, suffering from motor neurone disease, terminally ill, and facing an inevitably humiliating and disturbing death.[8] No longer physically capable of ending her own life without help, she needed the assistance of her husband to enable her to commit suicide when her ordeal became intolerable for her. Devoted to her, he was willing to assist, but she, equally devoted to him, did not wish him to be at risk of prosecution if he did so. The focus of her approach was the DPP's consent. She sought an assurance from the DPP that her husband would not be prosecuted if, in these circumstances, he assisted her to commit suicide; in effect, immunity from prosecution. The DPP declined to give any such assurance, arguing that in any event he would have no authority to give the assurances sought by Mrs Pretty. Mrs Pretty failed to establish any breach of Convention rights. There was broad consensus that the DPP had no suspending or dispensing power. Lord Hobhouse explained that

> the procedure of seeking to by-pass the ordinary operation of our system of criminal justice by raising questions of law and applying for judicial review of 'decisions' of the DPP cannot be approved and should be firmly discouraged. It undermines the proper and fair management of our criminal justice system.

I have yet to see any convincing contradiction of this assessment.

Mrs Pretty took her case to Strasbourg.[9] Neither the criminalisation of assisted suicide nor the DPP's refusal to grant Mrs Pretty's husband immunity in advance violated her Convention rights. Nevertheless the court was 'not prepared to exclude' that Mrs Pretty's entitlement to respect for her private life under Article 8(1) was

---

[8] *R (Pretty) v Director of Public Prosecutions* [2002] 1 AC 800.
[9] *Pretty v United Kingdom* (2002) 35 EHRR 1.

interfered with, adding that the interference 'may be justified' as 'necessary in a democratic society' under Article 8(2). This analysis left the door ajar.

However, before considering the case of Mrs Purdy, I must slightly digress to Daniel James, a fit, healthy young man aged 23 who suffered catastrophic injuries during rugby training. He did not wish to live. His life was ended at the Dignitas clinic in Switzerland. As far as I can recollect, catastrophic as his injuries were, he was not at immediate risk of death. His parents had assisted him to achieve his objective. The Director announced that there was sufficient evidence to justify a prosecution, but that it would not be in the public interest to do so. The decision and the reasoning were published in full.

And so to the case of Debbie Purdy. Again, she was a woman of full mental capacity, wheelchair-bound as a result of primary progressive multiple sclerosis, with an incurable and deteriorating condition which would mean that her life would become increasingly unbearable. When that happened, she wished to end her own life. Again, as an act of devotion, her husband was willing to assist her to commit suicide when her life became unendurable to her. The 'immunity' route had been closed by the decision in *Pretty*, and Mrs Purdy directed her criticism at the Director's failure to promulgate a specific policy, explaining the circumstances he would take into account in deciding whether or not to consent.

Only the House of Lords could revisit the decision in *Pretty*. Mrs Purdy's appeal against the refusal of the Divisional Court and Court of Appeal (where I declare that I presided) to grant her judicial review was successful.[10] The House of Lords was free to depart from its own decision in *Pretty*, and the decision reflected the observations of the Strasbourg court about how respect for the right to private life under Article 8 was engaged. It was not submitted that the court should not be involved in deciding whether it was appropriate or necessary for the DPP to issue the guidance. In the result the DPP was required to promulgate an offence-specific policy identifying the features to be taken into account in deciding whether or not to consent to a prosecution for assisted suicide.

Although what Mrs Pretty was seeking (an undertaking that her husband would not be prosecuted) and what Mrs Purdy was seeking (guidance of sufficient clarity to enable her and her husband to decide whether he would be likely to be prosecuted) were distinct,

---

[10]   *R (Purdy) v Director of Public Prosecutions* [2010] 1 AC 245.

in reality, both were intending to secure that they and their husbands should know in advance that the husbands would not be prosecuted for a crime which they had not yet committed and which had, inevitably, not been investigated.

Unsurprisingly, and acting with proper deference to the court, the DPP issued offence-specific guidance as directed by the House of Lords.

Concern was expressed about the issue of these guidelines. They were described by the Falconer Commission as 'exceptional' just because by identifying the circumstances in which a prosecution was justified in the public interest, they addressed not 'the exceptional or unexpected case' but rather 'the most common manifestation of the conduct that is criminalised'.[11] The guidelines therefore took 'a whole identifiable category of case outside the ambit of the criminal justice process'.

The Commission continued, with considerable force, that the decision about whether 'the law should be changed ... is not being made by ... Parliament...' because the effect of being forced to issue guidelines means the DPP has to decide on the extent of the law, 'and to whom it applies'. In strong but measured language the opinion was expressed that the issuing of the guidelines involved breaking an essential ingredient of the rule of law—that society was ruled 'by laws not men'. This, in different language, was Lord Hobhouse's point.

Valid though the criticism may be, where did the fault lie? Plainly not with the DPP. He was simply doing what he was required to do by the House of Lords in its judicial capacity. Why should the House of Lords, now the Supreme Court, be exonerated from blame? Because time and time again, almost indeed times without number, the judiciary, to the extent that the judiciary ever does implore Parliament to do anything, has implored the legislature to address this problem of profound individual and personal and social importance. The line is unbroken. Not merely through *Pretty* and *Purdy*, but through cases like *Inglis*,[12] where a mother, compelled by compassion for her severely injured son, murdered him, and *Bland*,[13] where one of the victims of the Hillsborough disaster was left in a permanent vegetative state, and the question arose, putting it crudely and harshly, whether the machine that was sustaining his life should be turned

---

[11] Falconer Committee, *Report on Assisted Dying* (2012).
[12] *R v Inglis* [2001] 1 WLR 1110.
[13] *Airedale NHS Trust v Bland* [1993] AC 789.

off. And yet, despite an incessant clamour from senior judges, the simple question whether assisting suicide should be decriminal-ised, and the circumstances in which it should be decriminalised, have not been fully addressed in our representative assembly.

And so, inevitably, the issue once again returned, via judicial review litigation, eventually to the House of Lords. This time, how-ever, neither claimant was suffering from a life-threatening condi-tion. Tony Nicklinson had suffered a stroke which left him suffering the terrible consequences of 'locked-in syndrome'.[14] His life was insupportable to him, and he wished to bring it to an end, but the consequences of his stroke meant that he could only end his own life by refusing all food and liquid—in other words, by starving himself to death. The other alternative was for him to take a lethal drug himself, using a machine which he could activate personally by using an eye blink computer. As the law stood, if the doctor had physically provided him with the drug, the doctor would have been guilty of murder, and if he had provided the drug so that Mr Nick-linson could operate the machine by eye blink computer, he would be guilty of assisting his suicide.

The second case, known as *M*, involved a man virtually unable to move following a brain stem stroke. He would have been fit to travel to Dignitas to take his own life. His wife was a nurse. The poignancy of the situations which can arise in cases like these is illustrated by the fact that, devoted as she was to him, and willing as she was to provide him with all the love and compassion and comfort as he ended his life, she herself was not prepared to assist him to die. When the High Court refused Mr Nicklinson the relief he was seeking, he died six days later from pneumonia, after he had refused to take food. His widow was added as a party to the case, and another man, Paul Lamb, also suffering from locked-in syndrome, was added to the proceedings as a claimant.

Again, without going through the decisions of the courts on the way up to the Supreme Court, perhaps I am allowed to refer to my own judgment in the Court of Appeal:

> The repeated mantra that, if the law is to be changed, it must be changed by parliament, does not demonstrate judicial abnegation of our responsi-bilities, but rather highlights fundamental constitutional principles.

In December 2013 nine Justices of the Supreme Court considered the decision. All nine Justices gave their own judgments. The fact

---

[14] *R (Nicklinson and Another) v Ministry of Justice* [2014] UKSC 38.

that it took over six months for them to be promulgated is an indication of how carefully they addressed the profound issues to which these cases give rise. Let me try to summarise the conclusions. The Justices divided five to four on whether or not the Supreme Court was constitutionally vested with power to make a declaration that the law relating to assisted suicide was incompatible with Article 8 of the Convention. Three held that it did have the constitutional authority to make such a declaration, but that it was, to use Lord Neuberger's phrase, 'institutionally inappropriate at this juncture'. Two Justices asserted that the court not only enjoyed the necessary authority, but that it should make the declaration now. The law, in Lady Hale's judgment, was 'not compatible with Convention rights'. Four Justices held that the issue should be resolved by Parliament and that it would be inappropriate to consider granting a declaration of incompatibility. In Lord Sumption's words,

> The issue is an inherently legislative issue for parliament, as the representative body in our constitution, to decide.

The court as a whole distinguished between its authority to require the DPP to publish offence-specific policy guidance (as required in *Purdy*) and the content of any such policy, once published (which fell within the ambit of the authority and responsibility of the DPP).

A number of thoughts.

The Supreme Court has reminded us that before any hearing at Strasbourg it may conclude that legislation creating a criminal offence may be incompatible with the Convention. It is not necessary for this purpose that the European Court itself should have given any judgment to this effect. In itself that is an interesting development. However, the present claimants, or later claimants, may yet go to Strasbourg for a declaration that the legislation is— not may be—incompatible with the Convention—that is, in agreement with the two Justices who have concluded that it is. Is that what we want? Whatever may happen, Parliament has now been invited to address the issue of the circumstances in which assisting suicide should continue to be criminalised. I repeat, Parliament may, of course, address the problem and decide that the present law reflects the public interest; equally it may conclude that amendment is needed. What I venture to suggest is that, now that the issue of incompatibility has been raised, our sovereign Parliament really cannot, and should not, ignore the pleas by the courts for the issue to be addressed.

It is the very essence of our constitution that it is for Parliament to act, as I have said before, as the conscience of the nation, as it did in the 60s and 70s of the last century. If nothing is done by Parliament, the Supreme Court and/or European court at Strasbourg may decide that the present legislation is incompatible with the Convention rights, not only of those who are seeking to reform the law, but of each and every citizen in this country, including those who are supportive of the present law. There is a serious danger that we are now very close to a limbo arrangement, with the Supreme Court declaring that a criminal statute is incompatible with the right to private life. What then would be the position of the DPP if and when a case arises which, according to present guidelines, would merit a prosecution in the public interest? Should she, when deciding whether to consent or not, take account of judicial declarations of incompatibility? Should prosecutorial decisions of this kind be influenced by judicial observations which cannot themselves amend or repeal primary legislation? None of this is fanciful. You can be sure that if a declaration of incompatibility were made then, an 'abuse of process' argument would be mounted against any such prosecution.

Where would all this controversy leave the delicate relationship between the legislature and the judiciary? In a constitution in which the sovereignty of Parliament remains fundamental, the Supreme Court would develop characteristics of a constitutional court, yet without the authority of a constitutional court—like that of say Canada—to nullify a statutory provision, or to in effect require that Parliament should do so. In Canada, however, the constitutional arrangement is very different. In a very recent judgment, *Carter*,[15] the Supreme Court of Canada held that the absolute prohibition on assisted suicide was inconsistent with Canada's own Charter of Rights and Freedoms. To the extent that these provisions prohibited physician-assisted death in the particular circumstances of the case, they were void, but the declaration of invalidity was suspended for 12 months. By the constitution of Canada this judicial decision obliges the legislative arm of the constitution to address the problem.

In the meantime, our own constitutional arrangements, which limit the authority of the judiciary to persuasion, cajoling, encouraging, imploring Parliament to address its constitutional responsibilities to decide the principles that should govern the society in which

---

[15] *Carter and Others v Canada (Attorney-General)* 2015 SCC 5.

we live, now extends to jurisdiction to make a declaration that a criminal statute, currently in force in this jurisdiction, is incompatible with Convention rights, but, nevertheless, not unenforceable. Where legal certainty is required, uncertainty will prevail.

Finally, perhaps, coming back to the moral questions, we should think of those for whom the misfortunes of life have created these appalling dilemmas. Are they and their families, and potentially each and every one of us and our families, not entitled to require statutory clarification of the precise nature of the involvement of the criminal law in this most sensitive of areas of human life? It is difficult to imagine that proposals like the recent Assisted Dying Bill in the House of Lords, limiting the changes to the criminal law, with various safeguards, to those who are within six months of death, can possibly represent the limit of how far the amendment of legislation will go if it were to prevail at all. If we were, subject to all the safeguards, to permit someone acting entirely altruistically, and out of a sense of compassion or devotion, or both, to help someone within six months of death to hasten that death, would we really refuse that relief for help given to an individual suffering from an appalling condition which, because life expectancy is not greatly reduced, may have to be endured for years, if not decades? Are compassion and love to be treated as entries in an accountant's ledger?

These moral and constitutional issues will be with us for many years yet.

Liberties and Rights

Equality before the Law

This lecture was given as the final keynote address at the Commonwealth Law Conference held in Cape Town, 2013.

T HIS MEETING HAS taken place in South Africa. That is about the most obvious, and to the extent that anything obvious is daft, the daftest observation in this conference. But I want to emphasise the point from the outset. First, however, hasn't it been a triumphant conference? The triumph has had many different facets. We can pause to admire the hard work and wise decision-making of the organisers, the high quality of the speakers, the immense kindness of those who looked after us, the pleasantness of the facilities. The programme has been wonderful and we have been spoilt for choice about which of the different sessions to attend. All this should be acknowledged.

But at this stage of the conference I do not think there is any point in trying to point to individual items and highlight them. Well, perhaps there is one. And it has a resonance for each and every one of us, from whichever country we come. Never take the rule of law for granted. Never, ever. The best of constitutions can be subverted. The democratic process itself can, as it did with Hitler in Nazi Germany, bring an evil dictator to power. As a result unnumbered millions died—millions in concentration camps, millions fighting to rid the world of the wickedness he had spawned. It all stemmed from the subversion of the democratic process. Yesterday those brave lawyers from Zimbabwe and Sri Lanka reminded us of the need for eternal vigilance. We, as lawyers, have the trained eyes to see, and the trained lips to voice, the alarm signals. We have a particular responsibility to be vigilant.

I have however tried to discern in my own mind what has made this conference so particularly special to me. What is it about this particular conference that has been so successful? I offer you very personal thoughts, and I offer them with respect. I do not intend to be controversial, and I certainly do not intend to cause any offence. But surely the starting point is that this conference has taken place here, in Cape Town, in South Africa.

It is easy to overlook its most obvious feature. This vast group of common lawyers, judges, advocates, academics, researchers, men and women of unimpeachable intellectual quality and professional integrity, has gathered together without reference to the colour of their skins, and we have shared our views and experiences. Perhaps most significantly of all, we have shared exactly the same spaces, sitting side by side in conference meetings, and enjoying our food at the same tables, men and women of all races, men and women of every skin colour.

This has happened here in South Africa where, not so very long ago, the colour of your skin, not your qualities as a human being, decided everything about the life you would lead, and the human company that you could keep, in a country where the law itself negated the principle of equality before the law.

One of my hobbies is cricket, which, like the common law, is another manifestation of events which started off in a tiny off-shore island on the edge of Europe, which has crossed the oceans, although not perhaps with quite the same success as the common law. There are many more important things than cricket. It is in the end only a game. But because cricket is one of my hobbies, one of my heroes is a South African. In those days the colour of his skin defined him as a Cape Coloured. With the support of the people who lived near and around him, he had the courage to go to England where, because of his own skill, and solely on his own merits, he was eventually selected to play cricket for England. In 1968 he played a magnificent innings against Australia, in the summer before a winter tour of South Africa was due to take place. In the entire history of the game, seen in purely batsmanship terms, there undoubtedly have been greater feats of batsmanship, but there has never been a more important innings in terms of its impact on history. His innings was a triumph on a personal level. He would now be selected to return to play in his own country as a man whose skin was not white against an all-white South African team, before segregated spectators—the achievement of his ultimate ambition. For the authorities who ruled this country in those days he could not and must not be allowed to do so. The story of pressures and corruption is told in a number of different accounts, but none better than Peter Oborne's carefully researched study.[1] From it I derived the words of the Prime Minister of South Africa at that time, translated into English:

> Over my dead body will we allow a black man, a coloured man, an Indian man to become a Springbok, whether it be in rugby, cricket, football, you name it.

[1] Peter Oborne, *Basil D'Oliveira: Cricket and Controversy* (London, 2005).

And so the tour was called off. Skill and ability had nothing to do with it: a black man could not play rugby, nor cricket, nor football for his own country. Nor could a Coloured man. Nor could an Indian man.

English is a language of extreme delicacy and great subtlety.

Let me give you an example. If I say, 'I am a white man', let us be clear that 'white' is an adjective. It simply describes the colour of my skin. But, on the level of apartheid, it meant that the colour of my skin defined me. It became the most important thing about me. In apartheid times, that absurd fact defined your very humanity. Yet if I say, 'my skin is white', that is a true fact, but it tells you absolutely nothing about the human being I am: all my qualities, all my deficiencies. In fact, described in this way, the colour of my skin is of total irrelevance. It doesn't tell you anything at all. It is an incidental fact of less than trivial importance. It would be of no importance if the colour of my skin was white, black, green, red or blue—you might look at me, but you would not judge my humanity. And if we are to be judged equally before the law, that is how skin colour must be seen. Not as a matter of convention or convenience, nor even, valuable as it is, as a right provided by a written constitution, but as a matter of principle so fundamental that it cannot be changed, so that if it is changed, no matter what the pretensions of that state to embrace the rule of law, the rule of law is shattered.

As I emphasise, cricket is only a game, and Basil D'Oliveira was free to walk about the country in England, into and out of the same public places as his white-skinned fellow cricketers, many of whom became his closest friends. He died recently in England, garlanded with well-earned admiration, respect and affection.

At the time these events opened the eyes of well-meaning people all over the world about something—not very much—of the realities of apartheid South Africa. Even a number of well-meaning people never really understood it. But they baulked at the astonishing proposition that a man could not play cricket—after all, just a game—in South Africa, against white South Africans, just because of the colour of his skin. He could not even walk onto the pitch with them. But this was only cricket, it was not life. And, of course, what happened to D'Oliveira was trivial compared to the fate of those who were executed and incarcerated, and those who lived under a law which, in the spurious interests of protecting the public from acts of terrorism, meant that you could be locked up for 90 days in solitary confinement without being charged, and on your release after the 90th day, be rearrested, and again locked up in solitary confinement for a further 90 days, and so on. As Judge Pillai asked us to note, it was of course legal, lawful, in the sense that it was the law enacted by the body in the constitution vested with responsibility for creating the law. The law countenanced what Justice Albie Sachs, himself a victim of it, described as 'state terrorism'.

The law, as enacted, perverted the very simple principle that we are all equal before the law. I hope that I may be forgiven for appearing to be making a discordant note, but I have detected a tendency in the public mind—perhaps outside South Africa rather than in it, but many of us here today do not come from South Africa, and perhaps because of the overwhelming impact of Robben Island and all it stood for—to overlook that women, too, were victims of this state terrorism, not simply because their men suffered directly, but because they too endured direct hardship.

Let me briefly underline that women as well as men were subjected to torture. The horror of isolation for long periods is described by Emma Mashinini, detained in 1981 in Pretoria. Can you imagine the self-torture and sense of guilt as she recalled the face of her youngest daughter, struggling and struggling ('struggle' is her word) because she could not remember the name of her little girl? This agony went on for days. If you read her description, it was an emotional crucifixion.[2] I could not read her own words out to you without tears coming to my eyes, and to yours too. My single point is that women as well as men tasted the ashes of anguish and desolation.

Eventually, this horror came to an end. Nevertheless, can we please remember that it is still less than 20 years since free elections were first held in South Africa. I can remember my own sense of awe, watching as vast lines of people who had never been able to vote before queued patiently, enfranchised at last. Those television pictures are engraved on my memory. And within a year legislation was drafted to create a Truth and Reconciliation Commission. The purpose was to establish the gross violations of human rights, which is too broad a phrase to describe the whole story, because it fails to capture the daily, repeated instances of man's inhumanity to man—that is, let us be clear, individual man's inhumanity to an individual man or woman—all committed between 1960 and 1993.

I can only speak as an observer, and I hope I have not got this wrong, I understand that this Commission was the product of the new constitutional arrangement. The purpose was to ensure that just because the full facts would be made public, the overwhelming

---

[2] David Schalkwyk, *Hamlet's Dreams: The Robben Island Shakespeare* (London, 2013).

public response thereafter would be to reject any system which would allow events like these to reoccur. The story is told in many different places, but for myself, *Country of My Skull*[3] by Antjie Krog will remain one of the most disturbing books I have ever read.

The judgment of Ismail Mahomed, then Deputy President of the Constitutional Court, who became the first Chief Justice of South Africa whose skin colour was black, described the conflicting principles that were involved in the creation of the amnesty allowed to the perpetrators of state brutality. If I may quote from his judgment about this Act:

> Secrecy and authoritarianism have concealed the truth in little crevices of obscurity in our history. Records are not easily accessible, witnesses are often unknown, dead, unavailable or unwilling. All that often effectively remains is the truth of wounded memories of loved ones sharing instinctive suspicions, deep and traumatising to the survivors but otherwise incapable of translating themselves into objective and corroborative evidence which could survive the rigors of law.

The search for the truth, which was what

> the victims of repression seek so desperately to know, is in the circumstances, much more likely to be forthcoming if those responsible for such monstrous misdeeds are encouraged to disclose the whole truth with the incentive that they will not receive the punishment which they undoubtedly deserve ... With that incentive, what might unfold are objectives fundamental to the ethos of a new constitutional order.[4]

I am speaking here with due humility. This is not my country. Self-evidently I was never a victim of state terrorism. Quite what those who were such victims, and their families, think is, I suspect, buried in the innermost recesses of the mind, to which we consign our most dreadful moments. Whether every victim agreed with the process, it is clear that the main objective was to secure the peaceful future of the country, and this outweighed any other considerations. It was a high-risk strategy and it was not inevitable that it would have the desired result. This conference proves that it did.

I mean not the slightest disrespect to Nelson Mandela, a man who I believe to have been one of the greatest human beings of this, or the last, or indeed any previous century, but, as with my reference to women, I pause to reflect that he was not alone. But this objective was identified by Nelson Mandela himself, quoting on his release

---

[3] Antjie Krog, *Country of My Skull: Guilt, Sorrow, and the Limits of Forgiveness in the New South Africa* (London, 1998).
[4] Quoted in Albie Sachs, *The Strange Alchemy of Life and Law* (Oxford, 2009).

in Cape Town in 1990 from his own speech made in court in Johannesburg in 1964, as he was about to start his quarter of a century and more in custody, cherishing

> an ideal of a democratic and free society in which all persons live together in harmony with equal opportunities. It is an ideal which I hope to live for, and to see realised. But *[addressing the judge]* my Lord, if needs be, it is an ideal for which I am prepared to die.

Notice, as long ago as 1964, facing a possible death sentence, the emphasis on living in harmony and equality. Isn't it a blessing that he lived to see the realisation of his ideal?

One of the books—and for a time just about the only book—available to those imprisoned on Robben Island was the *Robben Island Shakespeare*, also known as the *Robben Island Bible*,[5] because the political prisoner to whom it belonged was able to keep it, and then let his co-prisoners see it from time to time, when he persuaded his warders that the book he was reading was a religious Hindu bible. On the text, 34 of those prisoners marked particular passages which appealed to them. In that book, signed NR Mandela, we find this passage:

> Cowards die many times before their deaths:
> The valiant never taste of death but once.
> Of all the wonders that I yet have heard,
> It seems to me most strange that men should fear,
> Seeing that death, a necessary end,
> Will come when it will come.[6]

He dated this entry 16 December 1977. For those of you who do not know your history of South Africa, the very date itself is significant: it was the holy day for Afrikaaners, the date of the Battle of Blood River, the day when the Trekkers, many of whose descendants supported apartheid, prayed to God, promising that if they were given victory against huge odds, the day of the battle would be kept forever as a holy day.

Mr Mandela fully appreciated the significance of the date. 16 December was the date deliberately chosen for the start of explosions 15 or so years earlier. In the book, to write 16 December was a gesture of defiance.

During World War II Winston Churchill gave this advice to the world. In war, 'resolution'; in defeat, 'defiance'; in victory,

---

[5] See n 2 above.
[6] William Shakespeare, *Julius Caesar*, II.ii.32–37.

'magnanimity'; in peace, 'goodwill'. In the life of Nelson Mandela and those who underwent similar experiences, and in the work of the Truth and Reconciliation Commission, that thunderous advice was fully implemented. Indeed I cannot think of a better example.

These were not abstract ideas occurring in an academic discussion. This was the harsh reality. I have not been trying to encapsulate the ghastliness of conditions on Robben Island or indeed of events 20 years ago for their own sakes. Nor could I if I tried. Nevertheless, I believe that there is even more to all this, although there need not be any more to it because it is quite enough in itself, than the successful struggle against oppression. The success of that struggle, and the way in which the immediate aftermath was approached in South Africa, achieved something of far wider importance than was ever realised at the time. Quite apart from the achievement of a peaceful change in government and the establishment of a new constitution—both remarkable achievements for South Africa itself, achievements of the nation of South Africa alone—here an example was provided to the world of the peaceful restoration of equality before the law and the unacceptability of discrimination, not merely on the grounds of skin colour, but also race and creed and gender and sexual orientation and family background: indeed of discrimination in all the many forms in which it may manifest itself.

We all learned from it. The entire world learned from it. It was a lesson in humanity, for humanity, enriching us all. The removal of discrimination which underpins the principle of equality before the law, or the impartiality of the law, or the even-handedness required of the law, which is my basic theme today.

The rule of law is a phrase which has spawned many children. We can all make it say many things, and even the greatest jurists among us struggle from time to time to define precisely what we do mean. But as lawyers we rather understand when the rule of law is applied, and recognise it, and understand and recognise when it is not. But if we are looking for one crucial ingredient in the rule of law it is that we must live in a society in which every citizen is treated equally by the law. It is not a complete answer, because, as we have noted, in a dictatorship every citizen, or virtually every citizen except for the dictator's friends and family, is treated equally, but equally disgracefully. On proper examination therefore, their equality rests in the dismal fact that although there may be law, the rule of law is an outcast. In any society, some are richer, whether from birth or by acquisition, wiser, or indeed physically stronger, and others are impoverished, or stupid, or weak, so that in all these sorts of respects, it is absurd to consider that they are all the same. They are not. But neither money nor wisdom nor strength nor social position nor political or financial power should ever attract special privileges or special treatment from the law. The poor man at his gate is entitled to treatment equal to that of a president or prime minister.

We must be treated equally. That does not mean we must be treated identically, but, as I emphasise, equally. The difference is subtle, but important. You may say that a young man born into privilege who commits a crime deserves heavier punishment than a young man of similar age with all the disadvantages of a dreadful start in life, who has had no opportunity to learn any better. Whatever you may say, this is a simple example of the individualism which is also a necessary ingredient of the rule of law. We are dealing with individuals, not some group or groups, and if we start approaching cases on the basis of a group or groups, then some in the groups will be treated unjustly. Pause for a moment to reflect that, if we are not very careful indeed, if the law starts to treat one group rather than each individual comprised in it differently from another group—we are starting a very dangerous journey of which the very evil of apartheid was the ultimate culmination. Perhaps therefore we should identify the principle more clearly: perhaps it is better expressed by asserting that none of the considerations which can lead to prejudice against an individual citizen has the remotest relevance to the way in which the courts should deal with him or her or his or her case. So skin colour, race, gender, religious creed, sexual orientation and family background must be totally excluded from consideration in the judicial process.

We aim to do justice, according to the oath I took, 'without fear or favour, affection or ill-will'. A similar oath is taken by every judge in the common law world. It means, but it does not simply mean, that the judge must be courageous in facing possible personal threats whether from individuals or officers of the state; it goes much further. What the oath means is that, whether all those untoward threats are absent or present, the judge must be blind to prejudice: impartial, fair, balanced, with a true appreciation of the common humanity which binds us all and which we have all—every one of us—inherited. In that way we ensure equality before the law.

Ultimately that is the basis for the achievement of every human right, an issue which has been a major topic of discussion throughout this conference. Let us just examine it. Do we ignore the poisoned river because it is the poor, rather than the middle classes, who live and suffer in proximity to it? Of course not. Do we ignore the unlawful arrest of an individual who has been charged with a dreadful offence, or indeed who has been demonised by society? Of course not. Do we allow freedom of speech only to those who agree with and express views which we share? Of course not. A human right that is not universally available to every citizen in the country is a contradiction in terms. It is equality before the law that underpins the concept and ultimate achievement of the rights bestowed upon us by our common humanity.

Perhaps then, above all, above all else, this conference in Cape Town has underlined for me that of all the many facets of the rule of law, we must remain resolved that whatever the colour of our skin, race, creed, gender, or whatever it might be, the starting principle for the rule of law is that, in law, we are equal, and that it is the fundamental obligation of the law to treat us so. Here in Cape Town we have been vividly reminded by the living recent history of South Africa that this indeed must be and must remain our common purpose, and that we must be vigilant to maintain it.

Human Rights: Today and Tomorrow

This was the Mabel Strickland Memorial Lecture given in Malta in March 2014.

I WAS BORN on 19 May 1941 in what was then KG V hospital, a few hundred yards down the road from here, and on the edge of the Grand Harbour. It was a date of no importance to anyone except my mother, a young Maltese woman married to an Englishman, and of course to him. Luckily we all survived yet one more bombing raid where, on this occasion, the bombs landed and exploded in the hospital grounds and struck parts of the hospital itself. A few yards either way, and I should not be here giving this lecture. It was a very early lesson, although I did not know it, that life is full of chances, and that when today we contemplate tomorrow, probably the most important line ever written by William Shakespeare was 'What's to come is still unsure'.

Well, here I am, and unlike so many, we survived the siege. I am immensely proud of my Maltese origins. I am truly half Maltese. When I became Lord Judge I insisted that the basic colours of my coat of arms should be the red and white of Malta, of course without the George Cross awarded to the Island peoples. Whenever I have the chance, I proclaim my Maltese origins. And I have done so all over the world.

Maybe this was drummed into me by my mother, who used to tell my sister and me to remember that we were half Maltese—'and the best half too'. But it was my father too. Perhaps his shared wartime experience was what filled him with admiration, affection and indeed love for Malta.

Tonight, in this audience, apart from my mother herself, there are a number of Maltese people to whom I am especially indebted. Of course, they include my mother's brothers with whom we lived for some years after the war when my father was ill, and their families. If I may I would like to mention Mother Calleja Gera, who taught me my first elementary maths; and my first teacher at St Edward's College, Miss Elizabeth Parnis, who unfortunately cannot be here tonight, from whom I learned the value of concentration; and Mr Cachia Caruana, who later became Headmaster at St Edward's, but in my day tried to teach me maths, without any great success, and the importance of contributing to any organisation or team of which you were a part as best you could.

There is however one rather more important reason for remembering 19 May 1941. The *Times of Malta* was printed on that day. The *Times of Malta* was printed every single day of the war. And we must remember that it was not a modern communications system, it was the old-fashioned piece-by-piece creation of the blocks, and the application of ink to them, and paper over the blocks, all skilled hand work, that produced the newspaper. Even when the premises of the *Times of Malta* were bombed, the paper was published. Unfailingly. Without the break of a single day. In what was then the most bombed place on earth Mabel Strickland and, let us not forget them, the men who worked for her in those cramped, dusty and dangerous premises flew the flag of indomitability and defiance which symbolised the character of those who lived in and defended our island fortress.

In a foreword written by His Royal Highness the Duke of Edinburgh to a recent biography about Mabel Strickland,[1] he observed that she was 'One of Malta's great personalities of the 20th century'. The fact that not everyone agreed with her, and that she certainly did not agree with everyone else, does not diminish her standing or reputation. It is strange how after they have died, we come increasingly to admire men and women who spoke up for their principles even when others, sometimes vehemently, disagreed with them. It is indeed an honour for me to be giving this lecture in memory of a remarkable woman. And, perhaps we should notice, a remarkable *woman*, who became editor of the *Times of Malta* as long ago as 1935.

Human Rights. That's the title of this lecture. We all get used to new names, but perhaps because we now have a Convention on Human Rights, and indeed a European Court of Human Rights, whose role and function in a democratic country are themselves a matter for a lengthy lecture, and almost certainly a controversial one, we nowadays speak of human rights as if it is a sudden modern invention. It is not. Human rights encapsulate what our forefathers, our fathers and grandfathers before us described when they

---

[1] Joan Alexander, *The Life of Mabel Strickland, the Uncrowned Queen of Malta* (Malta, 1996).

were talking about freedom and liberty, and much blood was shed to preserve them. Human rights were not newly minted at the end of the last war. The Convention on Human Rights was largely written by British lawyers for a war-torn, concentration camp filled Europe. Nothing brought this reality more closely home to me than a meeting with a judge from Belgium at an international seminar. She told me that she remembered the British coming to liberate Brussels. She had been 5 years old. For the whole of her life she had wished they had come six weeks earlier. She explained that six weeks before the British arrived, without so much as the mythical knock on the door, her father was taken from them in the middle of the night, and they never saw him again. 'You see, we're Jewish.' If you examine the terms of the Convention, it reflected principles of the common law which were already well established. Freedom of speech, freedom from arrest without reasonable cause shown, the value of family life, the prohibition on torture, open trial and open justice, your right to enjoy your property—these are all nowadays human rights which were once described as our liberties. Whatever words you choose to use to describe them, the application of these principles today demonstrates that we are living in a civilised community; their disapplication means that we are not.

The story of Mabel Strickland enables me to highlight two distinctive features of human rights today. In Western Europe, but not throughout the entire world, we have surely noticed at last that half the human race is female. Well, that fact is pretty obvious to anyone, even in the most savage and primitive community, but it has consequences for us which, dealing with it very shortly, means that we have to recognise that although he may not have known it, when Rousseau was speaking about the 'Rights of Man', he was equally speaking of the rights of women, and that when we speak of Human Rights we are including, not excluding, the female half of the population of the world. It would be manifestly unjust to do so, but equally a folly, because it fails to recognise the talent, energy, capacity and leadership qualities with which women are no less blessed than men. You may not read it in many of the texts which set out, or purport to set out, the various human rights to which we are entitled, but in my view, equality of opportunity, like equality before the law, is fundamental to any society which espouses the concept of human rights. Indeed I would go further: without equality in both of these respects, any reference to human rights is so much hot air.

The point about a right is that it is an entitlement. It is not a matter of grace, by which someone in authority picks and chooses who will be the beneficiary of his, or the government's, patronising kindness. If that is all it is, then on the whole the patronising kindness is bestowed on those who support the government of the day, or fall within the favoured groups, and those who do not are excluded. Those who are gifted by favour can, however, see it stripped away in a moment on a whim. So for them, too, it is not a right. Any society which embraces the concept of human rights must therefore espouse equality before the law. And that in its turn requires an independent judiciary to enforce our rights and an independent press to observe that our rights are indeed being observed.

What I am driving at is that human rights do not exist in a vacuum. They are not mere words on a piece of paper, sounding attractive but ultimately bereft of meaning. What is the value of a right written on a piece of paper if it cannot, when push comes to shove, be protected and, if necessary, enforced. As one of our great political thinkers, John Locke, wrote in his *Treatise on Government* in the late seventeenth century, 'Where law ends, tyranny begins'. Tyranny is not confined to the obvious dictators, like Hitler or Mussolini or Stalin, or that extraordinary regime in North Korea. It extends to the danger of what Thomas Jefferson was later to describe as 'the tyranny of the majority'—the danger of crushing the rights that should be enjoyed by those who for the time being are unpopular or in public disfavour.

In 2015 we, in England, and I suspect throughout the world, will be celebrating the sealing of Magna Carta. It is sometimes forgotten that one of the most important clauses in the Great Charter was clause 61, which provided that if the king did not abide by the Charter, the obligations of obedience and fealty to him were for the time being discharged. Shortly afterwards, our great thirteenth-century judge, Henry Bracton, explained: '*Quod Rex non debet esse sub homine, sed sub Deo et lege*': the king was not under any man, but under—*sub*—God and the laws. In summary, there could therefore be no room for absolute power, and those charged with the responsibility of governing the country had to do so in accordance with its laws and the rights of the subject. The dispute went backwards and forwards for hundreds of years, and culminated in the execution of Charles I, who stood for the principle that '*Lex est Rex Loquens*': the king speaks the law. The privileges which we nowadays take for granted, like freedom of speech in Parliament, were not rights, but his to give, and therefore his to take away, at his own will; exactly as I explained a few minutes earlier, not rights of the subject, but acts of grace by the ruler. However, once you have established that the government of the day—whatever form that rule may take—is subject to the law, you are very close to establishing that everyone is answerable to the law, and ultimately equal before it.

That provides very fertile soil in which to plant the principle of human rights. Indeed the first modern right asserted in Magna Carta was the right not to be imprisoned or executed without a prior judgment in accordance with the law of the land, and the further right that justice would not be sold, or denied, or delayed. And indeed some of the remaining clauses emphasise the desperate cry for the speedy and efficient administration of justice. In *Hamlet* Shakespeare identifies the law's delays as one of the curses to which humanity can be subjected.

So, equality before the law, and a system by which you can obtain speedy redress against any infringement of your rights, or your freedoms, represent the foundation for any societal human rights. And this is true today, and will continue to be true tomorrow. These principles are fundamental. We sometimes say, perhaps a little loosely, that some rights are inalienable or absolute. I agree: some, like the right to justice, are indeed inalienable, but every inalienable right is itself an illustration of the equality before the law principle. They belong to us all, equally. One such principle is that no one, whoever he or she is, should be sentenced without trial—never, ever—and this process must be a public process so that whenever an individual is on trial, the system of justice is itself, equally, on trial. But we need to exercise a little caution with the idea of 'absolute' rights, because on occasions there is a danger of overlooking the impact of upholding a claimed absolute right on the rights of others. Even what is sometimes called the fundamental right is not absolute.

If a man came into this hall carrying a gun, and started firing it at someone here in the audience, then, in self-defence, or to protect the right of other people to life, his immediate killing may be justified. But if you think about it, that killing, the destruction of his right to life, is based on the protection of the right to life of others. So when we talk about rights we have to remember that every right that we assert for ourselves is equally shared by every other citizen, and that the implementation and enforcement of our own rights does not automatically follow if its implementation or enforcement destroys or infringes the rights of others. Take another example: we are entitled to a private life. The officials of the state cannot come trampling into our homes to see that we are living in accordance with some dictated rules. As one of my predecessors, Edward Coke, explained in the seventeenth century, an Englishman's home is his castle, his ultimate refuge. William Pitt the Elder gloried in the fact that even a hovel, into which the rain and the wind could enter, could not be entered by the King of England himself. But my right to privacy does not, I think, extend to viewing material showing children, or indeed any other human, male or female, being subjected to the most foul kinds of abuse. My right to look at whatever I like has to be tempered by recognising that my predilections will harm others. Just think about tonight. If the lights in this hall all suddenly failed, and then someone ran in to this crowded space shouting, 'Fire, fire', so that there was a rush for the doors and people were hurt and injured: would we think that his right to freedom of speech entitled him to say those words?

We sometimes contrast rights with responsibilities, and I accept the antithesis, but there is something even more profound. It is the principle of equality before the law. In short, each one of our rights has to be constrained or tempered by the equal entitlement of others to their own human rights, and our mutual obligations to recognise them. Those who rely on and extol human rights sometimes fail to understand that this is a necessary corollary of the principle.

Can I just go a little further? Our responsibilities as citizens are of course first and foremost to our families—to our children and our parents in particular; but nevertheless, and I regard it as an essential feature of the ethos of human rights, we must also be alert to circumstances or proposals which may undermine the principle of equality before the law. We must, of course, do what we can to prevent them happening today, but it is when I turn to tomorrow that we have to be most on our guard.

At the very outset of this lecture I said, in the context of the life of Mabel Strickland, that there were two particular aspects that I wished to highlight. I did not think it valuable to you to simply set out a list of all the very many declarations or conventions that set out lists in varying terms of what are described as rights. But there is a United Nations declaration, indeed there are many different declarations, and there is a European Convention on Human Rights, and many others. Effectively they say much the same thing. As I said, they are declarations of our liberties and our freedoms. By not referring to them in detail, I am not trivialising them. I am avoiding you listening to me for five and a half hours.

I began this lecture by first noticing how remarkable it was that she led the *Times of Malta* through the war—a woman at a time when women were rarely vested with public responsibility. Now I can come to the second, which is that her life exemplified the importance of an independent press. Perhaps I may be allowed a personal thought, as I reminisce about my Maltese grandfather, Anthony Micallef. As I said at the beginning, I lived with my maternal grandparents for a long time when my father was ill. Children absorb so much more from the ordinary hurly burly of family life than we can possibly imagine. Even as a small boy I realised that my grandfather believed very passionately in the right of freedom of speech. His newspaper, the now sadly departed *Bulletin*, was determinedly not in thrall to any political party or group. My father, too, passionately believed in freedom of speech; he thought that our minds expanded through discussion of controversial issues. So perhaps built into my own genes both from my Maltese grandfather and my English father is a belief in 'the first freedom' identified by President Roosevelt towards the end of the war. Of course freedom of speech is the public manifestation of something that simply cannot be controlled by anyone, which is freedom of thought. But just as freedom of speech is the public manifestation of freedom of thought, so an independent press is the manifestation of communal freedom of speech.

We have our own obligations as citizens to recognise when the principle of equality before the law is at risk. The reality is that given our day-to-day responsibilities, it is difficult for us to spot these dangers. However, I believe this to be one of the most essential functions of an independent press: to spot and identify and publicise, and make us, as citizens, think, not so that we agree with a particular line taken by a particular newspaper or television programme, but think for ourselves whether we agree that there is a real threat, and if so what is to be done about it.

For my own part the changes in society that lie ahead—the manmade changes, not those forced upon us by famine or drought or natural disaster—will arise from the revolution in technology and communications. When Gutenberg invented the printing press in the mid-fifteenth century, that created a revolution. Nowadays we can all read, we can inform ourselves, we can form our opinions. Before the printing press the ability to read was the privilege of very few, and the rest of society had to rely on the words of those who could read—and they, of course, could read things as they wished. But the changes in information technology are already astonishing, and we have not yet come to terms with them. Largely I do not think that many of us understand them, and although there is much to be said in favour of this new world, it does undoubtedly give rise to dangers. Can you remember that Facebook, Twitter and Google are still not 10 years old, and indeed that they are already becoming out of date. Yet there are machines, or there is the technology available, to concentrate every single item of human knowledge into a small machine, no better, no bigger than this hand. This will be a remarkable change, and it will give governments and large organisations, and even individuals, the power to know more about us than it is healthy that they should know. I do not subscribe to the thinking that proceeds on the basis that if you have nothing to fear you have nothing to hide. For me, the officials of the state, including judges, are public servants. I should not have to answer to them unless I am suspected of breaking the law. We therefore need to have our eyes peeled to this manifestation of man's brilliance, of man's scientific inventiveness and where it will be taking us. We are all going to know very much more about each other than we do currently, and I do not mean harmless gossip. What is more, the officials of state are going to know so much more. Is this what we want? Remember that if we think that it is a good idea for the officials of state to know a lot about other people, then by the same token they will get to know a great deal about us. I am concerned about our private lives, and our family lives, and our working lives, if we do not think carefully about the power that modern technology is going to put into the hands of others. And there is a feature of our freedoms or rights which is sometimes overlooked, and that is that their preservation is indivisible. Once you allow our rights to be undermined in one aspect, the same pernicious influence comes to bear on the others. The principles can become distorted.

We are indeed all equal before the law. Whatever legislation is enacted in our different democracies, it will apply to everyone. The question which then arises is whether the fact that we are equal before the law is sufficient to ensure the security of our rights. I do not think that it is. What I have said is that without equality before the law the reference to human rights is so much hot air. I have not said that equality before the law is a sufficient guarantee or security for our rights. Of itself, it is not. It is the starting point, not the finishing point. And I suggest that we shall have to beware of the tendency in governments of all kinds, even those entirely based on a commitment to democratic principles and the rule of law, to suggest that increasing powers should be placed in the hands of authority. You will have to listen, as no doubt I shall, to arguments based on what those who propose legislation will say is 'necessity'. We must beware of such arguments. Occasionally, of course, some restrictions on our rights are indeed 'necessary'. In times of war, we must focus on victory, and against an implacable enemy, victory as soon as possible, even if some of what we would regard as absolute rights in peacetime may, for the time being, have to be sacrificed. The word 'necessary' in this context can be given too broad an ambit and I suggest that when we see any proposals which are said to be 'necessary', or when any similar word is used to describe them, we should remember William Pitt the Younger, Britain's youngest Prime Minister:

> Necessity is the justification for every infringement of human liberty. It is the argument of tyrants, and the creed of slaves.

So whatever tomorrow may bring, we shall continue to need an independent judiciary to enforce our human rights, or to adjudicate between competing human rights, and an independent press to identify possible abuses or dangers which do not find their way before the courts. We cannot leave it entirely to the judiciary and the media, and abdicate our own responsibilities. The greatest possible danger to the rights which are so precious to us is our own indifference, our assumption that it will all be all right. We think, this is England, this is Malta, and we forget that there were those in Germany in the 1930s who thought this is Germany, and Hitler came to power by subverting the democratic process. The great Irish advocate John Philpot Curran told us in 1790:

> The condition upon which God hath given liberty to man is eternal vigilance; which condition if he break, servitude is at once the consequence of his crime, and the punishment of his guilt.

Do not misunderstand me. I am not suggesting—whether here in Malta, or indeed in Britain—that there is any immediate threat to our liberties, or that there are political parties in either country today which will threaten them. But the future is long as well as short, and when Shakespeare said 'What's to come is still unsure', he was not meaning tomorrow, not literally tomorrow, but the future, and that is what I mean. We, not other people, are responsible for safeguarding our rights, and the rights of our children and grandchildren. In the end, we are not simply addressing high sounding constitutional arrangements or declarations. Every dictatorship has at least one of those. We are not addressing noble, lofty sentiments. 'Peace in our time' remain four of the saddest words ever spoken in the English language.

In the end, the preservation of our rights and liberties is about us, and how deeply we cherish the liberties and rights for which our parents and grandparents fought and starved and died.

It really is up to us.

The Judiciary and the Media

*This was the Lionel Cohen Lecture given at the Hebrew University of
Jerusalem in March 2011, first published in the Israel Law Review (2011).*

I AM AN English judge speaking in Jerusalem at a lecture to honour the memory of an Englishman who was the first member of
the English Jewish Community to be appointed to the House of
Lords, now the Supreme Court of the United Kingdom. That was
60 years ago, in 1951. So this is an important anniversary.

This evening, I am seeking to highlight some of the issues which
relate to the role of the media, and the role of the judiciary in
upholding the rule of law, and the interaction of their relationships
in a democratic society which respects the rule of law. My experience is British, but my intention is to address questions which arise
in any civilised democracy. The essential principles are unaffected
by geography.

My overwhelming belief is that the most emphatic feature of the
relationship between the judiciary and the media is that the independence of the judiciary and the independence of the media are
both fundamental to the continued exercise, and indeed the survival, of the liberties which we sometimes take for granted. I have
said before, and I do not apologise for saying it again, that these are
critical independences which are linked, but separate. As far as I can
discover, there never has been any community in the world in which
an independent press flourishes while the judiciary is subservient
to the executive or government, or where an independent judiciary
is allowed to perform its true constitutional function while, at the
same time, the press is fettered by the executive. Try as I can, I can
find no such community. And this serves to reinforce my essential
feeling, that in any community which is governed by the rule of law,
the independence of the media and the independence of the judiciary are both of crucial importance to the liberties of the community
at large. Both must be preserved. And when I speak of preservation
I do not mean preserved like a museum piece, mildly tolerated as
somewhat idiosyncratic vestiges of an interesting but ancient past;
rather I mean preserved in the sense that Archbishop Fénelon urged
the value of moderation, but moderation not as an insipid response
for beliefs not very strongly held, but rather moderation at white

heat. The preservation of both independences involves white heat commitment.

But, and it is a very important but, what I am not saying is that the independence of the judiciary should somehow reduce the responsibility of the press to offer reasoned criticism of judges and their decisions, or that judges should be inhibited when applying the law as they find it to be, and even when the media does not like it. That is because the law in a democratic country binds the judges just as much as it binds the media.

There is this important further emphasis. Our independences mean that we are independent of each other as well as the executive or other authority of the state. Sometimes tensions are inevitable. Sometimes criticisms by one side or the other are unfair, or are thought by the recipient of the criticism to be unfair. Sometimes, perhaps, we are not as alert as we should be to the realities of the way in which each of us must perform our functions within constitutional arrangements based on the rule of law. So these twin independences—independent, of course, of each other—are fundamental to communities where there is a proper respect for the rule of law. I am not today seeking to address the quite different considerations which can arise in countries which are not blessed with this respect. These independences provide the context in which questions like defamation, reporting restrictions, websites, tweeting, confidentiality and privacy claims, undercover reporting, investigative reporting and freedom of information and the modern buzzword in England, superinjunctions, are all engaged. Each of these is perhaps worth a lecture on its own, and I do not propose to give you one on each of them. But they do indicate how wide and how important to society as a whole the engagement between the judiciary and the media must be, and how greatly it impacts on the day-to-day lives of our communities.

There are two further overarching themes. For us to be blessed with an independent media, the independent media has to survive. This is not a charity. We are dealing with businesses. If they are insolvent, the printing presses (or the modern equivalent) cannot roll. The same applies to television, save where there is a form of public funding. Public funding itself is a great problem. What would be devastating, in my mind, is a not unimaginable situation by which the local newspaper may die, to be replaced by some sort of handout from the local authority, no doubt extolling everything done by the authority, and silent about its errors. The public will not be properly informed by spin doctors employed on behalf of the government of the day, or local authorities. So, the survival of these businesses is crucial. It is no good considering the independence of the press, if there is no press to be independent.

My second theme is that some of these financial considerations have to be examined in the context of the way in which the modern world of communication is developing. We are living in the middle of a technological revolution. You will be interested to remember that in 1984 the Police and Criminal Evidence Act was enacted. This made very careful, structured provision for the retention of fingerprints, intimate samples and samples generally, and their destruction. The legislation did not include any reference to DNA profiles or biometric data. Suddenly DNA evidence arrived. It has become crucial. Its impact has been amazing. This new knowledge has enabled the guilty who would otherwise have escaped justice to be convicted, and the innocent who have been the victims of injustice to be acquitted. Similarly with the technology which applies to the world of communications. It is already astounding, and I suspect that the technology that lies ahead will have impacts on the way in which all our lives are lived, not least in the context of the development and survival of the media, which in truth are unimaginable. But whether we can imagine the future or not, and perhaps more so if we cannot, it has to be a future in which, whatever changes may occur, an independent media will survive.

So, as we face a new technological revolution, let us go back to the start of all this, with a few thoughts, to give a sense of historical perspective to our technological revolution.

Gutenberg has a lot to answer for. Yet he, and Caxton, and others, produced what we now take for granted, but at the time was an invention of cataclysmic consequences: the printing press. The invention of the printing press is one of the seminal moments in the history of the world which, because there have been others since, is nowadays in danger of being underestimated. Imagine a world in which every single copy of the Bible in existence had laboriously, painstakingly—and sometimes gloriously in its embellishments— been copied out word by word by hand. Imagine a world in which every idea had to be communicated orally. Imagine the change: the Bible in print, capable of being read by an increasingly literate population, increasingly literate because they did have the printed book. Imagine Copernicus in 1543, having printed *Revolutions of the Celestial Orbs*—instead of telling the world that the earth was not the centre of the universe—restricted to paternal chats around the table with his family in Poland.

As you allow your imaginations to wander, remember, and this is certainly not imagination, how the authorities sought very urgently to control the demon they believed that Gutenberg and others had released. The Tridentine Index was but one example. There was a new College of Propaganda. '*Libertas credendi perniciosa est: namnihil aliud est quam libertas errands.*' Freedom of belief is pernicious because it only allowed for the freedom to be wrong.

In England control of the press was established by a Star Chamber Order of 1586.[1] Strict limits were set on the number of printers who were allowed to practice, the number of presses they could own, and the numbers they could employ. Every book had to be licensed. And to make sure this worked, authority was granted to the Company of Stationers to damage and destroy any presses which were not conformable to the Star Chamber Order. Archbishop Laud, who was one of those most vehemently in support of the control of the printing press, bemoaned the old days, for now the members of the Stationers Company became interested only in gain, with the result that some of the workmanship was so slovenly that a 1631 edition of the Bible printed the seventh commandment so that it read:

Thou shalt commit adultery.

Late Elizabethan and early Stuart England was a ferment of ideas. Religion and politics, profound questions of constitutional importance, such as whether '*rex est lex*' or '*rex est lex loquens*' and whether the king was subject to the law. Tracts, papers and sermons, and, perhaps most symbolic of all, John Lilburne smuggling an account of his sufferings at the behest of the Star Chamber for the distribution of copies of an unlicensed pamphlet, known as *A Work of the Beast*, gave wings to the press. From this ferment the press—that is, the press as we now know it—not the machines which printed papers and tracks and sermons, gradually emerged. To begin with they were known as Corantos. I cannot resist the observation that it was soon being said that something was as true as a Coranto—meaning that it was all lies, or from some words written in the early seventeenth century about the Corantos:

Ordinarily they have as many lies as lines. They are new and old in five days ... they meddle with other men's affairs.... if they write good news of our side it is seldom true; but if it is bad it is almost too true. I wish them to write either not at all, or less, or more true: the best news is when we hear no news.

---

[1] See generally Robert Hargreaves, *The First Freedom: A History of Free Speech* (Stroud, 2002).

I do so because the issue of the irresponsible press, the press that should perhaps be curbed, the press that is not conformable, the press that is intrusive and unreliable, is not itself a new story. Tempting as it is, we must beware the demon trap. The price that must be paid for an independent press means that it will sometimes be irresponsible, and be inaccurate, and be not conformable. That is what independence means: but most important of all not conformable to the executive. My belief is that the freedom of the press is no less than an aspect of the first freedom—in President Roosevelt's memorable phrase—which every citizen enjoys: freedom of speech.

I love the story—true story—of the Bow Street magistrate in London who in the middle of the last world war had before him six Peace Pledge Union members who were charged under, I believe, the then Public Order Act with distributing pacifist literature at a time of national peril when conscientious objection to warfare was hardly a popular cause. The charges were dismissed. The magistrate observed:

> This is a free country. We are fighting to keep it a free country, as I understand it.

I do so hope that that judicial observation, made at such a time, continues to inform all those who would seek to legislate in ways which hinder or restrain our freedoms to speak as we believe, and to express unpopular opinions. Mind you, I do not go as far as Samuel Johnson, who summarised the problem in this way.

> Every man has a right to utter what he thinks truth, and every other man has a right to knock him down for it.

That, I would suggest, goes a little too far. And equally, of course, we have to be careful not to find ourselves, in Oliver Wendell Holmes' example, seeking to defend the freedom of an individual to yell out untruthfully, 'Fire, fire' in a crowded theatre so that in a panic to get out injury and death are occasioned. But to resume:

From these strange beginnings there gradually emerged our media, the role of the newspaper man, and many years later newspaper woman, and the press as we know it today, at any rate before the invention of the television. And at the same time, some elements of the constitutional arrangements relating to judges and the judiciary can begin to be discerned. The Civil War in England established that the king was not above the law, the law was not the king speaking, and after Charles I had been beheaded, and his son James II thrown out, the principle of security of judicial tenure was established in England. Judges could not be dismissed from office on the whim of the king, or hold office for only so long as he thought they were behaving properly. It was a far cry from the incarceration of Sir Edward Coke, Chief Justice, in the Tower of London and the deprivation of his office in 1616.

It would be comforting and pleasant to say that looking back over the history since those turbulent times, the relationship between the judiciary and the press—and from now on I shall include all elements of public communication, including the television as 'the media'—had always been relaxed and pleasant and without unfair criticism on either side, with words or judgments only ever offered in a spirit of constructive co-operation—but that would not be true. There was a very long way to go. In reality the main dispute was between the press and Parliament. The House of Commons in the eighteenth century continually asserted that any printed account of their discussions was an offence which merited severe punishment. This was the classic example of the assertion of a privilege embraced to meet one problem, that of an over-powerful monarch, being deployed long after the monarch had ceased to exercise any significant authority, with the privilege being defended in part just because it was a privilege. For example, in 1760 four newspapers reported that a vote of thanks had been given to Admiral Hawke following the naval victory of great significance at Quiberon Bay. Yet this was described by the House of Commons as a 'high indignity'.

Then along came John Wilkes. In 1762, in a newspaper called *The North Briton*, he wrote the great clarion call, the trumpet sound, the immortal words:

> The liberty of the press is the birthright of a Briton, and is justly esteemed the firmest bulwark of the liberties of this country.

Remove the word 'Briton' and it applies to every civilised country which embraces the rule of law.

The phrase was adapted by Lord Bingham of Cornhill, then Lord Chief Justice, when he spoke of 'that fair trial which is the birthright of every British citizen'.[2]

Remove the word 'British' and this too applies to any civilised country. If, as I believe, Lord Bingham was deliberately echoing the language used by John Wilkes 250 or so years earlier, it was a compliment, imitation being the sincerest from of flattery, that John Wilkes himself would have found astonishing. But, and it is a crucial but, it is to be observed that Wilkes was describing the liberty of

---

[2] *R v Bentley* [2001] 1 Cr App R 307.

the press as the birthright of each citizen, not, we must notice, the birthright of the owners of the newspaper in question, or the editors, or the journalists, or the publishers. This leads me to wonder how he would have addressed the stark question: whether the rights of the press as a whole should prevail over the right of the individual citizen to a fair trial. I suspect his answer might surprise those who, like me, regard him as a man like the rest of us, with many flaws, but of truly heroic qualities. This in truth is where the crunch comes; where the judicial system and the proper functioning of the media interact and on occasions conflict.

It is important to my thinking to emphasise that the role of the judiciary is to ensure that justice is done according to law within whichever system, in whichever field, one citizen is seeking redress or justice, or is subject to criticism or prosecution. Judges are servants of the community. They are vested with responsibilities, and very wide powers, as servants of the community. They are not human beings vested with innate authority or deprived of the universal human characteristic, of fallibility. When they exercise their office, they are exercising it as officers of justice. The wisdom of Montaigne, at the end of his great three volumes of *Essays*, applies to judges and all those in authority of any kind. They should have in mind at all times,

> No matter how high the throne upon which we are sitting, we are always sitting on our own backside.[3]

In the exercise of these functions, as you all appreciate, the judge cannot allow his or her own individual preferences or prejudices to prevail. He cannot, because he has been the subject of a scurrilous article in a newspaper, resolve litigation against the press if that is not what the law requires, and he cannot find for the press just because he has received a commendation from it. If we all gave judgment in accordance with our personal preferences, just think of the chaos and uncertainty that would follow. Indeed we would, if we did that, be in breach of our judicial oath 'to do right … in accordance with the law'.

So when the clashes come between the media and the judiciary, the issue is not personal. The judgment does not represent a judicial whim. When a judge finds for one side or the other, he is not reflecting a personal predilection. When he imposes a sentence, he does so

---

[3] Michel de Montaigne, *The Complete Essays*, translated by MA Screech (Harmondsworth, 1991).

in accordance with sentencing principle, or guidance, or statute. He may, of course, be wrong, but that is not because he is exercising a personal preference in a way which is open to criticism, but because he has mistakenly applied the law as he believes it to be, or, no less likely, he may be right because he has applied the law as it is, when it appears to the media that the consequences of the law correctly applied are inappropriate or wrong.

There are occasions when criticism is made by the media of the judiciary—sometimes vituperative personal criticism, sometimes unjust personal criticism—when the criticism should be directed at the legal principles which bind the judge. With the advantage of some clear thinking legal journalists, as well as a greater effort by or on behalf of the judiciary to engage with these issues, I believe that there is a greater understanding of these matters among the media in England than there used to be, although the understanding is not yet as universal as I should like it to be. The problem with direct personal criticism which is unfair is first, of course, that it is unfair; second, that it is difficult if not impossible for the judge to answer, because inevitably it would mean commenting on a case which he had tried or decided, when everything that needs to be said about the decision should have been dealt with in the judgment, so that for the judge that must be the end of it; and finally, and perhaps in the end most importantly, if we are discussing the independence of the media and the judiciary, because of its corrosive long-term effect on the public's view of the judiciary and the exercise of its functions.

This is not a deferential age, and I do not want it ever to revert to deference. But it does matter to the welfare of the community, and the preservation of the independence of the judiciary, that the confidence of the community in its judiciary should not be undermined. If it is undermined, then it becomes that much less difficult for the government of the day, or the legislature (and in a democratic society, who knows what the will of the electorate may produce at any election?), to introduce legislation which gradually restricts the discretion available to be exercised by a judge and eventually, in effect, instructs him on how his responsibilities should be exercised. What price then the independence of the judiciary? How then will the citizen be sure that when he takes on the government of the day, or the large institutions of the state, the judge before whom the litigation is being conducted is truly independent of the government or the large institution?

Perhaps in England one of the most powerful examples of the potential difficulty arises in the context of the Human Rights Act of 1998 and the incorporation of the European Convention on Human Rights into domestic law. The Convention, when originally written, was produced for a war-torn Europe in which a man or woman could be removed from home without warning and, for no reason except the wish or whim of someone exercising authority, taken to a concentration camp. This audience needs no memory jolting on this subject from me. The Convention was designed for the basic protections which were provided, and had for some years been provided, at common law. No arrest without reasonable grounds. No incarceration without due judicial process. And so on. Largely British lawyers wrote it, and if you read the Convention carefully you will see the ancient strands of common law in it. And then in the 1998 Act it was incorporated into our law. And it has resulted in a number of judgments which have excited huge criticism. Indeed the words 'Human Rights' are sometimes described in language which might suggest that they stand not for the noblest ideals, but, using polite language, as woolly nonsense. Now that is a point of view. In a free country, it is a view which one is entitled to express. And it can be expressed in the media as by the couple having a chat together over a pint of beer in the pub, or a glass of wine in the winebar.

What, however needs to be examined, in the criticism of 'Human Rights' and the judgments made by reference to them, is that the incorporation of the Convention, and the statutory requirement that the decisions of the European Court of Justice must be applied (whether we judges in the United Kingdom agree with them or not), and the decisions of the European Court of Human Rights must be taken into account, represents the law of the United Kingdom as decided in Parliament by the ordinary legislative process. Judges are *obliged* to apply the legislation enacted by our sovereign Parliament, and the European Communities Act 1972 and the Human Rights Act 1998 are two such Acts. No more and no less.

In my view these misunderstandings should be avoided, and the opportunity for them reduced. That is not to say that justifiable criticism should not be made of judges. That is not to say that judicial decisions should be immune to criticism. But when the judiciary is criticised in the media, it should be on the basis of an understanding of the limits or obligations imposed by the law on the judge.

We must go further: so it is that in England, judges with administrative responsibilities—for example, the senior judge in the Crown

Court of, say, Leeds or Manchester—are encouraged to have a working relationship with the editors of the local newspapers, so that if for example it appears that a judge in his sentencing remarks has said something outrageous or absurd, at least before this goes into print, it can be checked that he has indeed said that which was attributed to him, or that if he did, there was a context which explains it. A record of what the judge actually said should be made available. In that way what might be a misguided headline is avoided. On the other hand, if the judge did indeed utter a remark which, whatever the context, was absurd or stupid or revealing a prejudice, why then, it should be reported, and criticised for absurdity, stupidity or prejudice.

Again, a habit seemed to be developing some 10 years or so ago of the practice known as 'doorstepping' of judges who had given a controversial decision. You all know what I mean. But, with the assistance of the Press Complaints Commission, and the co-operation of newspaper editors, the practice has largely died down. The reason why it developed was ignorance on the part of reporters of the fact that a judge cannot comment on his decision. There is no point in doorstepping a judge who cannot, and is not permitted to, explain why he decided or spoke as he did. If the judge is not permitted to speak then doorstepping him is oppressive because it cannot produce any further public information.

Again, some 10 years or so ago, shortly after it was founded, the Society of Editors was increasingly, and if I may say so, justifiably concerned at the number of orders being made up and down the country, the effect of which was to prevent reporting of this or that case, or this or that feature of it. Some of these orders undoubtedly contravened the principle of open justice and did not fall within the exceptions to that principle. On the other hand it is not realistic for a newspaper in serving a court in some place remote from London to take immediate proceedings to set the order aside, not least because the proceedings in question might well be over before the process could be begun. And in any event, it all costs money at a time when newspapers are not flush with it. So between us, the judiciary and lawyers from the media worked together to produce easily read, manageable text for use in the Crown Court and the Magistrates' Court in which the essential principles were set out. They have become valuable handbooks, used regularly whenever a question of reporting restrictions arises up and down the country. And it is open to a newspaper reporter, a representative of a local newspaper, to draw the attention of the court to the content of these guides, so as to avoid the expense of employing lawyers for the purpose. The result is that fewer inappropriate reporting restrictions are imposed—or if they are, they are quickly removed, without the independence of either being diminished.

Another vexed topic is the world of superinjunctions. A superinjunction is an order made that the very fact of the injunction should remain confidential. In some respects it is a sensible precaution. If, for example, a business has discovered that a fraud is being perpetrated on it by two or three of its employees, and injunctive relief is sought to prevent any further consequent damage to the business, the disclosure of the fact that such an order has been made may itself add to the damage which has already occurred. So the business might be better off without the injunction, in which case the fraudsters would continue to enjoy the benefits of their dishonesty. When, however, the issue of the superinjunction comes to be examined in the context of injunctions sought by well-known figures to protect their privacy, the issue becomes more difficult. The reasoning is the same, but privacy law is itself in a state of development. As I speak, the Master of the Rolls is chairing a committee to examine the way in which superinjunctions should and should not work. The committee includes judges, barristers and solicitors representing both the interests of the media and those whose work includes the representation of men and women who have sought or are likely to seek such superinjunctions. The committee should report before the end of April. When its report becomes available the superinjunction issue will be examined. It is an example of sensible, practical co-operation between the judiciary and representatives of the media, the object of which is to ensure that processes, or a sensible discussion of issues of concern to the media, can be examined at the highest level in the judiciary, in effect round the table, for both increased mutual understanding and, if possible, resolution.

Of course, none of these arrangements and none of the discussions can alter existing legal principles. They have no legislative authority. And if anyone thought that the existing law could be suspended or dispensed with, they simply have to remember the fate of our King James II, who was thrown out for exercising the 'pretended power' to do so. But more often than not what is required is sensible recognition that without the judiciary or the media giving up one fraction of their necessary independences of each other, they can nevertheless examine problems of importance to one or other of them or indeed to both of them, and no longer pretend, as I think was sometimes pretended not so very long ago, that these problems do not exist or hope that they will somehow blow away in some gentle breeze.

I speak only for myself, but I very much doubt if there is any judge in England and Wales who does not recognise the crucial importance played in our affairs by an independent press—crucial not only to the wider public in the entire political arena, but crucial to the administration of justice. Now is not the time for me to go through the time-honoured reasons. But one, perhaps, is enough. It was Pliny the Younger who in Roman times pointed out to us that when we are sitting in judgment, we judges are ourselves on trial. The presence of the media in our courts represents the public's entitlement to assess whether justice is being done. And it is not just an emotional reaction that leads us to become immensely troubled by the operation of secret justice. It is principle. It is not enough to demand open justice when it suits you, or for causes which you deem to be appropriate. The principle of open justice has to apply to those who may be unpopular. It is rather the same as freedom of speech. It is all well and good proclaiming the freedom of speech of those who speak words with which you agree. The greater difficulty is to preach freedom of speech for those whose words you find repulsive. So the principle is open justice—that justice should be done openly—but the primary function of the courts is indeed to do justice. That is the paramount requirement. And we need to take care not be too mollycoddled about this, not too prissy about it. Of course there are occasions when the media, like the judges, make mistakes. Occasionally they go too far. Then perhaps we would be wise to remember the eloquent plea made by Oliver Cromwell in 1650, just before he himself dispensed with Parliament and assumed dictatorial powers at least as great as those claimed by Charles I, and which he enforced more effectively, and rapidly forgot everything that he had written in this letter:

> Your pretended fear lest error should come in, is like a man who would keep all wine out of the country, lest men should be drunk. It would be found an unjust and unwise jealousy to deprive a man of his natural liberty upon a supposition he may abuse it.[4]

The last few years have, without there being any great Commission into the problem, and perhaps without very many people appreciating that the process has been continuing, and its width, seen a careful re-analysis of huge areas of the work of the courts where for one

---

[4] Letter to Walter Dundas, Governor of Edinburgh Castle, 12 September 1650.

reason or another there has been a lack of understanding between the judiciary and the media, and where apparent restrictions on reporting have been gradually developing, in effect, because of the concerns expressed by Oliver Cromwell that you should prevent the drinking of wine because some would get drunk.

I have already touched on the co-operation between the Society of Editors and the judiciary for the production of guides to reporting restrictions in the Crown Court and the Magistrates' Court. I have also referred to the committee examining superinjunctions. I have publicly expressed my profound concern that London has been described as the libel capital of the world. And in a sense, whether this is true or not, like so many aspects of the administration of justice, if that is the perception it is in truth as alarming as if were true. In recent judgments we have re-affirmed the entitlement to express honest opinions without running foul of an action for defamation.[5] Lord Justice Jackson's report,[6] criticised in many quarters, has sought to address the dire financial consequences of the unsuccessful defence by the media of defamation proceedings. And now, last week, a further consultation, this time on the initiative of the government in relation to defamation, has been announced.[7] We have recently affirmed the right of the media to attend cases before the Court of Protection, the court that protects the interests of those with disabilities that mean they cannot conduct their own affairs, and the Family Division is re-examining the way in which greater openness in proceedings in relation to children should obtain.

Can I just pause there for a moment. This is a particularly sensitive area, because cases involving children are profoundly sensitive, and the problems are stark. On the face of it there can be nothing more private than the way in which unhappy parents themselves sort out the arrangements for their children if for any reason they become estranged. They only go to court when they have been unable to do so. When they do, the disputes often become bitter. Sometimes children are used as a weapon by one parent against another. These are private law cases, and it is perfectly arguable and indeed the law provides that the proceedings should remain private, not least because of the potential harm to the children. On the other hand, public law cases can involve decisions which on the basis of expert

---

[5] *British Chiropractic Association v Singh* [2010] EWCA Civ 350; *Joseph and Others v Spiller and Others* [2010] UK SC 53.
[6] *Review of Civil Litigation Costs: Final Report* (2009).
[7] Draft Defamation Bill: Consultation (2011).

evidence can result in findings of significant ill-treatment of a child or children by one or other parent with, in some cases, a conclusion which deprives one parent of access to the child or children. These are proceedings brought by authorities rather than disputes between the parents. To deprive a parent of access to his or her child is an order of profound magnitude both for the parents and for the child. So the case for openness is much greater. Such a draconian order should only be made after a fair trial, after a trial which can be perceived to have been fair. However, what possible advantage is there to anyone in publishing the identity of the parent against whom such an order has been made, leading inevitably to the identification of the child who has been subjected to abuse of such a kind that access to the parent in question is prohibited? For this purpose, it cannot matter whether the child is the child of a well-known public figure, or someone who would never interest even the most local of local newspapers. If the same process was taking place at a criminal trial, and the child was an alleged victim of sexual abuse by a parent, the trial would take place in open court, but the child's identity would be protected by complainant anonymity, which includes the prohibition on reporting which would enable a 'jigsaw' identification of the child. But then let us look further: in a laudable attempt to protect the interest of a child or children who would be harmed by the public revelation that their father had committed criminal offences involving child pornography (not involving his own children), a father was made subject to an anonymity order. We took the view that this decision was wrong.[8] We had to face the reality that, as the judgment indicated, 'the criminal activities of a parent can bring misery, shame and disadvantage to their innocent children' but if we permitted this restriction on reporting, we would be 'countenancing a substantial erosion of the principle of open justice', including the free reporting of criminal trials and the proper identification of those convicted and sentenced in them. So, in that case the anonymity order relating to the father was removed.

I have discussed these issues in the context of children because they exemplify why the answer to the question whether reporting restrictions of any kind should be imposed is not always straightforward. And it does not help the discussion that the phrase 'gagging orders' is applied indiscriminately as if the judge is always to blame, even where the restrictions on reporting are entirely based on statute, where statute prohibits reporting, and the judge has

---

[8] *Re Trinity Mirror plc* (2008) QB 770.

no alternative. As I have already pointed out, the judge cannot dispense with statutory provisions which provide for closed proceedings in relation to national security in the context of the Special Immigration Appeals Commission Act and the review by a court of control orders—that is, special provision for those suspected of involvement in terrorist activities where the evidence depends on material obtained through or by investigation which either cannot be disclosed because statute prevents it (Regulation of Investigatory Powers Act 2000) or because disclosure of the sources of material would either endanger those from whom it was obtained, or reveal information to potential terrorists which would enable them to avoid detection. On other occasions the judge is vested with a discretionary responsibility to examine whether to impose a restriction on reporting. This is where conflicting principles clash. The interests of the litigant in putting matters fully and frankly before the court, and the inhibiting effect of the presence of the media, and the equally powerful interests of the media in ensuring open justice, and the paramount need to ensure that justice is done, must be painstakingly balanced.

Finally, on this aspect, back to where I began. The world of communications is changing fast. Gutenberg has had his hour. Some four or five centuries of hour, but the consequence of his invention—the availability to all of the printed word—is being overtaken by a new world. Imagine buying a newspaper, and as you read through it, you discover that by using a piece of modern technology you can go and get much more newspaper online. In today's world, I am sure that this is a necessary ingredient for a successful newspaper. On the other hand, the need for care with the online information is no less acute than it is for the publication. Naturally enough, care is taken with the newspaper to avoid defamatory statements where they cannot be justified, but is the same care available to be exercised for the online information? It must be. And let us look to communications out of court. I wonder how many of you in this audience have the latest smartphone, the fourth generation of telephone technology, the ability through your telephone to contact and use the entire internet system, and indeed to receive advertisements on your telephone. If the results of one company, recently published, may be anything to go by, fewer and fewer books are being bought, and fewer and fewer CDs; access to both is through modern technology. We know all this from a brief examination of communications out of court. It is now possible, as you know, for a contemporaneous report of what is being said to be put up on a television screen as the words are spoken, or, more realistically, three or four seconds after they have been spoken. So we come to the problem of Twitter, which I use as a general name to cover all kinds of live text-based communications in the modern world. The quill pen and ink went out of court when the fountain pen was invented, and candles were replaced by electric light, slowly, but now we take electricity for granted. At present interim guidance on Tweeting in court has been given, for the purposes of a consultation into the use of modern technology and its impact on the processes of the court.[9] Obviously I must wait for the end of the consultation, but can anyone doubt that the issues of the impact of modern technology both as they apply to the judicial system and as they apply to the world of the media, and indeed as they impinge on the relationship of both the judiciary and the media, should be examined now rather than later? The speed of what is happening is quite remarkable. I have already emphasised that in my view an independent media will survive, but we—and I mean both the judiciary and the media—may have to be re-thinking many of the ways in which we do our work. Whatever the result of the consultation, and whatever guidance is promulgated after its conclusion, I have no doubt that it will have to be re-visited, and re-visited again, because as fast as we keep up with the developments, the developments themselves will be expanding. Ultimately, of course, we must be doing justice in the courts, and we must be doing open justice. My fervent hope is that the advance of new technology will make it easier for the media to be 'present' in court, and that the present trend for fewer and fewer reporters in every court will come to an end, or at any rate, that court proceedings will be reported.

I have commented publicly on other occasions on the potential impact of modern technology on the system of jury trials. Putting it briefly, there is not only the problem of the jury accessing information through the internet, but there is also the ability, long term, of the present generation of youngsters, who use technology at school, and who learn much more from looking at their screens than from listening to their teachers, adapting to the current arrangements for jury service. For present purposes, and in the context of what I have been discussing today, there is another element to technology which merits early thinking and long-term vigilance.

[9] Consultation on the Use of Live, Text-Based Forms of Communications from Court for the Purposes of Fair and Accurate Reporting (2010).

I put it this way because of the title of a book by Professor Susskind, the IT adviser to the Lord Chief Justice, entitled *The End of Lawyers?*[10] It is a convincing analysis of the likely consequences of modern technology for the operation of the legal professions. It is not an assertion that it will be the end of the lawyers, but a question whether it will be the end of lawyers. My concern can be summarised in this brief way. I do not intend to be portentous. I am not a wailing Cassandra, although people tend to forget that Cassandra was right that the great horse outside the walls of Troy was a trick, but as the world of technology changes, we should be aware of and— I do not put it any higher than this—alert to the possible impact of communication systems which today we cannot even imagine, on court processes. Of course we—judiciary and media—must use all the technology available to us to ensure speedy justice, ease of communication, and all the many advantages which may come our way. But we do also have to be alert to any possible infringement, even innocent and unintended, on the principle that justice must be done in a public forum, to which the public, or the media, has access. What I am saying is that if ever there may indeed be the end of lawyers, it cannot mean the end of public justice.

Perhaps most of all, what I have endeavoured to convey in this lecture is that the days when the possibility of communication between the judiciary and the media was regarded as anathema, and wholly wrong in principle, have gone forever. This is a world of communication in which, without any infringement of the mutual independences of the judiciary and the media, they can and should speak to each other, so as to ensure the open administration of justice and the preservation of two independences of cardinal importance to the rule of law.

---

[10] Richard Susskind, *The End of Lawyers? Rethinking the Nature of Legal Services* (Oxford, 2008).

Press Regulation

This was the 13th Annual Justice Lecture, given in October 2011.

IT IS NOT customary for judges to speak publicly about great issues of the moment, at any rate if there may be the slightest political tinge to the discussion. Nevertheless the topic I have decided to address at this meeting is the press, in the light of virtually daily discussion about the rights and wrongs of press behaviour, and the possibility of greater regulation, and in particular the Leveson Inquiry. This is not a talk about the law of privacy, or anything to do with it. That would be entirely out of order, if only because the issue might arise in court next week, or the week after, or maybe in a few months' time. My only concern is press regulation.

Of course, I may come to regret this decision anyway. First, because I am speaking now, and will not have heard the material drawn to Leveson LJ's attention. So I do not know what he will decide to recommend, and his recommendations may not coincide with the views I express today. But in view of some critical comments made recently about Leveson LJ and his involvement with the Inquiry I should explain that when I was consulted, as the statute requires, about the most suitable judge, after discussing it with my most senior colleagues I was the person responsible for putting his name forward as the right person to conduct it. I asked him if he would be prepared to do it. Like me he had no illusions about the burden he would be undertaking. As judges are, he was prepared to accept it. If he is the wrong judge to conduct the Inquiry, that is not his responsibility, but mine. I have the utmost confidence in him.

The terms of reference are daunting. It is no good fooling ourselves that he has not trodden into a minefield. He is required to make recommendations for a new, more effective policy and regulatory regime which supports the integrity and freedom of the press and its independence, including from government, while encouraging the highest ethical and professional standards. When you listen to those words, and they are only a very small part of the remit, I suspect that it may have occurred to you that this is quite a task. Already the criticisms have come fast and clear. Criticisms of the structure or structures of his Inquiry or the roles and experience of the membership of those who will assist him, and indeed his approach to, for example, the open public meetings which have already taken place. These are questions which are open to argument and discussion, and those who disagree with him are entitled to express their contrary views. He has however already been subjected to criticism in personal terms, to which he cannot respond. That hardly advances the debate. And it overlooks that in being prepared to accept this burdensome responsibility, Leveson LJ's obligation is to inquire and make recommendations. He is not providing a judgment which is binding on anyone in any way. When his Inquiry is completed and his recommendations are made, it will then be for Parliament to consider whether legislation is necessary, and if so what form it should take. No one has handed even this distinguished judge a blank sheet of paper upon which to promulgate regulations or constraints on the press, whether collectively, or on a single newspaper. Knowing him as I do, he wants the utmost possible public debate of the issues, not least because he recognises their great public importance.

The debate has now started. The objective must be a discussion about the issues, with, if possible, practical solutions in mind. By speaking today, I am myself engaging in the debate.

My decision to speak now is fortified because, long before the current controversy and concentrated focus on the press arose, I expressed my views publicly on a number of occasions. My views are well enough known to those with any interest in them. On the essential principle they are unchanged. And if some of you have heard me before on the subject, or read my words, bear with me. This is a time for me to repeat and emphasise them. My proposition is simply stated.

In a country governed by the rule of law the independence of the press is a constitutional necessity. The principle has not, as far as I can recall, been directly and expressly embedded in statute, although you can look about and from time to time find references in statute to the principle of freedom of expression. We do not have a written constitution, or at least we do not have a constitution which is wholly in writing. The fact that there is nothing in statute which states expressly that the independence of the press is a constitutional principle does not diminish the principle. Anyway, solemn sounding words do not always do the trick. In 1791 in the newly minted United States of America, with its written constitution, an amendment was carried through all the processes necessary for a constitutional amendment and provided that 'congress shall make no law ... abridging the freedom of speech, or of the press'.

It all sounds very obvious. But for the subsequent years in the United States itself there was turmoil and turbulence about precisely what even these apparently clear, unequivocal words actually meant. So let us look at the same point from a different angle; in this country we take the principle of judicial independence for granted. The constitutional obligation on the government to uphold this principle was not enacted in statute until the Constitutional Reform Act 2005. That does not mean that the principle was in any doubt, or in any way incomplete before that date. That is one of the blessings of a constitution which is not defined by a written instrument. Such principles can also be founded in a nation's history.

Given his clashes with the judiciary of his time, the spirit of John Wilkes would chuckle at the thought that a judge, no less, should cite the immortal words written in 1762 in the *North Briton*:

> The liberty of the press is the birthright of a Briton, and is justly esteemed the firmest bulwark of the liberties of this country.

We embrace that statement. The significance of what John Wilkes said was not, as those connected with the media sometimes suggest, that the statement is upholding the liberty of the press. That is undoubtedly a direct consequence of what John Wilkes said, but in reality on close examination what he was saying was much more profound. He was asserting that the liberty of the press is the birthright of every citizen, that is, the community as a whole. It is the birthright of the citizen that the press should be independent. It is therefore not a right of one section of the community, not just a sectional right. It is the right of the community as a whole. It is, if you like, our right, the right of every citizen. And that is why, if you accept it as I do, the independence of the press is not only a constitutional necessity, it is a constitutional principle.

We should perhaps draw attention to Article 10 of the European Convention on Human Rights, which encompassed what was believed to be common law principles at the time it was written in 1950. Article 10 provides the right to freedom of expression. Interestingly, it did not prevent the state from requiring that broadcasting, television or cinema enterprises should be licensed, but this potential restriction was not extended to the press. Ideas and information may be imparted without interference by public authority, unless limitations are imposed for identified specific policy reasons. None of those reasons for limiting the imparting of information ever extends to information with which the government or authorities of the day, or indeed a large body of citizens, may disagree or view with distaste. All this may lack the inspiring quality of John Wilkes. But it is making the same point.

There is an element of introspection in my expression of these views. Again, I am saying nothing new. I have said what I am about to say time and time again. The independence of the judiciary and the independence of the media are both fundamental to the continued exercise, and indeed the survival, of the liberties which we sometimes take for granted. These are critical independences which are linked, but separate. As far as I can discover, there has never been and there is no community in the world in which an independent press flourishes while the judiciary is subservient to the executive or government, or where an independent judiciary is allowed to perform its true constitutional function while, at the same time, the press is fettered by the executive.

In the sense that I have identified a community of interest, I should declare it. Although judges are frequently the victims of press criticism, sometimes indeed of wholly unjustified press criticism, the constitutional arrangements which underpin the independence of the press provide support for the principle of an independent judiciary, just as an independent judiciary supports the principle of an independent press. These are 'twin independences', each of us utterly independent of the other, but both fundamental to the welfare of the community as a whole.

A word about practical realities. An independent press, or one or other of its constituents, will from time to time behave appallingly, or employ individuals who in order to pursue a story will commit criminal offences. No editors, I think, have ever advocated that they are entitled to some special journalistic privilege if they do so, immunising them or their employees from criminal prosecution. Of course not. So that is not the issue.

An independent press, or one or other of its constituents, will also from time to time behave if not criminally, then with scandalous cruelty and unfairness, leaving victims stranded in a welter of public contempt and hatred or uncovenanted distress. But on the very same day, one of the other constituent parts of the independent press may reveal a public scandal. The scandal of telephone hacking which took the form of cruelty and insensitivity to one family, and ultimately led to the setting up of the Leveson Inquiry, was uncovered and revealed by a different constituent part of the press. The first of these scandals—the cruelty and unfairness—should never happen. The second—the revelation of a public scandal—must be allowed to continue to happen. My own view is that the public value of the second is priceless. Whatever means of regulation are designed to reduce the occasions of unacceptable behaviour by elements of the press, they must not simultaneously, even if accidentally, diminish or dilute the ability and power of the press to reveal and highlight true public scandals or misconduct.

Any system of regulation which is consistent with an independent press—and no other system would be acceptable—must be achieved in the context of two realities of modern life which are rather removed from the high-flown rhetoric. First, the press is no more exempt from the rapidly changing technological world of communication than the rest of us. That does not mean that when we are seeking to identify the standards which should govern the press, we should equate them with the lowest common factor to be found in communication systems. But it does lead to the further consideration. There can be no independent press if the independent press cannot survive in the marketplace. The different newspapers have to sell, and they sell in greater or lesser numbers as the public chooses to buy the product. And as the public chooses to buy, so the advertisers will pay for advertising space. Whether we call it choice, or competition, we need a press which responds to the demands of everyone who buy newspapers. And of course, it is part of the exercise of our own constitutional freedoms that we should be able to choose for ourselves the newspapers we buy and read. We are not cut from identical cloth.

It is no secret that the press, both in the country and nationally, faces huge financial problems. So, again getting away from the rhetoric, if there is no press to be independent, the issue of an independent press might become entirely academic: a wonderfully interesting topic for a PhD thesis 25 years after the last independent newspaper had closed down.

And there is this further consideration. We shall not then lack printed news material. It will be plied through our letterboxes and our computer systems. It will consist of the handouts prepared at the expense of the taxpayer by government, government departments, and the various different authorities which are central to our lives. While we tend to concentrate on the risk of emasculation of the independent press by regulation and statute, we need to be no less keenly aware of the risks to it provided by financial pressures and technological advances.

In the end, all these issues are for public discussion. Leveson LJ has made clear that he wants these issues to be discussed as publicly as possible. In the end, he will have to make recommendations.

The greater the extent of public debate, the more likely that he will have all the different considerations in mind, and the greater his opportunity to listen to and understand some of the conflicting interests, the better informed his Inquiry is likely to be.

The conundrum which faces us, and Leveson LJ in particular, is how best to avoid dilution of the essential constitutional principles. It would be easy, on the basis of a number of disturbing instances in recent times, to say that self-regulation has failed. Let me examine this, recognising that some very sad examples of press misbehaviour have happened.

First, crime is crime. If and when crime is committed by reporters with or without the support and encouragement of an editor, it should be investigated, and if on the available evidence there is a reasonable prospect of a successful prosecution, he or they are prosecuted. We do not say that the General Medical Council and self-regulation have failed when, as sometimes happens, a doctor sexually molests one or more of his patients, or, like Dr Shipman, murders them.

The Press Complaints Commission is now 20 years old. Not long after its 10th birthday the Media Committee of the House of Commons pointed out that the PCC has neither authority nor resources 'other than what is ceded voluntarily to it by the press industry'. Membership is not obligatory. The Commission has no investigative power. In reality it has no disciplinary power. When it works, as most of the time it does, it is because the press itself is prepared to comply with its rulings, not because it is under legal compulsion to do so. Its main role, and I do not seek to diminish it with faint praise, is to provide a sort of ombudsman/mediation service between the newspaper and an individual or group which is aggrieved by an article. It cannot award compensation. To criticise the PCC for failing to exercise powers it does not have is rather like criticising a judge who passes what appears to be a lenient sentence, when his power to pass a longer sentence is curtailed.

Nevertheless the PCC has been subjected to a number of criticisms. I repeat, I am deliberately not commenting on them, or whether they are justified. The point I want to advance is different. Even if they are fully justified, the criticisms of themselves do not automatically exclude self-regulation or a form of self-regulation in the future. In other words, it does not follow that we should jump from the present system to government regulation or regulation by a government appointed body which would give ultimate power to government. I hasten to add that I will be equally unenthusiastic about regulatory control in the hands of the judiciary. That would diminish the twin independencies about which I spoke a few minutes ago.

We must remember that, whatever lies ahead, the ordinary law of the land will continue. Crime will be crime. Injunctive relief where appropriate, with alleged breaches of any Code available to be deployed in argument in support of the application. Contempt of court powers will remain. So will liability to damages for breach of confidence and defamation.

May I offer just a few thoughts, very brief, on how the PCC might be strengthened. What should be its new powers? Perhaps the first question is whether it should continue to be called the PCC. Is the brand's name too damaged? I shall call it an improved PCC, by which I mean a more powerful body. It is immediately attractive to suggest all sorts of controlling and disciplinary powers being vested in the new body—that it must not be a toothless tiger. But we need to be careful. There is no point in a toothless tiger, but the concept of giving what would in effect be censorship and licensing powers over a constituent part of the press to a body vested with responsibilities for the whole of the press should set alarm bells ringing. And the problems would be aggravated by the fact that in a self-regulatory body, at least some of the members will be editors of rival competing newspapers, and this might then call into question the fairness of any such adjudicating system. Should the body have power to prevent publication, or should its role be limited to remedies for publication outwith the Code?

The first responsibility of the new PCC would be, of course, to continue the conciliatory/mediation work which is so successfully carried out now. But consideration would have to be given to whether it would be vested with power to make express findings that the code then current had been broken, and if so to direct the terms of any apology or appropriate article in the offending newspaper, and if the power is granted, to make an order for compensation. Two further points. The new PCC—that is the new body currently in my contemplation in any new system of self-regulation—must be all-inclusive. You might perhaps be willing to discount a news sheet circulated to about 25 people, but any national or regional paper would have to be included. In short, any new PCC would require to have whatever authority is given to it over the entire newspaper industry, not on a self-selecting number of newspapers.

The final point for mention, just for this afternoon, is the issue of the appointment of the membership of the new regulatory body. I suggest that the sensible approach would be to avoid all government involvement in the process. The choice of members and their removal should similarly be independent of government. Again the structures would arise for discussion. There are a very large number of bodies operating in the public interest which are independent of government. One example is the Bar Standards Board. Another is the Judicial Appointments Commission. It is, of course, essential to the way in which any of this may work that the membership should include a significant number of editors, and/ or representatives of the newspaper industry as well as what I shall describe as 'civilians'. All I am saying is that structures like these are not beyond the realm of achievement.

I have, as is obvious, joined the debate. If he were here, I expect that Leveson LJ would say that none of these issues is straightforward. And I would agree with him. But we all need to think, and think very hard, about how to assist the debate.

The Welsh Language: Some Reflections

This was the Hywel Dda Institute Founding Lecture given at Swansea University in June 2011, but updated by the results of the 2011 census for a lecture given to the Association of London Welsh Lawyers in June 2013. For those who are not Welsh, it may seem a little strange to find this lecture in the section of the book dealing with Rights; for a Welsh man or woman it would be insulting to put it anywhere else.

IT HAS BEEN and continues to be an honour and privilege to have been Lord Chief Justice of Wales, and I shall carry the warmth of that honour into the happiest memories that old age may bring. Every man and woman who is Welsh is heir to an important heritage. That is true whether you speak a single word of Welsh or not. So that, of course, is all of you. You have a responsibility to help guard it.

Notwithstanding all the discussions on devolution, all the high profile of devolution, all the education, all the teaching Welsh to children in Wales, the 2011 census reveals that in the previous 10 years in Wales the number and proportion of people aged 3 and over able to speak Welsh had declined. The proportion of those able to speak decreased from 20.8% to 19.0%. Nearly three-quarters of the population, 73.3%, had no Welsh language skills in 2011, an increase from 71.6%. Please think what this means. Nearly three-quarters of Welsh men and women and children have no Welsh language skills. That is why I have returned to this subject. In 2011 we were all bright eyed and bushy tailed about the issue: the future was saved. We now appreciate that the battle has yet to be won.

Much of the story that I am going to narrate reflects no credit, indeed reflects discredit on England, but the latest figures cannot be blamed on her.

The blame attached to England is encapsulated in the haunting words of RS Thomas,[1] the poet of Aberdaron, a great poet, lamenting that he could not express himself in his native language, Welsh.

---

[1] *The Collected Works of RS Thomas, 1945–1990* (London, 2011).

England, what have you done to make the speech
My fathers used a stranger to my lips,
An offence to the ear, a shackle on the tongue...

How could this be? How could this happen?

The answer to these questions involves scholarship of a depth which I do not have, and knowledge on a scale of which I am ignorant. But let me offer a few tentative thoughts on the subject, largely historic.

Let us begin at the beginning, perhaps with Thomas Hobbes in *Leviathan*:

The general use of Speech is to transfer our Mental Discourse into Verbal; or Trayne of our Thoughts, into a Trayne of Words.

It is systems of words, commonly shared among the group, that identify a tribe, or a community, or, using modern language, a nation. We know that animals of the same kind communicate with each other, but it is only the human animal that turns the noises into distinguishable and consistent sounds. It was not until I became a grandfather that I appreciated the extraordinary facility of the human brain, which, put starkly, comes to this. If the child in the cot or in his or her mother's arms hears mother or father speaking English, then the sounds which will eventually emerge will be the English language; if Swahili, then Swahili; if Mandarin, then Mandarin; if Welsh, then Welsh. As a father I think I took this for granted. As a grandfather it has struck me as utterly miraculous. The acquisition of this method of communication between human beings which we take for granted is indeed a miracle.

This is not a lecture about miracles, but the starting point of a lecture on this type of topic needs to emphasise how crucial the issue of language is to the very survival of the human race, and therefore to national and tribal survival. I could have not started nearer the beginning than the acquisition of language by a child. Nevertheless these miraculous processes underpinned the survival of Welsh.

Let me begin at 1215. Magna Carta. We shall celebrate it in style. At least I hope we will.

I am sure you are all familiar with article 56:

If we have deprived or dispossessed any Welsh men of lands, liberties, or anything else in England or in Wales, without the lawful judgement of their equals, these are at once to be returned to them ... English law shall apply to holdings of land in England, Welsh law to those in Wales, and the law of the Marches to those in the Marches.

Article 57 deals with the deprivation or dispossession of Welsh people of any thing without lawful judgement, allowing a respite for their return until after a crusade is completed, but on return from crusade, or if the crusade is abandoned, it continues:

> We will at once do full justice according to the laws of Wales and the said regions.

Welsh law—Magna Carta 1215 asserts that the law of Wales is distinct from that of England.

Now I must move to a different starting point. Completely at random (as no doubt you will all believe) I pick 1244, 30 years later. During that year it was pointed out to the royal Justiciar visiting South Wales:

> It is not easy in our region to reward or restrain the Welsh, unless this is done by someone of their own tongue.

The inference is inescapable. As well as Welsh law, the Welsh language was endemic. What else was this recording except that 800 years ago the people of Wales were speaking Welsh and that the language of Wales was readily identifiable? It was the unique and thriving tongue in which these men and women expressed themselves. To put it into context, by now William Marshal had already built his great castles at Chepstow, Newport and Pembroke.

Right in the middle of the great castle-building programme of Edward I, a few years later, we find a record in the Welsh Assize Roll of 1277–84 which includes this poignant lament:

> All Christians have laws and customs in their own lands; even the Jews in England have laws among the English; we had our immutable laws and customs in our land until the English took them away after the last war.

I hope no one here will misunderstand me when I say that the reference to the Jews must have been entirely deliberate. In medieval Christian communities Jews were treated appallingly. So the reference to Jews was deliberate: what this meant was that we in Wales were being treated even worse than that. Magna Carta or not, we have been robbed of our own laws and customs, laws among others of Hywel Dda.

In the wake of the great castles of North Wales, there is one further significant feature to notice. Perhaps inevitably, it was not just castles. There was in addition settlement by what we should describe as colonists. It was not a coincidence that in 1284 charters were granted to a large number of towns, including Flint, Rhuddlan, Conwy, Caenarfon, Criccieth and Harlech, and in the calendar of ancient petitions we had a protest from the colonists 'that so many Welsh are lodged near the town on the outside that they disturb the profit and market of the English'.

That complaint came from Rhuddlan. So the castles themselves, intimidating though they were, were attracting communities of men and women from Wales, no doubt looking for work, and food, speaking their own established Welsh language.

In 1295 Edward I declared that the invading French intended to eliminate English—a piece of propaganda revived by his grandson Edward III. But what was English? It was not English as we know it.

When we are looking back at medieval times, in the context of language, we must pause and understand the medieval world. At this date in England society was multilingual. French was still the language of the nobility and the aristocracy. Men spoke and on occasion wrote in French to demonstrate their high status and education. The language of the Court was French or Norman French. There had been no Shakespeare, no Authorised Version of the Bible; the concept of national identity in England was far from secure. What we can discern are trends.

Despite its Latin title, *Cursor Mundi* was written in English in about 1300. It demanded that each country should have its own language. Plainly that would apply to Wales. In 1323 a defendant to a charge of theft, claiming to be a cleric, refused to answer save in English. He was asked if he knew how to speak in Latin or in French. He said that he was English, and English born, and therefore he would speak in his mother tongue; he refused to speak anything but English. The end result was that he was treated as not entering any plea at all and visited with that terror, *peine forte et dure*: a sharp stone was pushed under his back, a flat object, like a door, was placed on top of him and then weights were added until his ribs burst and the breath was crushed out of him. This heroic martyr helps to underline that the issue of language is not some quirky product of a modern pressure group. It would matter—it does matter—to men and women of every nation.

Next I come to a statute, this time written in French, but using its English title: the Pleadings in English Act of 1362.

This declared its purpose.

(2) ... the said laws and customs that rather shall be perceived and known, and better understood in the tongue used in the said realm, and by so much every man on the said realm may the better govern themselves without offending of the law, and better keep, safe, and defend his heritage and possessions:

And the remedy:

> (3) And in diverse regions and countries, where the King, the nobles, and others of the said realm have been, good governance and full right is done to every person, because that their laws and customs be learned and used in the tongue of that country.

So there it was—statutory recognition in Parliament of the importance that the laws and usages of the community should be properly understood by the members of the community, and that the language used to enforce the laws and customs should be the language used by the members of the community itself. The ideal was noble. There was no great rush to enforce it in England, but English was developing at great speed, and the French and Latin and old Anglo Saxon components were gradually moulding together. English was, to use Robert Burchfield's delectable phrase, a language of 'amazing hospitality'[2]—and so it remains, constantly developing, constantly taking new words in from all cultures, and at the same time establishing itself across the world. I shall return to this consideration at the end of the lecture.

But again, going back to the fourteenth century, none of this was clear. Indeed for the 'establishment' in England it can be argued that the use of the local or native language was regarded as something of a threat. For example, as the fourteenth century was turning into the fifteenth, it was declared that the sacrament of the Mass was not to be discussed in the vernacular, and as for the Bible in English, that did not come up for discussion, save in the sense that monks and scholars were allowed to use it if authorised. Wycliffe's Bible in English was not welcome. In England the language of dissent was English.

Throughout this period, Welsh, as far as I can see, continued to flourish. There was no reason why the language should not have continued to be used and to develop in Wales. According to Miri Rubin,[3] even the English Marcher lords 'developed a great liking for the sounds and generic diversity of Welsh poetry; for the Welsh cywyddau ... for the elegy or the ode'. She quotes, and I do, Ieuan Llwyd ab Ieuan's elegy for his beloved wife Angharad on her death:

> A fitting pain, a shower of tears wets me,
> My cheek is sallow and withered by languishing grief;
> ... sad work for the sight, the long enforced weeping;
> Woeful work of longing, the memory of Angharad.

---

[2] RW Birchfield, *The English Language* (London, 2006).
[3] Miri Rubin, *The Hollow Crown* (London, 2005).

The quotation is, as you have heard, in English. Someone will one day recite to me how it sounds in Welsh. A poem of haunting beauty, written long before the poetry of Wyatt or Howard or Shakespeare, evidence that the language of Wales was thriving, and vivid, and perhaps, in one word, communicative. And there was no reason why it should not have continued to thrive.

Until we come to the Tudors. The Tudors. A Welsh monarch on the throne. His son half Welsh. All should have been well.

The Laws in Wales Act of 1535, sometimes called the Act of Union, was the main provision directly connected with Wales enacted by the Reformation Parliament, one of the most momentous in our history. It asserted that the 'imperial crown' of England 'incorporated and united and annexed Wales' into the 'Realm of England'. In passing, note that the same language was used in the statute which was to govern religion, the Act in Restraint of Appeals, a year or two earlier, which declared that 'this England is an Empire'. Henry VIII had some grand ideas—on the Continent foreigners tended to believe that all Englishmen had tails and were usually drunk.

Now to the justification, or explanation, for the Law of Wales Act:

> The People of the same Dominion have and do daily use a speech nothing like, nor consonant to the natural Mother Tongue used within this Realm.

Of course, this was typical Tudor hypocrisy, and you will gradually discern that I am not a great admirer of loveable, bluff old Henry VIII with his six wives. It was undoubtedly true that Welsh was not a speech used in England. But it was used in Wales. There it was the natural mother tongue. And so, having unified Wales to England, the statute went on to provide:

> That from henceforth no Person or Persons that use the Welsh Speech or Language shall have or enjoy any Manner Office or Fees within this Realm of England, Wales or other the King's dominions. Upon pain of forfeiting the said office or fees, unless he or they use the English speech or tongue.

So either you spoke English or you were excluded from public life in your own country, or any office, including judicial office; you would not advance in the world. Yet who in the end does not hope for some improvement in his life, for greater opportunities for his children? In Wales it all seemed to depend on the abandonment of the use of language which, if Welsh, you learned to articulate when your mother and father spoke to you when you were a baby. It was an 'outrage'. That was the word I used in my own judgment

in *Williams v Cowell* in July 1999.[4] To my mind it was made worse
by the utter hypocrisy of the further statutory requirement that in
courts in Wales, and contrary to the provisions of the 1362 Act,
Welsh people were prohibited from using their own language. What
had happened to the principle established nearly 200 years earlier
in the 1362 Act?

The reality is that the later half of the reign of Henry VIII was
filled with outrages. He was, after all, the Supreme Head of the
Church, and believed himself to be God's lieutenant on Earth. And
so, as with every tyrant, his personal wishes coincided with those
of the Almighty. It is a shattering potion. The dissolution of the
monasteries—not the reform of monasteries which were sick, or
corrupt, or venal, or crammed with immorality, which had begun in
Cardinal Wolsey's time, but the complete dissolution of centuries-
old places of worship, and assistance, and education, and learning—was but one huge act of criminal damage. All that I am getting
at is encapsulated in the exercise in terrorism which followed his
personal promise—the king's personal promise—the promise of
God's anointed—to Robert Aske that when those who joined the
Pilgrimage of Grace dispersed, they would be pardoned, and he
would hold Parliament at York with 'free election of knights and
burgesses'. Contrast those welcome assurances with his unequivocal orders to the Duke of Norfolk:

> You shall, in any wise, call such dreadful execution to be done upon a
> good number of the inhabitants of every town, village, and hamlet, that
> have offended in this rebellion, as well as by the hanging of them up on
> trees as by the quartering of them ... as they be a fearful spectacle of all
> other hereafter ...

And not long afterwards the Statute of Proclamations enacted what
we now, with disparagement, describe as Henry VIII clauses, granting powers to the king, in effect, without parliamentary approval.
Rule by executive regulation: this remains a pernicious danger to
the rule of law, and in recent years the habit has revived. We should
be very watchful.

Wales was not alone in its suffering at the hands of this Tudor
king. Indeed Magna Carta was not imprinted on his soul. I do not
offer these observations in order to imply that the Laws in Wales Act
was less than an outrage. That is what it was. But it was one outrage among a number of other outrages. And it is my belief that this

---

[4] [2000] 1 WLR 187.

single Act of Parliament, and its consequences, was ultimately more damaging to the language of Wales, and its use in Wales, than the more dramatic, attention-seeking castles of the Plantagenet kings.

To reinforce this thought, we should remember that this was a time of wide political and religious ferment. All over Europe the Bible was being translated into the vernacular, with printing presses churning out numerous copies of it to be read by people familiar with their own language. In the reign of Elizabeth I the right to read the Bible in English was firmly established; and, no less important, she authorised the publication of the Bible in Welsh in 1588, to join the Welsh translation of the Prayer Book in the churches of Wales. Again, the inference is plain. In Wales, when the Laws in Wales Act 1535 was enacted, the Welsh language was in common use. Otherwise why provide for the Bible in Welsh? Doesn't this underline the hypocrisy of the 1535 Act?

The decision that the Bible should be published in Welsh was another crucial moment. It must have contributed, in communities where the Christian religion retained its vitality, to the very survival of the Welsh language. It is not cynical, but maybe perhaps it is, that on one view this meant that it was acceptable for Welsh speakers to accumulate their treasures in Heaven, provided they did nothing which might allow them to accumulate treasure on Earth.

And the impact, very gradually, of the first 1535 Act was the destruction of the Welsh language in large parts of the country. Perhaps 'destruction' is not the right word. Perhaps it was an enervating process, gradual decline by desuetude. To speak Welsh was not the way forward to advancement. Nevertheless loyalty to the Welsh language continued. So, in 1830 the absorption of the legal system of Wales into that of England was completed when the Courts of Great Sessions of Wales were abolished altogether, and the old Assize system which had operated in England was now applied in Wales. But these courts had survived for 300 years after Henry VIII. And in 1846 the county courts in England and Wales were created, with a county court boundary system, which meant that some were entirely in Wales, and one spanned Wales and some of the English bordering counties. I think it significant that it was recognised that where possible judges who were acquainted with the Welsh language should be appointed to the county courts of Wales. It means, of course, that again it was recognised that in some parts of Wales, at any rate, the language continued in common use, and it also underlined that by the mid-nineteenth century, at any rate, whatever Henry VIII might have ordered, the Welsh language had been and was inevitably going to be used in some areas of court business.

As Professor Gwynedd Parry demonstrates in his fascinating biography of Sir David Hughes Parry, Caernarvonshire remained 'a fortress and a bastion for the Welsh language'.[5] He supports his thesis by referring to the 1891 census figures which show that more than 65% of the population of Caernarfonshire spoke *only* Welsh, and only about 10% could not speak Welsh at all. Taking Wales as a whole, something like 30% could speak *only* Welsh. In the small rural parishes of North Wales, it is highly probable that the entire population spoke Welsh. What is consistent with the census figures is perhaps demonstrated by the *Government Report on Education in Wales* published in 1847. It speaks of 'The mockery of an English trial of a Welsh criminal by a Welsh jury, addressed by counsel and judge in English'. It was 'too gross and shocking to need comment. It is nevertheless a mockery which must continue until the people are taught the English language ...'

Note that the problem is attributed to the Welsh not understanding English, not the English not understanding Welsh.

In Victorian England, even early Victorian England, it does not appear to have occurred to anyone that the solution might be the repeal of the Laws in Wales Act. And that, in truth, is unsurprising. These were the years of Empire; not Henry VIII's empire, but the British Empire, to which in all its manifestations, good as well as bad—and there were many good manifestations—people from Wales made their own contributions. To this day there are still areas in Argentina where Welsh is spoken. However, whatever may have been happening in Caernarvonshire, or for that matter in Argentina, in the South, in the Valleys, Welsh was in serious decline, and indeed it was declining in the North too. There were many factors.

This remarkable decline in the use of the Welsh language coincided with the extraordinary changes in social and industrial history of the nineteenth and early half of the last century, for example the industrial revolution, the economic disasters of the 20s and 30s, and two destructive world wars, in particular the First World War. There were more insidious changes. The use of Welsh by children in Wales was actively discouraged. By active I do not mean correction, but punishment: punishment meted out not only by teachers who were English, but by teachers who were Welsh, who honestly believed

---

[5] R Gwynedd Parry, *David Hughes Parry: A Jurist in Society* (Cardiff, 2010), which was invaluable to me when preparing the later part of this lecture.

that for the children to speak Welsh would damage their chances of progress. And, of course, Welsh was not taught in schools. From now on survival depended entirely on mothers and fathers speaking Welsh to their children. By the 1971 census, by contrast with 1891, the number of Welsh speakers throughout Wales was reduced to 20% of the population, so 80% did not speak the language at all, and even in what Professor Gwynedd Parry describes as the 'solid heartlands' the figure was down to 60%. The language of Wales had gone from being a language of the majority to the language of the minority. That seems to me to be a sad story.

The result is summarised in a memorandum written by a prosecuting counsel in the trial of Saunders Lewis and two others in October 1936 for arson at an RAF school on the Llyn Peninsula. He pointed out:

> The King's Commission is written only in English ... no mention of Wales is made and in the entire ceremonial the existence of such a place as Wales is ignored.

The judge rejected the applications of three fluent Welsh speakers to address the court in Welsh. It is said that generally he was utterly contemptuous of them. The jury did not agree its verdicts. They were re-tried at the Old Bailey and convicted.

After the trial, a petition was launched at the Eisteddfod in Cardiff in August 1938. It asserted that the statutes of Henry VIII were 'a source of injustice and indignity to British subjects whose native language is Welsh ...'

The prayer of the petitioners was for an Act of Parliament that would place 'the Welsh language on a footing of equality with the English language in all proceedings connected with the administration of justice and of public services in Wales'. Mark these words.

As ever, the terrible consequences of war produce some unanticipated results. The Nazi conquest of Europe brought many refugees to our shores—Resistance fighters from Holland and Norway and France among them. Arrangements were made for these individuals to be tried, when charged, in courts in which their own language was used. Yet this was not then available in Wales. Then in October 1942 the Welsh Courts Act 1942 repealed the language clause in the Laws of Wales Act 1535. One of my predecessors, Lord Caldecote, commented in April 1943 that Welsh was

> a foreign language to me and, to tell you the truth, I do not know that I feel very sympathetic to this plan for keeping alive, what, like Erse and Gaelic, is really a dying language.

I do not think that the fact that bombs were falling in London provides any excuse; but it demonstrates that it took a huge amount of energy, and a vast amount of commitment, and dedication, and determination, to halt the decline of the use of Welsh, and now to ensure its revival.

The 1942 Act did not treat Welsh as equal with English. It permitted the use of Welsh to a party or witness who believed that he would be at a disadvantage if forced to use English when his natural language of communication was Welsh. Nevertheless even in Wales not everyone agreed with this measure. For example, the Associated Law Society of Wales protested that such a measure was brought forward 'in time of war'. But enacted it was.

It was in the context of subsidiary legislation prescribing forms of oaths in Welsh that this enactment was considered in *The Queen v Merthyr Tydfil Justices, ex parte Jenkins*[6] when the Divisional Court considered the case of a schoolmaster, fluent in English, charged with driving without a licence, asserting that he would not plead to the charges until they were put to him in the Welsh language. Pleas of 'not guilty' were entered. He then sought to cross-examine a police witness in Welsh, and was not allowed to do so. When he gave evidence he was allowed to give it in Welsh. He was convicted. He relied on section 1 of the 1942 Act and asked for his convictions to be quashed because he had been denied his rights.

It did not help before the Divisional Court that it was conceded—as it had to be—on his behalf that he had no defence to the charges. That is an unpromising foundation for a successful appeal. From his observations it is clear that Lord Parker, Chief Justice was not unsympathetic, but given the absence of any defence, the appeal could not be allowed. A Welsh judge, Mr Justice Glyn Jones, took the same view. Mr Justice Widgery, another of my predecessors, expounded his view in the context of his experience of having spent the summer on circuit in Wales:

> It is quite clear that the proper language for the court proceedings in Wales is the English language.

The use of Welsh impeded 'the efficient administration of justice in Wales'. He went on to describe the very limited rights given by the 1942 Act, and concluded that

> language difficulties which arise in Wales can be dealt with by discretionary arrangements for an interpreter, precisely in the same way as

---

[6] [1967] 1 All ER 636.

language difficulties at the Central Criminal Court are dealt with when the accused is a Pole.

So the 1942 Act had not delivered the official recognition for Welsh sought by many leading figures—but, as I have underlined, not all influential figures—in Welsh public life.

In *Evans v Thomas*,[7] a completed nomination paper for a candidate for election as a county councillor was completed in Welsh, and rejected by the county returning officer on that ground. It was not 'in the prescribed form as laid down by statute'. The only other candidate was therefore elected. The petition was for that election to be declared void. Everyone involved understood and read Welsh, including the claimant, the elected candidate and the returning officer.

The Divisional Court decided that the 1942 Act had not authorised the use of the Welsh language in a nomination paper. Winn LJ said:

> It is desirable that it should be clearly appreciated that the court is no more concerned ... with any general question of the status of Welsh as a national language than it is to animadvert on the reasons or emotions which inspired the petitioners' refusal to employ English in their nomination paper.

I do detect in this judgment a measure of sympathy.

It is not difficult to understand why those who were campaigning for Welsh to be treated on the basis of equality were disappointed with the Act. It is only fair to the judges in these cases to indicate that a proper statutory interpretation of the Act left them with no choice. The alternative construction was not realistically available. But, even looking back on what is still the not so distant past, is it perhaps too much to have asked for at least a level of understanding of the issues, and a little less sense of disparagement in the disposal of the argument? Indeed Sir David Hughes Parry was driven to dismiss Widgery J's remarks as language which can 'be fairly interpreted by lay men to carry a bias, Anglo-Saxon nineteenth century political flavour'.[8] In short, the future Lord Chief Justice was given a 'wigging'.

And so we come to the Welsh Language Act 1967. Perhaps we should pause for a minute. There was a new judicial understanding afoot, exemplified in the quashing by the Court of Appeal of a sentence of imprisonment imposed on students from Aberystwyth

---

[7] [1962] 3 All ER 108.
[8] See R Gwynedd Parry, n 5 above.

who disrupted a very high profile defamation trial to register a protest in support of the Welsh language. The trial judge sent them to
prison for three months. Within a week their appeal was allowed.
They were released and bound over to keep the peace and to be on
good behaviour. At the time of this demonstration I had recently been
called to the Bar, and I remember the case very well. It was indeed
one of those demonstrations that really matter, perhaps because the
tide of history was flowing in the right direction. Notwithstanding
their clear and deliberate contempt of court, Lord Denning and his
colleagues were not unsympathetic.

Lord Denning pointed out:

> These young people are no ordinary criminals. There is no violence, dis-
> honesty or vice in them. On the contrary, there was much that we should
> applaud. They wish to do all they can to preserve the Welsh language.
> Well may they be proud of it. It is the language of the Bards—of the poets
> and the singers—more melodious by far than our rough English tongue.[9]

Professor Parry points out that perhaps Lord Denning was drawing
on his own experiences as a young officer attached to the 38th Welsh
Division in France in 1918, when he was shoulder to shoulder with
Welsh soldiers digging trenches under continuous shell fire.

The Welsh Language Act 1967 expanded the use of the Welsh language in courts by permitting any party or witness or other person
'who desires to use it' to do so. It was no longer necessary to demonstrate need, or disadvantage, or difficulty with the use of English.
The individual could choose for himself or herself. It was not what
we may describe nowadays as the 'full Monty', and in particular did
not fully implement the principle of total equality between English
and Welsh in courts in Wales. And it was not directed to wider
aspects of public life. But, and this is an important but, perhaps at
the time it was as far as it could realistically go. When considering an
Act of Parliament, realism includes political realities, and it must be
acknowledged that there were many Welsh men and women living
in Wales who did not share the zeal for the Welsh language which
enthused, for example, the students from Aberystwyth.

And finally for the present, we come to the Welsh Language Act
1993. This proclaims the principle that:

> In the conduct of public business and the administration of justice in
> Wales the English and Welsh languages should be treated on the basis of
> equality ...

---

[9] *Morris v Crown Office* (1970) 2 QB 114.

The principle is clear and simple. The trumpet has sounded. The 'outrage' of the 1535 Act has, at long last, been eradicated. All this was confirmed in the Government of Wales Act 1998, which created the National Assembly for Wales and underlined the principle that where 'both appropriate in the circumstances and reasonably practicable', the English and Welsh languages should be treated 'on a basis of equality'.

The petition launched in Cardiff in August 1938 has been answered. At last. I have said before, and I repeat, that the judiciary applies this principle of equality. In a court in Wales, if the litigant, or the witness, wishes to use the Welsh language, then he or she has an absolute right to do so; it is not a discretion vested in the judge, it is an entitlement vested in the citizen. All documents relating to processes in court are available in both languages. Many judges who sit in Wales are fluent Welsh speakers; so are something like 250 magistrates; many more judges and magistrates have the language skills, even if not fluency. And there will be more.

Of course, this is not the end of the story. As a judge I have no better insight into the future than anyone else, and moreover, as a judge I shall not make observations about what can truly be described as political issues. The way in which Welsh will be used in Wales—and I do not merely mean its official status, but include its actual use in day-to-day transactions and for communications between citizens of Wales—is a political and social question. But for the foreseeable future, I believe that the survival of the Welsh language is assured.

But there is corollary to the truism that the future is uncertain, that 'what's to come is still unsure', and that is that you cannot foretell the future. So we must pause at the moment of assurance and remind ourselves that Welsh must survive in an international environment in which English is, if not the dominant language, then certainly one of the dominant languages of the world, and likely to remain so. In a world of new and extraordinary methods of communication, that is a consideration which should not be overlooked. I do most earnestly hope that the disappointing figures I gave you at the beginning do not presage the impact of this new world, but watch it.

How do I end this quick dash through 800 years of history? The thoughts are very simple. The language of Wales is a precious heritage. It has survived. But there is no room for relaxed smugness. Its survival is thanks to a relatively small number of people who over many centuries stood by it, probably against their own economic and social self-interest, teaching it to their children. When I visit

Aberdaron, as I frequently do when on holiday in North Wales, I offer a metaphorical little bow to RS Thomas. If the language his fathers used was ever again to become a stranger to his lips, or an offence to the ear, or a shackle on the tongue, all the effort and sacrifice made by those men and women would have been in vain. But never take the future for granted. Speaking as Lord Chief Justice of Wales, I can only urge you to safeguard your language. Safeguard it well. Even if you do not speak a word of it, guard it well.

Administration of Justice

The Art of Advocacy

This lecture, sometimes in more or less identical terms, sometimes in a much shorter version, has been given to a wide variety of legal audiences, reflecting my personal experience as an advocate and observing advocacy over very many years. This particular lecture was given at the Singapore Academy of Law in September 2012. It was published in the Singapore Academy of Law Journal *(2013).*

High-quality advocacy is fundamental to the forensic process, whether in an adversarial or inquisitorial system, for the administration of justice. However, the practice of advocacy is not confined to the law courts. It is going on all the time. Advertisements represent an attempt to persuade us to buy, to do, or not to do something. At meetings, whether in the office or in the legislature, and even from time to time at home, someone is trying to persuade someone else of something. We do not describe these processes of persuasion as advocacy, but that, on analysis, is what they are. That said, I do not recommend the deployment of forensic techniques which work in the process of litigation in discussions and arguments at home. Spouses and teenage children in particular do not always respond positively to cross-examination by lawyer husbands or wives or parents.

I AM GRATEFUL for the honour that has been done to me in inviting me to deliver this annual lecture. My wife Judith and I are privileged to be here and, if I may say so, we have already been shown huge kindness and much traditional courtesy.

Coming here, to a country which, by its history and geography, is one of the world's great hubs of air and sea routes—small in size but vast in achievement and aspiration—reminds me of my own place of birth on a tiny island, which has for centuries been a hub and the heart of Western European civilisation, but where classical Arabic is the native tongue—the island of Malta.

My mother is Maltese. I was born in Malta during the war, in the middle of a bombing raid. Once Malta, like Singapore, was part of the British Empire. Now, like Singapore, it is an independent and proud Republic. And there is an astonishing symmetry about this. I saw your flag. The flag of Malta is also red and white with a remarkable embellishment in the corner (the George Cross); only the Malta flag is the other way around. But isn't it extraordinary that

I should come all this way and there is this link? Now, both of those communities—both your community and the community of Malta, and, for that matter, the community in Britain—are fortunate: the rule of law prevails.

I am just going to repeat those words because they can be far too easily taken for granted. In all these three communities, the rule of law prevails. Let us pause and be grateful.

For today's purposes I shall identify one irreducible aspect of the rule of law, and it is this: an independent legal profession appearing as advocates before independent judges, in a relationship that is marked by mutual respect. That is my thesis.

Advocacy is not a matter of nationality. Every community throughout history has found its great advocates. You all remember Ancient Greece, Demosthenes teaching himself to be an advocate by going down to the seashore and speaking with pebbles in his mouth, above the sound of the waves, so as to make sure his voice could be heard in the assemblies in Athens where thousands of people would meet. He appreciated that the advocate's voice was a weapon that would be absolutely useless if it could not be heard.

But why I was asked to speak about advocacy baffles me. I once went to the House of Lords;[1] I am going to use words which no advocate should ever use but I did to myself then, and I say again, I went to the House of Lords with a cast-iron winner, on a point of statutory construction that I could not lose. My opponent stood up (he was the appellant) and within one minute, certainly no more, one of the learned Law Lords leant back in his chair, opened his arms wide, yawned slightly and said, 'When I was on the Law Commission, what we meant this statute to provide was ... ', then he went on with a meaning that was the precise opposite of what the statute actually said. In this way, I lost a certain winner, and I lost it five–nil. Within two years, the House of Lords, some of whom were the same members who had thrown me down five–nil, said that the decision was to be confined to its very narrow and particular facts.[2] In other words, they had been talking rubbish two years earlier. But on that occasion, I was not the advocate. So what it comes to is that the person addressing you today had lost a certain winner, which two years later the House of Lords said he should have won. What sort of advocate is that? So I went and became a judge. And having

[1] *R v Ayres* [1984] AC 447.
[2] *R v Cooke* [1986] AC 909.

established my absence of credentials, I think I'd better go home now. So I will. Cheerio!

Well, I have decided to stay. You have been kind to us; I'd better give the lecture. Just a word or two about context though: wherever I use the word 'his' or 'her', I always include 'she' in 'he', and 'court', where I use it, includes arbitration or tribunal. Although the programme refers to five separate headings to this lecture, I am dealing with them compendiously.

So let me come back to my basic thesis. Great damage to the administration can be done when there is an absence of mutual respect between the judge and each of the advocates. Of course, we all know, you all know, some advocates are better than others. You can't say this but I can—we also all know that some judges are better than others. That's the reality of life. We also know, do we not, that there are sometimes personality clashes between advocates, just as there are, on occasions, personality clashes between a judge and an advocate. Of course, all this is true; we are dealing with human beings. But the essential feature that I am driving at is this: there must be what I shall describe as institutional respect. Justice is better served when there is a degree of professional harmony between the legal profession and the judicial office holders.

Lord Bingham of Cornhill, one of my predecessors, went rather further than I would have gone, quoting an observation of the philosopher Piero Calamandrei:[3]

> The judicial process will have approached perfection when the discussion between judge and lawyer is as free and natural as that between persons, mutually respecting each other, who try to explain their points of view for the common good. Such an arrangement would be a loss for forensic oratory but a gain for justice.

Now you don't very often disagree with Lord Bingham; certainly I don't. But I respectfully disagree that there can be a discussion of the kind envisaged in this quotation. There are, of course, formalities within the processes of law that are essential to the orderly discharge of business. More importantly, whether in a criminal or a civil case, the advocate is acting for a client. The judge has to listen to rival cases and make up his mind between them. The role of the advocate is dual. The advocate has obligations to the court but it is the undoubted responsibility, as your Chief Justice has just indicated, of every advocate to advance the case of the client, however

---

[3] Piero Calamandrei, *The Eulogy of Judges* (Princeton, 1942).

unpopular it may be, in its best light and to the best of the advocate's ability. It is a process involving high-quality advocacy on both sides of the case—the prosecution and defence, plaintiff and defendant—which produces the answer required by truth and by law. That is the judicial objective.

So the crucial words in the quotation are 'mutual respect'. That is an expectation that the judge is entitled to have from every advocate, and every advocate is entitled to receive that from the judge: an expectation based on the clear understanding of each other's different responsibilities in the administration of justice, but not too cosy—not as cosy as Piero Calamandrei had implied.

Perhaps in the end he overlooked that litigation is not a symposium between distinguished commentators in a great academic institution, but a legal process that, so far as the parties involved are concerned, will involve answers that provide life-changing consequences such as the deprivation of liberty, punishment, financial disaster, the removal of children from one or other parent.

And as judges in this overall context, we have to remember that the simultaneous duties of the advocate—to the court and to the client—can create very difficult problems of professional judgement, and that, in any event, there is a principle of legal professional privilege, which means that the judge cannot know the whole story or the particular pressures under which the advocate is working. Before we seek to criticise the advocate, we need to remind ourselves not only of the problems that we can see for ourselves, but also, more importantly, that we probably do not have the fullest idea of all the problems the advocate is currently facing. As for the advocates, there are advocates, might I suggest with the greatest possible respect, who perhaps on occasion fail to appreciate that the answer to many cases is neither as straightforward nor as simple as the advocate on one side or the other thinks that it really must be. Perhaps all the advocates here will respect the problem identified by King James VI. It's a lecture in itself. But in the early part of his reign at the start of the seventeenth century, he decided that he should exercise a judicial function; after all, the king is the fountain of justice—so he would sit as a judge. He discovered what every judge in every jurisdiction very rapidly recognises. I quote:

> I could get on very well hearing one side only, but when both sides have been heard, by my soul, I know not which is right.[4]

---

[4] Quoted by John Hostettler in *Champions of the Rule of Law* (Hook, 2011).

Perhaps I can sum it up in this way: when I was in practice at the Bar, the worst sort of judge was the sort who knew all the answers. When I became a judge, I discovered that the worst sort of advocate was the one who thought I was completely stupid and thick. Both tended to bully rather than persuade. And if nothing else, advocacy is the art of persuasion. Notice it is an art, not a science. If there is one message I can give, and I do give it time and time again, it is that advocacy is a most personal, individual skill, with different forensic techniques, which have to marry up with and be consistent with the character and personality of the man or woman advancing the case. Let me give an example. If you need a major operation, say, to your leg, there will be a large number of surgeons specialising in the field, available to help and advise you. Each will have his or her own bedside manner. Each will help you before the operation with their bedside manner—or hopefully will help you with their bedside manner; most surgeons I have had to deal with have terrified me in advance but let's let that part pass—and then after the operation, assist you in its aftermath. Their bedside manner is a reflection of their personalities and characters. But that is not the operation. The actual process—and of course I am simplifying—of cutting into your leg and into the body and working away at the complex structures found there proceeds in a way that, allowing for the minutest variation in technique, is more or less identical. And it all takes place in private in an operating theatre.

Please don't misunderstand me. I am not, of course, referring to pioneering operations, to operations that go just that little further than ever before because medical science has advanced. That is a different matter. Nor am I decrying the care, skill and professionalism involved. But the operation itself is not personal in the sense that the personality and character of the surgeon have a direct impact on the processes. Now let us take advocacy. Identify any difficult criminal trial. You can find 10 good-quality advocates to defend the case or to prosecute it. Each of them, if they are any good, will study the papers, think about the case, reflect on how to approach it, and come to court and present the case as each of them judges best. And this is true, whether the case is criminal, civil, family, planning, tribunal, first instance, arbitration, appeal court, or any of the myriad of tribunals in front of which advocates may appear. There are many good advocates. But they do their cases differently.

To begin with, the advocate has to be comfortable with his own way of doing things, with his own personality, with his own style and attitude to the case, his way of dealing with the judge and the witnesses—all are reflective of his personality and character. And he is carrying out his responsibilities in public; indeed, just about everything an advocate does is done publicly. His client is not under anaesthetic; he is there, observing it all for himself. So are all his colleagues, and believe me, colleagues spot your professional forensic blunders as soon as you make them. I always used to hear a titter when I made mine; that was my learned friend making the most of it at my expense. I never tittered in reply, of course; you understand, I was a gentleman.

So the profession of advocates is working in public, in a constantly changing and fluid forensic situation over which, no matter how much preparation the advocate has made, he has no complete control, and indeed in which, if he is over prepared, he may stick too long to the script, clutching it like a child with a cuddly comforting toy. The best advocates respect and understand the imperative of the moment, they are alert to its needs and they are flexible to the changing momentum in a case. Sometimes these changes are very subtle, apparently tiny movements in the atmosphere. But you never quite know what answer will be given, or the way in which a piece of evidence that you anticipate will emerge. And you have to be ready for it. You—that is, the advocate—have to be ready for it. Fully prepared, but not over prepared. Anticipating the improbable, but unable to predict what form the improbability will actually take, but flexible enough to cope with whatever form it may take. This is why it is about you, about the individual, the human being who is wearing the robes of the advocates' profession.

These are the sorts of reasons why I describe advocacy as an art. The truth is that persuasion is an art. And I want to give you examples of persuasiveness that have absolutely nothing to do with the court process but illustrate it. I have used these examples before, and I make no apology for doing so again. I am going back to some research into 'D-Day' in 1944. I know you have your disaster history of the 1939 to 1945 war—so have we. This history may not be as vivid for you as it is for us in Europe, but in summary, Nazi Germany had overcome the entire continent of Europe, and to relieve Europe of the thrall of Nazism, an invasion of Europe was planned. It succeeded, but my goodness, it was a most remarkable success, and the opportunity for failure was enormous. But huge numbers of men were gathered together to sail across the Channel to die in order to save Europe. And here are the words of three different commanders to the men under their command. All of them, of course, united in fear and apprehension of what lay ahead, and all knowing that there were going to be many casualties.

The first commander said:

> Look to the left of you, look to the right of you, there is only going to be one of you left after the first week in Normandy.

The second said:

> What you are going through for the next few days, you won't change for a million dollars, but you won't want to go through it very often. For most of you, this is going to be the first time you are going into combat. Remember that you are going in to kill, or you will be killed.

The third pulled out a large commando knife, flourished it above his head and shouted:

> Before I see the dawn of another day, I am going to stick this knife into the heart of the meanest, dirtiest, filthiest Nazi in Europe.[5]

Let's pause. I am talking about persuasiveness. The first commander was factually correct. The casualties were going to be—and they were, in fact—horrific. The second tried to suggest, by way of inspiration, that they were all going into something of an adventure, a once-in-a-lifetime adventure. The third was utterly unrealistic because he knew, and the men he was addressing also knew, that the meanest, filthiest Nazi of all and all his close allies were nowhere near the coast of France, let alone the coast of Normandy, but bunkered down in Berlin.

Now relate this to the trial system. For a judge sitting on his own, perhaps the second of these efforts could have represented the most persuasive advocacy. For a trial by jury—still our system, although I know perfectly well not yours—perhaps the third. And for a court of appeal of three judges, perhaps the first was best. Each tribunal demands different advocacy techniques.

And returning to the quotations, the significant feature is that the words chosen by the three commanders were addressed to groups of men who were in identical positions of fear and apprehension, and the commanders themselves, when all is said and done, were young men too. They were crossing the Channel with their men, their risks were identical to their men and, no doubt, they were equally apprehensive and frightened. So what each of them said was a reflection of his own personality, of how he felt able to inspire them at a moment of profound responsibility, at a time when he was in deep apprehension. In other words, they used words that their personalities led them to use.

---

[5] All quoted by Antony Beevor in *D-Day: The Battle for Normandy* (Harmondsworth, 2010).

The advocate cannot be anything other than his own man. He cannot be somebody else. He cannot be trained to advocate in a way that is not a reflection of his/her own personality.

We are, as I emphasise, talking about persuasiveness; persuading the tribunal. The point of construction of tax law or a charter party is quite different from a criminal trial arising from a homicide, which may or may not have occurred in unreasonable or excessive self-defence. Of course, before any tribunal, there is nothing like standing still most of the time; keeping your hands out of your pockets always; not waving your hands about like a conductor who has the Valkyrie to conduct when Wagner is really blasting away. That is no good. The judge is looking at your hands and wondering when they are going to fall off. Look at the court, if possible, engage the eye of the judge, speak clearly, modulate your voice; remember your voice, your crucial weapon; modulate the speed at which you speak. Occasionally when you are losing the court's attention, just drop your voice, not shout.

And then as some of you are doing now, you lean forward to hear what on earth is coming next. Unless you have bored the court into somnolence, the judge will lean forward to try and pick up what you are saying, then you return to speak more loudly. If, of course, you bored the judge into narcolepsy, I'm afraid you're not going to be very good because you should have spotted that at an earlier stage. Silence—silence has its important moments. The pause can highlight that moment, and can add great emphasis; much greater than the shouted word.

May I respectfully suggest to you, particularly to the young among you: don't forget to listen. Listen for the hesitation in the evidence of the witness, listen for the issue that seems to be interesting judges in the Court of Appeal and with which your opponent seems to be having some difficulty. Listen to what your client is telling you. I found that out when I had clients who suffered major personal injuries, usually in car accidents in the days before you had a head-rest, whose spines were broken at the back of the neck. You wanted to hear what they were not telling you. You wanted to hear what the catastrophe had done to ruin their lives and which they were not prepared to talk about until they decided they could trust you.

Listen, listen. Don't bury your head in your papers. If you do, you will miss these important moments. And I repeat, don't forget the pause. If you have a good but slightly complex legal point, let it sink into the judge's mind. Give his mind time to work, to mull over, to chew over the complex point you're making. And if you are cross-examining a difficult witness who you have reason to believe and, your instructions tell you, is not telling the whole truth, a pause by you will often lead the witness to want to fill the silent gap, and in doing so, he may give something away that he might rather have kept hidden.

One of the great advocates of my early days was an Irishman called James Comyn. He was appearing before Lord Denning, famous in England, and I suspect throughout the world, for his concern of the man we describe as 'the little man'. Comyn was appearing in front of Denning in the Court of Appeal on an absolutely hopeless appeal for a tenant against the landlord, and he began knowing that there was very little law on his side, if any. These were his few opening words:

> In this case, I appear for an 87-year-old widow, whose husband was killed in the last war, and she'd lived in this house where he left her to go and fight for his country, ever since.

'Come, come, Mr Comyn,' said Denning, 'This is a court of law, not a court of sympathy.'

And there was then a long pause. Comyn did not break into it. He let it linger and linger, waiting for the moment. And then Denning filled the gap: 'How old did you say this poor old widow was?' That was fabulous advocacy—not rushed or forced, just fabulous advocacy.

In this pantheon of advocacy, I offer you two further stories. Just about every common law jurisdiction claims this first one for its own, and for all I know, you here in Singapore may claim it for yourselves. If you do, I apologise, but it always raises a laugh on these occasions.

The advocate for the appellant opened his case in this way: 'My Lords, in this appeal, there are three points. One is arguable, the second is not arguable, the third is overwhelming.' The court responded, in the calm, sensible, balanced way judges do, 'Well, why don't you tell us what your overwhelming point is?' 'Aha,' said the advocate, 'That is for your Lordships to discover.'

It is a great story. I love it, I tell it at every opportunity. Now why? There are here a large number of advocates of distinction and promise as well as many judges. And we all titter because that is a story in which the advocate has undoubtedly outsmarted the court. But to what end? Was this the best way to persuade the court to find for him and his client? The answer to that is 'no'. So it is a good story and it was bad advocacy.

Let me now come to a different approach in our Court of Appeal Criminal Division. This is a story from England. It was told to me by the Lord Justice of Appeal who was presiding in a very busy court on a very busy day when things had taken a long time, and the court was in a hurry to complete its list. And, in truth, it was rather a hopeless appeal against sentence. A young counsel stood up, and within minutes—I am sure your judges don't do this in Singapore, but in England I am afraid we do—the court was intervening, interrupting, 'Oh, what about so and so. Have you thought about this? Have you thought about that? Well, why not? Three bags full.' On and on they went at counsel, and suddenly—again the way it happens in England but, of course, not here in Singapore—they all had to pause for breath. So they did. The counsel said quietly, but firmly:

> My Lords, I know I am not going to get this aeroplane off the runway, but could you at least allow me to drive it out of the hangar?

Sublime advocacy. It stopped the court in its tracks. It made the court listen. And the Lord Justice involved told me, 'He was marvellous, he never did get his plane off the runway, because there was nothing in his case, but it was marvellous.' The court was put in its place, and the advocate was serving the interests of his client. He behaved courteously, firmly, respectfully, and with mutual respect, the court recognised that he was right and they were wrong, and from that moment on, treated him with the respect to which he was entitled.

One of problems of the modern world is that time has not expanded proportionately to the material being created in every aspect of our lives. I could go on about that, but I won't because there are still only 24 hours in a day, and 60 minutes in the hour. The legal system is affected in the same way as other parts of our society. Our trials—I am speaking now about England and Wales—are taking longer and longer, and the technique of advocacy has become much more diffuse. Certainly in England, modern advocacy doesn't seem to have much use for Rudyard Kipling's six wonderful friends. I read long transcripts of questioning of witnesses which, for a start, very rarely contain a question, which virtually never reflect his advice and which I strongly commend to you all:

> I keep six honest serving men
> (They taught me all I knew);
> Their names are What and Why and When
> and How and Where and Who.[6]

---

[6] Rudyard Kipling, 'I Keep Six Honest Serving Men' from 'The Elephant's Child', *Just So Stories* (first published 1902).

Virtually any question in any court can begin with those words, and for the purposes of cross-examination perhaps the word 'did' could be added to them and, of course, on occasion, the 'why' can become 'why not'. 'Did you so and so and so and so? Why?' Or, depending on the answer, 'Why not?' Much better than just charging in; ask the question beginning with those words.

We must be far more austere in our system, and I suspect throughout the world, in our use of time. There is a fairly simple principle, which I endeavour to encourage at home. And it is this: neither the advocates nor the parties to any form of litigation, whether criminal, civil, family or whatever, are entitled to take as much time as they like to develop their cases. Time is a resource. It is a finite resource. It is perhaps the most certainly finite of resources. Of course, both sides are entitled to a reasonable opportunity—a reasonable opportunity to deal with the case against them, to present and advance their own cases. But where a case takes longer than reasonably necessary, it presents a huge disadvantage to the litigants, in terms of nervous energy and costs, and it has a knock-on effect for all the other cases waiting to be heard.

Ultimately, it begins to undermine confidence in the administration of justice. I would like to think that throughout the common law world, we can persuade judges and advocates of this fundamental precept: that it is a confusion to regard the length of time taken by the case as any evidence of the quality of the advocacy involved. I quite understand that if a lawyer has to spend days, weeks or months preparing a case, he will think that the length of the trial should bear some proportionate length to the care, time and trouble he has taken. But surely the point of preparation includes work designed to exclude what doesn't really matter very much. If you have one authority from your Supreme Court that established the principle, why do you need 10 that make the same point in different language? I was, you say, too busy to write a short letter; the same with arguments.

Now one of the reasons why our cases take longer is, of course, the increasing length of our judgments. That's not the responsibility of the advocate. I am speaking now for us in Britain, but again I don't think the problem is confined to Britain. It may not apply here, but there are certainly common law countries where it does. Judgments are not academic disquisitions, nor are they arguments of counsel. Judgments are the legal principles which the court has applied after the advocate has identified the legal principle that he wishes the court to apply. If necessary, where an existing principle has been modified or extended, it sets out precisely why and the basis for the modification or extension. The judgment explains to both sides who has won and lost, and why. And just because the court has chosen not to deal expressly with the endless elaborations of argument, or indeed every submission advanced or every authority referred to by one side or another, it does not mean that the court has ignored them. If they are not referred to in the judgment, it is because the judge has decided that they have no bearing on the ultimate outcome. Don't be offended if your lengthy argument produces a two-paragraph judgment; it is not personal.

Much the same point indeed perhaps arises even more strongly with the written arguments, which in England we call the skeleton argument. This is a remarkable change to the common law tradition, which is founded on orality. Now let's look at that as a form of advocacy. This is the written persuasion. The pen, or nowadays the modern technology—a computer, or modern technology in different forms—being used to produce something for the judge to see and read, rather than the voice being used for the judge to hear. I am not sure I dare say this but I am going to. Whichever you use, the advocate needs to engage the brain.

For these written arguments have developed their own technique; there is much more flesh on the skeleton than there ever used to be. Obviously, when a judge reads a prepared written argument, he will be impressed. Let me tell you about me. I read the appellant's written argument. By the time I turn the last page, I think, 'Well, he's going to win. Let's go, that's it.' It is obvious and clear. But then I am a fair-minded judge and I think, 'Well, I'd better read the other side's case.' And I read the written argument for the respondent. When I finish reading that, I think, 'Wow, he's got to win.' So it is advocacy. However, like oral advocacy, the art of preparing a written submission is more subtle than it looks. Mad thought! The document should be prepared for the purposes of the court. It is the court that is being persuaded to help the judge to find for your client. Sometimes I believe—I have said this in England and I have never had anybody challenge me—that in England these arguments are written for the client, so that the client can think that the big fat fee he is paying for the advocate is fully justified. And so they go on and on and on. Because if you just write a skeleton argument saying the appellant should win because the judge has not applied the rule in *Foss v Harbottle*,[7] he'll wonder why he was paying you

---

[7] (1843) 67 ER 189.

all those thousands of pounds. Sometimes in the cases of countries with divided professions, they are written to impress the solicitor who is instructing the advocate. The problem therefore can sometimes be a lack of focus. Please allow me to repeat myself. The objective is to persuade the court, not to impress anyone else. I am also going to enjoy saying this: whether you like it or not (I am looking at the advocates in the hall), judges are just ordinary human beings. And you know something about ordinary human beings? They tend to listen more carefully and follow more closely the advocate who seems to them to have thought carefully about his submission and to advance submissions with real weight, rather than those that look as though they are grandstanding to somebody else.

The written submission has had some unexpected consequences. Some advocates who are masters of the written submission are not as good when it comes to oral presentation. An increasing habit we have—and I do suggest to you that you don't allow it to develop here—is the habit of the advocate reading his submission. And this habit can lead to the destruction of the oral process. Your voice can command attention, it is your weapon; but it can also cause boredom. Your PowerPoint presentation may reveal that you're fantastically adept with modern technology, but make sure it doesn't diminish your advocacy.

Let me offer this to you:

> Do your Lordships have my skeleton argument? You do? I thank you so much. I am looking at paragraph, no … sorry, so sorry My Lord, paragraph 47. Erm, does Your Lordship have it [to the second judge] … No, paragraph 47. Right. 'Fourscore and seven years ago, our fathers brought forth on this continent a new nation, conceived in liberty and dedicated to the propositions all men are created …' Am I going too fast for your Lordships—oh I am going too slowly. I am so sorry, I'll move on. 'Now we are engaged in a great civil war, we've come to dedicate a proportion of that field to the final resting place for those who gave their lives …'

And so, one of the great speeches of history can be destroyed by an advocate reading his submission. Would any of you listen to any of that? Would Abraham Lincoln have ever, ever been known of in that context if he had delivered his speech in Gettysburg in that way? Of course not.

Two brilliantly written arguments, and the judge does not know which side is right. What's the advocate to do? One of them must be wrong. One of the arguments must be flawed. The advocate's responsibility is to identify the flaw, to reveal the leap in a logic that slides over the difficulty in the argument. Now this ability in the advocate to deal with issues that trouble the court in the context of written submissions is much harder than it looks. It requires at least as much preparation as the written argument. And I want to offer one piece of advice that many advocates at home do not seem to have mastered. I suspect it's something to do with training. Of course, you will think about how to advance your own case. That is elementary. Sometimes you get so enmeshed in this part of the process that you fail to think through where your own case is at its weakest, and where your opponent's is at its strongest. Concentrate on those issues. Be ready with the answer at the hearing. When I was at the Bar, I asked myself this question before going into court. I regret that I wasn't able to find an answer to this particular question when I went to the House of Lords and lost five–nil. Because here's the question: 'If I were the judge in this case, what would I ask me?' It is a very salutary lesson. Your own case, brilliant, frills, whizbangs and all, but what about the weakness in it? What's the judge going to ask me to deal with? He knows all the good points.

The average advocate can deal with all the points in his own case and advance them. The best advocates have thought about and are ready to deal with and address the aspects of their opponent's case at its strongest, and their own case where it is weak and problematic. This is integral, if I may say so, to the preparation and quality of preparation of every argument, whether written or oral.

In the end, however one dresses it up, we are, are we not, in the judicial process, engaged in doing justice according to law. The quality of this process is heavily dependent on the quality of the advocates who appear before us in our courts. It really is as simple as that. The importance of the role of the advocate in contemporary systems is completely undiminished. It is not one jot less important now than it used to be. Techniques may have changed, with modern technology, modern methods, the use of the PowerPoint and so on. The modern world, with all the dramatic, revolutionary changes with which we are becoming familiar, has not altered these principles. Indeed, in some respects, the importance of the quality of the advocates has been enhanced, not least because the law has become so very much more complicated. But important as all this is, the basic techniques of persuasion, flexibility, of alertness to the moment, and most of all, of the advocate being the advocate that his or her personality and character makes them, is unchanged. And 70 years later, any advocate will continue to recognise the reality of the observation of Justice Jackson of the US Supreme Court, who said that when he was in practice as an advocate, he had three arguments ready for every court appearance. Now that sounds too good to be true, until he goes on to say that the three were these:

> First, came the one that I planned—as I thought, logical, coherent, complete. Second, was the one actually presented—interrupted, incoherent, disjointed, disappointing. The third was the utterly devastating argument that I thought of after going to bed that night.

I must come to an end, but before I do, I hope that some of the more mature members of this audience will allow me briefly to address the younger members of the audience.

I was an advocate for 25 years. I absolutely loved that profession. The daily combination of responsibility and stimulation meant that some days, of course, were good; things went well. Some days things didn't go so well and maybe you learnt a lesson. But I never remember a single dull day. I don't remember driving off to court without feeling the adrenalin start to run. I made lifelong friendships with those who were my opponents, competing for work with me. And however their capabilities varied—some were outstandingly wonderful and some were less good, with only one exception that I have never forgotten and I will take with me to my grave—every single one was a man or woman of personal integrity. Isn't that a wonderful way to spend your life, with such people around you, doing such work?

The advocacy profession had never been easy. But nothing that is easy has ever been worth very much. And you cannot succeed in anything unless you try and you put your whole heart and soul into it. Please, if you want to be an advocate, don't be put off by the difficulties. I am perfectly well aware of them, and perfectly well aware of them at home. It has always been very difficult to get started. It is very difficult to maintain a practice; people are choosy.

But in the end, in life, you have to live with yourself. Now imagine that you backed off something you really want to do. You have to live with yourself for the next 50 years or so. You have to live with, 'I didn't have the guts.' Imagine if you do your best and it doesn't work out. 'Well, I gave it my best shot.' And perhaps no less important for those of you for whom it works and on whom luck has shone, and if you do succeed—there will be times when the luck has shone on you and not on somebody else who is competing with you for the same work—do remain humble. It is not all down to you. Luck is involved. And perhaps I'd better end by saying good luck to all of you.

Trial by Jury

This lecture was delivered in Belfast in November 2010 as the Judicial Studies Board Lecture. We can become romantic and sentimental about trial by jury, but, as I emphasise at the outset of this lecture, the principle is immensely precious. Over the centuries the system of trial by jury has evolved. For example, by contrast with earlier days, everyone (including every woman) on the electoral roll is eligible for jury service. So, as the world changes, if the jury system is to survive, it must address the changing world. Modern technology, and the new methods of communication, will impact on the jury system as it will on just about every other aspect of life. This lecture sought to address some of the issues.

L OVELY AS IT is to be here with you, you did not invite me to take up your time with a catalogue of good jury stories extolling the virtues of trial by jury, or indeed reminding ourselves of the moments when perhaps it could politely be said that the jury was taking an idiosyncratic view of a case, or a piece of the evidence, or indeed for that matter of the trial judge.

My starting point is simple. Everything in my own personal career, both at the Bar and then on the Bench, has served to demonstrate the value of our jury system, and the reason for its pre-eminence in our constitutional arrangements for the administration of criminal justice. The jury system ensures that in our jurisdiction no one can be convicted of a serious crime or subjected to a lengthy term of imprisonment unless he has admitted his guilt in open and public court, or a body of his fellow citizens has considered the evidence and satisfied themselves on the basis of that evidence that they are sure of his guilt.

None of this is to say that the jury system cannot be subverted, and in this jurisdiction above all, you need no reminder from me of how the jury system can be subverted. Subversion can be generic, and it can be individual. But the fact that remedies have to be found for subversion does not alter the essential reality that the jury system has a resonance for us, and indeed for every common law system which has embraced it, which it is difficult to underestimate and unwise to ignore.

That is not to say that different systems of trial are unfair or lack legitimacy. After all, in our jurisdiction the overwhelming majority of criminal cases are decided by lay magistrates. In your jurisdiction, the Diplock Courts have been, and are, regarded as a model of how a trial of serious offences can take place without a jury, and that such a process provides a fair trial and a reasoned judgment explaining the reasons for the verdict. It is perhaps worth underlining the tribute paid by Lord Trimble to the judiciary in this jurisdiction in September 2007 when, in the House of Lords, in the context of an expression of what he described as distaste for non-jury trials, he said:

> I do not share that approach at all. In this debate, it is appropriate that we record our appreciation of the judges in Northern Ireland who, during the past 30 years, have sat in Diplock courts in very difficult circumstances. Despite the difficulties and dangers they have managed during that time to achieve a good result. That must be said.[1]

And much of the basis for support for the jury system is just factually wrong. For example, Magna Carta is said to have established the right. You cannot forget—well, some of you will not remember—the great moment when Tony Hancock was replicating the juryman in the famous *Twelve Angry Men* film:

> Think of your roots,
> Think of your history.
> Magna Carta, did she die in vain?

It may be bad history, but in the context of criminal justice in very many ways perception is a fact, a real fact, and perceptions matter hugely.

It is not an accident that for very many years now there has been a widespread belief, crossing all political and social lines, that from the time when the jury system ceased to be trial by immediate neighbours who would know the facts, and the responsibility for the verdict was vested in the jury as a body examining the evidence, the system has helped to ensure the administration of justice as well as the preservation of civil liberties. As long ago as 1618 the Great Charter for Virginia, drafted by Sir Edwin Sandys, established the rights of settlers in the new colonies and the plantations, and their children, and provided guarantees for trial by jury. And it was the removal of the right to trial by jury in the Stamp Act in 1765 that triggered the concerns of those then described as the colonists in the

---

[1] Justice and Security (Northern Ireland) Bill, 20 February 2007.

United States of America. What I am driving at is that we must not assume that our national devotion to the principle of trial by jury is newly minted.

In his remarkable and outstanding *Review of the Criminal Courts of England and Wales*, published in October 2001, my friend Robin Auld (Lord Justice Auld) questioned the ability of jurors to acquit 'in defiance of the law and disregard of their oath'. This, he argued, was more than illogical, rather it was a 'blatant affront to the legal process'. The role of the jury was to find the facts as they are and apply the law to those facts, not to substitute 'their view of the propriety of the law for that of Parliament or its enforcement for that of its appointed executive, still less on what may be irrational, secret and unchallengeable grounds'.

Of course, in one sense Robin is absolutely right. Jurors should apply the law in accordance with the directions of the judge. As you would expect with Robin, he makes a number of telling points. What, for example, about prejudices in the jury room that may lead to perverse acquittals, for example in a sexual offence where a number of misconceptions relating to the issue of consent to sexual activity tended to reflect a dangerous combination of ignorance and prejudice which deprived the victim of justice?

I see all that; nevertheless the jury system does provide a safeguard against oppression and dictatorship. It is not a guarantee, because of course a dangerous dictatorship—and all dictatorships are dangerous—could as easily pervert our constitutional arrangements as they could our democratic principles, by ensuring that although jury trial was preserved, juries would be 'packed' with malleable and frightened individuals. All that is true. But even in a democracy, it is possible for the legislature to create potentially oppressive and unjust criminal laws. The very fact that such laws will be exposed to the scrutiny of a jury in the event of a prosecution may—and for my own purposes 'may' is enough—cause the legislature to pause and reflect on whether it is wise to enact such a law. It is one small aspect of the very subtle relationships which govern the operation of our society and the well-being of the community.

I want to address three specific questions relating to jury trial and the impact of modern technology which I believe need to be addressed, and which I do not think have yet been sufficiently addressed.

I have spoken publicly on this subject, but not here, and in any event my thinking on the subject has been developing, in truth, as technology itself has developed.

(1) The jury system depends on 12 good citizens and true, selected at random, coming to court and listening to the case. 'Listen' is a crucial word, although increasingly jurors are also required to assimilate documents. But we all know that orality, the spoken word, is at the heart of the system. Witnesses are asked questions which they answer. Counsel address the jury. Judges give directions, increasingly summarised in writing, in the form of guides to verdict, and so on, but essentially the process is an oral one.

Let me now consider my grandchildren. Not perhaps the youngest two, but the teenagers. They are technologically proficient. Much of their schoolwork is done by absorbing information from machines. They consult and refer to the internet. When they do so they are not listening. They do not, as we did, sit in class for 40 minutes listening to the masters and mistresses providing us with information. They are provided with information in written form, which they assimilate into their own technology.

Now, what this form of education lacks is training in the ability to sit still and listen, and I emphasise, listen and think, I repeat, listen and think simultaneously, for prolonged periods. Yet that is an essential requirement for every juror.

But, assume they are naturally gifted with this ability, that they can learn it from life as life goes on (although in truth the lives that they will lead will be even more technology based than their current days at school). How long before they seek for all the evidential questions on which they have to make up their minds to be provided in ways which adopt modern technology? And here I am speaking not of today, but of 10 or 20 years' time, and none of us need much reminder of the speed with which technology has been developing. Now, of course, in our current processes we have assimilated modern technology, and in major trials much material is made available to jurors on screens. But in the end, what will they make of a process which becomes screen and paper and illustration and mockup when, as is so often the case, the task of the fact finder is to decide where the truth lies when two witnesses are telling dramatically different stories? Was the child indecently assaulted, or is it a fabrication? Was the sexual activity consensual, or not? And we all know—do we not—of cases which on paper look very strong against the defendant, which as the trial unfolds, through oral testimony and cross-examination, demonstrate that the entire prosecution case was structured on paper, and is no stronger than paper.

(2) Next there is the problem of the jury consulting the internet. You all know of the kinds of directions that we give. They are in

truth no more than a development of what we have always said to jurors about discussing the case with others, and the reasons why that should not happen. As you all know, but they may not appreciate, this is to do with the fairness of the trial, and the preservation of the principle that the trial must be fair. So we give clear directions to the jury that they should not consult the internet. Sometimes, I am told, they find this difficult to believe. Not least because they are so accustomed to looking at the internet. Huge numbers of people visit the internet to discover whether the symptoms from which they are suffering may be an indication of a profound disease. The search for information is genuine. Its object is to discover answers. So if you have such a habit in the context of your health, or that of your family, you will inevitably be tempted to consult the internet to see if you can get further assistance in the achievement of the difficult task of doing justice in the trial in which you are participating.

We have recently suggested that in the light of the research by Professor Cheryl Thomas,[2] who came to speak to you some months ago, the collective responsibility of the jury extends to the good behaviour of each member of the jury. Maybe we must go much further.

It is of particular concern that her research suggested that jurors are developing the habit of looking on the internet for information about the case they are trying. Professor Thomas asked whether the jurors were just looking for information, or whether they then went on and discussed the case on social networking sites. It is significant that this search for information appears to be greater in high-profile cases than in, if I may call them so, standard cases. In high-profile cases something like one in four said they had seen information on the internet, although, interestingly enough, only 12%—one in eight—said they actually looked for it. In the more standard cases, 13% said they saw the information, although only 5% admitted to looking. One wonders at the number of times any jury man or woman can *accidentally* have stumbled across information about the case they are trying when using the internet for other purposes. What we do not know is how far this search or innocent accidental stumbling across information went, or how the technology was used, if at all. But all her research is consistent with the fact that from time to time judges receive information which shows that a juror has consulted the internet. Once received, this information has to be investigated, and an investigation involves an examination

---

[2] *Are Juries Fair?*, Ministry of Justice Research Series (London, 2010).

of the question whether an individual juror did so, and the extent to which the jury as a whole may have been contaminated.

At present I am aware of a case where allegations of rape and serious sexual activity involving middle-aged women when they were very young girls and a defendant who was adamantly denying the allegations was brought to an end when the judge felt obliged to discharge the jury because of internet research.

The case demonstrates one of the fundamental problems. This trial will have to start again. This is not a mere formality. A retrial is not a non-event. Those women will have to give their stories in public, again. The defendant, too, will have to give his evidence again and then await the outcome of the trial. It is arguable—and until I hear the argument I obviously have an open mind, but it is at least arguable—that for a juror to examine the internet for information relating to the case is a contempt of court, and a criminal contempt. If it is, and if nevertheless jurors continue to ignore the directions given by judges at the outset of the case that they should not consult the internet, one consequence of the use—or rather misuse—of modern technology in the course of the trial would be that they may be liable to a finding of contempt of court, and indeed a sentence.

Now I suspect that this is a problem which we have not fully addressed until now, and that is why I am raising it with you for your consideration, and for a judicial discussion of these issues. What we seem to do at the moment is assume that the occasions when jurors go on the internet for information are rare indeed. It is therefore easy to brush them aside as odd moments of aberration. I wonder whether we will still be thinking that a year or two from now. Professor Thomas suggests that we should be thinking of it immediately. I respectfully agree.

I should just add that I must record my entire disagreement with the view of the former Director of Public Prosecutions in England and Wales, now Lord MacDonald, that judges are 'giving up trying to stop jurors using Google, Facebook and Twitter to access potentially false and prejudicial' information about defendants. He is reported as suggesting that a trial should not be invalidated if jurors are found to have conducted online research while a case is in progress. The thesis, as reported in the *Guardian* newspaper,[3] is that we should expect jurors to follow directions to try the case on the evidence, but to assume that there will be occasions when online research will take place, and that this should not 'invalidate a trial'.

[3] 4 October 2010.

Where he and I are agreed is that this is an issue of great sensitivity. I would find it wholly unacceptable to create a system in which every juror, once sworn, had somehow to allow access to his or her private systems, so as to enable some authority (which authority?) to make sure that the internet was not consulted. In any event, that would be pretty pointless, because they could go to an internet café if they were so minded. But I do believe that if it is not addressed, the misuse of the internet represents a threat to the jury system, which depends, and rightly depends, on evidence provided in court which the defendant can hear and if necessary challenge. He is not to be convicted on the basis of material which from his point of view is secret material—not only secret material, which is bad enough, but material which may be inaccurate and could also be false. Sight of such material will create conscious—or, perhaps more pernicious, unconscious—prejudice. In any event it is fundamental that the defendant should be able to address it. And we must not assume that this prohibition against the misuse of the internet is designed only for the protection of defendants. The victim of an alleged crime is equally entitled to a completely fair trial. All of us, and the community as a whole which is represented by the 12 members of the jury, have an interest in ensuring that juries return verdicts which are true to the evidence produced in court. If there is to be a system of open justice—and how can anyone brought up in our traditions envisage criminal proceedings behind closed doors—what has to be 'open' is the evidence on which the verdict depends. So we cannot accept that the use of the internet, or rather its misuse, should be acknowledged, and treated as an ineradicable fact of life, or that a Nelsonian blind eye should be turned to it or the possibility that it is happening.

I have to be blunt about this, but in my view, if the jury system is to survive as the system for a fair trial in which we all believe and which we all support, the misuse of the internet by jurors must stop. And I think we must spell this out to them yet more clearly. It must be provided in the information received by every potential juror. It must be reflected in the video which jurors see before they start a trial. Judges must continue to direct juries in unequivocal terms from the very outset of the trial. And I should like the notice in jury rooms which identifies potential contempt of court arising from discussions outside the jury room of their debates, to be extended to any form of reference to the internet.

My final observation in this context is this. To date, the way in which we have addressed these problems is, where necessary, to discharge the juror, or where the jury as a whole has been contaminated as a result of what an individual juror has done, to discharge the whole jury. But this is a luxury. And I am not focusing exclusively on the cost of a trial, although given our current financial circumstances, the cost of the trial actually matters. I am focusing on the problem of an increased number of retrials, or more than one trial leading to a verdict, and in every such case, quite apart from the financial cost, the cost of delays to other cases which need to be tried, whether for the sake of the witnesses and victims or the defendants, some of whom will be in custody, and ultimately for the sake of the witnesses, victims and defendants of the case where the jury has to be discharged and a fresh trial start. These are significant costs. They cannot be counted in pound notes, but as you know, the emotional trauma will be considerable. And let me offer a pertinent example.

The allegation is that a girl of 12 has been badly molested sexually. The problem recurs: is the best course of action immediate treatment and psychiatric attention to enable the child to come to terms with how to live with the experience? Or is the primary need for the protection of society that a man who has perpetrated such an offence should be tried as quickly as possible, and if the evidence is sufficient, convicted and sentenced? Sometimes we know that the process of rehabilitation for the victim can make it easier for the offender to escape justice. This audience does not need me to expand on why. Which is in the public interest? How can the public interest be improved if the processes which are already subject to delay, are subjected to the further delay and trauma of retrials?

That these risks are not merely theoretical is demonstrated by *Thakrar*,[4] where the search of the internet by a member of the jury provided him with apparent information about the defendant's previous convictions, which in fact was completely false, and he conveyed this information to the other members of the jury. They remained silent until after the defendant had given evidence. This information only came to light because the jurors asked a question of the judge about why they had heard nothing about those convictions. If the question had not been asked, the defendant might have been convicted on a wholly false basis, and no one would have been any the wiser.

In the end the issue for discussion is whether, in the light of the latest research, we have to be yet more emphatic against the use of the internet, and whether nowadays the direction to the jury should be backed up with an express warning that breach of the order might

---

[4] *R v Thakrar* [2008] EWCA Crim 2359.

constitute a contempt of court, and whether one day it may become necessary to decide if it is indeed a contempt, and then to treat it with the seriousness it requires, depending on the consequences to the ongoing trial.

(3) May I come to a third consideration to which modern technology gives rise. Its importance to the jury system is not immediately obvious, and its ramifications are much wider. The impact of Twitter and other social media, as they are called, on the criminal courts has hardly yet arisen for consideration. You all know what Twitter is. Twitter may be accessed from any device which is internet enabled with the correct software, and most modern mobile phones are compatible with Twitter. Of course the court has jurisdiction to regulate all behaviour in court, and the ambit of the law of contempt of court extends to the internet, unofficial blogs, emails and websites and so on. That, however, begs the question of whether and if so what form of regulation is appropriate. Twitter technology has come into existence long after the law of contempt and reporting of proceedings was developed or enacted. It involves an engagement between the legal processes and live text-based broadcasts directly from within the courtroom. For the purposes of this lecture—and I emphasise that I am not giving legal advice to anyone—I could not find a statutory prohibition on text-based remote transmission of material from a courtroom, whether transmitted by an internet-enabled mobile phone, or a laptop computer, or in any other way. Yet section 9 of the 1981 Contempt of Court Act prohibits the use in court of any tape recorder or other instrument for recording sound, except with the leave of the court. Does this extend to Twitter? Arguably, at any rate, no. But should it? This question has yet to be decided, and the decision may have a considerable impact on our processes.

How is the principle of open justice compatible with preventing an ongoing, live, text-based dialogue being sent to the outside world from a courtroom? If a reporter or member of the public is permitted to write notes to himself or herself in court, and then 'file them' from a telephone outside the court, what is the qualitative difference if they are permitted to do so when sitting in court by, say, sending a email? If it is possible to file a story via email from a laptop in court, then why is Twitter any different? On the other hand tape-recordings are prohibited by statute. Why is Twitter in the form of text-based transmission of material from court any different?

These are, as I say, questions for thought. In considering them we have to remember that 'tweets' stay on the internet, and allowing court-based tweeting is likely to increase the potential for prejudicial material regarding the defendant or a witness becoming available on the internet. Thus, it will be possible for tweets originating from an earlier trial involving a defendant, when a retrial has been ordered, to be retrieved by a mischievous juror—or indeed a journalist—in the context of the second trial. And the next problem is that even if a tweet originating in the courtroom itself may indeed be a 'fair and accurate' observation or report, the responses of other users of the Twitter system may not be. The publication of a defendant's previous convictions, or for that matter a victim's previous convictions, when the judge has ruled them inadmissible provides a classic example. There is no way for us to control these responses, so that gives rise to questions of how to limit the potential damage to trials and their fairness.

My instinctive response is that the criminal trial process must always be open. I use the word 'instinctive', but in truth it is deeper than that; it is visceral. But not all tweeting comes from within the court. It is, I have no doubt, all too easy for campaigners for one cause or another, to bombard the system with tweets which are intended to seek to influence the outcome of the hearing. Some of it will be well meaning, and some pernicious: if it is a campaign, it is unlikely to be balanced, and more likely to be prejudicial to one side or the other.

We cannot stop people tweeting, but if jurors look at such material, the risks to the fairness of the trial will be very serious, and ultimately the openness of the trial process, on which we all rely, would be damaged.

We must always welcome new technology. When jury trials began there was no electricity; there were no typewriters; people came to court by foot or on horseback. We now use technology for many purposes, to the public advantage. We do turn on lights; we even put some heating into the building. So judges are not antediluvian. We welcome advances in technology, provided that we are its masters, and it is our tool and servant. But we need to examine the impact on our jury system with great care, and with an increasing need for urgency, just because technology is developing at an astonishing rate.

Can I bring these thoughts to a conclusion. We must not assume that we would always and in every circumstance discharge the jury following information that the internet has been used. In *R v Thompson and Others*[5] we suggested that the approach should be as follows:

> Just as it would in any other instance where it was satisfied that extraneous material had been introduced, the approach of this court is to make inquiries into the material. If, on examination, this material strikes at the fairness of the trial, because the jury has considered material adverse to the defendant with which he has had no or no proper opportunity to deal, the conviction is likely to be unsafe ... If the material does not affect the safety of the conviction, the appeal will fail.

This, of course, can only apply after conviction, not before. We have no means of knowing in the event of an acquittal whether it was unfair because the jury or a juror had made inquiries into material adverse to the prosecution's case or the prosecution witnesses which would have struck at the fairness of the trial.

In *Thompson* we also offered suggestions as to the way in which jurors should be directed to approach the internet, recognising that although the internet was part of their daily lives, the case which they were trying should not be researched on the internet, or discussed on the internet on social networking sites, any more than it should be researched with, or discussed amongst, friends or family, and for the same reason. The result might affect their decision, whether consciously or unconsciously, so that neither side at trial would know the considerations which might be entering into their deliberations and would therefore not be able to address submissions about it.

> This would represent a departure from the basic principle which requires that the defendant be tried on the evidence admitted and heard by them in court.

We recommended a direction on which the principle is explained in terms which do not merely imply that the judge is making a polite request, but which make it clear that he is giving an order necessary for the fair conduct of the trial. Such a direction will naturally fall to be given at the outset of the trial, in the same way as the direction as to the collective responsibility addressed earlier in the judgment.

... *[The lecture went on to address the decision of the Grand Chamber of the European Court of Human Rights in* Taxquet v Belgium*]*[6] ...

---

[5] [2011] 1 WLR 200.
[6] [2010] ECHR 1806.

The Belgian government asked for the issues to be re-heard by the Grand Chamber. The re-hearing took place in October 2009. As I have said, the judgment was delivered today, and I have tried to absorb it during the flight over to Belfast ...

My immediate impression is that the Grand Chamber has understood the essential features of the jury system as it operates in our jurisdiction and, for that matter, in the Republic, with whom I know you are about to have an exchange of views. Indeed if I may say so, the arguments advanced on behalf of Ireland before the Grand Chamber were extremely powerful, beginning with the proposition that this was the method of trial which defendants and the public actually wanted. What seems to me to be clear from the judgment is that a properly structured summing up followed by a verdict of the jury, which is confined to the verdict, provide an ample understanding to the defendant, and to the public, of the reasons why the jury decided that the case against the defendant has been proved. What is more, there is nothing in the judgment of the Grand Chamber which suggests that it is a necessary step to achieving the objective that the directions in the summing up must be reduced to writing. Adequate oral directions are as acceptable as adequate written directions.

In short, the decision of the Grand Chamber is that within our jury system it does not follow that the verdicts given by juries are unreasoned, or that the defendant is ignorant of the reasons. This, it seems to me on proper analysis, is a judgment which endorses our system of trial by jury in the context of the performance by the judge of his well understood responsibilities, and the ability of the Court of Appeal Criminal Division to examine every aspect of this performance.

Our trial process is trial by an independent and impartial judge as well as an independent and impartial jury. You do not need me to set out the responsibilities of the judge. But in the context we are considering the judge has a number of obligations which include ensuring that admissible evidence only is deployed before the jury, and that even if the evidence is admissible in law, if its prejudicial effect outweighs its probative value, it should be excluded. He must also ensure that cases do not proceed to the jury where a reasonable jury could not properly convict. But all that pales into insignificance compared to the summing up. Directions of law are given. The facts are summarised. The summary of the facts includes identification of the issues, and the way in which the decisions reached by the jury on fact dovetail with the directions of law. In reality nowadays, as

Lord Justice Hooper aptly put it in a recent lecture, the summing up can be seen as a 'judgment ... on the central issues in dispute'.[7]

* * *

Since this lecture was given, the use of Twitter from court by journalists has been addressed (*Practice Guidance (Court Proceedings: Live Text-Based Communications) (No 2)* [2012] 1 WLR). In *Attorney General v Fraill* [2011] 2 Crim App R 271 and *Attorney General v Dallas* [2012] 1 WLR 991 the Divisional Court exercised its powers vis-a-vis contempt of court in relation to jurors who had conducted improper communications or research in defiance of express judicial orders. In an important paper from the Law Commission, *Contempt of Court (1): Juror Misconduct and Internet Publications* [2013] Law Com No 340, recommendations relating to modern media and juror misconduct as part of the general law relating to contempt of court were addressed. The issues raised in this lecture continued to resonate, and sections 68–77 of the Criminal Justice and Courts Act 2015 implemented many, but not all, of the recommendations of the Law Commission.

---

[7] Lecture in Middle Temple Hall, October 2010.

Half a Century of Change:
The Evidence of Child Victims

This was the first Toulmin Lecture in Law & Psychiatry, given in memory of His Honour Judge John Toulmin QC at King's College London in March 2013.

JOHN TOULMIN WAS my friend. He was a man who had many friends. Their vast number did not diminish the depth of friendship enjoyed by each and every one of us. His friends came from all over the world. Friendship with him knew no bounds of distance or nationality or race. Among many institutions and organisations which enjoyed his support, he gave distinguished service to King's College London. I am indebted to the College, but, if I may say so, even more to Carolyn Toulmin for doing me the honour of inviting me to give the first lecture in celebration of the memory of a distinguished jurist and a fine man.

I have chosen to use the occasion to offer some reflections on the way in which the approach to the evidence of children, and in particular children who are the victims of crime, has changed during the last 50 or so years since John and I were called to the Bar. 'Children' is used broadly, to cover children who are very small and teenagers too—all separate individuals, of course. And perhaps I should add that the focus of this lecture is the child victim of crime, usually sexual crime, but sometimes violent crime and sometimes neglect.

Perhaps I may be allowed to begin by repeating thoughts I have expressed on earlier occasions. Whether you approach the issue from the traditional common law 'adversarial' process, or the equally traditional continental 'inquisitorial' process (and that is a lecture in itself), justice cannot be done without witnesses. In Deuteronomy there is a passionate call for 'heaven and earth to witness against you this day if you did evil in the sight of God'. Heaven and earth now includes all kinds of modern technology, including, for example, CCTV cameras and DNA profiling, both sources of evidence which were inconceivable in biblical times. There will be advances in technology which, like the prophet who wrote Deuteronomy, we have not begun to contemplate; but, for the present and the immediate future certainly, for justice to be done, accurate and honest witnesses are required.

It is not an accident that one of the Ten Commandments prohibits the bearing of false witness. As drafted, it prohibits the false allegation. No one should be criminalised by falsehood.

We do all remember the precise wording of the seventh Commandment, don't we? Thou shalt not bear false witness 'against', or, as it is sometimes written, 'on', thy neighbour. Read like a statute it does not expressly prohibit the bearing of false witness by the false denial of a truthful allegation. But surely, if not within the express language of the Commandment, it should follow by necessary implication. But does it? There is a problem here. For the guilty defendant, and there are very few guilty defendants of any smattering of acuity who do not know that they are guilty of molesting a child, the truth is not always the objective. Many plead 'not guilty' when they know perfectly well that they are. For such a defendant the objective is that the truth should not emerge. So, the administration of justice requires honest and accurate witnesses to secure the conviction of the guilty defendant, but the guilty defendant has no corresponding obligation to be honest and accurate. He should be—of course, he should be, but his objective is to escape justice.

Yet, and it is a very important yet, not every defendant is guilty. An innocent defendant does want the truth to emerge. False allegations are sometimes made. Sometimes indeed they are made by children. We cannot avoid that stark reality. The defendant is deemed to be innocent until proved guilty. There can be no compromise with that principle, and when we examine the myriad of problems attached to the evidence of the child victims of crime, we cannot, even by implication, compromise with that principle. The object of any reforms and improvements in our processes is not directed to 'getting the defendant convicted', but to doing the best we can to make sure that the guilty defendant, and only the guilty defendant, is convicted.

So our trial processes when John and I started in practice, and our trial processes today have this much, if not a great deal more, in common. They must cater for the truthful and the untruthful child witness and the guilty and the innocent defendant. And the processes mean that those vested with responsibilities for making these decisions do not know in advance which is which. This constant collision of crucial interests has always been, and I believe will inevitably always continue to be, integral to any system for the administration of criminal justice, and each generation is always seeking to do its best to reconcile the divergent interests.

And there is a separate, crucial problem about any process designed to bring the criminal who has molested a child to justice. Assume that the child is telling the truth: which is the better course for the child—the court process, with an uncertain outcome if there is to be a trial, or appropriate psychiatric or psychological treatment for the child? And if both are appropriate, in which order should they take place? Which consideration should have the priority? And similarly, if the child is not telling the truth, who is to assuage the consequences for the untruthful child, who sometimes honestly believes by the time he is giving evidence that he has been telling the truth, as well as the child witness who, for whatever reason, has deliberately lied; and how to address the consequences of such events for the innocent defendant, wrongly charged and facing conviction and prison?

For lawyers the focus has tended to be the court process, not for its own sake, but for the sake of justice, and the sake of bringing the process to an end in a verdict. For the psychiatrist, or psychologist, the focus is the welfare of the child, unless of course the psychiatrist or psychologist has an innocent defendant as his patient.

I believe that this is an area where high quality research is needed. Do we know—indeed has anyone ever bothered to find out—how the child sees it all, not at the point when the decision is being made, but, say, 10 years later? Which would have been the better course? I am told by my good friends Joyce Plotnikoff and Richard Woolfson that no research in this country has yet examined the impact on child witnesses years after their court appearances. There is a study as long ago as 2005 in the USA which followed up 200 young victims of sexual assault 12 years after trial. The broad findings were that the extent of distress while waiting to testify and while actually testifying predicated poor psychological adjustment in later life. But I am not sure that this is very surprising. Work has been done on the more or less immediate aftermath of the trial process, but I am thinking of the long term, and whether, for example, there may be a level of maturity or immaturity, or whether the level of seriousness of the offence described by the child, provide indicators about which process should come first. Of course such long-term research would be extremely difficult and sensitive, and many victims will not want to resuscitate the past, whether the experience of being molested or indeed giving evidence. They may have formed new relationships, and not told their partners of what happened in their youth. All that said, I believe the reality is that we do not know—actually know—what is best. What I am prepared to say for certain is that the quicker the court process is completed, the better for the long-term interests of the child.

My very strong impression from my early days as a young barrister at Quarter Sessions or Assizes is that there were relatively few trials of sexual crime: relatively, that is, to today, when many such cases crowd into our Crown Court lists, a significant proportion. Nowadays there are cases of historic sexual allegations, which in themselves are an indictment of the processes which discouraged or effectively disenfranchised the young from coming forward. We are, I believe, catching up with the consequences of the problems ignored or created by earlier generations. So our lists are filled up not only with contemporary crimes involving our current generation of children, but with the generations of child victims, now mature adults, who for whatever reason did not come within the purview of the criminal justice system contemporaneous with their childhood.

Perhaps I can give an example from my own very early experience. I was briefed to defend a father charged with committing incest with his daughters. The sequence is not pleasant to relate but in the course of a lecture like this the reality cannot be avoided. The case came from a very remote part of the country. After the wife had borne many children, effectively with her acquiescence, the father started using his daughters as his sexual outlet. Three girls. On the basis of their comments, he started on each when they reached about 15. When he was arrested he made a full confession. I still remember their arrival at court—everyone through the same entrance, you will remember, and on this occasion mother, father and the three young women, the oldest of whom was now about 19 or 20. My client rejected my advice that he should face up to the responsibilities he had accepted when interviewed. The case was called on. He went into the dock. The first young woman was called into the witness box. Having given her name and address, she burst into tears. She refused to give evidence against her father. Exactly the same happened with the second girl, and then again the third of them. All just burst into tears. No evidence came from any of them. The father was acquitted.

And so this family all returned back together to their remote village. To this day I wonder whatever became of them, and their children in turn. No doubt other cases contributed to my profound sense that we were getting it wrong and the commitment that I made to myself that I would offer such support as I could to those who identified the need for changes.

Some are here tonight, and I regard them with personal affection and professional respect.

Let us just go back to those days, and ask ourselves why so many historic sexual abuse cases are now emerging. In part at least it is because those who were children then were not listened to. Are any of you old enough to remember that 'children should be seen and not heard'? Of course this was to do with manners, to do with children not showing off, and so on, but maybe, just maybe, this line of thinking encouraged the thought that children were not worth listening to, and not to be believed when they made allegations of sexual molestation which earlier generations refused to countenance as a reality. Let us assume that the child had got past all the woes and tribulations of actually getting someone in authority to even begin to accept the possibility that the complaints were true. Let us come to court. Rules of admissibility designed, of course, as a safeguard to protect the innocent from wrongful conviction simply closed the door to many of them. If one looks through the reported criminal cases of the '60s '70s and indeed the '80s, very few involved cases of child sexual abuse. That is due to a combination of two factors. The first is that so few cases were brought, and the second that when they were brought, so few resulted in convictions. And indeed if you look yet more closely, you will find that many of the appeals involving this kind of case were directed to the problems of corroboration, and its complexities.

The Law Reports reflected the reality. Do you remember the competency test? Children below some notional fixed age could not give evidence. It was said by one of my predecessors, Lord Goddard, just a few years before John and I came into practice, that it is 'ridiculous' to suggest that a jury could attach 'any value' to the evidence of a 5-year-old child. Notice, 'ridiculous'; 'any value'.[1] Indeed the same point was repeated as recently as 1987.[2] And if they were older than whatever the notional age was, they were tested to see whether they understood the importance of telling the truth, and the test had religious connotations.

My much admired friend, Professor John Spencer of Cambridge University, highlighted the way in which our remoter ancestors decided whether a child was competent by finding two examples.[3] I shall read these to you, not only because one of them is shocking,

---

[1] *R v Wallwork* (1958) 42 Cr App R 153.
[2] *R v Wright* (1987) 90 Cr App R 91.
[3] JR Spencer and Rhona Flin, *The Evidence of Children: The Law and the Psychology* (London, 1990).

but also because it is so shocking that it is difficult not to titter. But if you do titter you will not titter in fun; you will titter in shock.

Judge: suppose you should tell a lie, do you know who is the father of liars?

13-year-old boy: Yes.

Judge: Who is it?

Boy: The devil.

Judge: If you should tell a lie, do you know what will become of you?

Boy: Yes.

Judge: What if you should swear to a lie? If you should call God to witness to a lie what would become of you then?

Boy: I should go to hell fire.

It is no comfort that the judge in question was the notorious Judge Jeffreys. Justice Maule, in the middle of the next century, was rather more gentle.

Judge: And if you do always tell the truth, where will you go when you die?

Little girl: Up to heaven sir.

Judge: And what will become of you if you tell lies?

Little girl: I shall go down to the naughty place, sir.

Judge: Are you quite sure of that?

Little girl: Yes, sir.

Judge: Let her be sworn, it is quite clear she knows more than I do.

It was not until the Criminal Justice Act 1988 that it was appreciated, and became the law, that a proper understanding of the duty to speak the truth was just as valuable to the process as an understanding of the nature of the religious oath.

If during the police investigation it was thought that the children would pass these tests, they arrived at court. A building into which they had never been before, walking through the same door as the man they were accusing, and waiting in the same public area as that man, and his family if they were there, and in some cases if the man in question was, say, a stepfather, far too often with their mother on his not their side. They were called into court, into the witness box. Sometimes they could only just see over the edge, and when they looked, close by, because that was the design in courts those days, the defendant could be seen watching them, and then months after the incident or incidents, without being allowed to read or be reminded of their original statements, and which would not be looked at by the jury at any stage unless, extremely foolishly, counsel for the defendant 'put them' in evidence—which you never did—they gave their accounts of what happened.

As Professor Spencer points out, this meant that having first been questioned by someone who wanted them to say one thing, they were then cross-examined by another person who wanted to make them say the opposite. All that surmounted, the judge then had to give the jury a corroboration warning which was couched in language which inevitably meant that he was reminding the jury that the evidence of the child was to be treated as untrustworthy. Judges incanted observations like it was 'dangerous to convict' or 'you must exercise very great care indeed', and 'these allegations are easy to make and difficult to refute'. Distress, if any were seen, did not provide corroboration. The jury was warned to be very careful about distress: it could be easily feigned, and the only complaint made by the child that could be admitted must have been made very close, 'recently', to the offence, otherwise it was 'hearsay' and even when it was admitted as 'recent' evidence, it did not constitute corroboration, but rather showed consistency, only consistency. And one unsworn child could not corroborate another. It is awful to say it, but if you were a paedophile with an interest in very young children, who could not be sworn as witnesses, no matter how many of them there were, they could not corroborate each other.

Some of you may think that all this is exaggerated; I assure you that it is not.

And let us just keep going round to the end of this cycle. Nothing in the court process amounted to any encouragement to the process of investigation if and when the child made a complaint. And I hate to imagine how many children there were who complained of molestation or who were or knew that they would be, if they did complain, subjected to corporal punishment of one kind or another for telling lies about nice old Mr so and so, the history master.

In 1990 Lord Lane, with his usual penetrating analysis, overruled the decision of Lord Goddard in 1990, observing 'a change of attitude by Parliament, reflecting in its turn a change of attitude by the public in general to the acceptability of the evidence of young children and of increasing belief that the testimony of young children, when all precautions have been taken, may be just as reliable as that of their elders'.[4]

As ever with Lord Lane, one needs to concentrate on the message. He was saying that the public generally did not, or were not prepared to, accept the evidence of young children, and doubted whether their evidence would or could be as reliable as that of adults. And the reality is that there were still plenty of intelligent educated adults about in this country for whom the light had not dawned.

With the solemn ritual of investigating competence, with reference to God in an age in which such references were not always comforting, taking place in a solemn building with solemn people all around, all significantly older, all looking and indeed being people in authority over them, the belief was that children would be so compelled with the solemnity of it all that they would solemnly tell the truth. No one articulated any concern about how much more likely the child would be to freeze up or, no better, to become confused. Nor did anyone reflect that perhaps the very last thing any child who had been sexually molested would wish to do would be to tell a whole crowd of strangers in an unfamiliar place about something dirty and nasty that had happened. Forgive me for making this personal, but just think about how embarrassing it was for every one of you to talk about sexual matters to your parents. I can remember my very dearly beloved father being deeply embarrassed as he tried to explain the facts of life to me. Looking back on it I had no idea what he was talking about. My point however is that he, the adult, was embarrassed at the conversation. And children, and that is what I was, sense these things without being told.

We do of course have to remember that they were living then and we are living now. It was not very long since incest had been criminalised. It was generally thought that in law a man could not rape his wife. A husband could claim damages for adultery from a man with whom his wife had had an affair or with whom she began to live. You could only get divorced if you could prove a matrimonial offence. And if you had committed adultery yourself, you had to ask the court to exercise its discretion in your favour.

So perhaps my most solemn warning to all of us here tonight is this: we may be horrified about what happened then, but we need

[4] *R v Z* [1990] 2 QB 355.

a little humility ourselves. We need to be very sure indeed that our grandchildren, 50 years from now, may not be astounded, and appalled, at the way we do things now. What we are doing reflects what we believe to be the best that we can; or perhaps putting it another way, we are striving to do the best that we can. Fifty years from now they may not see it this way. Like us, our forefathers were acting in the best of good faith. They were just wrong.

Perhaps our forefathers either did not or could not believe that these things happened. As Lord Lane observed, perhaps they started with an assumption that a complaint was untrue. How much did they know of children anyway? For very many years, certainly in the time my father and many of your fathers were children, everyone believed that because children had no memory of events that happened to them before they were 3 years old, whatever did happen to them did not matter. Very few realised that those first 3 years of childhood were absolutely crucial to a child's development. And the difference between being cocooned in love and cocooned in misery at the start of life leaves indelible marks on character and personality.

You know perfectly well that I cannot and would not comment on any individual case. But does it come as any surprise that really from all over the world awful stories about mistreatment of youngsters are beginning to be allowed to emerge, and I include this country, and the United States, and the Republic of Ireland? And all credit to those who are prepared to allow for the fact that the older generation got it wrong, and that children who were indeed subject to dreadful abuse, both physical and sexual, and of course emotional abuse without redress, have, at last, as adults, found their voices. And let us not be foolish: men, and a few women, with a perverted sexual interest in children and youngsters are born in every country of the world. In some of them these sad stories have not yet begun to emerge.

And yet, as a case I have done recently underlined for me, for some victims, even years later, having a voice at last represents some kind of therapy—being believed is invaluable—and there will be others who were forced into silence in those days, for whom even having to think about finding a voice creates painful memories which they do not wish to reopen. You will find cases where three or four members of a family were abused years earlier, and when one decides to tell the story, one or more of his or her siblings will tell their own story, and yet one or more of the other siblings will not. Many of those families are deeply divided all these years later, all part of the ongoing consequences of the earlier abuse and either disbelief in the complaint, or fear of making it.

I have a vivid memory of one case, but it exemplified many, where the complainant, a woman in her early 30s, made a complaint, not because she really had any wish to have her stepfather, now an old man, sent to prison for many years, but because she wanted her mother, to whom she had complained when she was very young, to acknowledge that she, the mother, should have supported her daughter, not her husband.

Recognising some of the deficiencies of the old system is, of course, but a first step; recognition is not improvement. Can we just cast about, back into the 1980s? Few of you here will remember the phenomenal battle that went on before we introduced into the interrogation process by police officers of a suspect, that rather simple, outdated device called a tape recording machine. My clients, interviewed by police officers, tended to produce entirely coherent statements of confession, with a middle, a beginning and an end, all in their own language, all unprompted, and my clients turned out to see me, and somehow were so intimidated that they were inarticulate, virtually illiterate, quite incapable of stringing a sentence together. Nevertheless, although everyone knew something was going wrong, there was profound suspicion of and objection to the use of the tape recorder. We now take it, and a video recording of the defendant being interviewed, entirely for granted. We know exactly what he said, the precise context in which he said it, and the question he was answering.

Much the same battle raged over the possible use of a video-link for children's evidence. I reminded myself of an article written by John Spencer in 1987. As ever he delivers knock-out blows with a humorous punch. The arguments against the use of a live video-link were that to do so would be 'alien to the traditions of British justice—which, as every lawyer knows, is the Envy of the World', which John describes as a 'puzzling observation'. But he was making a more simple point. If, as they just had, two Israeli security officers were allowed to give evidence from behind a thick oak screen against a terrorist who attempted to blow up a Jumbo Jet then surely that could be permitted when a 'terrified little child' would be giving evidence.

He ended:

If the basic traditions of British justice really require the Colin James Evanses of the paedophile world to confront their 4-year-old accusers face to face, even if this makes it impossible to get a word of evidence out of them, it is the traditions of British justice which need re-examining, not the video-link proposal.[5]

This conservatism formed part of the context. So you have to see the opposition as part of the context in which Tom Pigot, the Common Serjeant of London, was invited to write a report on the use of video recordings of interviews of child victims to be treated as admissible evidence at criminal trials. With his team in 1989 he produced a seminal report, a wake-up call, remarkably clear about its recommendations and prescient for the future.[6] Recommending the admissibility of video recording, he and his Committee suggested that 'a fundamental change of attitude towards children in the legal context is now required'. They added that the courts should be 'more receptive to children'. I have little doubt that they influenced the remarks made by Lord Lane shortly afterwards. Nevertheless they went on to point out that there were very many practical, legal and penal issues which would require re-examination in the light of modern conditions and research.

If I may jump ahead, we now know that the video recording of the account given by very young children indeed—not their oral testimony in the witness box in court—can provide very compelling evidence, perhaps not least because many of them are too young to be guileful.

The take-up for the Pigot reforms was slow, not wildly enthusiastic, and some were directly opposed. I remember a huge debate, still continuing, about whether allowing a child to give evidence through a screen diminished the impact of his or her evidence, thus leading juries to acquit when, so it was contended, if the child had given evidence from the witness box, they might well have convicted. Research suggested otherwise, but I believe that much the most significant feature was the quality and size of the screen available in the particular court. Over the years, with support from learned academics, energetic campaigners and enthusiastic researchers, with weight added by the NSPCC and Victim Support, judicial training and lawyers practising in this field, very many improvements have taken place. Society has changed; the attitude of society to complaints by children has changed. People recognise in a way they did not that these things, sadly, unfortunately, do happen. And that they

---

[5] 'Video Technology and the Law of Evidence' [1987] *Criminal Law Review*. Evans 'had a hideous record as a child molester' and had murdered a 4-year-old child.

[6] Home Office Advisory Group on Video Evidence (known as the Pigot Committee), 1989, chaired by His Honour Judge Pigot QC, the Common Sarjeant of London.

can cause devastating damage. All this is admirable, and 25 years from now I suspect that there will be fewer historic cases from the present needing trial in about 2030 than there are now, which go back to the 1970s and 1980s.

You will not be helped by a recital of the arrangements for the evidence of children. You will find them in all the text books under the rubric 'Special Measures'. I am no longer very happy with describing them in this way. That was fair enough when we were trying to bring home the importance of addressing these new measures which were, at that time, special. Now they are a perfectly normal, ordinary part of the procedural safeguards provided for vulnerable witnesses. In effect, by statute, all witnesses under 18 are entitled to them. They include:

— Video-recorded evidence-in-chief
— Giving evidence by live-link, accompanied by a supporter
— Screening the witness from the defendant
— Removal of wigs and gowns
— Examination through an intermediary
— Provision of aids to communication

Of course the anonymity of the child witness is now long established, and there are significant changes to the layout of courts, so that the child does not come through the same door as the defendant, and is kept in a place where he or she can neither see nor be seen by the defendant and his supporters.

All this has made for dramatic improvement. Alongside the growing public recognition that children can give reliable evidence, the processes to enable them to do so have been greatly improved. But the process is not complete.

We are talking about a lot of children going to court. We do not actually know precisely how many young witnesses give evidence, and from the statistics we do have, we do not know how many of the witnesses were themselves victims of the alleged crime, or witnesses to crimes in which other people, including adults of course, were victims. In 2008/9 the CPS statistics indicated that about 48,000 children were called to give evidence at court; a couple of years earlier the Witness Service supported over 30,000 young witnesses at court in England and Wales. In 2012 the joint inspection report on the experience of young victims and witnesses suggested that in a 12-month period about 33,000 children and young adults under the age of 18 years would be involved in giving evidence at a criminal trial. So we are not talking small numbers. Let us take the lowest figure, 30,000. Let us postulate what I believe to be the absurdity that half of them will suffer no concern or long-term effect from giving evidence. That still leaves a very large number of individual children who will have been damaged. It does seem to me, however, that we really should have properly gathered statistics of the number of child victims who are involved in the criminal justice process. And they should be divided into those who make complaints and provide evidence, which are followed by a confession and early guilty plea; those who provide the same evidence, and attend court and are then greeted by a last-minute guilty plea; and, most important of all, those who provide evidence and attend court and give live evidence at a trial. Desirable although this is, on Budget Day particularly, I should perhaps add a footnote: staff at court have been cut; staff in the CPS have been cut; everywhere there are budgetary restraints. We have to beware of the temptation to think that because improvements are desirable they come at no cost for those responsible for their implementation.

This lecture is already too long, and I have in mind to develop some of the themes which I am going to address in a Law Reform lecture in the autumn.[7] I suggest that in these 50 years of change, what we have actually recognised is that there are many different ways of enabling the evidence of a child witness to be fairly considered by a court, without representing any change to the proper protections available to the defendant. I do mean 'proper' protections; I discard artificial protection. Just because a change does not coincide with the way we have always done things does not mean that it should be rejected. We should be considering each individual child as the individual he or she is, at the age and with the levels of the maturity that he or she has, alleging whatever form of crime of which he or she has been the victim. Do proposed changes cause unfair prejudice to the defendant? If so, of course, they cannot happen. If however they make it more likely to enable the truth to emerge, whether favourable or unfavourable to the defendant, then let it be done. The truth is the objective.

There is an urgent need to address what is sometimes described as Pigot 2, the second half of the recommendation that the whole of the child's evidence, in-chief, and then, after a fair opportunity for that evidence to be considered by the defendant and his legal advisors, immediate cross-examination, be video recorded and in due course presented to the jury. I have heard numerous objections

---

[7] See 'The Evidence of Child Victims: The Next Stage', this volume, p 225.

and obstacles. Yes, it is true that in a few cases, proper disclosure at a later stage in the process may reveal information about which the cross-examiner was ignorant at the time. But surely all we need to do is introduce a measure of flexibility. If the interests of justice require a further cross-examination, so be it; as to when and where it should take place, appropriate arrangements can be made. I shall be astonished if section 28 of the 1999 Act (which contains the necessary permissive provision) is not implemented within a few years. And we shall all be astounded by what all the fuss was about.

There are four brief further points. First, we have yet to establish the full use of the intermediary systems in these cases. Second, we have not yet fully answered the question whether it is necessary for the child witness ever to come to court at all, and whether for some of them, at any rate, attendance at trial cannot be arranged in a more congenial place, with necessary safeguards to ensure judicial control over the trial process and the safeguarding of the interests of the defendant. Third, we have not yet established full judicial insistence that questions to a young witness should be open-ended. What are described as tag questions are unacceptable. Indeed the modern technique of cross-examination, which I deprecate generally, is particularly damaging in cases involving young witnesses. That is a long assertion, followed by 'did he?' or 'did you?' or sometimes not even a question, but raising the voice in an inflexive questioning tone. Fourth, we must make sure that all the provisions which have been introduced as best practice are in fact implemented.

The end result is this: give or take a year or two, in John Toulmin's first 25 years in practice the way in which the evidence of children and teenagers was addressed remained rooted in the practices and misunderstandings which applied when he started in practice. During the last 25 years there have been remarkable changes—perhaps indeed, if one compares the processes which obtained at the start of his career with those which are in place now, revolutionary changes. That is profoundly welcome. That is a very strange thing for a Lord Chief Justice to be saying, but the revolution in our processes, the necessary revolution in our processes, is not yet over. But then, given that so much has been achieved without unfairly prejudicing the position of the defendant, we must confidently expect this revolution to continue.

I think that I have just heard John's voice from over my shoulder saying 'I entirely agree'.

The Evidence of Child Victims: The Next Stage

This was the Law Reform Committee Lecture given in London in November 2013, following my retirement in September of that year.

FOR THOSE WHO look back as I can on the changes in the arrangements for children involved in the criminal justice process once they reach the courts, we have made remarkable progress. For an earlier generation the description 'revolutionary' would come to mind, and it would be accurate.

For others, impatient for further improvements in these arrangements, there is still a long way to go. So even if the description 'revolutionary' may be accurate, the revolution is awaiting its fulfilment by some Napoleon or other, not a description to which I have ever aspired. Anyway I have been banished to the judicial equivalent of St Helena.

I agree with both views, without the slightest embarrassment. They are not inconsistent or contradictory. We have indeed come a long way, but we still have a long way to go. This lecture is not about where we were and how far we have come. I addressed those questions and why I have been concerned about the way in which children were treated in the criminal justice process from my earliest days in practice at the Bar at Quarter Sessions 50 years ago, and the pioneering efforts of others, in my Toulmin Lecture in Law and Psychiatry entitled 'Half a Century of Change: The Evidence of Child Victims' given in March 2013 at King's College London.[1]

My broad thesis is that the day will surely come, and in my view it has already arrived, when the requirement for the physical presence of a child witness or victim in the court building will be regarded as an antediluvian hangover from laughable, far-off days of the quill pen and the ink well.

The importance of the issue is underlined when we remember that we are talking about many, many children, not the odd isolated few. Taking any sort of analysis of the research produced by the CPS and

---

[1] See this volume, p 211.

Witness Service and joint inspections, it is reasonable for us to anticipate that next year, 2014, something like 40,000 or more children and very young adults will give evidence in criminal cases. Many of them will be complainants. Their ages will vary from very small children indeed to teenagers. Think of all those young lives. This is an annual figure. Our long-term ambition must be that not one single one of those lives will be distorted by the forensic process, and that the impact on them of the unhappy events of which they speak will not be exacerbated by the process. It is a considerable ambition, perhaps unrealistic, but then perhaps our ambition should be that the number of children whose lives are distorted by the forensic process shall be reduced and then kept to an irreducible minimum.

Perhaps I should add that I am not in this lecture directing attention to issues which arise from the investigation into the complaint by the police, or the local authority, or the prosecutorial decisions, or the preparation and assembly of appropriate evidence for a trial. My observations in this lecture are confined to the court process, although the ambition which I have just identified should apply equally to every single one of the different agencies involved in this process. And I am confining myself to the court processes in criminal cases, but these cases are difficult and sensitive in the family justice system as well.

As the figures I have just given you demonstrate, the evidence of children is integral and sometimes vital to the administration of criminal justice. They are witnesses and victims of crime, and they are sometimes defendants. Like adults they can assist in the quest for truth, and sometimes they can obscure it. Like adults, they can sometimes be right and sometimes be wrong. But they are not adults. They are not even little adults. Indeed they are not even a miniature of the adult into which the child will eventually grow. We are heartbroken by the recent pictures of small children bereft of parents and family and home and hope as a result of the typhoon in the Philippines, but we do not see the children shown in these pictures as small adults. We see them as the children they are. Who can forget the haunting photograph of the child in Vietnam who had suffered Napalm burns? Do we remember a little adult, or a small child? So it must be in the forensic process.

The position of the child defendant is more complex. At present I do not see how the child should be deprived of the right to be present in court when he or she is the defendant, and anyway there is a very strong argument that the defendant should always be present in a process which is focused on his alleged guilt. Whether the child should have an opportunity to waive his or her presence is a different question, but subject to that important consideration, and the practical consequences of the application of the broad principle that the presence of the defendant is an essential feature of the trial process, I do not see why the processes which protect the child witness or victim should not be available to the child defendant. To my mind it is not just a question of equality of arms, it is simply that the defendant who is a child is a child, like the complainant who is a child. Neither is a little adult. But for today's purposes the focus is the child victim.

The reference to the child defendant enables me to begin by emphasising at the outset that, quite apart from the presumption of innocence, I am not advocating, and we have not and should never introduce, change on the basis that the object of the trial process is simply to confirm the guilt of the defendant or that the failure to achieve a conviction represents a failure of the forensic process. Sometimes, even after the most careful process, in which justice is done to every witness, the evidence is simply not good enough for the jury to be sure of guilt. However, it is easy to overlook that the defendant is sometimes truly innocent. He is not always guilty. False complaints are made. It follows that the complainant is not always a victim. However we approach further changes to our processes, none of us would want to enhance the risk that a truly innocent defendant and his—and it virtually is always he or him—family, including his own children, should carry the stigma of his paedophilia and he be sentenced to imprisonment for an offence he has not committed. Who then would be the victims?

These disasters can and do happen. So the processes must cater for the truthful child and the untruthful or mistaken child. That represents a considerable challenge when we also know perfectly well that any step designed to protect the innocent from a miscarriage of justice is equally available to be used, and certainly will be used, by the defendant who is guilty and determined that justice will miscarry in his acquittal. And there is this further problem. If having taken advantage of every available procedural step the guilty defendant is convicted, the processes intended to safeguard the innocent defendant are then called into question for every case, to the potential disadvantage of other innocent defendants. Yet we must be careful to avoid any kind of populist rush to do away with proper safeguards for the innocent.

In what follows, I have these considerations firmly in mind, and never, at any stage, overlook them. My objective is rather old-fashioned. What I shall suggest is designed to enable the guilty defendant to plead guilty as early as possible, and if there is to be a trial, for the verdict to be the true verdict according to the evidence. For that purpose the evidence must be given in the best and clearest way possible. That involves recognition of the intellectual and emotional limitations of children, and the need for the processes of the court to reduce their consequent disadvantages.

Looking back at it now, some of the older principles which we have already rejected were based on antiquated beliefs in which the trial processes reflected contemporary understanding and ideas. Folklore is probably the best description of ideas that worked their way into the judicial system. Perhaps it may have been science too. After all, experts believed once that the earth was flat, and indeed that the earth was the centre of the universe which spun around us in awed progression. Centuries ago it was believed that a woman who became pregnant following a rape could not have been unwilling; similarly if she did not immediately raise a hue and cry. When I began at the Bar the direction given by the judge in cases of sexual complaint, whether by children or by adults, required the complainant to be approached as if the devil himself might have inspired him or her to lie or fantasise, and offered them remarkable temptations to feign distress when they felt none, and had no reason to be distressed. So directions were given to the jury that were intended to convey—and whether intended to convey or not, certainly would have conveyed—that there was somehow research, or in the words of the Pigot Report, 'official information that children who say they have been abused are far more likely to be untruthful than the knowledge and experience of the jury might indicate to them'.[2] If 20 otherwise unconnected children who could not under the rules then in force be sworn, and who each independently spoke of abusive experiences at the hands of the same adult, none could provide any support for any of the others even if the possibility of collusion or contamination could be excluded. Without corroboration, in a very formal sense, the case would not even go to trial. Until relatively recently it was generally believed that because little children had no recollection of what had happened to them in the early months of their lives, what they could not recollect was of no importance to their development. Today we appreciate the critical impact on every aspect of every child's future of those vital early

---

[2] Home Office Advisory Group on Video Evidence, 1989, chaired by His Honour Judge Pigot QC, the Common Serjeant of London.

months: how damaging they can be or, alternatively, how sustaining they will remain throughout life.

Perhaps it was a reflection of this myth that led Lord Goddard, one of my predecessors, to observe that it was ridiculous to suggest that a jury could derive any value from the evidence of a child of 5 years—a view repeated in 1987, but demolished by Lord Lane shortly afterwards. Notice Lord Goddard's words, 'ridiculous', and 'any value'. Now we don't hesitate. You know all about *R v Barker*[3] and I shall return to it.

While addressing the issue of myth busters, it does no harm for the judiciary and legal professions, and for that matter the whole of society, to acknowledge the contribution made to myth busting by academics and researchers, and in this particular field, supported by the efforts of charitable organisations like the NSPCC, Barnardo's and ChildLine, all deeply concerned with the welfare, in its broadest sense, of children.

Neither judges nor the judicial system can be slaves to the latest fad or fashion, or indeed to the enthusiastic efforts of committed pressure groups. Fads and fashions change. Pressure groups do not always avoid tunnel vision, but our new-found knowledge on issues affecting the evidence of children did not come down to us via a flash from the heavens. There was much solid digging here on earth. And perhaps, too, we should not overlook the contribution of open justice. One facet of the application of that principle has been fair and accurate reporting and greater understanding to us of some of the harsh and objectionable realities.

I can also say something that I could not perhaps have said two months ago. It is to highlight the remarkably positive approach by the judiciary at all levels to these issues. We have co-operated with the research and those interested in these issues for many years. The training video for judges demonstrating good practice when children were giving evidence, first promulgated in 1997 as '*A Case for Balance*', involved an energetic participation of judges and barristers, now many of them on the Bench. Similarly with the next video, '*A Case for Special Measures relating to the Needs and Treatment of Vulnerable Witnesses*', now over 10 years old. The implementation of the statutory provisions relating to special measures once they came into force was clear and unequivocal. In the Court of Appeal Criminal Division we have advanced as far as we can without legislative intervention to address these issues, as we did in *Barker*

---

[3] *R v Barker* [2010] EWCA Crim 4.

and other cases to which I shall come. The Criminal Procedure Rules Committee with its wide-ranging representation has reflected this greater understanding of the issues, and the Judicial College has issued guidance. The process is ongoing, with Fulford LJ and Judge Cahill QC continuing to undertake responsibility on behalf of the Lord Chief Justice to address and improve the arrangements for vulnerable witnesses in criminal trials. The Ground Rule Hearings are well established. The objective is to sort out what the problems are, identify them, and then, subject to the judge's ruling, how they must be resolved and the trial conducted. What points are sought to be advanced on the defendant's behalf? Are they, using the word comprehensively, 'admissible'? If so, how should they be advanced? Inevitably, differently for each child, and differently, depending whether the child is 14 or 7 years old. Quite apart from physical age, and at least as important, what are the particular characteristics of the child to which attention should be directed?

Of course, there are individual cases where the trial judge has not got it right, or where he or she has been too patient and less interventional than appropriate. We cannot avoid individual errors or eradicate errors made in individual cases, nor can we produce a system that is error-proof. But each error is instructive, and we are learning from them.

Let me return to *Barker*. Perhaps the first point to grasp about the evidence of that very small child is that in the Court of Appeal we were in as good a position as the jury to assess her evidence in chief. We saw exactly the same evidence as they did. We found it equally compelling. This reminds me that some years ago at the time of the Runciman Commission[4] I ventured the suggestion that the technology that then enabled police interviews to be tape recorded, and videoed, should be used at every stage of the trial for the purpose of recording the evidence of every witness. My objective was that in place of the dry transcript of any relevant evidence, the Court of Appeal could be put more closely in the position of the jury assessing the credibility of the witnesses. In short, if there were grounds for concern about the credibility assessment, the court should not be forced into the incantation that as the jury had seen the witness, any further argument before the Court of Appeal was closed down. That was not one of my ideas that succeeded in establishing any roots.

---

[4] Home Office, *Report of the Royal Commission on Criminal Justice* (Com 2263), 1993, chaired by Lord Runciman.

There would be potential problems about the constitutional primacy of the jury, and the Court of Appeal interfering with its findings. Nowadays, too, argument would undoubtedly be mixed up with the issues surrounding televising criminal trials. Be all that as it may, ultimately it is the court that is responsible for ensuring the safety of any conviction. How can it best perform that function? Enough of failed ideas. Nevertheless I do not think it arrogant to suggest that in the world of modern technology, my proposal from far-off days will eventually find its way into the Criminal Procedure Rules and the judicial process.

Let us return to children, and my original thesis. With the exception of the child defendant, whose position for reasons I have already given is much more problematic, why should it be assumed that the child victim or witness should be physically present at court to give evidence? Once you accept, and we have accepted, that the jury does not have to see the child physically present in the court itself, but can do justice by examining the evidence of the child in chief via a video recording, and then observe the cross-examination at what is no longer a face-to-face confrontation with the defendant's advocate, but instead a long-distance encounter between them through the use of modern technology, why does the child have to be present in the court? Of course I recognise that the judge must be in charge of the process, and I also recognise that there may be occasions when it is for some reason or another necessary for the child to be present at court. It may even be that on some occasions the search for the truth may be diminished if the child were absent. Fine, bring the child to court. But the assumption should be that the child will not come to court, and that instead he or she will go to a safe quiet place, if necessary with the court usher, assuming there is one, or with a trained member of Witness Support, who goes to that safe place to ensure that all proper precautions are taken to avoid influence or interference, with the judge in constant communication with that supporter. I should add in parenthesis that the arrangements by which responsibility for young witnesses' support is being moved from the Ministry of Justice to the area of responsibility of police commissioners need very careful attention. But, coming out of the parenthesis, what I am saying is that perhaps for these purposes the court should come to the witness. Perhaps the mountain should shift itself. That would indeed be a special measure.

These words are constantly used in the forensic process. We must soon get away from the idea that for child witnesses, as for other vulnerable witnesses, there should be special measures to govern the arrangements for their evidence. This was a convenient statutory label, but it has had its day. These special measures are no longer truly special at all. They are commonplace. They do not represent concessions patronisingly offered to the vulnerable. They must surely now be regarded as the normal steps available to enable the truth to emerge. My concern is that the use of the convenient shorthand may contribute to an inappropriate state of mind. If any description is needed, surely 'protective' is more accurate than 'special'.

Maybe that state of mind—we must offer special measures—contributed to the stunning sloth with which Pigot[5] was implemented, or more accurately partially implemented. *Jarndyce v Jarndyce*[6] was fiction based on fact, but compared with the non-implementation of the whole of Pigot, that notorious litigation moved quite quickly. Pigot reported in 1989. With no great rush many of the reforms recommended by the committee have been implemented, to no disadvantages to the defendant, certainly none to the innocent defendant. Perhaps we should pause to observe how far-sighted Pigot was. We must remember that the report was produced during the days when the old-fashioned committal for trial was part of the process, and that it reflected an approach to technology which, by current standards, was in its infancy. All that said, I am unaware of any case in which protective measures were used and which for that reason alone resulted in a miscarriage of justice.

Nevertheless the proposal which was at the heart of the entire package still has not been implemented. In essence the whole of the child's evidence, including any cross-examination, should take place out of court and be recorded in advance of the trial, and should then be admitted as the child's evidence. The necessary legislative provisions for what I shall describe as full Pigot were enacted in the 1999 Youth Justice and Criminal Justice Act. But they were not brought into force until very recently, when we now have three pilots. I have no objection to the pilots. Indeed I welcome them. In Leeds, Liverpool and Kingston we have appropriate courts in which to identify and sort out complications relating to the necessary equipment, its efficient working, early disclosure issues, defence engagements, and the like. I do not suggest that the implementation of the full Pigot can be achieved with the stroke of

---

[5] See n 2 above.
[6] Charles Dickens, *Bleak House* (1853).

the pen, and both the judiciary and the advocates will have to adapt to it. Again, I do not suggest that there will not be hiccoughs and difficulties, but I regard implementation as inevitable.

I venture to notice, with some disbelief, that Pigot 2, that is the admissible recorded pre-trial cross-examination process, was introduced in Western Australia in 1992, yet left in our own legislative in-tray for nearly a quarter of a century. It is now admissible in most of the states of Australia, which like many here were highly sceptical of what their colleagues in Western Australia were doing. For those of you who are concerned about any possible unfairness to the defendant, the fairness of the processes has been fully tested in Australia, and their effectiveness was confirmed by the Australian Law Reform Commission analysis of 2010.[7]

In summary it identifies, among other benefits, improvements in the quality and reliability of the evidence ... Do you want me to repeat that? Well I shall anyway.... Improvements in the quality and reliability of the evidence. That is what we are about, is it not? But there are other advantages too. These include better pre-trial decision-making by both sides—in other words, the prosecutorial decision whether to proceed, and the plea to be offered by the defendant, are both better informed. If there is to be a trial, the pre-trial management is clearer. The analysis further identifies how Pigot 2 minimises the forensic abuse of children, not I hasten to add deliberate abuse, but consequential abuse. That, too, seems to me to be a crucial consideration.

Of course we have to recognise the possibility that even after this process has been deployed, the interests of justice may require a further opportunity for cross-examination of the witness. Things meriting attention do sometimes emerge, of which the defendant could have had no notice at the time when cross-examination took place. The interests of justice require flexibility, and they must always prevail. But the reality is, as with all these changes, that once they become embedded in the forensic system, and everyone is used to them, the occasions when the opportunity for further cross-examination will be sought will gradually diminish until the occasions become truly exceptional.

I should add, in response to one concern expressed to me by a number of different people, that I regard pre-trial cross-examination as cross-examination for the purposes of Article 6 of the Convention

---

[7] Australia Law Reform Committee, *Seen and Heard: Priority for Children in the Legal Progress*, ALRC 1997, Report No 84.

or any other article. In my view it is a fair and sufficient opportunity to test the evidence of the witness. It may not—and I hope
that when Pigot 2 is introduced it will not—involve what I shall
describe as forensic posturing, and that comment, which too frequently poses as cross-examination, will be disincentivised. Why
on earth should I use a long word when a short one will do? Comment posing as cross-examination must stop. Although I shall
ignore my own injunction today, so must repetition. For example,
in the modern world we have had to become accustomed to cases
involving multi-defendants, allegedly involved in sexual abuse of
young women. It is entirely reasonable that matters which go to the
creditworthiness of a complainant should, assuming that she is old
enough to comprehend the issues under examination, be analysed
in the process of cross-examination. But once is, and should be,
enough. In other words, where there is a single defendant, repetition should not be permitted, and the idea of repetition does not
become more attractive, merely because the repetition is offered by
a number of different counsel in a multi-handed case. There is no
possible justification for the witness being driven through the same
process by the successive advocates for the remaining defendants.
That is not a process required to enable justice to be done, nor to
ensure the fair trial of each defendant.

The impact on the forensic process of the decisions of the Court of
Appeal in *R v Barker*, *R v Edwards*,[8] *R v W and M*,[9] *R v Wills*[10] and
more recently *R v Farooqi*[11] has not yet been fully appreciated, and
the principles contained in them already apply before the implementation of Pigot 2. Taken together, they have effected a major
change in the way in which cross-examination should be undertaken. I strongly urge anyone involved in criminal trials, whether
as judge or advocate, to understand the impact of these decisions,
and their implications. They represent current legal principles, and
have been reflected in the latest edition of the Criminal Procedure
Rules issued on 3 October this year.

I warned you that I should repeat myself. Perhaps I may be
allowed a few more comments about comment, which is no more
than pre-final speech speechifying to the jury. This is not newfound
jurisprudence. Over 200 years ago, in a treason trial, in which,

[8] [2011] EWCA Crim 3028.
[9] [2010] EWCA Crim 1926.
[10] [2011] EWCA Crim 1938.
[11] [2013] EWCA Crim 1649.

exceptionally, defence counsel were permitted to address the jury, Eyre CJ observed to counsel:

> I am sorry to interrupt you, but your questions ought not to be accompanied with those sort of comments: they are the proper subject of observation when the defence is made. The business of cross-examination is to ask all sorts of acts, to probe a witness as closely as you can: but it is not the object of a cross-examination to introduce the sort of periphrasis as you have just done.[12]

My *Shorter Oxford Dictionary* illuminated my own ignorance about periphrasis: it is 'a roundabout way of speaking'. But, apart from the comment issue, the cases taken together underline the simple proposition that the objective of cross-examination is to investigate the truth by questions which must be clearly understood by the witness, and which must therefore take full account of his or her maturity, and for the child, that he or she is indeed a child, not a little adult.

With respect, and I mean that in a non-forensic sense, to those brought up on and indeed teaching advocacy techniques based on what I shall describe as pre-*Barker* techniques, they must be rethought. Complicated tagged questions, double and triple negatives, and comment, along with the accompanying paraphernalia for all of them, are no longer available. The advocate should go into the criminal trial anticipating that the judges will apply the legal principles to be derived from this group of authorities. And perhaps for the avoidance of doubt I should underline that it will apply to Pigot 2 when it comes into force, and no less throughout to prosecution advocates, some of whom approach their task of cross-examining the defendant as if cross-examination, are synonymous.

We need to go a little deeper. Quite apart from speechifying, the modern technique of cross-examination often hopes to persuade a witness to agree with something that he, the witness, does not necessarily believe to be wholly truthful. Contrast 'Did you eat a banana?' with 'You ate a banana, didn't you?' Or 'Did you hit him first?' with 'You hit him first, didn't you?' I introduce ridiculous examples for the purpose of illustration. The first of that pair of questions seems to me to be entirely appropriate, just because each of them is indeed a question. The second in each pair does not consist of a simple question, which might just as easily have been asked as 'Didn't you

---

[12] *Hardy's Case* (1794) 24 State Trials 199.

eat a banana?' or 'Didn't you hit him first?' Closely analysed, the second of each pair consists of an assertion by the advocate, apparently giving evidence or expressing an opinion, which is then followed up by a question. It is probably old-fashioned to believe that advocates should not be making assertions of fact, or stating their opinions, even if the assertions represent their client's instructions, or the opinions are consequent on those instructions. Just because it is old-fashioned, it does not necessarily follow that it is wrong. But in cases which we are currently considering, the problem with cross-examination along the lines of the mixed assertion and question is that they are made, from the point of view of the child witness, by a person in apparent authority with whom many children would naturally be inclined to agree. Carried to levels which might be perfectly acceptable if the witness under cross-examination is a mature individual, questioning of this kind can constitute bullying of a child. And finally, this method of cross-examination can too readily develop into the kind of comment and speechifying which is unacceptable. So, this technique of cross-examination needs to be carefully monitored.

As you will all appreciate, the use of intermediaries is now established. As is so often the case with change, there was much misunderstanding about intermediaries and their functions, and indeed it is not too exaggerated to say that much suspicion about them was engendered. Intermediaries do not interfere with the process of cross-examination. They are not supporters of the witness. They are neutral and independent, offering assistance to the court and responsible to the court. Their presence is designed to assist the judge and the advocates and the witness to ensure that they all understand each other. Take a simple little word like 'fib'. We all think we know what it means. But do we all think it means the same thing? Does it apply to any kind of lie—the deliberate malevolent lie, and what is sometimes described as the 'white lie', the little lie told to avoid causing umbrage and offence—or does it apply only to the deliberate falsehood? Or is it just a refined middle-class word, quite meaningless to many children? If you are not all using the same word, with the same comprehension of its true meaning, misunderstanding and therefore a false impression of what it is that the child witness is seeking to convey, or agree with, are inevitable. Intermediaries perform a valuable function which it is not open to the judge to perform without, at any rate, giving the appearance, if the judge acts entirely on his or her own initiative, of partiality.

When the full Pigot has been achieved, there will be a number of consequences, and they are not unimportant. Let me immediately identify two. First, if the evidence of the complainant is completed and completed long before the trial actually begins, then the entire atmosphere surrounding the trial will change. I suspect the emotional content of the subsequent trial will be reduced. The cross-examination will have been completed away from the inevitable tension of court, and the inevitable wish of both sides to make an immediate impact on the decision-making body, the jury. I have no doubt that we shall hear for ages the advocates on both sides suggesting at the subsequent trial that they are dealing with *Hamlet* without the prince, but it will be part of a new and different process. It will be a trial taking place months after the evidence of the main witness for the prosecution will have been completed.

The second consequence is, in a sense, more important. Where the child has been a victim, the question which always arises is how best to enable the child to come to terms with, or get over, or accommodate within his or her life, the events which he or she has described. In the Toulmin Lecture I asked for consideration to be given to research into the question whether child victims should complete their evidence before treatment is undertaken, or rather be provided with the necessary treatment as soon as possible, irrespective of whether or not their evidence has already been given. This is always a desperately important factor for the child's future. I believe that the full Pigot will make the decision much easier. Provided the cross-examination is completed fairly soon after the evidence in chief, then treatment can be undertaken immediately.

Perhaps I should add a third factor, revolutionary I know, but if we assume that the full Pigot is introduced in cases involving child victims, then there will be a powerful case for it to apply to many other victims, particularly of sexual offences. Perhaps, therefore, we are at the very beginning of what will become a significant change in the entire trial process, a consequence of modern technology, properly applied to the administration of justice, and for my own part, as I emphasise, without increasing the possibility that an innocent defendant might be convicted.

I must come to an end, but I do not think I can end on a bland note. The objective of the criminal trial is that justice should be done, that the innocent should be acquitted, and that so far as possible evidence proving that the guilty defendant is indeed guilty should be produced to enable the guilty defendant to consider his plea, and if he persists in his denial, available to prove his guilt. Our system is adversarial. It depends on the proposition that the results of the adversarial system will represent justice. But we have to face the reality that if the adversarial system does not produce justice—that is, justice to everyone involved in the process—it will have to be re-examined, and it should be re-examined. If it fails to do justice, then the system needs to be changed.

At present I see no reason to suggest that the adversarial system should be modified so as to provide, for example, for cross-examination to be conducted by a court-appointed advocate to investigate creditworthiness, or adding to the responsibilities of the intermediary some kind of facilitator or expert role, some kind of neutral examiner responsibility—a proposal, let it be noted, supported by the majority of the Pigot committee.

I have great faith in the adaptability of our system, and the ability of all those involved in it, whether judges or advocates, to recognise when change is necessary. The changes during my own professional career underline why my faith is justified. I do very much hope that my successor, or two or three down the line, is not required to give the Law Reform Lecture explaining why the system which I value no longer has any place in their modern world because it is no longer achieving justice.

Expert Evidence and Accreditation

I cannot find a note which tells me where and when I delivered this lecture, but I think it was given to the Institute of Expert Witnesses; judging from the material, it must have been given in about 2004.

MY PURPOSE IN this morning's address is to take a broad look at some of the issues relating to expert evidence, perhaps reminding ourselves of the difficulties inherent in any system of law in which expert evidence is admissible. And that must mean any proper system of law. Without expert evidence, justice could not be done in our courts, or in the courts of any civilised country. However with expert evidence difficulties are absolutely inevitable, because if we knew which of them is right and which wrong then, in reality, we should not need experts. So what are we after?

> If matters arise in our law which concern other sciences or faculties we commonly apply for the aid of that science or faculty which it concerns. This is a commendable thing in our law. For thereby it appears that we do not dismiss all other sciences but our own, but we approve of them and encourage them as things worthy of commendation.

The language is surprisingly modern. Yet the words were used in a judgment as long ago as 1553.[1] If the premise is that the issue of expert evidence is a delicate and difficult subject, the starting point is that we must all approach the discussion with humility. All of us, without exception, must do so.

In medieval times it was well understood that if a woman became pregnant, she could not have been the victim of rape. In 1491, many of us knew perfectly well that the earth was flat. If in 1553 Nicholas Copernicus had come into court and explained that the Sun was at the centre of our universe and that the Earth orbited around it, if lucky, he would have been laughed out of court; and if unlucky, locked up for heresy. And, and this is the point to emphasise, the judge, and the jury, and everyone in court, and assuming that there had been national television, every expert on television would have agreed. He was either a lunatic, or inspired by the devil;

---

[1] *Buckley v Rice-Thomas* (1554) 1 Plow 118.

and whichever it may have been, he was certainly and undoubtedly wrong. And the same view would have been taken in the courts in France, or Spain, or any of the German principalities, or indeed anywhere in Europe.

Yet, as we now know, they were all wrong. Even the great Aristotle was wrong. So—horror of horrors—was the 19th psalm when it referred to the Sun in these terms:

His going forth is from the end of Heaven

And his circuit unto the end of it.

It took great courage to challenge the accepted wisdom. If for no other reason Galileo's name will be immortalised as long as the human spirit survives. I am indebted to Robert Hargreaves' wonderful book, *The First Freedom*,[2] for this summary of how Galileo's

contribution to the emancipation of the human mind has lived on, though it would be other lands and other cultures that built on his stubborn and sometimes belligerent insistence that material facts and the laws of science were to be established by independent enquiry, unfettered by the power of any outside authority to overrule them. Like Socrates before him, he showed that mere authority cannot suppress the search for truth. The lead he gave set scientific enquiry on a course it has followed for three and a half centuries, and engendered a passion for truth that gave the eighteenth-century Enlightenment its motto. *Sapere aude*—dare to know.

Note the emphasis on the passion for truth.

So, that is what we are after: the search for knowledge with a passion for the truth, always open to the possibility that one generation's certainty may in the end turn out to be wrong. Note, however, the way I put it. 'The possibility'; 'may be wrong'. Just because science is new it does not follow that it is right. Recent research may come to the wrong conclusions or point us in the wrong directions. So you do not discard old knowledge in the way that the consumer society discards its wrapping. It would be so easy if old knowledge was always right, or indeed always wrong, and new knowledge always wrong, or always right.

Anyone here could amply take up a day on this theme. Generally, acceptance that knowledge has indeed advanced has not come cheaply or easily. New ideas are not always received with enthusiasm; sometimes they are positively rejected. Hence the need for humility, all round.

---

[2] Robert Hargreaves, *The First Freedom: A History of Free Speech* (Stroud, 2002).

There is no avoiding the simple reality that we need expert evidence in court, just as we need experts in our daily lives. If my roof is leaking, or my car is broken, or I am unwell, I need an expert to help me. And if you were to compile a book of the number of leaking roofs that were mended, or broken cars that were mended, or patients who visited their doctors, whose condition was accurately diagnosed and sensibly treated, the successes would be multitudinous when set against the occasions of disappointment or disaster.

There is, however, this crucial distinction. Out of court the expert is following his profession—exercising his judgement. In court he is part of a system in which the issue is in dispute, helping another expert or decision-making body to resolve the difference. In court, the judge is striving to discover the truth; in a criminal case so far as it can, so is the jury. But not everyone involved in litigation is always striving for the truth. The guilty defendant certainly does not want justice to be done. He has a positive interest in justice not being done. He is almost certainly telling lies to his lawyers, and his instructions about events which form the basis of expert evidence called on his behalf are likely to be tainted. In cases involving the future of children, the judge is often given conflicting versions of events, one of which may well be inaccurate or incomplete, either deliberately, or because of the understandable emotional sensitivities which can distort memory or create amnesia. Perhaps therefore the first task for any expert, in whatever litigation, called by whichever side, is that he or she must maintain a judicial sense of realism and dispassion and neutrality.

Both at the Bar and as a judge, I have seen experts demonstrate this essential quality, and the complete integrity that led them to offer evidence to the court which was inimical to the interest of the side which had first instructed and called them. We should not underestimate the pressures on a witness, expert or otherwise, who has supported one side or the other, to not change his mind. Nor should we, as judges, underestimate the difficulties which are imposed on expert witnesses to express themselves in language which is appropriate to the forensic arena, but which involves concepts which may not be truly susceptible to such treatment. And we may all just push the expert forward to give a little more 'helpful' evidence which leads him to stray off the true field of his expertise. The process, after all, requires a judge or jury to decide between experts, and an expert who is able to produce a favourable impression based on stance, demeanour, confidence, voice, and so on, may have a disproportionate advantage over his hesitant, contemplative colleague whose expertise is, in truth, just that fraction deeper or wider, and who, if the entire process were confined to paper, and he was allowed a week to reflect on questions from the other side, might produce the more accurate responses. And finally, we simply cannot ignore the fact that, just like an honest identifying witness, an expert of undoubted integrity and experience in his speciality may sometimes be wrong.

It has not taken rocket science to discern the two essential questions about expert evidence. The first is whether the expert is right. That involves assessing his (or her) means of knowledge and experience, as well as any material which tends to contradict him. The second is whether his integrity in the very broadest sense, in relation to every aspect of the detail of his evidence, is total.

All this leads me to reflect that we live in an age of increased specialisation. It is virtually impossible to nourish a successful practice as a general common lawyer. When I began at the Bar the specialisation was advocacy. Nowadays it is very difficult to be regarded as an expert, even in personal injury work. Leading counsel are increasingly sought for their expertise in medical negligence cases, or architectural negligence, or solicitors' negligence. The general surgeon will gradually give way to the specialist ankle, knee and hip surgeon. And a mining engineer and a mechanical engineer and a computer engineer are all engineers, but what they have in common is the description of their profession, rather than their specialist expertise. So we need more and more experts in court, just as we need more and more specialists in our daily lives. So we shall be using more and more expert witnesses.

As I understand it, the police service nationally holds on record a list of over 2,000 expert witnesses. Of course some come on and join the list while others leave it, for any number of reasons, including retirement, or a challenge to their expertise. But it is a very large number of potential expert witnesses. We are therefore not addressing a tiny offshoot of the justice system. The expert witness is integral to it.

Accreditation is the current buzz-word. We need to be careful not to assume that because it is a very long word, it can carry a very heavy weight. We must not over-burden or rush it. It may well constitute part of the answer, but in my view it certainly does not constitute the whole answer.

I start with four propositions. First, absence of accreditation cannot be regarded as a disqualification from an individual acting as an expert witness. It is the court which decides whether a witness is to be treated as an expert, or not.

Second, if there is to be a system of accreditation, it needs to be a system rather than a series of different bodies going about what is perceived to be the same problem in different ways.

Third, the success of any accreditation system would depend on the quality of the accreditors, and at the level at which accreditation would be pitched.

And perhaps, finally, a cautious reminder that even the best system of accreditation would still leave the occasional fallible expert, and the occasional over-committed expert. Accreditation would not do away with the fallibility which marks each of us as individuals, and each and every system for which and within which we work.

Let me amplify all that. I simply do not see how it would be right or possible to achieve a system in which individuals who are treated as experts in their particular professions or occupations are to be denied the opportunity to give evidence as experts, or that the parties who wish to call them as experts may be prevented from doing so, merely because they have not been signed up by or signed up voluntarily to a system of accreditation. We have to be realistic. We cannot say, for example, of a consultant surgeon, a Fellow of the Royal College of Surgeons currently in practice, that he is not to be permitted to give evidence of matters within his speciality if he or she is not accredited. Ignoring the court's role, notice my words, 'not to be permitted'—that means disqualified. In last week's *Times* it was reported that a substantial number of individuals were admitted as Fellows of the Royal Society of Chemistry. They are entitled to use the letters FRSC. Who would be entitled to refuse to accredit such an individual if accreditation was sought? Do we anticipate some exams? And if so, which busy consultant surgeon would be prepared to undergo whatever tests were thought appropriate? After all, integrity, and a commitment to the qualities and tradition of a profession, are the hallmarks of every professional.

Then, again, we have cases in which particular expertise is required in the most narrow field of science. I once tried a case of murder where the tiniest of snails, effectively invisible to the naked eye, was found in the tread of the sole of a trainer. It mattered to the case that the snail could not survive away from running water. In short, it was a very narrow area of specialisation, with very few experts in the field, and such experts would very rarely be needed to give evidence. Accreditation for them would be a pointless exercise. And, what is more, in such a specialist field, it would be difficult to find experts to be responsible for accreditation who were themselves any wiser or more experienced than the expert whose credentials were being tested. What is more, would anyone have accredited Copernicus, or Galileo?

We need to think further on whether there should be automatic qualification based on practical experience or professional qualifications, or whether indeed accreditation is a distinct process. For example, section 12(2) of the Mental Health Act identifies a form of speciality among medical practitioners whose evidence is needed before the court can make a hospital order. I mean no discourtesy to those who have been granted the qualification, but it does not represent the pinnacle of forensic psychiatric expertise. That requires much more. It leads me, in parenthesis, to another observation. Although I was a practitioner in the field, I have to confess that I had not myself fully appreciated the limitations of this statutory qualification. This came home to me when I became a full-time judge running criminal justice training. So we also need to address the issue of training the judiciary, in criminal cases, in how to train or inform the jury of the true significance of the expert's qualifications. Perhaps a well-trained judge can ask the necessary questions.

Next any system has to be managed and run. What I am driving at is that there is no point in a system of accreditation if the process gets bogged down in bureaucracy. And what is more, if there is to be such a system, it is unlikely to be of huge benefit if the expert starts his evidence by describing all 19 organisations by which he or she is accredited. Who then evaluates those accreditors?

I now turn to some further aspects of accreditation which perhaps may be worth thought.

— The ideal expert witness knows his subject. However much theory and however many papers written by other people he can quote, it is always better for him to be practising in the field of his expertise, or only just recently retired from it. A few years away from practice, at a time when so many areas of speciality are zooming ahead, a commitment to being an expert witness rather than an expert practitioner is disadvantageous.

— It is the mark of a true expert that he is called by both sides. In other words, the expert should not become known as a plaintiffs' expert or a defendants' expert, or a prosecution or defence expert. Some do. Some are always called on the same side. They sometimes begin to appear to be hired guns. By way of analogy, I happen to think that barristers in criminal practice should appear both for the prosecution and the defence. It is easier for a barrister to remember that things can go wrong in a police station if his clients instruct him from time to time that they have done. Similarly, it is wise for a barrister to be reminded that things often go right, and according to the book in the police station. His judgement is better if he has continuing experience on both sides.

— And of course, there must be no cheating. Obviously, I am not here referring to downright deliberate lies or manipulation of material: more to emphasising the critical words in the oath, 'the whole truth and nothing but the truth'. Good experts know this perfectly well, and do not do it. If the evidence drifts into an area about which the expert can give some evidence, but which is outside his precise field of expertise, the temptation to give the evidence without a warning must be resisted. Of course, having to say 'I don't know' or even 'This is on the fringes of my expertise', and to do so in public, particularly at a time when everyone in court may be hanging on every word, is difficult. But we expect an advocate to tell the court of authorities which contradict his own case. And advocates do. In court, we rely on them and are justified in doing so. We are entitled to expect that expert witnesses will not step outside their true expertise. They are 'officers of the court'. They really must not give evidence, or conceal evidence, in order to produce the result which they 'know' will be right because that is what their side wants.

— And I wonder whether we need to be much more alert to the occasions when the expert lets himself or his profession down. If a police officer's evidence has been disbelieved, he is liable to be cross-examined about that occasion whenever his credibility is called into question. If an expert has been disbelieved, whether on the basis that he has told lies, or that his expertise is in doubt, the same rules of evidence apply. How do we find out? How do we find out about the occasions in the Family Division, in cases involving children, which are held in chambers, that a particular expert has been disbelieved? How can we equate the privacy which cases involving children require with publication of occasions of concern? Ought there to be a central registry, to which information of this kind should be sent? And someone working at the registry to make the information, and the relevant judgments, available? Would such a registry be more valuable than accreditation? Or at least as valuable? Both would help, but if we had sufficient funds only to have one rather than the other, which should come first?

I must stop. Perhaps I could end by drawing attention to one of the concerns that has struck me with increasing force when reflecting on this topic. A number of different organisations are working on the issues with which today's meeting is concerned. It is not until you start thinking about it and make enquiry that the full extent becomes apparent. Thus we have just had the report from Baroness Kennedy on *Sudden Unexpected Deaths in Infancy*.[3] Shortly the Legal Services Commission will put out a consultation paper on the use of experts. In reality, this is the way the tide is running—and when a tide is running, the opportunity to use it must not be lost. There are many more examples, and my concern—and I should like this meeting, and similar meetings, to address it—is that the end product of all these initiatives must be a cohesive system for dealing with expert evidence. There is no monopoly of wisdom on these matters. If any system is to be workable, a series of different initiatives will have to be brought together for analysis, and examination, to produce the most efficient system we can devise.

---

[3] Royal College of Pathologists and Royal College of Paediatrics and Child Health, *Sudden Unexpected Deaths in Infancy* (2004).

Miscarriages of Justice

This lecture was given to the Netherlands Council for the Judiciary at The Hague in November 2007. As the text shows, I was invited to The Hague to discuss possible arrangements for rectifying miscarriages of justice and quashing unsafe convictions.

IT IS A privilege for me as an English judge to be addressing this distinguished gathering in such magnificent surroundings. 1648, when this church started being built, is a date of great significance to you here in the Netherlands.

It was in 1648, using the old method of calculating, when the year did not end on 31st December, that in England we removed the king's head from his shoulders in January 1648 (as it now is, 1649), and demonstrated that no one was above the law. So it is important for us too.

I am not coming to The Hague to tell you how to do anything at all. That would be an impertinence. I am coming to The Hague to pay my respects to an old friend, Bert van Delden, as he reaches retirement from his present distinguished post. I shall reflect a while with you on one judicial quality which never receives the attention it deserves. To be a good judge we need many attributes. We need to be intelligent, knowledgeable about the law but wise about the ways of the world, sensitive to others from different backgrounds to our own, fair and open-minded and balanced, independent in spirit, courageous to do what we believe to be right even when that will be unpopular, whether with politicians, the executive, or the media; but to all these ingredients and others, I add the requirements of judicial modesty and humility.

In this magnificent church I have not come to preach to you. If I wanted to preach I would ascend up to the pulpit. I want to talk about that vital quality, judicial humility, and the need for us, as judges, to remember how Montaigne put it in his great work,[1] which I suspect is hardly ever read these days, at the end, when he said 'no matter how high the throne on which you sit, you're always

---

[1] Michel de Montaigne, *The Complete Essays*, trans MA Screech (Harmondsworth, 1991).

sitting on your own backside', although I suspect that in the original French he used a rather coarser word than 'backside'.

The most powerful judges in the world may be the most powerful judges in the world, but they are and remain human beings, sitting on their own backsides, with the capacity for error, for mistake, for fallibility, that is part of our common humanity. No trumpets blow for judicial modesty and humility, but they are nonetheless noble judicial qualities shared by the best of judges.

No one exemplifies these characteristics better than Bert van Delden himself. Indeed he is not a man to blow his own trumpet. He is not a man to shout and draw attention to himself. But when he speaks you want to hear what he is saying. When he speaks you are listening to a man whose words do not obscure his meaning. When he speaks it is to get good things done, whether at home or in Europe generally, not to bask in self-glorification.

Bert has had a remarkable career, and indeed he is not yet disappearing into that gentle goodnight of retirement. You will know all about his curriculum vitae, and it would be insulting to you for me to rehearse it.

In the end what matters about a man is the man himself. However distinguished his career, whatever his public reputation and fame, every man, and for that matter every woman, in the end has to live with himself or herself, and with his or her own conscience. By that ultimate test, I am sure that Bert should be entirely at peace with himself.

The issue that I want to address is a profoundly important one to any individual exercising judicial power. And we have to face the fact that that is what we are doing. Exercising power. The power to lock up an individual, to deprive him of his liberty, even for 24 hours, is a desperately important power. It has to be exercised with great circumspection. It demands not only intelligence, but integrity. All of us involved in the administration of justice are committed to a simple principle, which is that in every case before our courts, justice will be done according to law. When I became a judge, I took an ancient oath that I would 'do right to all manner of people according to the laws and usages of this realm, without fear or favour, affection or ill will'.

Notice, do right—not vague; positively *do right.*

That oath reflects the aspiration of every judge in any civilised country, and it reflects his hope that every other judge sitting in his jurisdiction will have the same ambition. And yet, however determined we all are to ensure that justice is done, there have been, and there will continue to be, occasions when justice miscarries. The evidence before the court may be incorrect, sometimes deliberately misleading and untruthful, sometimes just simply mistaken, but coming from an apparently convincing source or witness. Sometimes, too, acting in good conscience, the decision-making body, that is the court, composed as it is of human beings, just gets it wrong. It is, of course, a miscarriage of justice if a guilty man is acquitted, but the most troublesome to all our consciences is the miscarriage of justice which leads to punishment and incarceration of a truly innocent individual. And I suspect that each and every such case is painful not only to those pre-eminently involved in it, that is those responsible for the erroneous decision, but it is also painful to every judge, whose personal conscience is afflicted by the enormity of what has happened. Yet every judge knows that any error his colleague made today may be one he will make tomorrow. That is why we need judicial humility.

As you probably appreciate, in England and Wales our criminal justice system is very different from your own. In any serious criminal cases we have a system of trial by jury. The judge himself plays no part in the decision whether the defendant is to be acquitted or convicted. My experience has demonstrated that juries take their duties as seriously as professional judges do. They do their utmost to return what we call a true verdict according to the evidence. In our system, the pre-eminence of the jury means that the Court of Appeal does not interfere with their verdict unless there are good grounds for doing so. Unless there is fresh evidence, the grounds are almost always judicial error. That means that there is a public judgment, criticising the judge for the error. That is painful for him, but that, as the saying is, goes with the territory. That is the job. We cannot hide our mistakes, or expect a higher court to keep them hidden.

I repeat, judges do not make the decision whether a defendant is guilty or not. That is exclusively the province of the jury. Actually that is not quite what a jury does. What it decides is whether the defendant is proved by the evidence to be guilty of the crime alleged. In the Court of Appeal we are never, or virtually never, considering whether the jury was right or wrong. We are considering whether there was evidence to justify the jury's conclusions. In particular we are not considering whether the defendant found guilty by the jury was guilty or innocent. We are only considering whether the conviction is safe. However, whatever the system, jury, judge alone, group of judges, mixed judge and jury, whatever the system, from time to time it produces an injustice and then within each system there is an appeal process, and in every system the process of appeal is different. Our appeal system requires the Court of Appeal to quash a conviction if we think that the conviction may be unsafe.

Notice this does not involve a conclusion that the defendant is in fact an innocent man. A conviction may be unsafe because the jury has been misdirected by the judge. It may be unsafe because the process which brought the individual to court was itself flawed, and the officers of state behaved in such a way that the rule of law itself was undermined. In other words, the system accepts that individuals who are truly guilty may nevertheless be entitled to have their convictions quashed. So it does not necessarily follow from a successful appeal that the decision to quash the conviction means that a truly innocent man was convicted in the first place. It is enough that the conviction is thought to be unsafe. If it is, it must be quashed. We also have the power, and often exercise it, then to order a fresh trial before a new judge and jury. All the evidence is examined, the old and any new evidence, and the jury then returns its verdict.

Our processes have never been foolproof. There are a number of cases where evidence which emerges after trial may cast doubt not only on the safety of the conviction, but which shows that the defendant is and always was truly innocent. We have just been reminded of the shocking case of Stefan Kiszko. He was convicted of murdering a small child. He served 16 years in prison. Fresh evidence emerged at the end of that period of a scientific nature which demonstrated that, and I am paraphrasing a very long story, one of the crucial pieces of evidence against him, sperm found on the child's underclothes, could not have come from him. His conviction was quashed in 1991 or 1992. A few weeks ago, another man went on trial for the same murder. Basing itself largely on the developments in the science of DNA, the prosecution successfully established the link between him and the murdered child. Kiszko's conviction represented a terrible and desperately sad miscarriage of justice.

Every country, and every judicial system, has its Kiszko cases. Sometimes they will be just as high profile, sometimes less so. Any judge who asserts that his system of justice never has had its Kiszko cases is, with great respect, blind to the realities. With the best will in the world, no system is perfect. It cannot be.

Apart from anything else we are learning all the time. How many experts would have given evidence in 1490 that the world was round? Endless professors from Leyden University, Bert's alma mater, and Cambridge University, my own, would have come to tell the jury what their eyes tell them anyway. The earth was flat. Who on earth in any court in Europe in, say, 1550 or 1560 would have believed Copernicus and Galileo that the earth moved round the sun, not the sun and stars around the earth? They would have been laughed at. Indeed in Galileo's case, it was much worse. He was tried for heresy. We now know that he was right. The story of human error is an old one. I sometimes wonder what special factors about the way we do things now in 2007, and what we believe to be plainly obvious, will be revealed as the years go by to have been wrong. But it is not just experts, it is every aspect of human life which is open to the possibility of error. It is an essential part of the human condition that we are fallible. The institutions created by and run by human beings are themselves subject to the same human fallibility.

And yet in court we still have to act on evidence. We cannot give our decisions based on some broad understanding of the potential for human fallibility. We are after all required to make a decision. We are in post and it is our duty to give judgment, not to avoid it, not to lack the necessary judicial courage to say what we think. We cannot be judges and evade our responsibilities. We cannot be judges and take the cowardly way out.

In England we first acknowledged the possibility of error in the criminal justice system relating to jury cases exactly 100 years ago this year. The Court of Criminal Appeal was created. I have touched briefly on its remit, as it currently stands. More important for recent purposes was the creation of the Criminal Cases Review Commission, exactly 10 years ago, in 1997.

It is important to remember that in our system the defendant was only permitted to use the process of appeal against conviction once. After that, he depended on the exercise of what used to be described as the Royal Prerogative of mercy. In practice, certainly since the beginning of the last century, that meant that there was a small department in the Home Office which was charged with examining convictions in the light of any fresh evidence that might become available. It was not a satisfactory process. The number of cases referred to the Court through it was very small.

The creation of the Commission publicly acknowledged not only the possibility of fresh evidence arising in any case, which is always a potential ground for appeal, but identified the body that should be properly resourced to exercise an independent function, in among other things, the examination of the actual evidence at trial as well as fresh evidence in close detail, indeed every aspect of the investigation of the crime, and the trial process itself. The Commission resulted from some brilliant thinking at a time of great public concern arising from unsafe convictions following IRA atrocities. It was a time of great ferment. Not surprisingly, there was considerable public disquiet. There were some pretty strange ideas floating about, which largely consisted of setting up some new body, consisting of the great and the good (whoever they are), who would somehow be able to tell whether a conviction was safe or not, largely on the basis of what was being reported in the newspapers and on the television. That was not a very sound idea. It was not only judges who thought that that particular idea was not a very sound one.

Those who supported the idea of the new Commission, and this would be true of any such body created in any country, believed that it must be an independent body, independent of political or media pressure and altogether independent of judicial control. It could not be the judiciary investigating the way the system operated in an individual case.

But, at the same time, it would only be constitutionally acceptable if the Commission itself was given no power to take ultimate judicial decisions. These were to remain and do remain the exclusive responsibility of the Court of Appeal. That remains the only body vested with power to interfere with the verdict of a jury. Constitutionally the structure is impeccable.

So the Commission is not a court, although it operates within the statutory framework which governs the jurisdiction of the Court of Appeal. It is linked to the Court of Appeal in two ways. First, it can refer any conviction, however old, to the Court of Appeal whether or not there have been one or more unsuccessful previous appeals. It also is available to the court when we need help, when the case before us reveals reasons for concern which perhaps have not been fully investigated by the prosecution and/or the appellant, and we invite the Commission to conduct appropriate investigations.

There are a number of important features about the Commission which are worth underlining. Its responsibility is to consider and decide not whether a conviction is a safe conviction, but whether to refer a conviction to the court for the court to make that decision. The question for the Commission is whether there is a real possibility that the conviction will be considered unsafe by the Court of Appeal. That is crucial to our system, and I would suggest to any new Commission, or its equivalent in any country. In the end the decisions must be made by a court, and as I have said, in England convictions returned by a jury can only be interfered with by the Court of Appeal. (For present purposes, I shall not go into the system of appeals from magistrates' courts, but the route is to a higher court, known as the Crown Court, and the Commission can refer convictions returned by magistrates' courts to the Crown Court.)

Appointment to the Commission is made by the Queen. That coincides with judicial appointment, and reflects the reality that the Commission has a quasi-judicial function. On the other hand appointment to the Commission is not a permanent appointment. No one can serve on the Commission for more than 10 years, and some serve for less. The staff of course include lawyers to give advice, and one third of the Commission must be lawyers, and two thirds of them must have some experience of the criminal justice system. Every commissioner will have had a different professional lifetime experience—an accountant, a nurse and former National Health Service Chief Executive, an investigative journalist, and the like. They are also men and women chosen not merely for their integrity, but for their independence of mind.

The Commission may refer a case where the appeal process has taken place and where, but for the Commission, it would effectively be exhausted.

What produces an unsafe conviction? I suppose ultimately this means that something has gone wrong somewhere along the process of investigation or trial itself. You can identify a number of factors for yourselves, but let me suggest a few examples.

— Confessions to a crime which are later proved to be unreliable, whether because of unfair pressures exerted on the defendant, or indeed his inadequacy, neither of which were properly appreciated at the time.
— Improper practice by the investigating authorities which only comes to light at a later stage.
— Unreliable testimony by an apparently reliable witness. An example from a recent case: complaints of sexual misconduct, denied adamantly by the defendant, but on the face of them reliable, were made by a young woman who was subsequently proved to have made false complaints on other occasions, unearthed by the Commission. This of course did not prove she was lying about this particular case, but it meant that her reliability as a complainant in sexual cases was doubtful.
— Flawed expert evidence, dividing itself into two areas. First, whether a crime was committed at all. For example, did the mother murder her babies, or was their death the result of

natural but as yet still unknown causes? In other words, Galileo again, in cases where the prosecution relied heavily on a world-renowned authority in this particular field. It is hard to imagine a worse torture for a mother than to lose her babies through death, and then find herself convicted and sentenced to imprisonment for life for having murdered them when she did not, when the deaths were natural.[2] The second is where there is no doubt the crime has been committed, but the expert evidence at trial no longer bears the weight which was attached to it. Another recent example was the significance of a speck of gunshot residue found on the defendant's clothing. Those of you who watch any English television will know of the cold-blooded shooting of Jill Dando. New evidence suggests that the prosecution case attached more evidence to that speck of residue than it deserved. The conviction was therefore unsafe, and there will be a new trial.

The examples could continue indefinitely.

As you appreciate, the Commission is granted power to investigate the circumstances of a conviction in a totally independent role. If it decides that a conviction should be referred to the court, then it makes its own observations, and of course sends copies of its report to both the defendant and the prosecution as well as the court. Thereafter the defendant becomes the appellant, usually using the evidence and witnesses found by the Commission. Indeed on occasions, when the prosecution sees the results of the Commission's investigation, it immediately accepts that the conviction is unsafe.

One reason for requiring the commissioners to be men and women of independent mind is that they receive well over a thousand cases from convicted defendants every year. Some of these defendants are professional criminals, and they are perfectly well able to put pressure on the Commission, or at any rate to try to. Some defendants' families will never accept his guilt, and they too, understandably if they believe genuinely that the defendant is innocent, will also try to apply pressure. In any one year the Commission refers to the court about 4 per cent of the cases referred to it. So there has to be, and there is, a dispassionate objectivity in the way they go about their work. When a conviction is referred, over the last 10 years, the court has tended to quash about two thirds of the cases referred, leaving the convictions to stand in about one third. Mathematics is

---

[2] *R v Cannings* [2004] EWCA Crim 1 provides but one example.

a dangerous master in this field, and we need to be careful about statistics. But, in the period 2006–7 the convictions of 39 individuals were heard by the court, and 25 of them were quashed as unsafe. In many cases that is the end of it. In others there were or will be new trials, where the case will be investigated again, and it is reasonable to expect, and experience has shown, that often, but by no means always, the new jury will return a conviction. But that conviction is safe whereas the first one was not.

Judges throughout our system welcome the Commission's work. It is a hugely valuable weapon in the fight—yes fight—to avoid and prevent, but if necessary to admit and acknowledge, that a conviction thought to be safe at the time when it was returned has turned out not to be so. And as a court, we invite the Commission, because we have the power to do so, to conduct investigations at the behest of the court, where we have concerns about the quality of the work being done by either side. The senior judiciary has complete faith in the integrity and quality of the work of the Commission, which is carried out to the very highest possible standards. When, as judges, we say 'thank you' to the Commission for its work, that is not simply a token gesture of gratitude.

That does not mean that we always agree with the Commission. That is simple to understand. The Commission exercises a different function to the court. As I have explained, they refer cases where there is a real possibility that the conviction may be unsafe, but we quash only those which we conclude are unsafe. But whether we agree or disagree, as judges, both here, and at home, and in any civilised country, surely we should welcome light being thrown into any dark corners, and indeed we do. And by doing so, we make it less likely that a truly innocent man who has been convicted will remain convicted of a crime he did not commit.

A very important question arises. It is perhaps best expressed in this way. Has the creation of the Commission damaged public confidence in the judiciary or indeed in the jury system? That is a serious point—although surely no one could justify keeping a man in prison if he may not be guilty, simply in order to avoid damage to the public image and standing of judges and juries.

For what it is worth, and as far as I know there is no research on the subject, my strong impression is after a little understandable early excitement, the public has come to view the Commission as an integral part of the administration of justice—no more, no less. Like the trial judge himself, or the jury itself, it is now one of our safeguards—a new safeguard admittedly—but a safeguard against wrongdoing and error. As to the jury system, public confidence is unshaken. We retain an intuitive belief in the jury system. Criticise it, and we leap 800 years back to Magna Carta and what we regard as the immensely valuable concomitant of the jury system, which is the direct involvement, in every serious case where the defendant pleads not guilty, of 12 members of the public chosen at random to involve themselves in and be involved in their own criminal justice system. I am not here to explain the jury system, but I can assure you that the Commission's work has not eroded public confidence in it.

May I end where I began.

I have not come to preach, to tell you that what we do in England is perfect. Far from it. The issue for you is how you address this question here in the Netherlands. You cannot dig up a plant that grows in a foreign country, and examine its roots, and then stick it into a hole in the ground in your own. It will not flourish. How you address the question in the Netherlands depends on your history, your history as a nation, the route which took you from where it all began to where you are now. It involves your existing system for the administration of justice, and your own judicial structures. It would be utterly presumptuous of me, who was not brought up to it, to attempt to tell you how you should plant a Commission, and what shape it should take. So I have not done so. You must choose the plant, which must be suitable for the ground in which you hope it will grow. My objective has been to stimulate your own thoughts about these issues by offering you a few tentative thoughts from across the Channel. And so we say farewell to Bert, a man, a great man, who would have adorned the judicial system of any civilised country but who is, at it happens, an ornament of your own.

The Sentencing Decision

This lecture was given at Birmingham University in March 2009. I have given a virtually identical lecture on numerous occasions, both before and since, reflective of the public interest and concern about sentencing decisions. The 'Adam and Eve' analogy first struck me in the very early 1990s, and I have used it ever since. I have also heard of others using it. What has struck me during the many years I have given this or a similar lecture is that the responses of my audiences to the questions posed to them demonstrate that there is a continuing gap between the facts relating to sentence and public (mis)conceptions of those facts.

THIS IS A subject about which I have spoken publicly on a number of occasions, and I do not apologise for repeating what I have said before.

Whenever I speak on the subject of the sentencing decision I remember how the best stories always start at the beginning. You cannot go nearer the beginning than the Book of Genesis. It was in the Garden of Eden that the first crime was committed and the first sentence was imposed.

Let me give you a thumbnail picture of the case.

Adam knew that eating the apple was expressly forbidden, but knowing that it was forbidden he deliberately involved himself in the crime. It is true that he did not know the likely range of sentence, but neither the Human Rights Act nor the European Convention on Human Rights had been propounded. In the Garden of Eden everything was perfect and these rights were not needed. So for what his counsel described in mitigation as 'picking an apple', just one small wizened little apple, probably tomorrow's windfall, he was expelled from the Garden of Eden, and we, his progeny, have been subjected to tribulations and sadnesses ever since.

There is another side to the story, of course. Listening to his counsel, the sentence sounds manifestly excessive—such horrendous consequences for scrumping a single apple. But you have to remember the prosecution case against him in Eden Crown Court. It was not that he had pinched a little apple, and eaten it. His crime was to be seeking power—power in the form of knowledge, power enough to make him equal with God or Godlike. So this was not just eating a small, wizened little apple. This was a deliberate challenge to the rule of law and the cause of irreparable damage to the whole fabric of creation. All our consequent tribulations and sadnesses are down to him. On this view no punishment could adequately make up for the heinousness of his crime. Hanging would be too good for him. How shocking that he was given a complete let-off, literally allowed to walk free, straight out of court into the world.

Let us consider Eve. Was the punishment unfair to her? Although guilty, according to her counsel she had been led astray by Adam. He was the one who knew the secret of the apple; she did not really fully appreciate it. Her husband was very domineering, and God hadn't really trusted her with the information which he had given to Adam—and moreover an unknown defendant incited her.

That would have been quite tricky mitigation to advance— to blame a serpent or snake would have taken forensic skill. Was she incited? Did she incite Adam? Which of them was to blame? Would you remember such facts as you acquired about the case, two days or even two hours after you had read them in the paper? And which facts would you remember if some months later a 'Free Eve' campaign were mounted? Or would you simply be left with an impression of the case which confirmed your own prejudices and the line adopted by the editor of the newspaper you happened to choose to read. Your view would almost certainly depend therefore on whether you read the *Heavenly Times*, or the *Guardian Angel*, or the *Daily Hail*.

But for today's purposes should there have been any distinction between the two defendants in the Crown Court? Was either of them more culpable? The sentencer did not see any difference. They had the same sentence. And now to the crucial question: did the sentence do any good? However you approach the answer, that Draconian penalty certainly did not stop crime, and in the next generation one of their sons killed the other. The pre-sentence report for Mr Cain would certainly have blamed his parents' criminal background. What chance did he have? Perhaps you should blame the judge for the sentence? Could you argue that the first homicide in history was the fault of the judge in Eden Crown Court who was not too lenient, but far too severe? Should the judge perhaps have given them a warning? A clang of the gates of Paradise with them outside, for maybe three months, with a solemn warning when they returned: 'Now you know what it is like outside. Any further offences and next time you will be out for good.' Would that have worked? Would their experience outside Paradise contaminate their innocence beyond restoration?

It's all there in the first book of the Bible, the Book of Genesis. It's easier to get hold of than Bracton or Glanville or any of our great medieval law writers. There it is. The first crime. The first sentence. The consequences of the first crime. The consequences of the first sentencing decision. Like every such decision, it was a unique decision; like every unique decision, it had and contributed to a wider context. But if, on your way home, you choose to discuss any of the issues to which this lecture may give rise, you will see, on examination, that the issues then were very similar to the issues which arise in the sentencing decision in court today.

You will of course have spotted one crucial difference. There was not then, and by definition could not have been at the time the first crime was committed, the kind of fear of crime which is present in our society.

This consideration presents us all with a problem. I emphasise the 'us' because the 'us' is you and me, it is the judges and magistrates. If the fear—that is, the fear that we live in a dangerous society—is well founded, it must be addressed head-on. Society must be protected. The causes of crime must be understood and addressed. There is no short-term, easy fix. Mistrust anyone who suggests by implication that there may be. We need to be thinking now about how to wean those of today's children who are likely to fall into criminal ways in their teens away from that risk. But the part played by the sentencing judge in this process is limited.

Before an offender can be sentenced, he must be convicted of an offence. The judge does not walk the beat. He does not investigate the crime: that is for police officers with all the assistance they can receive. Nor does the judge bring the perpetrator of an offence to court: that depends on the police investigation and the willingness of witnesses to come forward and the decision of the CPS that he should be prosecuted. Judges do not decide whether the offender should be prosecuted, or cautioned. Unless the defendant pleads guilty, in any case in the Crown Court, juries, not judges, decide that question.

The two most important features of effective crime prevention are totally out of the hands of sentencing judges. Without being sentimental the first is childhood, upbringing, nurturing and education, and the love and discipline or loving discipline which, as I have said on a previous occasion, should be the birthright of every child, but is not. The second is the deterrent effect of the certainty or the near certainty that if you commit a crime you will in the end be caught, brought to justice and prosecuted to conviction. If you do not believe that is likely to happen, there is very little chance that you will think twice before committing an offence. And we then must ensure that—and this is where the judge starts to get involved—every guilty defendant who goes to court is frightened at the prospect of being sentenced.

None of this is rocket science, but unless we bear it in mind from time to time, there is a danger that it will be overlooked.

But can I return to the second feature which is critical to all these discussions. It is the public perception of crime. Whether the perception is right or is wrong, perception is an undeniable fact.

First, a word of warning. Always treat any statistics anyone gives you, including me, relating to crime, with care. Always examine precisely what the statistic is about.

The *British Crime Survey* for 2007/8 is quite an interesting piece of research and gives us a thumbnail picture of public perception. Something like 50,000 people are asked questions. Compare that with the sort of number used by pollsters to tell us what the public think of the current standing of our political parties.

In 2007/8, when 6,000 people were questioned specifically on the subject, the results showed this: 75% believed that sentences handed down by the courts were either too lenient or much too lenient, only 20% thought they were about right, and 2% that they were too tough. The remaining 3% were 'don't knows'. That itself is interesting. When political polls are taken the 'don't knows' are rarely as low as 3%.

Now that is a profoundly alarming statistic. We judges are public servants. We serve the community. Three-quarters of the population believe that we are not doing the job that we should be doing: sentencing with sufficient firmness. There are huge consequences to this perception, potentially profoundly damaging to our community.

So I am going to test you, each of you. The point of this exercise is to examine what you believe, and, set against what you believe, what the true facts are.

Now, no cheating.

1. What percentage of serious sexual offences against children occur in their own homes or in the home of the offender who is known to them?
2. What percentage of murders are committed by strangers?
3. In 2007 how many men aged 21 or over were
    (a)   convicted of dwelling house burglary
    (b)   sent to prison (in percentage terms)?

4. How many men aged 21 or over were
    (a) convicted of robbery
    (b) sent to prison (in percentage terms)?
5. How many men aged 21 or over were
    (a) convicted of rape
    (b) sentenced to imprisonment (in percentage terms)
    (c) and what was the average sentence?
6. What percentage of crimes recorded in the Crime Survey to which I have just referred involved crimes of violence of any kind, including all cases of robbery and including violent crimes where no injury at all was inflicted?

Now to the answers.[1]

1. The percentage of serious sexual offences against children occurring in their own homes or the home of the offender known to them is 80%.
2. Strangers to the victim commit 30% of all homicides. Even if we assume that the 15% of homicide cases for which there is no known suspect were all strangers, still that would mean that more than half the victims of murder know their killer.
3. 6,711 adult men were convicted of dwelling house burglary. 59% of them were sent to prison.
4. 2,652 men were convicted of robbery. 82% were sent to prison.
5. 707 men were convicted of rape. 97% were sent to prison, the remainder to secure hospitals. The average sentence was seven years' imprisonment.
6. Violence accounted, in round figures, for 20%.

Let us just look at some further information.

Let us take the case of rape. The *British Crime Survey* discovered that 34% of those questioned thought that less than half of those convicted of rape were sent to prison; another third (32%) thought that between 51% and 80% of rapists were sent to prison; only one third thought that over 80% of rapists went to prison.

In relation to robbery, the vast majority underestimated the proportion of those convicted of robbery who are sent to prison, well over half believing that the proportion of those so sentenced was below 45%. As to burglary, 82% thought that 50% or fewer house burglars were sent to prison. 8% had the figure right at between 51% and 70%, and 7% thought the figure would be over 70%. As to

---

[1] The answers were accurate when I gave them.

violence, where the true answer is 20%, the public thought that the figure was 50%. In other words they thought that 50% of all crime involved crimes of violence. Is it any wonder people are frightened?

This is a profoundly alarming story. If a large proportion of the population believe that significant numbers of rapists and robbers and burglars are not sent to prison, then it is hardly surprising that 75% of them believe that the sentences handed down by the courts are too lenient. And if I didn't know that all rapists, the overwhelming majority of adult robbers, and a large percentage of adult dwelling house burglars were sent to prison, I would not think that judges were doing a very good job, and I would think that they were being much too lenient.

You are an intelligent audience of people who have bothered to come out on a miserable Wednesday night. You are therefore interested in the subject, and many of you are informed about it. On that basis I should hope that most of you got seven or eight right answers.

What is strange about the perception is that we are currently living in a time when the prison population has rocketed so that the prisons are filled to overflowing. Some 10 years ago, Lord Bingham, then Lord Chief Justice, made this remark, commenting on the extraordinary paradox 'that judges and magistrates have been roundly criticised for over lenient sentencing during a period when they have been sending more defendants to prison, for longer periods, than at any time in the last 40 years'.

That was when there were 70,000 in prison. The actual numbers now are over 80,000, but more important, the population in prison has never been so high, either in terms of the proportion of the population overall or in absolute numbers.

Why do people get it wrong? Why do you, those few of you who did, score, say, less than 7 out of 10? Why is there this vast discrepancy between the fact and the perception?

Let me show you some headlines and figures from newspapers, written on the same day, following the publication of information to do with sentencing. These are typical.[2]

If you are wrong, you are probably in very good company. But that is how you receive your information about sentencing. It depends on which paper you come to read.

So how does a sentencing judge come to deal with the sentencing decision? There is nothing more difficult in the whole judicial process than the sentencing decision. Every single case is different.

---

[2] The newspaper extracts were taken during the week preceding the lecture.

The common law purposes have now been put into statutory form. We have section 142 and section 143 of the Criminal Justice Act 2003. The purposes identified by Parliament are as follows.

The relevant parts of section 142 and section 143 read:

Section 142(1)

Any court dealing with an offender in respect of his offence must have regard to the following purposes of sentencing —

(a) the punishment of offenders,
(b) the reduction of crime (including its reduction by deterrence),
(c) the reform and rehabilitation of offenders,
(d) the protection of the public, and
(e) the making of reparation by offenders to persons affected by their offences.

Section 143(1)

In considering the seriousness of any offence, the court must consider the offender's culpability in committing the offence and any harm which the offence caused, was intended to cause or might foreseeably have caused.

Who could argue with any of those?

All these purposes have to be balanced in each sentencing decision. In section 142 the purposes of sentencing are not described by Parliament as having any particular priority over each other. Not only is none more important than any other but these purposes are not always consistent. Reform and rehabilitation and punishment do not always go together. They are not always likely to produce the same conclusion. In addition, there are three further essential factors in issue, sometimes themselves conflicting, while the judge seeks to balance out the purposes of the sentence.

— First, there is the crime itself, and how it is perceived in contemporary society.
— Second, there is the victim, and the impact (note that word) of the crime on the victim.
— Third, there is the defendant, and the circumstances in which he came to commit the crime, and his or her attitude to the crime.

Not all of these three factors are objective. Indeed, two of them include at least an element of the subjective.

And finally, bear this in mind: any fool can sentence a piece of paper. A judge or magistrate is sentencing a live human being where another live human being has had to suffer the consequences of the crime.

So, let me analyse those three factors in more detail.

First, the crime itself. That is, the crime admitted, or proved. If a man is charged with seven offences of indecent assault, but only convicted of one, it is obvious to us that he can only be sentenced for the one. He cannot be sentenced for the other six. You cannot be sentenced for something you are not convicted of.

I emphasise the attitude of contemporary society, because public attitudes constantly change. I was told recently that in the sixteenth century, Henry VIII's Parliament—the Reformation Parliament—invented a new penalty for blasphemy: being boiled alive. Even Tudor England thought this was too much. Nowadays, blasphemy is so constant that we do not even notice it. In the eighteenth century it was not considered a crime to trick someone into parting with their goods or money. If you were stupid enough to be gulled, that was your fault. Too bad. When I started at the Bar, drink driving was not regarded as a serious offence—indeed juries simply never convicted. And that is why the law was changed to tests based on blood and urine samples and breath tests. Very many cases of causing death by dangerous driving were dealt with by a fine and short disqualification. The change in attitude during my time in practice has been dramatic. The maximum sentence has gone from two years to five, to ten, to fourteen.

Note my emphasis on our contemporary British society here.

As an example, a judge from India who had tried the most serious cases, and imposed the death penalty, attended a judicial seminar. We were discussing the case of a man who, finding his wife in bed with her lover, of whom he was totally unaware, armed himself with a shotgun and fired it at the lover's legs, causing very serious injury. Our view was that this was a serious offence, discounted for the element of provocation. The judge from India was horrified that we were contemplating a custodial sentence. Her view was that this man's actions had been to protect the honour of his family. We are English judges, and we must try to reflect the views of the community which we serve, and their current attitudes, best reflected in any changes made by Parliament in maximum and minimum sentence levels.

Let's move on to section 143. All five of the purposes specified in section 142 have to be reflected in terms of assessing seriousness. Notice 'culpability ... any harm which the offence caused, was intended to cause, or might foreseeably have caused'.

There are many cases where something like this happens.

A man stabs another man with a knife. He intends to cause him a very serious injury. Fortunately there is an alert passer-by, and by the greatest good fortune and skilful surgery, the victim in the end escapes any long-term injury and makes a complete recovery. That happens. There is no doubt about the intention. He must have intended really serious harm.

This too happens. A couple of lads have a row about a girl in a pub, and step outside. One punches the other on the jaw, not intending any serious injury, and not a particularly hard blow. But the other has had a drink or two, and so he stumbles backwards and falls to the ground. Unfortunately he cracks his head on a large stone or pavement edge. There is no miracle. He dies. There is no doubt here about the catastrophic harm. But the intention was no more than a punch.

The first man is guilty of wounding with intent to cause grievous bodily harm. The second is guilty of manslaughter. He is a 'killer'—and that is how he will be described in the evening paper. And that is what he is. But you could ask yourself: which of those two men is morally more culpable? I won't answer the question. You answer for yourselves. Which is legally the more to blame? The second man has actually caused the death of another human being. That is a result of his actions, for which he and he alone is responsible. But to impose a sentence on him which takes account only of the death, without reflecting that the result was something way beyond anything he anticipated, or imagined, or tried to cause, would, I suggest, surely not be just.

Take another example of a really serious problem of driving. We all have experienced the idiot who drives too fast, quite oblivious to others, for long distances. You see him occasionally, steaming down the motorway, 10 yards from the car in front, blowing his horn and flashing his lights. A complete danger to everyone on the road at the time. Luckily there is no accident, no damage, and no injury, but that man is guilty of dangerous driving. Another man generally drives very well and carefully. One evening he is working late. But he knows that his wife isn't very well and the children are playing up. Not fully alert, he drives somewhat too fast, takes a corner too quickly, crosses to the other side of the road and crashes into another car coming the other way, killing one of the innocent passengers. He is guilty of causing death by dangerous driving.

Again, I ask the question, and do not supply the answer. Of those two men, which is morally more to blame? Parliament has made it clear that, in law, the second man is to be sentenced as if he is, potentially at least, now seven times more to blame than the first man. The maximum sentence for dangerous driving is two years. The maximum for death by dangerous driving is 14 years. Obviously, the death of the innocent passenger in the other car is a matter of utmost concern, and there is public outrage at such incidents. Nobody underestimates the feelings of the family. But if you are considering the appropriate range of sentence, you must—must you not?—consider not only the awful result, and the grieving members of the victim's family, but also the actual criminality involved. And indeed, this poses yet another question, which is whether the sentence should be affected because the deceased has left many grieving members of his family, or a few, or none: no one to mourn him at all. If we cannot ignore his death (and I am sure we cannot), should the sentence be longer if there are many who mourn him? Or if he or she was a wonderful, special person?

So, next, the victim. The impact on the victim of the crime.

For years, in some newspapers, judges were castigated for what were described as punitive sentences imposed for crimes of burglary, for attaching too much importance to offences against property, for which most victims were insured anyway, although many couldn't afford insurance. But the judges then, and now, and the community now, believe that burglary of the home is an offence against the person. It has a direct impact on the householder, whether or not she or he is in the house when it happens. The impact is not necessarily the monetary value. What about a wedding photograph, wantonly destroyed? Or perhaps the now-dead parents' wedding photograph. And what about the war medals, kept by the widow of someone who is now dead? I don't mean the Victoria Cross or the Military Cross or Military Medal, which have monetary value. I just mean the ordinary service medals. These, after all, are my parents, or for some of you at any rate, your grandparents. Those medals remind the widow of the story of the youth of her marriage. They tell of partings and fear; keeping things going by letter writing and then the return; he having seen, and probably done, terrible things; she having kept the home going; and then him coming home. The medals are worth 50p, if that, to the dishonest receiver at the car boot sale, but those medals tell her story, and in most cases they add far more in the scale than the stolen television, which on the face of it is worth far more money.

And remember, impact. The court is not exacting private revenge. And therefore it cannot be influenced by the private wishes of the victim about the penalty. That would make sentence depend not on the crime, but on how forgiving or otherwise the victim felt. And we must not assume the victim always wants revenge.

In a reported case,[3] two victims had identical interests. They were both the parents of a boy who had been killed by his friend in a car accident after they had been drinking together. One parent came to the Court of Appeal to seek the release of the boy who killed her son. The other parent had a diametrically opposed view. They were both victims. They both suffered an identical loss. If you address the question 'which of these victims' views should the court have followed?', you can quickly appreciate how the views of the victim cannot be determinative.

And so we move to the defendant.

The defendant nearly always makes a difference. This isn't namby-pamby psycho-babble. You are not sentencing a piece of paper. In some cases the defendant does not matter, because the sentence is mandatory. An armed criminal, blowing away a policeman who is in his way and might lead to him being caught, is sentenced to life imprisonment. But so is a spouse who, out of a sense of profound love and loyalty over many years, hastens the death of a pain-riddled husband or wife, thus avoiding months of anguish, but also curtailing life by that amount. Although they will not serve the same time, the actual sentence for murder for both is life imprisonment.

The judge listens to the mitigation. He sees the defendant. Sometimes the defendant is in tears. Are those tears of remorse—or self-pity? Is it insight into the impact of the crime on the victim? Is it understanding of the consequences to him or her? Should genuine remorse result in a reduced sentence? Why not? If the defendant is highly unlikely to offend again, is that to be taken into consideration? Again, why not? Do we not take into consideration the judicial view that the defendant is utterly callous, or sometimes proud of what he has done?

Or take sex crimes. The word 'paedophile' is now used indiscriminately. It is used to describe the evil pervert who does unmentionable and distressing things—and, I emphasise, distressing even to a judge who has had more than his or her fair share of exposure to human wickedness. And it is used to describe the defendant who puts his hand on a child's bottom in a crowded swimming pool, over her costume, and who is 16 years old, inarticulate, educationally

---

[3] *R v Nunn* [1996] 2 Cr App R (S) 136.

backward, and almost certainly the victim of abuse with not the slightest idea of how to behave.

You are the judge. You believe that the defendant in the latter case can receive help and advice, and that, from the community's point of view, the treatment he could receive, now, might stop him being a serial abuser when he is 35. You know, however, that a non-custodial sentence will cause outrage. What is the right sentence to impose on him? It takes judicial courage to pass what the judge believes to be the right sentence. More than one judge has had great distress caused to his family because of inaccurate coverage by the media of cases of this kind.

What about young offenders? Which of us did not make mistakes during our teenage years? Or indeed our university years? Or became involved in silly things that could have gone wrong—but luckily for us didn't? This is part of growing up. Is it advantageous to the public for young offenders to be sent to what are sometimes described as 'universities of crime'? Of course they must be punished for serious offences, but locking them up and throwing away the key is no sort of solution. You have to think and you then have to have the courage to do what you think is right.

For a judge there is justice and there is mercy. But mercy is not a quality currently in great demand.

I have a theory, not to be analysed now, that if the community as a whole believed, as it used to believe once, that each of us, in our time, will have to face a greater Judge than any on earth, for him to weigh our faults and our virtues in the balance, mercy might not have become so unfashionable. Isabella's plea in *Measure for Measure* says it all (the first three Acts are all about these issues):

> ... How would you be,
> If He, which is the top of judgment, should
> But judge you as you are? O, think on that;
> And mercy then will breathe within your lips,
> ...

Or more simply:

> Forgive us our trespasses, as we forgive those who trespass against us.

One further concern which every sentencing judge has to acknowledge when he imposes an apparently lenient sentence is the damaging effect of the way that decision will be perceived. And that perception really matters.

A lenient sentence may enable the offender to think that the time has not yet come to reform. A lenient sentence may also denigrate the victim in his or her own eyes, and give the impression of trivialising the crime. That is why it is imperative that reasons should always be given for an apparently lenient sentence, although whether the explanation finds its way into the newspapers is another question.

Can I come back to where I started? If there is a general perception in the community that sentences are over-lenient, then there will be a number of consequences:

— The guilty defendant will be less frightened than he should be.
— If victims believe that nothing will happen to the criminal, they will not report the crime. They will think it pointless. And so the criminal will get away with the crime, and be free to perpetrate another.
— The fear of crime will increase. This is socially destructive. I hope it does not happen to you but we all know an elderly person, or more than one, possibly our own relatives, who lock themselves into a virtual fortress at dusk, frightened of what the night might bring. That is a terribly sad way for anyone to end their days.
— Individuals who believe that offenders are not properly punished by the courts may take the law into their own hands and mete out violent retribution. There is a very short journey to mob or lynch law. That is no sort of law, and no sort of justice. In the end it will engulf the innocent as well as the guilty.
— A division grows up between the community and the judiciary who are its servants. That is bad in itself. Worse still, although we all recognise the importance of judicial independence, if the public perception is that judges are not doing the job expected of them, then the public itself will more readily tolerate politicians interfering in areas which traditionally, at any rate, have been regarded as matter for judges, who, independently of political pressures, are the ones who make the necessary decisions.
— Finally, history tends to show us that even in a community like ours, where there is a long tradition of powerful support for the concept of individual liberty, fear—whether fear of an outside enemy in wartime, or fear of the consequences of uncontrolled and unpunished crime—may lead to willing acceptance of measures which curtail our liberties. These will be said to be 'necessary' for public protection. If they are really necessary, that is what they are. However, we surely must examine them with minds that are uncluttered by misconceptions about the crime and the criminal justice system.

So, perception is a crucial fact. Perception of the sentencing process is critical. As critical as the actual facts. That is why your answers to the questions I posed you earlier really matter. If your answers were wrong, it is not your fault, but the fact that they were wrong remains critical.

Social conditions contribute to crime. So do drugs, alcohol and family breakdown. I simply record that I have seen emotional deprivation in the most prosperous of homes, and nobility of purpose and true appreciation of the worth of every member of the family in the poorest and most abject of physical surroundings.

The sentencing judge is involved right at the far end of the crime. The crime has been committed and the crime has a victim, and the offender has been caught and convicted. The judge has to try to reflect, in each and every case, on a series of conflicting interests, purposes and concerns, and to form a judgement about the just answer to each individual case. It is, I am sure you will understand, rarely of easy application. Indeed the sentencing decision is often the most difficult decision any judge has to make.[4]

[4] For some indication of the changed approach to sentencing during my professional life, see 'David Thomas', this volume, p 364.

The Judiciary

Judicial Independence and Responsibilities

This lecture was the final keynote address at the 2009 Commonwealth Law Conference, held in Hong Kong. It was first published by the Judicial Commission of New South Wales in The Judicial Review *(2009).*

N O ONE WHO had any reservations about the principle of judicial independence would be here. Indeed it has been the constant subtext of many of the discussions. So to begin with, at any rate, I am simply repeating what we all know. However, it bears constant repetition. First, because when we speak of judicial independence, and then speak of the rule of law, we tend to make it sound as if we have two separate concepts, when they are as closely intertwined as a mutually dependent and loving couple after many years of marriage, where one simply cannot survive without the other. And second, to remind us that we should never take either judicial independence or the rule of law for granted. It would indeed be unwise to assume that judicial independence is inviolable. There are among us today men and women of the Commonwealth, and in one particular case men and women who are no longer of the Commonwealth, who have direct experience that it is not. And in the light of their experiences, the rest of us have humbly to recognise how fortunate we all are. Nevertheless, eternal vigilance is a necessary price, worth paying, not exclusively by judges and lawyers, encased within that mythical ivory tower so beloved of pundits and commentators, who do not understand that our daily diet reveals all we need to know about the sadnesses and tribulations of humanity, and its capacity for good and evil. In truth vigilance is also a responsibility to be accepted by a free and independent media, as well as an alert community.

On an occasion at a meeting of judges in Europe I was describing why we in England are proud of the jury system. In a mildly jesting way I told the assembled company that the jury provided a safeguard against unacceptable laws. By way of an absurd example I suggested that if Parliament passed a law that said that all women with red hair should be sent to prison for 12 months, we would expect a jury to find anyone prosecuted under such an absurd law not guilty, even if the defendant's crowning glory was the striking red of a Titian painting. One of the Supreme Court judges of a western European country afterwards chided me in the most pleasant possible way. He reminded me that apart from the United Kingdom, not one of the countries represented at that meeting, and all were European democracies, had not at some time in the last century at least once, if not twice, been subject to their own home-grown dictators or their invading armies. The places where things have gone wrong include countries which believed that they were mature democracies, where these things did not and could not happen, but they did. But they did.

Recent events in Belgium underline this point. 'Fortisgate', as the affair came to be known, arose in consequence of the worldwide banking crisis. Fortis was Belgium's biggest financial service company until October 2008, when it found itself facing bankruptcy. Its bailout by the state led to legal proceedings, during the course of which it was found that the government had tried to influence the judges who were adjudicating on the legality of the proposed sell-off. The Minister of Justice was forced to resign when the Prime Minister admitted publicly that one of the Minister's officials had contacted the husband of a judge of the Court of Appeal on several occasions during the course of the litigation. It shocked the community, and we must all be glad that it did shock the community. We do not know all the facts, but we must agree with the Deputy Prime Minister who said that 'those who have done wrong must clearly take their responsibilities'.[1] If the judge listened to any of these blandishments without reporting it, she had, in my view, failed in her responsibilities.

This provides us with a recent salutary example that these things can happen, even in a mature democracy, where, and perhaps because, the principles are taken for granted. There was, of course, no physical intimidation, no threat to security of judicial tenure, none of the extremes of tyranny. But it is the first steps that have to be watched. The first incursion by the executive into impropriety. The first compromise by the judiciary with principle. We are all familiar with the employee who steals from his employer. The most difficult time is the first time the hand goes into the till. After that, each successive time is less difficult. The problem with the phrase

---

[1] D Charter, 'Belgian Prime Minister Yves Leterme offers resignation over bank crisis', Timesonline, 19 December 2008.

'eternal vigilance' is that it appears to focus on the long term. But the focus is the immediate, today, every day. The insidious dangers are no less threatening than the obvious ones, and for the judiciary to acquiesce in the first small, even tiny, steps, may ultimately be terminal.

The justification for judicial independence has been examined time without number by wiser jurists and philosophers than I. Convinced as I am that no formulation can be complete, but stimulated by the many splendid contributions to which I have listened at this wonderful Conference, may I offer this possible formulation for consideration. In a democratic country all power, however exercised in the community, must be founded on the rule of law. Therefore each and every exercise of political power must be accountable not only to the electorate at the ballot box, when elections take place, but also and at all times to the rule of law. Independent professions protect it. Independent press and media protect it. Ultimately, however, it is the judges who are the guardians of the rule of law. That is their prime responsibility.

They have a particular responsibility to protect the constitutional rights of each citizen, as well as the integrity of the constitution by which those rights exist. The judge therefore cannot be out for popularity. He—or she—cannot please everyone. He should never try to please anyone. That includes the judge himself. He should never use his office to confirm his predilections or to allow his prejudices to gain some kind of spurious judicial respectability. However, because he is not accountable to the electorate as the members of the legislature are, he is entitled to apply the relevant law, but only the relevant law, and although he must be aware of his powers, it is critical to the independent exercise of his responsibilities that he should fully recognise the limitations of his power. Having been entrusted with huge power, judges have an ultimate responsibility to see that when exercising the power vested in them, they use it lawfully in precisely the same way as they ensure that political and other powers vested in other institutions of the state are exercised lawfully.

Without independence, and without respect for judicial independence, these desirable, indeed elementary facets of a civilised community are threatened. At the same time, no individual, or group of individuals, nor even any judge, however high his office, has any dispensing power—that is, the power to set aside or disregard the law. In the middle of the seventeenth century, not long after the execution of a king who claimed that Rex is Lex, and after a public trial, Thomas Fuller observed, 'Be ye never so high, the law is above you'. Well the law is above any individual judge too. No individual judge is Lex either. The absence of any dispensing power was, and remains, fundamental to the rule of law. Judges cannot dispense with it. Parliament itself cannot dispense with it. None of our democratic institutions may do so. They are, of course, entitled to change it.

So where does this take us? The judge must apply the law as it is, not as he would wish it to be. But, and this is a very important but, judicial creativity—I deliberately do not use the undefined word 'activism'—is acceptable provided it is within the law. And this is where the common law has such strength. In the common law it has been accepted for a thousand years, indeed it is the essence of the common law, that judges may develop the law by applying its fundamental principles to new conditions and declaring them. If it were otherwise, the common law would have been an atrophied, rather quaint system of jurisprudence, confined to the small island off the coast of Europe where it originated, the subject of learned doctorates by university scholars rather than a body of law applied throughout the world, but adaptable and adapted to local conditions. Sometimes the common law finds new words to describe old principles. May I just go back to the hypothetical law that said that all women with red hair should be sent to prison for 12 months. Let us suppose that the government of the day acknowledged that juries would never convict, so that the statute was drafted to provide that trial in such cases should be the responsibility of the judge sitting without the jury. Would the judge be obliged to convict her? Ignoring mass judicial resignation, may I just suggest, because now is not the time to discuss it in detail, that you should watch out for a new emanation from the common law, based on long-established fundamental principles, so fundamental that nobody thought it worthwhile writing it down. The word, some of you will already have seen, but which you will all increasingly see, is 'constitutionality'. It is a word with a great future. In other words, if the executive wished the legislature to pass such an outrageous Act, it should do so in language that was so plain that the public conscience would be revolted, and the legislation fail, or if passed, the price would be paid at the next election.

In deciding every case, the judge must be free from any form of pressure, direct or indirect, which might interfere with or influence his obligation to decide the case before him or her in accordance with his honest judgement and according to law. The Bangalore

Principles of Judicial Conduct in June 1998, following a meeting of judges of the Commonwealth, explained the principle in these words:

> Judicial independence is a pre-requisite to the rule of law, and a fundamental guarantee of a fair trial. A judge shall therefore uphold and exemplify judicial independence in both its individual and institutional aspects.[2]

Or as Edmund Burke (who said publicly that the complaints in the 1770s of the then British colonists in what we now call the United States were entirely justified) once explained, the rule of law requires the 'cold neutrality of an impartial judge'.[3]

The concept of judicial independence carries with it the clearest possible understanding that the judge is not to be subjected by anyone—government, media, litigant—to fear or favour, or invited to display affection or exercise ill will towards one side or the other, or indeed anyone in his court. The judge must resist fear or favour, affection or ill will, in whatever form it may take. That is pressure from the outside. But the judge is responsible to his conscience and to the administration of justice to make sure that he is not allowing himself to be influenced in his judgment by even the tiniest twinges of fear or the mildest blandishments of possible favour. Judges know that sometimes their decisions will be greeted with derision and the most intense public hostility. Why should we pretend that that does not create pressure on the judge? It does. The judge's responsibility is to be impervious to it. Because if he allows his decision to be influenced by the possible consequences to him, or even to his family, he is allowing himself to be corrupted. That corruption has nothing to do with money. His judgment is flawed. Justice is tarnished. That, too, is an awesome responsibility.

It is therefore fundamental that there are no circumstances in which the executive may even appear to tell judges how cases should be decided. Even when the public agrees with the executive at the particular time in relation to the particular point, future public confidence that justice will be done impartially and independently will be eroded. In the end, I firmly believe that the public, even if dissatisfied with an individual decision in an individual case, wants its judiciary to be independent of the executive.

Something of the nature of the possible problems was highlighted at home in the context of a number of Control Orders issued under

---

[2] Bangalore Principles of Judicial Conduct 2002.
[3] *Brissot's Address to his Constituents* (1794), Translator's Preface.

the Prevention of Terrorism Act. This led a former Home Secretary publicly to criticise the 'total refusal' of the Law Lords to discuss the issues of principle involved in these matters, and for him to put forward the suggestion that it was time 'for the senior judiciary to engage in a serious and considered debate about how best legally to confront terrorism in modern circumstances'.[4] Accordingly he suggested that some 'proper discussion' would be very helpful between the Law Lords and the Home Secretary, in effect for the Law Lords to advise him about what steps might or might not be struck down. He made the point, and it is a fair one, that the idea that such discussions would corrupt the independence of the Law Lords would be 'risible'. I agree with him; it would not. I also quite understand that intelligent members of the public might themselves wonder why such discussions should not take place. But none of that is in point. Such discussions would have represented one of those tiny first steps of which we should beware. When this issue was ventilated before the House of Lords Select Committee on the Constitution (and this is not the House of Lords sitting in its judicial capacity) the Committee considered it essential that the members of the court 'should not even be perceived to have pre-judged an issue as a result of communications with the executive'.[5] In principle such discussions, even if not concealed from the public, would not, in their effect, be very different from the approaches to the judge in the Fortis case. Their motive might be different; but the consequences, in particular the damage to public confidence in the independence of the judiciary, would be the same.

This means we have to recognise not only when our independence is at risk, but when the perception of our independence may be at risk. We have to recognise that however ill-founded a perception may be in fact, perception itself is a fact. As it was once said, 'the judge who gives the right judgment while appearing not to do so may be thrice-blessed in Heaven but on Earth he is no use at all'.[6]

In England and Wales, judges, particularly senior judges, have hugely increased administrative burdens, in effect, consequent on the changes by which the Lord Chancellor ceased to be Head of the Judiciary in England and Wales and transferred many of his responsibilities to the Lord Chief Justice. Therefore, there has to be constant contact and communication between us. Without it the system

---

[4] House of Lords Select Committee on the Constitution, *Relations between the Executive, the Judiciary and Parliament*, 6th Report of Session 2006–07.

[5] ibid.

[6] Patrick Devlin, *The Judge* (Oxford, 1979).

would grind to a halt. Between us, however, we have to see that the increasing need for these discussions does not become too cosy. There is no difficulty when the Lord Chancellor and Secretary of State for Justice of the day happens, like the present incumbent, to be, by background and qualification and experience, thoroughly familiar with and understanding of the separation that there must be between him and the judges. There might be a different problem if one of his successors happened, like the former Home Secretary, not fully to appreciate some of the subtle and important refinements of principle. Section 3(5) of our Constitutional Reform Act 2005 expressly provides that 'the Lord Chancellor and other Ministers of the Crown must not seek to influence particular judicial decisions through any special access to the judiciary'. I am glad to see it set out in writing. But I suspect that if it were not written down, the principle of constitutionality would supply the missing words.

There are more mundane areas of responsibility which at a meeting like this I am not prepared to shirk. Judges are obliged, surely, to maintain their knowledge of the law, keeping up to date with its developments, whether through the courts or through the legislative process. That is a personal responsibility, both to learn, and to offer to teach from our own experience and by way of example. But it is not just a question of keeping our knowledge up to date. We must, as a body, throughout the Commonwealth, indeed anywhere where judges sit, address the problems created by the proliferation of paper, the endlessness of information, the length of our own judgments, the ability of lawyers to inundate the court with bumph, or paper by the trillion-load. This requires judges to manage their cases much more robustly. The proposals may involve technical procedural changes, but at heart they require judicial insistence on proper case management. We must train ourselves to take advantage of the technological developments so that our systems are improved by it, so that the judges are its masters and not its slaves, so that the judges run the cases and the cases do not run the judges. If we are not alert to this we will end up being overwhelmed by modern technology.

What I am driving at is that the judiciary has an institutional responsibility to ensure that inefficiencies in the legal system do not, as Lord Denning once remarked, 'turn justice sour'.[7] In 1215, when King John sealed the great Magna Carta, it was agreed: 'To no-one will we deny or delay right or justice.' Over the centuries, our

---

[7] *Allen v Sir Alfred McAlpine & Sons Ltd* [1968] 2 QB 229.

greatest writers have identified the consequences of inefficiency. In *Hamlet*, Shakespeare listed it among the 'whips and scorns of time'. At the very start of *Bleak House*, Charles Dickens identified its ability to exhaust finances, patience, courage and hope. Can you imagine anything worse than exhaustion of hope? And if hope is exhausted through the process of litigation, or a long-delayed criminal trial, how can we, as judges, disclaim any responsibility for it?

Judges therefore cannot distance themselves from some responsibility for inefficiency and delay. Others contribute to it. Resources, money, men and women of sufficient quality, a principled legal profession: these are all required to make a system more efficient. But in my view—and like everything I have said today it is a personal one—judges nowadays should accept a measure of responsibility to ensure that the court processes are as efficient as possible. This must be led and supported by the senior judiciary. For some this involves a re-think of culture. Judges really must not sit there and wait for the parties to present their cases. They must know the case each side intends to present, and prepare accordingly. And it can be done. For some years at home we suffered from what was described as the 'adjournment culture'. We have introduced much more stringent rules of procedure in both the criminal and civil courts. Huge amounts of residential training have been prepared for judges at every level. With this training we are gradually killing off the adjournment culture. It takes judicial effort; it involves professional co-operation. It takes time, and no one can do it alone. But we should remember how, after one very long hearing, with many adjournments, a judge in England complained that a case had taken him seven days to try. He then pointed out that that was one day longer than the Almighty himself needed to create the entire universe.

This is a new dynamic. But nowadays there is an increased expectation of everyone in positions of responsibility. Judges are not immune from it. Indeed we are part of it. And this leads me to say something, very briefly, about what judicial independence is not. It is not, and if it ever was it cannot continue to be, an excuse for judicial inefficiency or idleness. There are thousands, perhaps indeed hundreds of thousands, of judges of different kinds at different levels throughout the world. Some, I firmly believe a few, indeed a very, very few, but some, are not hard-working. Some are not wholly committed to their responsibilities. Taxed with the practical consequences to the public of their idleness and lack of commitment, they may wield the shield of independence. But for them, as a shield, it is paper thin. And we, fellow judges, must blow it aside. There is the public interest in blowing it aside. But there is this too: if we do not accept that responsibility, it will be unsurprising if others decide to try to take it from us. And then, there is a danger that a problematic circle would be complete. It would then be possible for a perfectly efficient judge, who had in one way or another crossed the government of the day, to find himself indicted for his idleness when the government was seeking to get rid of his independence of mind and spirit. We are not in comfortable territory here, but the principle of judicial independence cannot be divorced from judicial responsibility. In short, we must not permit the inadequacies of a few to provide an executive, attracted to the idea of limiting or interfering with judicial independence, with an excuse to interfere.

There is no time now to do more than identify further strands of the structures which contribute to judicial independence. But the appointments system should not be controlled by the executive, and the deployment of judges, the listing of cases in court, judicial training and the discipline of judges should be subject to judicial not executive control.

There are two final observations. A few years ago, I was speaking in Argentina, not long after the rule by their military government had come to an end. I hope you will forgive me for repeating something I said then. The critical aspect of judicial independence, underpinning the entire concept, is that although the principle of independence benefits the judge sitting in judgment, who must do what he or she believes to be right, undistracted and uninhibited, the overwhelming beneficiary is the community. When judges speak out as they do, in defence of this principle, they are not seeking to uphold some minor piece of flummery or privilege, which goes with their offices: they are speaking out in defence of the community's entitlement to have its disputes, particularly those with the government of the day, and the institutions of the community, heard before an impartial judge who is independent of them all. The principle must be defended, not for our own sake as judges, but for the sake of every community which truly embraces the rule of law. Among our tasks, we have to ensure that the rule of law applies to everyone equally, not only when the consequences of the decision will be greeted with acclamation, but also, and not one jot less so—indeed, perhaps even more so—when the decision will be greeted with the most intense executive or public hostility. In the end, all judges, wherever they exercise their offices, in whichever court or countries they sit, must accept this burdensome responsibility. Judicial independence and responsibility are therefore two sides of the same coin.

What this conference has shown us is how things have gone wrong in the past, and how they may go wrong, even when unanticipated, and the dreadful consequences for the community when the rule of law and the independence of the judiciary are subverted. During the discussions I was acutely aware of how fortunate most of us are, and how dreadful the loss of these principles is for some of us. We judges and lawyers from the Commonwealth who all, in our different ways, share the heritage and blessings of the common law, derive mutual support from each other. To those among you who struggle on through the darkest of nights desperately hoping for a new dawn, I have a message from a small church in the heart of England, in Leicestershire. It was four years after the king was executed. Oliver Cromwell had dispensed with Parliament. And in 1653 a brave man founded an Anglican church. This is what you read on the stone inside the church.

> In the year 1653 when all things sacred were throughout the nation either demolished or profaned, Sir Robert Shirley, Baronet founded this church; whose singular praise it is to have done the best of things in the worst of times and hoped in the most calamitous.[8]

To do the best of things in the worst of times, and to maintain hope in the face of catastrophe, is an ultimate test for any human being. It is a test that some of you have already passed. It is a test that I hope all of us would pass.

---

[8] Staunton Harold, Leicestershire.

Being a Judge Today (2013)

This was the Judicial College Lecture, given at Cardiff University in February 2013.

PERHAPS THE STARTING point is to underline how many changes there have been in my lifetime in the law. Let me give you a few examples.

My client was seeking a divorce on the grounds of his wife's adultery with the co-respondent. He also claimed £300 damages for her loss. If I had valued my wife at £300, I think she would have been justified in going off with the co-respondent. But it is laughable to think of this kind of monetary evaluation for the services of a wife, which incidentally did not operate the other way round. Perhaps, but it is unlikely, that meant a husband, unlike a wife, was valueless.

Another example: if you wanted a divorce and you yourself had committed adultery you had in your petition for divorce humbly to seek the exercise of the court's discretion in your favour notwithstanding your own adultery. You had to provide a full, frank, total admission of all the occasions when you had committed adultery yourself. And after you had given evidence, even if the case was undefended, an envelope was solemnly handed to the judge, who carefully opened it and read the contents. One of my clients was a sailor. He had committed adultery in 84 different ports throughout the world in 84 different countries, perhaps unsurprisingly, with completely unknown women. Nevertheless the list had to be written. By contrast, another petitioner, not my client, about whom I was told, came from rather a grand family in England, and his discretion statement included list upon list of the assembled nobility, beginning with duchesses, then listing countesses, the wives of barons, and the wives of mere knights, with only the odd commoner thrown in at the end. My point is that this was all solemnly part of the ritual which was required before you could get a divorce.

None of that avoided the rather difficult evidential point that what was said in the statement certainly proved that the person making the statement had been having sexual intercourse with someone, but surprisingly failed to prove that that someone had been having sexual intercourse with him.

Looking back on it, these are all funny. But I also had a client who, as an adult, committed buggery with another adult, in private. This was private consensual sex between adult men. He was sentenced to three years' imprisonment. I thought then and I still think that was a shocking sentence, but it reflected the times.

And, still in my time in practice, in *The Queen v Merthyr Tydfil Justices, ex parte Jenkins*[1] a future Lord Chief Justice expounded his view of the content of his experience of having spent the summer on circuit in Wales.

> It is quite clear that the proper language for the court proceedings in Wales is the English language.

Indeed the use of Welsh impeded 'the efficient administration of justice in Wales'. As to language difficulties which might arise in Wales, they could be dealt with 'by discretionary arrangements for an interpreter, precisely in the same way as language difficulties at the Central Criminal Court are dealt with when the accused is a Pole'.

So perhaps the most obvious example of changes is that here today in Cardiff the Lord Chief Justice is not the Lord Chief Justice of England, but since just before 2000, the Lord Chief Justice of England and Wales, and, I would add, in Wales, Lord Chief Justice of Wales and England. The examples I have given, and this last example in particular, symbolise that being a judge in the modern world has at its heart the notion that judges should understand the modern world, not embracing the latest fad or fashion, because these are ephemeral and short lived, and today's fashion inevitably gives way to tomorrow's fashion, but because where real change is apparent, the judicial system must understand, represent and respond to it. Here in Wales the modern judge must be alert to the developments of the legal life of Wales: not because he or she has a personal belief one way or another, but simply because the legal life of Wales is in flux and rapid development. Judges must not seek to push or to hold back, but they must be alert to what is happening.

This lecture is being given under the auspices of the Judicial College. It is now the Judicial College, not least because of yet another area of new understanding and arrangement. The men and women who sit in the tribunal system are exercising a judicial function, no less than those who sit in what I may describe as the ordinary courts of the land, the High Court, the Crown Court, and the county court

---

[1] [1967] 1 All ER 636.

as well as others. The new Judicial College simply brings together what were formerly the separate arrangements for judicial training of judges and tribunal judges. HMCTS is just that: Her Majesty's Service for Courts and Tribunals, a single service. So when I speak of judges, I am including judges who sit in tribunals. That, too, is a significant change. The modern judge may be sitting in a suit in a tribunal rather than in what we recognise as a court. And the modern judge may also be sitting as a magistrate, also in a suit, in something that does look like a court. In other words, the modern judge comes in all kinds of judicial shapes and sizes, with differing responsibilities, but ultimately committed to the administration of justice.

But I want to go back to those first days of the Judicial Studies Board. We are back in the late 1970s and early 1980s. I was appointed a Recorder of the Crown Court in 1976. I sat for two years as a Recorder before I received any training at all. I was simply a barrister practising on the Midland circuit who was thought to be up to the responsibility. The omission of training was no reflection of my remarkable talents: it was simply that there was no training at all. At the end of two years I was summoned to a brief seminar, held in the Court of the Lord Chief Justice, and a desultory exchange of views between a Lord Justice of Appeal and the judges and Recorders then took place. I can still remember that the main message of the day was that provided you said, and re-emphasised, that the decision on the facts was for the jury, it was open to the judge to make any comment, however damaging to the defendant, that the judge thought fit. In other words, the judge could run the trial on the basis that provided he repeated and emphasised that the jury was entitled to reject any comment made by him, he could make virtually any comment he liked. That is not how we do it these days.

What is more, in the first years after the Judicial Studies Board was formed, there was significant judicial antipathy towards the process. Many of us welcomed the training, but many did not. Many thought that this new-fangled idea constituted an interference with judicial independence. And notice the importance of the title of the organisation—it was Judicial 'Studies'—not what in truth it was, Judicial 'Training', and if you ask 'what's in a name?' the answer is a great deal. You do not reconcile those who are hostile to the idea if you demean them by implying that they might need training in the performance of their responsibilities.

I speak of these matters from personal knowledge, because I was part of a tiny team which ran the Judicial Studies Board in those far off days.

Let us briefly go back to those days. For some of you it will be inconceivable, but we are talking in the years before the Police and Criminal Evidence Act 1984 had come into force. The Judges' Rules were applied, their objective being to ensure that any evidence which might amount to a confession of guilt was properly obtained and accurately recorded. Police officers were believed to have the kind of memory that holds sway in the elephant kingdom. They were able hours later to remember verbatim the precise questions and answers of a conversation with the defendant. And my clients all seemed to be vested with the kind of intellectual quality of a professor of modern language when it came to their offering a free account, always in their own words, of their criminal activities. Logical, coherent, with a beginning, a middle and an end, none of it prompted.

I never detected very many such qualities in many of my clients. Often they were confused, and many inarticulate.

But here I can bring two threads together, making the same point. I can remember a very senior police officer who told me how much he would welcome the use of tape recordings during police interviews, and indeed, and these are days long ago, filming of the interview process. He was in a tiny minority. In the face of much opposition it was introduced. We can now be certain that we know exactly what the defendant said, and the context in which he said it, and the question he was answering, as well as the answer itself, which taken out of context could be immensely damaging. No one would wish to go back to the old days. What a welcome use of what was then at the forefront of modern technology. Most welcome to us all.

And the same applies to the Judicial College. Continuing education is integral to the working life of a judge. We all are sure of its value. Judges know that training has no bearing whatever on his or her independence. The process enables them to be better informed and therefore better able to discharge their responsibilities. Judges now book in to the seminars which are appropriate for their needs. They value continuing training and education. Being a judge in the modern world does not merely require such education and training, it requires a frame of mind in which these positive advantages are welcomed. And they are.

Before you rush to condemn the older generation of judges, perhaps you would bear in mind that they were simply reflective of what to them was the modern world. Their world was 'modern' to them, just as it was to all their contemporaries in all the professions. In their modern world football players in the First Division, now the Premier League, were paid £10 per week with a £2 bonus for a win and £1 for a draw. Men who had the honour of turning out to represent Wales at Cardiff Arms Park were amateurs. Woe betide you if anyone discovered that you were accepting money or benefits in kind; you were expelled. And in those days no one in the legal profession, or as far as I am aware in any other profession, had continuing education. What we now treat as common and obvious was not common and obvious then. And before we get too carried away with our own rectitude, bear this clearly in mind: that in 25 to 50 years' time, the Lord Chief Justice of Wales will be addressing just such a meeting as this in Cardiff, and there will be gasps of surprise at how extraordinary our processes and the way we do things now, were. Yet, of course subject to improvement, because we are always trying to reflect our best view of the best way things should be done. And if you examine this process more deeply, you end up, do you not, with this reflection. Just as judges must not follow fads and fashion, they must be alert to the practical realities of the world in which they live and understand it, and understand the realities with which those who appear in court have to grapple.

Put in this broad way, perhaps what I have just said is rather nebulous. There are a number of direct, concrete matters which fall within my broad proposition.

We need to address the impact of modern technology on our justice system, and in particular our criminal justice system. You may very well appreciate that we use modern technology in the Crown Court. But our system is different from the different police forces, and the Prison Service, and the Probation Service. So the different bodies cannot simply all send the relevant documents to each other by pressing a single button. We can ask ourselves, how could that possibly be? But where do you stop with modern technology? Twitter and Facebook are less than 10 years old. In other words, if I had being giving this lecture in, say, 2003, they would have been unheard of, and if heard of, of no moment, not least because our eyes were focused on the extraordinary constitutional changes that were going on. Do you remember? The Lord Chancellor to be abolished: that did not get through the House of Lords. But he ceased to be head of the judiciary. That responsibility passed to the Lord Chief Justice. No one bothered to ask the Lord Chief Justice what he thought about this proposal, let alone whether he agreed with it. Well, that is modern political life. And we have had a remarkable change in our constitutional arrangements, not just in the context of devolution in Wales and greater independence in Scotland, but in the context of the judiciary as the third arm of our constitution. The judiciary is no longer represented around the Cabinet table by a Minister whose function is to ensure that Cabinet decisions do not impinge on the independence of the judiciary, and the judiciary is no longer able to speak for itself in Parliament, because the right of the Lord Chief Justice to stand up and speak in Parliament has been abrogated. The impact of these constitutional changes has not yet been fully appreciated, and we must watch very closely how it develops.

Let us return to technology. So which piece of modern technology, as yet uncreated, of which we are all ignorant, will arrive to change the face of the administration of justice? I do not know, and, by definition, you do not know either. But we can be certain, can we not, that there will be dramatic changes, and that they will have, and should have, a dramatic impact on processes. We can be sure that the most modern technology today will be utterly out of date by 2025, if not significantly earlier. Should we, can we, go on with our time-honoured practices? The fact that they are time-honoured and tested gives them some merit, but they have not been tested against the possibilities which modern technology can open up. So how does the modern judge and the judicial system accommodate this extraordinary phenomenon, extraordinary, but unfixed and unknown?

We have to manage it: we cannot be insulated from it, any more than any other aspect of society. It is like the tide, coming in, eventually to fill every nook and cranny of society. Health, education, government, businesses large and small, football clubs, anything you care to think of does not merely need current IT, but needs vision about the uses to which IT can be deployed, enhancing, in our case, the administration of justice. Again, we have to be careful not to be after the latest fad or fashion; but we do have to examine, we certainly shall have to examine, whether the processes with which we have been familiar for generations can reflect the valuable assistance of modern technology without diminishing the quality of justice.

Let me just ramble. Do we need vast files of paper? Do we need so much focus on the oral tradition? In civil appeals, can all the material not be put onto a screen? In criminal appeals, unless there is fresh evidence, can the defendant not always be linked to the court by video, so as to avoid him a most uncomfortable journey, and the cost of fetching him to and from prison? Can we, perhaps most of all, recognise the dire danger of burying our system, our common law system, under mounds and mounds of so-called authorities—decided cases which are supposed to assist the judge by directing him or her to the relevant principle? If we could use modern technology to distil the essential principle to be applied by the court into two or three paragraphs, rather than two or three folders of so-called authorities, that would be a triumph. Let us remember that when the Incorporated Council of Law Reporting was set up in the mid-1860s, its purpose was to ensure proper reporting of cases which decided legal principle. Well, modern technology has produced the unreported, neutral citation judgment, which decides no legal principle, under which to bury the judge, so perhaps it may one day expiate its guilt and produce a new system for reporting cases which actually matter. And if I may say so, finally on this topic, let us not be beguiled by the latest sales talk into buying equipment which will be redundant in three or four years, after a massive capital expenditure: if we are investing vast sums of capital, can the word 'Flexibility' be built in to it?

Let me give a particular example of the impact of modern technology in the context of criminal trials. We already have too many cases where jurors ignore the directions of the trial judge that they should decide the case on the evidence presented to them and not seek information from whichever species of modern technology they choose to use. This is not an attempt by the judiciary to preserve a piece of flummery. You can all see, when you think about it, that it is elementary that if you are charged with a criminal offence, not only must your trial be held in public, but you should have an opportunity to deal with any evidence which is said to prove your guilt. You would be absolutely horrified if in today's processes you, as the defendant, were asked to leave court while some material, apparently damaging to you, was presented to the judge and jury. You would want to know what it was, and you would want to try and deal with it. The juror who seeks information outside the court process is doing just that: he or she is using material which is secret from you, and which you have no chance to address, to decide whether you are guilty or not. The same complaint could be made by someone who is the victim of crime. If you wish to preserve the jury system as it is, we need all the best technology that we can find to enable masses of evidence to be presented and all of the processes to be clearer, and simpler, and speedier. But just because technology is 'modern', its impact is not always to the public advantage. So we have to be careful to welcome the technology, and to learn how to handle it, but to handle it cautiously, so as to ensure that the administration of true justice is undiminished. If the jury system has to change because of modern technology, and over the centuries it has been susceptible to change, then this must not be done behind the scenes by a nod and wink, but must be addressed directly and explicitly in our legislative assemblies. It is those who work in these places, those we elect to represent us, who have the responsibility for making these decisions about the sort of society in which we and our children and grandchildren will live, and the rules which will be agreeable to them in their modern society. That, of course, is for the future.

And for the future, however it is addressed, the qualities we seek in a judge will be identical to those that we seek in a judge today. The eternal verities do not change. We make great demands of our judges. They must have wisdom, patience, a sense of practical realities, an understanding of people and the way of the world, fairness and balance, independence of mind and knowledge of the law, and a total commitment that justice should be administered according to the law. These are qualities which are needed by judges at whatever level they sit, and wherever they sit, giving judgment without fear or favour, affection or ill-will. But there are a number of particular further features which are sometimes overlooked.

First, a judge must have the ability to make up his or her mind and give a decision. Anyone can see a number of different possible solutions to a problem and different ways to address it. In many cases that is precisely why they have come to the judge: because they cannot agree it. The judge cannot take refuge in the answer being one thing or another: the judge must decide.

Second, judges have to make decisions that are profoundly unpleasant and have very serious consequences. But they have to make them. To send someone to prison when his spouse believes that he is innocent; to take children away from one or other, or even both, parents because it is no longer safe for them to be living with that parent; to tell the government of the day, or all the many authorities that have power over us, that they are acting unlawfully is a difficult responsibility. This is not a fun job. And you have to do it. The parties and the public are entitled to a decision from you. And you must give reasons for it. And you must give it to the best of your abilities. And you must give it even if you know that another court may take a different view.

Third, the modern judge is increasingly involved in what can be described as administration. The days are over when the judicial function was performed by the judge turning up at court at 9 o'clock, reading the papers for the day's work, going into court at 10 or 10.30, sitting the court hours, adjourning at 4.30 or thereabouts, working on the day's work in preparation for the summing up or the judgment and then going home. Many, many judges have out of court responsibilities. They are members of different Boards or Councils; they have pastoral responsibilities as Resident Judges, Designated Family Judges or Designated Civil Judges; they help with diversity issues; some of them work with schools and places of education. Ultimately, the administrative responsibilities devolve downwards from the Lord Chief Justice. Properly to perform his function, he has to deal with the Lord Chancellor, the Permanent Secretary of the Department and senior officials, other Ministers in the Department, and then all the Boards and bodies which work to make the system more efficient and more accountable, such as, for example, the Judicial Appointments Commission, and HMCTS. All of us help to ensure the efficiency and effectiveness of the system which the Lord Chancellor must provide to carry on the business of the courts. So the modern judge is likely to be involved directly or indirectly with many responsibilities out of court, which have nothing whatever to do with his or her judicial judgments. All this is new, but the burdens are likely to increase rather than diminish. Do not get me wrong: they add greatly to the interest of the job, but the time in which to do it does not increase. I am very grateful to the many judges up and down the country who are prepared to offer themselves to help ensure that the administration of justice runs efficiently, not merely when they are conducting their cases in court, but overall, in each of its many aspects.

So this leads to the final feature I wish to highlight. Judges must have moral courage or fortitude, in particular to make decisions that will not be popular with the politicians or the media or indeed the vast majority of the public. And judges have to defend the right to equality and fair treatment before the law of any individual citizen—even, and perhaps most of all, a citizen who is unpopular, currently demonised, currently beyond the pale. That is the rule of law, and in its practical application it is not always very popular. And, what is more, the judge cannot respond to personal criticism. This makes fortitude, an old-fashioned virtue, much underrated in our present society. Quiet fortitude, a requisite for the judge in the modern world.

But you will notice that none of these qualities have anything whatever to do with the gender of a human being, or the colour of the skin of the human being, or the sexual orientation, or the physical abilities, or the religion they follow, or their social origins. None of these matters have the slightest relevance to the identity of those we are seeking to persuade to take on judicial office, or indeed to the judiciary as a whole. We are still far from a diverse judiciary. I do not underestimate the value of diversity as an essential ingredient for its own sake; my view is however more intensely focused, and it is that diversity is a necessary requirement of the judiciary because the individuals best suited to judicial office include women just as much as men, include human beings whose skin is brown or black as well as white, include those whose social origins are the most humble, and include those who would not win a gold medal in 100 metres at the Olympics. None of these things matter. What matters is that the judiciary should be made up of individuals who are qualified for appointment and are of the highest calibre, vested with the qualities that make a good judge. We do after all vest in our judges considerable responsibilities, and power. Only the best will do.

Somehow or other the pool of candidates for appointment to judicial office is not as large or as wide as I would like it to be. Putting it bluntly, the larger the pool of those with an interest in judicial office, the greater potential for increasing quality in our judges. When I was studying to become a barrister the vast majority of those around me were white men. There were very few brave women breaking into what was then an overwhelmingly male profession. There were tiny, tiny numbers from ethnic minorities. None of this was special to the Bar. It was true of solicitors and consultants and major companies and indeed politicians, and, so far as men were concerned, white men formed the international cricket, soccer and rugby teams. That has changed and is changing and, I earnestly hope, will continue to change. But you have to start thinking about a judicial career very early. I want the young students at the University of Cardiff who are thinking of entering the legal profession, whether solicitors or barristers or indeed as members of CILEX, to think now, in the years when they are students, and while they are qualifying for their professions, to ask themselves whether after 20–25 years in their chosen profession, the judicial Bench might also represent an interesting new challenge. The old barriers have gone. The old doors are open. All that we need is for some of those from under-represented parts of our community, if they are good enough, to join the Bench. I am not looking for quotas. That is insulting.

We have far from resolved the diversity issue, but it is at least fair to say that in society today no one is surprised to come before a judge who is a woman, or whose skin colour is not white, or who needs a stick, or a wheelchair. That is progress, slow, slow, but progress towards the time when our diverse community is served by a diverse judiciary.

Ultimately being a judge in the modern world requires us to have and keep open minds about every single current and new facet affecting the lives of those who live in the same community which we as judges are privileged and proud to serve. We are serving the community. We have to understand their world. They are living in it today, and so are we.

Judicial Studies: Reflections on the Past and Thoughts for the Future

This Judicial Studies Board lecture was delivered at the Inner Temple in March 2010.

WHEN I FIRST joined the Judicial Studies Board (JSB), I did not anticipate giving this lecture. There was no JSB Lecture. There hardly was any JSB at all.

Harry Skinner led a small team, a very small team called the JSB. It consisted of him as Chairman, a young Tom Legg, a delightful magistrate (who always came to the meetings with a small dog), me, a secretary, and another youngster, David Thomas, who showed a little promise as an expert on sentencing, at a time when the only experts, so far as the judiciary were concerned, were judges.

The real target of the JSB was sentencing—consistency of sentencing—and that was what Peter Webster and Harry Skinner sought to drive at. Of all the people who used to be under constant attack by the participants at seminars for not respecting or for interfering with their judicial independence, Harry Skinner, and Peter Webster before him, never seemed to me to pose the slightest threat.

I had sat for two years as a Recorder before I received any training at all. The very first case I tried involved allegations that two police officers had accepted small bribes from motorists anxious to avoid prosecution. Even the burden of proof was the wrong way round. At my very first seminar in the Lord Chief Justice's Court, a distinguished Lord Justice, who later went on to the House of Lords, told us in unequivocal terms that, provided we directed the jury three or four times that the facts were for them, 'we'll support any comment you make about the facts'. Happy days indeed. Mind you, those were the days before PACE, when the Judges' Rules held sway. Police officers were believed to have memories that would have graced Einstein—able, all of them, to remember, verbatim, the precise questions and answers of a discussion which had taken place two or three hours earlier. And my clients had a remarkable intellectual prowess—the ability to dictate a logical, sequential confession of their criminal activities which suggested an intellectual capacity way beyond anything I could glean from my conference with them. Perhaps the temporary flowering of such brilliance was coincidental with the propensity of their heads to make unexpected voluntary contact with the doors of police cars, or the doors and walls of their cells. Then, when the effect of the blow wore off, they resumed their former levels.

What, I wonder, about our present system for the administration of justice will bring laughter from a collection like this audience in 20 years' time. If I have a wish it is that we should better address the consequences to children who have suffered abuse.[1] Should we always and immediately set about all the necessary processes to enable them to come to terms with their experiences, so better to ensure a full, rewarding, and, so far as humanly possible, an unscarred life? 'Yes' is the obvious answer, but is it still 'yes' if treating that as a priority reduces the chances of a proper conviction? The answer may still be 'yes', until we remember that if the perpetrator of the crime is not prosecuted and convicted, other children may become his victims. This is an acute dilemma, and even if you have, as we do have, a system by which judges, experienced both in criminal justice and family justice, make the decisions about which should come first in an individual case, the treatment or the trial, the decision that is made is made in the knowledge of the possible adverse consequences either way. I note that Baroness Stern discussed this subject in the context of rape victims in her recent 'Review into Rape Reporting in England and Wales'. It contains a valuable analysis of analogous issues, and repays close attention.

Perhaps in 20 years' time a different sort of laughter may greet the thought that the ascertainment of the truth could be best served in civil cases by taking as read a statement in chief which, so far as the court knew, had been drafted by solicitors and counsel, and re-drafted and re-drafted again, and polished up, and checked for possible difficult areas, and then re-drafted by them all again. I suppose such witness statements are more reliable than the confessions to which I referred earlier. Are they?

But if I may just go back to those early days in the JSB's life, they were very different times. Mobile phones did not exist. Some 50 or 60 judges and recorders were squashed into the accommodation at Roehampton, with one public telephone box to be shared between them all. And we all needed to use it. And I am told that one of

---

[1] See 'Half a Century of Change: The Evidence of Child Victims' and 'The Evidence of Child Victims: The Next Stage', this volume, pp 211 and 225.

my predecessors is extremely fortunate that his judicial career was not blighted when he climbed out of Roehampton and returned to his nearby home in Barnes.

From these days, and the developing history, I want to identify a number of specific moments, beyond the invention of the mobile phone, the email, and the Blackberry.

First, the meetings of the judges to discuss sentence revealed a significant difference of views about the correct approach to sentencing white-collar professionals who had committed offences of dishonesty to the disadvantage of their clients. For some judges the most serious feature was the breach of trust; for others the fact of the court appearance, public shame, and inevitability of striking off represented sufficient punishment. Harry Skinner, and Donald Farquarson, who took over from him, took the problem to the Lord Chief Justice, Geoffrey Lane. That difference of view produced the first true guideline case, *Barrick*,[2] in 1985, when—if my memory is right—Donald Farquarson and Di Tudor Price sat with Geoffrey Lane. That decision had a high impact on the judges, not merely for the guidance on sentencing. It demonstrated to them that their views and concerns, as expressed at the JSB, were understood by the senior judiciary, and that the JSB represented a form of communication between them. That was a very significant moment in establishing the credentials of the JSB with the judiciary.

It also had the long-term consequence that eventually culminated in the Sentencing Advisory Panel, the Sentencing Guidelines Council, and is now embodied in the Sentencing Council. That, I suspect, was not a consequence that Geoffrey Lane would have anticipated.

The second was the moment when the JSB was extended to take on civil and family work. Michael Mustill[3] had become chairman. At the very first meeting, he asked all of us sitting round the table to express whatever views we wished on the future development of the JSB. He listened to them all. And then, in what remains to me a vivid memory, he spoke without a note for something like 25 minutes about his aims and ambitions for the JSB. I suspect that no note of it was made. More's the pity. It was a stunning vision expressed with brilliant clarity. It would have been a seminal paper. He addressed the issue of diversity, and the way in which we had to ensure not only that people from ethnic minorities were treated

---

[2] *R v Barrick* (1985) 81 Cr App R 78.
[3] Sadly, the death of Lord Mustill on 24 April 2015 was announced while this book was in preparation.

equally, but in such a way that they themselves perceived that they were being treated equally. He also laid out his ambitions that, long term, there should be a Judicial College. That has been a consistent policy of the JSB for many years now. We are still waiting for the Judicial College, recently supported in the context of judicial appointments by Baroness Neuberger. It will happen.[4]

The third of these moments was when Henry Brooke came to a criminal seminar I was running at the time when the new Ethnic Minority Awareness Committee was formed. I offered Henry, and Trevor Hall, the opportunity to speak. Not all of you know Trevor Hall. He is black. I remember the sense of astonishment and disappointment and anger when he told the meeting that he, aged 37, had been stopped no less than 38 times while driving his car, or it may have been the other way round. No one any more thinks that these issues can merely be addressed on the basis of treating everyone with proper courtesy. We needed knowledge. We had, for example, to recognise that it was not an infallible indication of truthfulness for a witness to stand up straight and look the judge in the eye. Some witnesses would look down, not because they were shifty, but out of a sense of respect for the court. And, too, determined perjurers learned the trick of looking the judge in the eye.

There have been many critical moments in the development of the history of the JSB. I have identified these three from what now are early days, before the JSB got to its teens, as highly significant moments which I personally witnessed which led to and affected its development into much more than a body providing information for the use of judges, but a body which contributed to the modernisation of the judiciary.

In all my time the Judicial Studies Board has been the judiciary's great success story. It has had a series of remarkable chairmen, and when the time came, energetic, dedicated directors of studies. Everyone who served on any committee knew that it was a privilege to do so. So, I believe, do all those who worked at the JSB. It is thanks to all of them that it is the jewel in the judicial crown.

Continuing education is now regarded as an integral part of the working life of a judge by the judges themselves. The old days of resentment and complaint about interference with judicial independence have disappeared. It is interesting to notice that under the new arrangements of the judicial training strategy, by which judges

---

[4] The name 'Judicial College' was formally adopted in April 2011; however this is not yet Michael Mustill's vision.

choose the training they need from a prospectus published by the JSB, the response to the first prospectus published last September which covers seminars from April this year to March next has been nothing short of magnificent. 2067 judges have booked in to seminars: of the entire judicial family only 16 judges have failed either to book or to give an acceptable explanation for their inability to do so. I should not have forecast that in 1979. No one would.

One crucial reason for this glowing success is that—and it is important to emphasise—judges are responsible for the education and training of judges, and the judges in the JSB are as determinedly independent of mind as any judge who has ever attended one of their seminars. Of course outside assistance is sought, but the ultimate responsibility for the organisation of the seminars is with the judges themselves. And it is has been another constant feature that no one at the JSB is marking those who attend the seminars, in particular not the newly appointed judges. That policy was laid down at a very early stage. If individuals were chosen for judicial appointment, the role of the JSB was to train them, not to second-guess those responsible for the appointment. It makes for healthy seminars, and enables the participants to seek advice where they may otherwise be inhibited.

I want now to reflect for a little while on some of the issues relating to education and training which may be needed for judges some few years from now. In 1979 the European dimension had hardly crossed any of our paths; technology extended to the typewriter and the dictating machine; fee notes in chambers operated through a card system. It never crossed anyone's mind that the Lord Chancellor would be so suddenly, and discourteously to the judiciary, sidelined.

In making these reflections about the future it is essential for you to understand that I am not advocating—repeat not advocating—any particular changes. I am merely reflecting on how looking at it today things may develop, and doing so confident and in the certain knowledge that any forecasts are less reliable than any long-term weather forecast. That is why these are reflections. And what is more, I can only touch on a number of questions, each of which on its own could form the basis of a lecture. Indeed experts write books about our constitutional changes.

It might be questioned whether after the dramatic constitutional changes of which the Human Rights Act 1998 and the Constitutional Reform Act 2005 were but two, there is room for further change; perhaps more accurately, whether it might be as well to stop and see where we have arrived before considering further change. The changes have been revolutionary. Most of us were brought up on the British constitution identified by Bagehot and Dicey. The recent changes led Professor Bogdanor in *The New British Constitution* to observe that the constitution known to Bagehot is dead, and that Dicey's constitution is dying before our eyes.[5] He suggests that the constitutional reforms over the last 12 years have 'fundamentally altered the balance between the main institutions of Government—the legislature, the executive and the judiciary'. But his thesis is that the constitutional position is far from resolved. The constitutional arrangements continue in a state of flux.

Where then may we be going? The separation of powers has been enhanced. The Supreme Court is not the Judicial Committee of the House of Lords. Of itself, there is, in my view, no immediate change. As I have said before, the old—I mean former—Law Lords were not lambs who have, by virtue of becoming Supreme Court Justices, suddenly been transmogrified as lions. I suspect that anyone who studied the work of the House of Lords over these last years would agree that they had been lions all along. But there is a huge symbolism in the physical movement of the court out of the Houses of Parliament.

The 2005 Act acknowledges that the judiciary is a 'third branch of Government'. The principle of judicial independence is recorded in statute. Ministers are required to uphold the principle of judicial independence. Of course I am pleased about that. But I do not believe for one moment that the responsibility of the judiciary to maintain and if necessary insist on its independence of the executive has been reduced by one iota.

The creation of the Judicial Office for England and Wales, to support the judiciary when carrying out administrative functions, which were previously carried out by the Lord Chancellor's Department, was in truth a revolutionary step. Its creation underlined the new responsibilities of the judiciary. The office is in its infancy. It will grow to maturity. During that time, and perhaps in the immediate future, the future of the Tribunals system, currently in the form anticipated by Andrew Leggatt, will arise for reconsideration. Judges who sit in Tribunals are judges: they are not mini judges nor semi judges. They have identical judicial responsibilities to those vested in any other judge. I make no bones about my position. If they are judges, and I believe that they are, then in my view the

---

[5] Vernon Bogdanor, *The New British Constitution* (Oxford, 2009).

identical arrangements should apply to them as they do to any other judge in England and Wales.

The question whether the current Constitutional Reform Act arrangements will turn out to be set in stone, and remain unchanged for the next 25 years, or whether in five years' time we shall be looking back at the current arrangements and recognising that they were merely temporary, is open to question. We do not yet know. But as we are in a state of flux, let us just reflect briefly on some of the possibilities.

One significant question is whether HMCS should in future become the exclusive responsibility of the judiciary. That would be a mammoth change. What we do know is that if there is any move to increase the administrative burdens on the senior judiciary, by putting the entire system for which Her Majesty's Court Service is currently responsible into their hands, these arrangements must be implemented so as to ensure that senior judges will continue to sit in court producing judgments. Otherwise, I venture to suggest, it would be an indication of failure. The senior members of the judiciary cannot lead the judiciary by sitting in their offices, overwhelmed with administrative responsibilities: they must sit in court, deciding cases. And so the process is not to be contemplated without a very careful examination of the resources available to the judiciary to undertake these responsibilities, and an analysis of how such a change might properly fit into their contemporaneous context, that is, yet further changes in the constitutional arrangements.

Another feature running in synchronisation is to recognise, first, that increasing devolution within the United Kingdom almost certainly lies ahead, and that the current arrangements for the administration of justice in Wales may be very different in 10 years' time. Again, we are reading in our papers this very week of suggestions that the House of Lords, as the second constituent of Parliament, will be reformed into extinction. In the meantime, the Supreme Court has responsibility for addressing some of the consequences of the devolution arrangements. I shall not recite a long list of possible changes to our structures. You can think of them for yourselves. But they may all have knock-on effects, and, following the logic of the creation of the Supreme Court of the United Kingdom, the time may come when it will be proposed that there should be a more formal mechanism by which the judiciaries of Scotland and Northern Ireland as well as those of England and Wales, and the Supreme Court of the United Kingdom, should not only co-operate more closely together, but even that a formal constitutional body will be proposed, through which the different judiciaries should have open communication with the legislature and the executive, for formal discussion of matters of common interest, in something that I describe as a kind of Conseil d'Etat.

I am not advocating it. Changes of this kind would draw the judiciary too closely into policy-making decisions, and therefore political decisions. If so, the judiciary will become increasingly politicised, and a politicised judiciary is anathema to me, and I suspect to each and every one of you, not least because if we allow ourselves to become politicised, judicial independence will inevitably be threatened. But we should watch out for beguiling blandishments, and warn ourselves against them, although I do not recollect any blandishments at all, beguiling or otherwise, about the announcements that the Lord Chancellor would be abolished, or a couple of years later, that his department would take over the prisons. I do not for one moment imagine that they will come in the next 10 years, but as they say, a week in politics is a long time, and 20 years is eternity. It will be the young among you who will have to face up to these sorts of challenges arising from the uncertain and unfinalised form of our constitutional changes, and deal with them.

In 20 years' time I believe that the judiciary will be different from the judiciary trained today by the JSB. There are within Baroness Neuberger's report[6] a series of suggestions which could—I am suggesting no more than 'could'—produce a career judiciary. The example of some of the continental systems suggests to me that this is not a course to be embraced, because certainly some of those systems are at least beginning to open up the possibility of successful practitioners entering the judiciary later in their careers. But two significant changes seem to me inevitable.

First, we must create a system which stops potential applicants for judicial appointment in effect self-selecting themselves out of appointment, because they will not make an application, sadly believing that there is something about them—the wrong background, the wrong colour, the wrong gender—which means they think that any application is doomed to failure. Doing away with any such myths is a responsibility of the current judiciary, and in my view, comes within the ambit of the Judicial Studies Board. But not just the Judicial Studies Board. All current members of the judiciary must be involved.

---

[6] *Report of the Advisory Panel on Judicial Diversity 2010*, chaired by Baroness Neuberger.

The second change relates to judicial appraisal. We must tackle the lack of a system of appraisal. The day should come when everyone who is appointed as a full time judge should have been appraised when sitting as a part-time judge. Of course, every effort is made to ensure that only the best applicants, and those qualified for appointment, are appointed. But, dealing with it simplistically, what better evidence can there be than the evidence of how the individual in question behaves—and I do not merely mean whether he or she is pleasant and courteous, or not, but how the individual behaves in the overall discharge of his or her judicial responsibilities, showing patience, and humility, and fortitude, and wisdom, and balance, and fire, fired by an enthusiasm to do justice according to law. That information is available. We are not yet in a position to tap into it. The expense would be considerable. But it would, in my view, enhance the selection process, and improve the perception of the selection process. It is only if you believe, and I do not, that judicial skill is entirely intuitive, that you reject training and appraisal. That would raise questions about the true role of the JSB. I quite accept that attendance at seminars should not form part of an appraisal system. But in the context of a Judicial College, appraisal of individuals sitting in court might properly fall within the responsibilities of the JSB, perhaps in a newly created part of it.

All of these ambitions require focus on the Judicial College about which Michael Mustill spoke, now some 25 years ago. Such a College would serve to widen the pool from which judges are chosen, by attracting some of those who presently would self de-select and enabling others who are uncertain whether to seek judicial appointment at least to be better informed about it, and ultimately enable the system for appointment of judges to be improved, and ensure that once appointed their education will continue. At a time of financial stringency, it is quite unrealistic to anticipate the early creation of the College, fully fledged as Michael Mustill envisaged it, but it should remain, and I have no doubt that it will remain, a long-term ambition for the JSB.

And the JSB is bound to have to address Europe. Ignoring altogether the different views expressed by our political parties on the issues of Europe, and the Strasbourg court, and avoiding any inappropriate discussion of the topic, perhaps I should begin with the European Court of Justice. You all know that the decisions of that court bind us. That is a consequence of our domestic legislation. As a matter of statute the decisions of the European Court of Human Rights in Strasbourg do not bind our courts. The statutory obligation on our courts is to 'take account' of the decisions of the court in Strasbourg. Naturally, the decisions there must command our respect. It is certainly open to us to follow the reasoning, and if possible identify and apply the principle to be found in the decisions, particularly those of the Grand Chamber. But I venture to suggest that that is not because we are bound to do so, or because the Supreme Court is a court subordinate to the Strasbourg court, but because, having taken the Strasbourg decision into account and examined it, it is appropriate to do so. And that means it is not always appropriate to do so. What I respectfully suggest is that statute ensures that the final word does not rest with Strasbourg, but with our Supreme Court. But however that question is approached, the further development that has to be addressed is that the European Court of Justice is beginning to acquire jurisdiction over matters that would normally be regarded as matters not for Luxembourg but for Strasbourg. Before I come to it I want to express another concern.

Too many decisions from Strasbourg, and too many domestic decisions, are cited in argument, and, dare I say it, sometimes in our judgments. Part of this is a manifestation of the extraordinary way in which the forensic technique has changed, and part at any rate the result of the development of modern technology. All the cases on the point are assembled, and put into the skeleton argument. That skeleton argument is saved by counsel. When another case emerges, from whatever source, Europe or England and Wales, from any part of the European system, and even unreported cases in this jurisdiction, all join hands with and achieve spurious importance by being linked with reported cases already in the saved skeleton. The process is just too simple. And so the arguments grow like Topsy. Professor David Ormerod told me that he worked on the principle that in Smith and Hogan, which he now edits, for each case added, one is removed. Many skeleton arguments would be a lot shorter if the person responsible for them was required to write them out by hand. I also think that our bundles of papers would be radically cut, if the only documents looked at by the court were those which had been copied by hand. Wholly impracticable, of course.

With the decisions of the European Court, however, there are occasions of forensic blindness. Very often, too often, we are asked to consider decisions from Europe which have already been considered or must have been considered in the House of Lords or the Supreme Court. That is the decision which binds us all. After all, once the Supreme Court has considered decisions of the Court of

Appeal, the authority of those decisions is largely extinguished. Surely the same should apply to decisions from Europe. In other words, once the Supreme Court has considered the relevant decisions from Strasbourg, we need to employ a powerful self-denying ordinance against allowing further citation of decisions on the point which provide no more than an illustration of a principle which has been encapsulated in the decisions of the Supreme Court. Am I alone in thinking that we are being presented with far too many so-called authorities whether from Europe or domestically? We are, I believe, tending to forget that the point that matters in any authority that is cited to us is to discover, using the Latin, the ratio decidendi. If we cannot discern the ratio, the decision is not authority for anything. And surely the JSB will start teaching our judges to refuse to allow counsel to cite what are no more than decisions, often unreported, which do not help to identify the principle, but merely illustrate its application. It is surely up to us to start that process and to insist on it here and now, with immediate effect. If we do not get a grip we shall bury our system under a mass of paper.

The primary responsibility for saving the common law system of proceeding by precedent is primarily a matter for us as judges. And while we are about it, perhaps we should reflect on the way in which I detect that our Australian colleagues (and those from other common law countries) seem to be claiming bragging rights as the custodians of the common law. Do they have a point? Are we so focused on Strasbourg and the Convention that instead of incorporating Convention principles within and developing the common law accordingly, we are allowing the Convention to assume a priority over the common law. Or is it that we are just still on honeymoon with the Convention?

Can I turn to an additional element of the European dimension which will impinge both on us as judges and on the Judicial Studies Board. The European Union is about to expand not simply its influence but its jurisdiction over criminal matters. The European Arrest Warrant was, as we all know, the first major instrument of Community law in the area of criminal law. The impact of the European Union on criminal law is now increasing. The first significant change which will affect most criminal courts in this jurisdiction is the implementation of the *Framework Decision* on criminal convictions, which will take place on 15 August 2010. It will require domestic courts to take account of previous convictions recorded in the community in the same way as they take account of domestic previous convictions. A certificate of conviction is sufficient for this purpose. No doubt much attention will be paid to the method of verification of the European certificate of conviction, and so on, but the change, although not shattering in itself, provides a foretaste of things to come.

The EU has recently signed up to what is called a 'roadmap' of five areas of criminal procedure which must be addressed within the next five years to protect and guarantee the rights of EU citizens. I have no problem at all with the principle that there should be proper translation and interpretation for an EU citizen in another EU country, or with the right to information about his or her rights and the charges brought against them, or the right to legal advice, with special safeguards for vulnerable persons, or indeed a right to periodical review of the justification for pre-trial detention. None of that is new to us. They form part of domestic law, and they are also, effectively, part of the Convention. In general terms we have always assumed that within the European dimension, the fairness of trial processes, and of the trial itself, were the sole preserve of the Strasbourg court rather than the Luxembourg court. The Treaty of Lisbon has brought criminal justice matters to the core of the EU, and with it the jurisdiction of the Luxembourg court. The principle of qualified majority voting has been extended to measures relating to judicial co-operation in criminal matters, and so the time may come when the United Kingdom could find itself outside the majority, and therefore unable to influence the development of EU criminal justice policy. Under the Lisbon Treaty the United Kingdom will have to decide whether to opt in to new criminal justice instruments and whether to participate in the existing body of EU criminal justice and with it the jurisdiction of the Luxembourg court.

A number of specific matters arise, if this happens. All these changes will have to be considered in the context of our own adversarial criminal justice system, in which juries try the most serious cases, and an inquisitorial system which is available in most EU member states, where the jury lacks the constitutional primacy we give to it, and where, unlike this jurisdiction, there is a significant overlap between the career structures for judges and prosecutors. But, again, I do not have the time to develop an analysis of the potential consequences. I simply remind myself that decisions of the Luxembourg court on issues arising out of the Treaty of Lisbon, even to the extent that they involve criminal matters, would become binding on us all, if the right to opt in is exercised by the United Kingdom. And we may have the spectacle of the Strasbourg court ruling on problems which arise out of the consequences of our obligation to enforce binding decisions of the Luxembourg court. And these matters, I suggest, emphasise the need for us to approach the decisions in Strasbourg in the way which our domestic legislation requires.

The other feature of these potential developments in EU law, and the acknowledgement within the EU of the need to ensure its consistent application, is that judicial training will be involved. The *Stockholm Programme* sets out the strategy for justice for the next five years, and includes the pursuit of what are described as systematic European Training Schemes

> to be offered to judges, prosecutors, judicial staff, police and customs officers and border guards. The ambition for the Union and its member states should be that a substantive number of professions by 2015 will have participated in the European training or an exchange with another member state, ... for this purpose existing training institutions should in particular be used.

There are many arguments about the Lisbon Treaty, and indeed there has been much discussion among our political parties about the Convention. So I shall not enter further into turbulent political waters. It is, however, safe to anticipate that unless there are some dramatic changes, new and additional training requirements will be required before too long, and that the development of the European Union, and the extended jurisdiction of the European court in criminal matters, will have a significant impact domestically.

And so I come to technology. We must welcome modern technology. We must welcome scientific advances. DNA has been a remarkable success. It achieves the conviction of the guilty. It undoubtedly helps to clear the innocent. Recorded police interviews have done away with some of the nonsenses with which we once had to contend. Video recording of a child's evidence represents a huge step forward, provided that the method questioning of the child is carefully addressed. I am far from convinced that we have arrived at our ultimate destination here, but the combination of new technology with special measures does represent a significant step forward.

The impact of technology in the future led Professor Richard Susskind to write a book entitled *The End of Lawyers?*.[7] As he points out himself, the question mark is an important aspect of the title. He is not making any assertions. He is asking a question. And rather like me today, he is not providing definitive answers.

---

[7] Richard Susskind, *The End of Lawyers? Rethinking the Nature of Legal* Services (Oxford, rev edn 2010).

Let me begin at where we stand today ... No, will you allow me a reminisce about the time the Sputnik went up. At the time when I joined the JSB in 1984, did anyone in the legal profession, or indeed outside it, appreciate the technological changes that would hit us over the next 25 years? I doubt it. Did anyone anticipate that the good old cheque would be under threat? What I know about technological advances in the next 25 years is that we cannot begin to forecast where they will take us. What, however, is certain in my mind is that they will have a dramatic impact on all our lives, and inevitably, on the processes by which justice is administered.

First, a few words about the jury system. At the risk of repeating what I have said elsewhere,[8] the process by which the children of today are educated is very different from my own. I sat in class and listened, or tried to listen. In the listening process I absorbed information. It was, being utterly facile, a preparation for jury service. Jurors sit and listen. They may make notes, but the process involves absorbing information by listening. The learning process for my grandchildren involves very little listening. Largely it is visual, mainly screen based, but also book based. But listening is a much diminished aspect of the process.

I suggest that it is inevitable that the process by which we provide jurors with the material to enable them to form their decisions will have to change. If they are to perform their public function, they must be provided with the tools most suitable for them to do so, not those which were regarded as appropriate for earlier generations. This will have an inevitable impact on the trial process. And while we are about it, can we determine now, as we stand here today, that such changes will not take the form of bombarding juries with more and more material. One of the problems with modern technology is that it tends to generate more and more material—witness, the length of skeleton arguments and the numbers of cases referred to in them.

There is, however, a second potential for modern technology about which I think we must warn ourselves. Some of you will have heard of the Virtual Court. Very briefly. The defendant is arrested and charged in the normal way. Through an electronic diary system a slot is found for a hearing either that day or the next day. The defendant is either remanded or given conditional police bail, the condition being his appearance at the police station at the appropriate time for the hearing. The necessary paperwork is dealt with

---

[8] See 'Trial by Jury', this volume, p 198.

electronically. The court and the CPS and the defence are provided with the necessary materials. The defence solicitor may choose to attend the virtual hearing either with his client at the police station or at court while the defendant appears via a video link from the police station. The defendant then appears on a TV screen in a police interview room with a live link to the court. Proceedings then follow the usual pattern. The system has worked well in London, but it has yet to be used in large country areas. Much time and resource is saved. The number of out-of-court disposals is reduced, so matters are brought back into court. On the other hand the process is much less formal than the normal court appearance.

There are still plenty of teething troubles. I personally strongly favour the use of the virtual court system. But, and it is the 'but' that I want to trouble you with, although the virtual court represents a sensible, practical use of modern technology (and is therefore to be welcomed) we must watch and guard against the possibility that it will gradually develop into a system which will mean that we virtually do away with the court altogether. After all, if the defendant, and his solicitor, and the CPS, and the court can all be on video systems, as a matter of technology, so can everybody else. I do not want to see the day when the judge and every member of the jury is provided with the necessary technology, and the court hearing becomes a thing of the past. We would be then dealing with a system which is tantamount to closed justice. That would never be acceptable.

I am sorry that this has taken so long. There is much to reflect on, much to look forward to, and plenty to guard against. That is always the way with the future.

I am indebted, as I think we all are, to the Judicial Studies Board. As I said earlier, it is the success story of the system. And my personal belief is that over the next 30 years that success will become more deeply embedded than ever. But, as always, what's to come is still unsure.

Judicial Diversity

This speech was given at the Minority Lawyers Conference held in my Court in April 2009. It is typical of a number of speeches on this important issue which I have made over the years. Some will say that I am optimistic when I say that the barriers are broken. I believe that they are, although I also recognise that they have not been swept away. The harsh reality is that in the modern system of judicial appointments, no one who has not applied for judicial office can be appointed to it. That is sometimes a barrier. But for those who do apply, the only remaining barrier is the judgment to be made by the Judicial Appointments Commission: that of merit.

I T IS A privilege for me to be asked to address this conference. I know, I do know, that that is what many speakers start by saying, but I mean it. I have not come here to offer you all a speedy route to judicial office. I do not know any tricks. If I tried to pretend that I had easy answers, I would be trying to pretend to some major quality I do not have. Would you therefore allow me a few minutes to wish this conference well, to explain my own perspective and to share my thoughts with you on some of these issues, and offer you encouragement to consider a judicial career, whatever the difficulties?

The equality issue has been troublesome to me for many years. I have recounted to the Association of Women Judges my youthful amazement at a dinner my old circuit gave to the first woman High Court judge, Elizabeth Lane, who had been a member of the circuit for many years. Those of you who have heard it before will forgive me.

Elizabeth Lane stood up after some nice things had been said about her by the Circuit Leader and began by saying, 'Mr Recorder, this is the first time I have been allowed to dine in Mess'. Because she was a woman she had never done so before her appointment as a county court judge. By the time of her appointment to the High Court, women were permitted to dine in Mess. Her comment horrified me. It horrified others. Many of them were horrified that she should be so discourteous as to make the important point that she did. Others of us were horrified that that had been her experience, and admired her courage in drawing attention to it. When I told this story—which is completely true—to the Association of Women Judges, I noticed, sitting at the same table as me, a woman Silk who had been elected Leader of my old circuit, and at another table, a woman who had been the Recorder when I was Leader of the Circuit, and who was now one of its Presiding Judges. Today just about half of our lay magistrates, who try the vast majority of criminal cases in this country, are women. When Lizzie Lane was speaking, that prospect would have seemed risible. The tide is not always fast; sometimes it is very slow; but in the end the tide always wins.

The ethnicity question has a number of different facets. As a junior member of the Bar I used to wonder from time to time, when my client was black, and the judge, counsel, solicitors, jury, usher and prison officers were all white, how the defendant would feel. Putting myself in his position, how would I, as a white man, feel sitting in a dock in which the judge, counsel, solicitors, jury and dock officers were black? Would it feel better or worse if the court was a foreign court or a court in what I thought and was entitled to believe was my own country? Such questions focus the mind. Of course I did not endure the experience of my defendant client. But then, fortunately, I have not had to endure the experience of being a defendant in a criminal case. I hope that imagination was quite enough, and that in due course it led to my being able to claim proudly that it was when I was Chairman of the Judicial Studies Board Criminal Committee that I invited Henry Brooke to join me on the platform for the very first time ever, to address the issue of judicial behaviour towards litigants from the minority ethnic communities. Although some judges did not appreciate it, they needed help and advice. Many of them thought it enough to be well mannered. There was much to learn. Two of those who lent Henry help, Oba Nsugbe and Anesta Weekes, both now in well merited Silk, are here today. They will forgive me for reminding them that they were younger then than they are now. So, too, was I. It cannot have been easy for two young black barristers to address those bodies of white judges. I admired their courage and their balance. I still do. There are others like them. All this is now encapsulated in the Judicial Studies Board Equal Treatment Bench Book. A remarkable success.

So the journey has begun. There is a long way to go. It is not unreasonable to be impatient, to wish for progress to be more speedy. That after all is the point: if it is progress, the faster the better.

The essential principle seems to me to be encompassed in the language used by Thomas Jefferson in his Inaugural Address in 1801 when he said:

> Though the will of the majority is in all cases to prevail, that will to be rightful must be reasonable ... the minority possess their equal rights, which equal law must protect, and to violate would be oppression.

I have never shared the status of virtual sainthood bestowed on Thomas Jefferson as the author of the first rough draft of the American Declaration of Independence in which all men—not women—were stated to be created equal, but who deliberately failed to address the slavery question, which was later to haunt the United States and produce a Civil War in which 600,000 American—more than their total fatalities in the two world wars—died. But great principles can be expressed by flawed humanity. The point of this observation, as it applies to us today, is that members of minorities do indeed possess equal rights, and that there is an obligation on the law to protect those equal rights. Implicit in what he said was the concept that minorities should be entitled to equal opportunities, to be protected by equal law. Implicit it may have been then, but for the avoidance of doubt, we must declare it, and work for it, and ensure that in the legal profession we will and must achieve it.

That begs this further question. How does a society show to the minorities, and indeed the majority, that this principle of equality applies? Notice the way I put it. In the end it is no less important that the majority appreciate that it applies as that the minority should. That is because, majority and minority, we are all members of a single society.

Bare assertion will not do. There need to be outward signs which demonstrate that the principle is not merely accepted, but flourishing. If this virtue exists, then, like justice itself, it cannot be cloistered. Men and women from minority ethnic communities on the judicial Bench, or like Patricia Scotland, holding one of the most ancient offices in this country, demonstrate to everyone that in this respect, at any rate, we live in a civilised society. The ambition is that the time will come when it will be a matter of no surprise or moment for any litigant, or defendant, or witness, or jury member, that the colour of the judge's skin is not white.

The list of judicial qualities is a long one, and you can pick and choose among your favourites. You can also identify judicial failings, and no doubt you have all experienced examples of them. But what I have said before, and I do not hesitate to repeat now, is that none of the qualities have anything whatever to do with gender, or colour, or creed, or origins. Neither gender, nor colour, nor creed, nor origins has the slightest relevance to the identification of those most fitted to be judges or indeed to the judiciary as a whole. Justice is depicted blindfold. Like Justice itself, the selection process should be metaphorically blindfold. In the end your gender, the colour of your skin, your religious belief, or indeed your social origins, are all utterly irrelevant. It is the individual who is the judge, and it is he or she who carries the judicial responsibilities and the judicial burdens; the judicial conscience which governs all judges is utterly without colour.

As you all know, judges in this country are not appointed, or are very rarely appointed, to judicial office before the age of 40, or indeed in many cases before 50. This is significant. At the time when I was listening to Lizzie Lane, the vast majority, the overwhelming majority, of practitioners at the Bar, and the newcomers to the Bar were white men. Black and minority ethnic barristers were rare indeed. But perhaps I should add that much the same applied to all the other professions, and the City, and to public and political life, and indeed so far as the men were concerned, professional footballers and cricketers. Gradually, very gradually, in all these professions, including the law, a few brave souls launched themselves into what must have seemed an abyss. But by setting the example they did, and that others are now following, they increased the prospect that more will achieve judicial appointment. It is to encourage these processes that the Lord Chief Justice's Diversity Conference was held on 11 March this year. It is to encourage this process that my office—the Directorate of the Judicial Office—co-ordinates a judicial work shadowing scheme, a sort of judicial mini-pupilage open to all. It is for this reason that I supported the expansion into the categories of legal practice which qualify an individual for judicial office in the Tribunals, Courts and Enforcement Act. Fellows of the Institute of Legal Executives, Registered Trademark Attorneys and Registered Patent Attorneys qualify for judicial appointment. It is for this reason that I supported, and still enthusiastically support, the creation of the Judicial Appointments Commission as a statutory body for judicial appointments. In recommending the candidates for appointment, the JAC is required to have regard to one statutory criterion—that appointment should be made on the basis of merit for judicial office. I make no secret of the fact that I am an advocate of the merit test. Others disagree. My belief is that the public interest requires that the judiciary should be constituted of individuals of the highest possible calibre, and the single consideration for the selection panel must be to discover the person or persons most fitted to perform the office to which they are seeking appointment. Candidates must merit their place on the Bench whether as a magistrate, a part-time recorder or indeed for that matter a Law Lord.

Nowadays the number of black and minority candidates who enter the legal profession, whether as barristers or solicitors or fellows of the Institute, has been increasing year on year. This is a welcome trend. The pool of eligible candidates will in due course be much richer and much more diverse.

There nevertheless remain some serious and difficult questions, and these are issues which you will be addressing today. Do a sufficient number of black and minority ethnic candidates put themselves forward for appointment? If they do not, what is it that deters them? Do we need to increase the support to be offered to such candidates at the very earliest stages in their careers? Do we indeed need to increase the support to be offered to potential candidates, years before, when they are still at school? How do we encourage them to give serious consideration to a judicial career? Is there anything in the appointments process itself which can remedy the relative scarcity of such candidates? These are difficult questions. They are not confined to the legal profession. In truth there is a broad social problem.

It still takes courage to enter the legal profession. Many of those seeking to enter it have vast debts. Many barristers will not in the end find pupillages, let alone tenancies. Outside the large City firms, the solicitors' profession is not in ebullient health. Those doing criminal work will not be driving around in gold-plated Cadillacs. But if you have the determination and courage, notwithstanding all these difficulties, to go into practice as a barrister or solicitor or legal executive, you can aspire to a judicial career. Being a judge is not without its difficulties. The nature of the burdens and responsibilities means that it does not suit everyone.

But I have come here to give you a simple message. If you are legally qualified then you should not rule out the possibility of a judicial appointment. If you say to yourself, this is not for me, because I do not want to make those sorts of decision—I am not prepared to send someone to prison, or to order that a mother should give up her children—if you do not want to become a judge because by becoming a judge you are accepting that there are responsibilities which you do not have to accept if you are a barrister or a solicitor or a legal executive—well and good. But, please, do not ignore the possibility of a judicial career because you think that the colour of your skin, or your creed, or your origins or your sexual orientations may make you unsuitable, or ineligible, or indeed may mean that you will not be successful.

If I may be a little portentous. In life you have to live with yourself. Those of you who have got this far in the professions have had to make very difficult decisions about whether to go on, and you have done so. You have given it your best shot. And you will not, unlike those who have not pressed on as you have, have to spend the rest of your life regretting that you lacked the courage and determination to do what you wanted to do. The same is true for a judicial appointment. None of us wants to end our days regretting that we lacked the courage to try.

But there is, quite apart from your own personal position, a separate and important consideration. Our society is a diverse society. That is one of its glories. It is enriched by diversity. This diversity should be reflected in all areas of society. It should be reflected in the judiciary.

The journey to diversity is a long one. Progress is slow. It should be quicker. But it will come. It will come. I have a firm, indeed a passionate belief that our community will be enriched when the judiciary properly reflects its diversity. The tide is for diversity. The tide is inexorable, and in the end the tide always wins.

Personal Reflections

Celebration of the Diamond Jubilee of Her Majesty the Queen

Address delivered at Temple Church, 14 June 2012.

HERE IN THIS Mother Church of the Common Law—here in the then new building in the Winter of 1214/1215 where the Master of the Temple assisted King John and his rebellious barons to thrash out the terms of the settlement which reached its climax at Runnymede in June 1215, we are pausing for a moment to celebrate the Diamond Jubilee of Her Majesty Queen Elizabeth II, whose visits to the Temple Church are shown in the Service Sheet.

Perhaps we should begin by reflecting that during her long reign the momentum for change has been irresistible and the speed of change has been explosive. I venture to suggest that this has been a reign in which more has changed more rapidly for more people than ever before in the history of this nation, and indeed in the history of mankind. Yet during all that change, since 1952 our Head of State has been unchanged.

It is no exaggeration to suggest that during the celebrations the weekend before last there was an outpouring of affection, respect, admiration and joy for the Queen. Each member of the crowds had his own or her own personal reason for participating in the celebrations. There were those of my parents' generation, the generation which endured the casualties and hardships of the Second World War, who remembered the beautiful young Princess so vividly evoked in Winston Churchill's speech in February 1952, grieving for the loss of a beloved father, simultaneously assuming the mantle of heavy responsibility—and there were their great grandchildren, some of whom were too young to have any real idea about what was being celebrated, but who, as children do, were certainly willing to have fun if the grown ups were bright and cheerful.

Just about everything that could be said and written about Her Majesty was said and written—indeed on occasions much speculative psychobabble and creative impertinence about the royal family was relied on to make good any shortfall in the knowledge of the writer or the speaker.

Nevertheless in all that outpouring, in all the enthusiastic commentary, I missed any lengthy reference to an old-fashioned, nowadays much underrated quality—yet one of the cardinal virtues identified by the Christian faith: fortitude. If I may say so with the greatest respect, it is fortitude that has struck me as a particular feature of this long reign, and about which I want to say just a little more.

Why does this have anything to do with the Temple Church? The Church is filled now as it has been for hundreds of years with judges, former judges and part-time judges, men and women who have exercised or are exercising judicial responsibilities, and those who appear or appeared as advocates in front of those judges.

A month or so ago, I heard myself talking to the Judicial Appointments Commission and telling them that of course I wanted decent, patient and wise men and women to be appointed to the Bench, but I added, quite deliberately, that among all the positive qualities required of the candidates, they should look for fortitude. And why? Simply because every judge requires fortitude, inner strength. Judicial responsibilities are not easy. The decisions we have to make are sometimes profoundly painful. Sometimes it is necessary to sentence a man to imprisonment when you know that his wife and family believe passionately that he is innocent of the crime. Sometimes you have to separate children from one or other, or even both parents, a catastrophe to avoid a worse one, a decision which is life-changing for every single member of the family involved. Sometimes you have to safeguard the rights of a profoundly unpopular individual, sometimes indeed the rights of an individual who has been demonised. All these decisions create their own burdens, and some generate public opprobrium. Inner strength is needed to weather the storm that may follow, a storm which is sometimes more painful to the family of the judge than to the judge himself or herself, but for whom the pain suffered by the family creates a very special kind of pressure of its own. And of course, sometimes we reach the wrong decision, but without for one moment thereafter being able to take refuge in hesitation.

We cannot falter. We must keep on making our decisions, doing right, according to law, in every case, conscientiously, without fear or favour, affection or ill will. To do this case by case, day by day, year by year, requires inner strength and depth of character.

Fortitude is a virtue for which trumpets should be sounded, but because those who are blessed with it tend not to sound their own trumpets, it is in truth a self-effacing quality, perhaps overwhelmed by our modern tendency to relish and respond to the clarion call. And fortitude has a further ingredient which is not always fully in accordance with the modern world. Fortitude does not run with the ebbs and flows of easy popularity and the fickleness of fashion. It is neither time serving nor time pleasing. Whereas fashion is transient, and populism brief, fortitude takes its stand on principle and principle is unchanging.

Nowadays, unlike King John, Her Majesty the Queen does not sit in judgment, but the Crown remains the fountain of justice. We are not the Prime Minister's Judges, nor the Government's Judges, nor even the Parliament's Judges. We are Her Majesty's Judges.

During the long years of the reign we have been celebrating, inevitably, time's revolutions have sometimes produced moments of real difficulty, and indeed sharp criticism. So not every moment of the long reign has been comfortable. Fortitude has been needed. At all times.

Let me but take a simple example from last weekend. We all know that the Duke of Edinburgh was taken ill. Did it occur to us for one moment that the Queen would not attend the concert on Monday evening and the service at St Paul's on the Tuesday morning? Did it occur to anyone of us that at her age, bereft of her husband's support, she might just have found it a little troublesome, or perhaps have been unable to do both? I doubt if it occurred to any of us for one moment that she would not be there, as planned. Did it occur to you? Why ever not?

My answer is that this is a tiny example of why our current celebrations represent, among other things, the triumph of fortitude, and simultaneously, they underline how easy it is for fortitude to be taken for granted. It is fortitude that enabled the fulfilment of the solemn act of dedication and service made by the 21-year-old Princess Elizabeth in 1947. Surely, in this long reign we have been privileged to witness for ourselves an embodiment of this unsung, underrated, but spectacular human quality. For those involved in the administration of justice—in whatever capacity—this ancient church is the appropriate place in which to give thanks for it.

Catastrophic Spinal Injuries

This is the text of an after-dinner speech given to the Spinal Injuries Association in London in early 2010. It was published in the Journal of Personal Injury Law in February 2010. I have included it to acknowledge the personal inspiration given to me over many years by those who suffered, and members of the families of those who suffered, catastrophic personal injuries, either as a result of negligence during the birth process itself, or as a result of trauma at work or on the roads. I also include it as a tribute to my wife, whose professional career was spent treating babies and small children who had been born with or suffered sometimes catastrophic injuries and who, like me, was inspired by and in her case gave inspiration to so many children and their parents. An extract was published in The Times *on 28 December 2010 as part of its Christmas Charities Appeal following the catastrophic spinal injuries in a riding accident suffered by Melanie Reid, one of the regular commentators for* The Times. *Her articles since her accident continue to provide vivid reminders of many remarkable men and women.*

SOME OF YOU may know the fundraiser for the Spinal Injuries Association, John Fieldus. Fifty years ago last summer, John and I played in the same team in a cricket match at Lord's. In a successful stand for the sixth wicket, I was Monty Panesar; he scored about 70 beautifully struck runs. He was a superb rugby player at fly-half and centre, a wonderful athlete all round. Some 20 years later in a swimming accident he broke his spine. He cannot be here today because he is undergoing yet another operation. But his is a life remade.

When he asked me to speak tonight it was an invitation from a friend that I could not and did not want to refuse. And he linked it with the 35th anniversary of the founding of the Spinal Injuries Association. The Association represents a remarkable story of achievement and success, with practical and positive contributions to the welfare and well-being of those who have suffered spinal injuries. So may I thank you all for coming and supporting the Association and its officers and its objectives.

What has struck me over the years in practice is how much change there has been in relation to major spinal injuries since 1975. Looking back on it, the legal professions, whether the Bar, or solicitors or judiciary, lacked any real knowledge of the realities of these cases, not only for those who had suffered the catastrophic injuries themselves, but for all those who lived with and loved them and cared for them. Perhaps that is unfair. After all, many of these men in the legal profession, and in those days they were almost all men, had seen their friends killed, and wounded, and permanently maimed, so it is perhaps more accurate to say that knowledge had not percolated into the assessment of damages, or the harsh practical realities, and maybe that was the way things were done then. The legal profession had yet to be shaken by the likes of Bart Hellyer and Paul Bush, and many others. But there were other features too.

When I was a junior it was an absolute rule of the profession that the lay client was not seen at home. He or she came to chambers for a conference; if not there was no conference before the hearing. At the hearing itself, there were no access facilities of any kind. I vividly remember an elderly mother and father struggling with their spinally injured and extremely heavy son, a miner injured in a pit accident underground, carrying him up the stairs in the old Nottingham Assize Court, hurrying to avoid interrupting the arrival of the judge. After the hearing they had of course to get their son home—another exhausting, back-breaking journey for them, and for him. I believe court facilities are better now than they were then.

Shortly before I took Silk it was suggested to me by the late Patrick Bennett QC that the right place for a consultation in this kind of case was the plaintiff's home. And from the moment I took Silk I adopted that practice. I did not seek permission from the Bar Council. It was a revelation. I went to many different homes, some very prosperous, and some pretty abjectly poor, most somewhere in the middle. In the whole of my time in Silk I only left one house without feeling both humbled and inspired by the human spirit that I had observed. I remember the one because it was the only one. In that case—as I emphasised, one among many—I just felt sorry.

Many of my clients are still in my memory. I shall not name any of them, but just one will do as an example.

She was a very attractive young woman, who had been thrown out of a car, and broken her neck. Her fiancé still wanted to marry her. And after thinking it over long and hard she agreed. When I saw her with her husband at home she had, despite all the obvious difficulties which no one here will need me to explain, presented him with two children, and she was pregnant with a third. She mothered her two with a strength of character and personality that was quite undiminished by her injuries. I shall never forget her saying to me that there was no reason why the injuries she had sustained should prevent her husband becoming a father. None of you here will need me to spell out what the realities must have involved for her.

There were many lessons to be learned from these visits. If you saw your client at home you understood what they—that is, they as individuals—actually wanted, their aspirations and anxieties, their hopes and concerns, the sought-for improvements in their lives. You also learned—and perhaps this is the most important lesson for any lawyer with a seriously injured client—to listen out for what you were not being told, to listen out during those moments of silence. What is it about these catastrophic injuries that hurt my client so much that he or she cannot talk about them? In a young couple, perhaps the damage to the physical side of their relationship. In parents, concern about what will happen to the child when they are no longer available to help, or the pressure on the other siblings, perhaps burdened with responsibility which would impact on their own lives. Or perhaps simply, life expectation. Or the money running out. Or whatever it was. It could be anything at all. If you listen to what you are not being told you hear a great deal. The overwhelming requirement then was sensitivity, not because of the disability as such, but because you were treading into very private matters.

I took much that I learned from this experience to the Bench with me. I hope that first instance judges take time, after the litigation is over and the case is settled, to seek permission from both sides to talk to the injured man or woman and those who have come to court to support him or her. I always did—unless I was asked not to do so, and that did happen on one occasion. And that is a reminder that every one of these cases is the case of an individual. It is a case of such importance to them, and among many of the less pleasant manifestations of humankind which are the regular diet of criminal judges, cases like these remind you of the indomitable nature of the human spirit.

And then, along came the new periodic payments and structured settlements. I believe, although I am not claiming it, that I led my old friend James Hunt in what was the first structured settlement in this country. Our client was on the point of emigrating to the USA when he was injured. In the USA he had lawyers, and it was through them that he asked us to approach insurance companies to arrange a structured settlement. It was an idea whose time had not quite come then, but it did come, and it has come. What an improvement this is to the assessment of damages which used to be based on more or less speculative estimates of life expectation.

The business is unfinished. There have been huge developments. Simultaneously there has been, I believe, a vast change in the attitude of society to disability, whatever its source. I witness fewer occasions when people shout at individuals who are stuck in a wheelchair in the way that they did when I was young, as if they were just stupid. Along with the plusses come some problems. The problem of aging with a spinal cord injury includes skin deterioration, the wearing of joints, changes in bladder and bowel function. The care arrangements must focus on all these long-term consequences of increased life expectation. Despite the progress, therefore, the work of the Spinal Injuries Association is not yet finished—far from it.

Is it any wonder that I support the work of the Spinal Injuries Association? So much has been done, so much achieved in 35 years. But, I repeat, the business is unfinished. The battle is not over.

In the end, nothing, but nothing, replaces the human spirit. And I have come here tonight not only to thank you for coming, which I do; but to reflect with you, and if you will allow me on your behalf to acknowledge what every one of us involved in work in which catastrophic personal injuries has experienced. We have all been enriched personally by our involvement in this work, and by evidence we have seen of courage, and fortitude, and determination, and the indomitability of the human spirit. And tonight that is what we are celebrating.

History of the Middle Temple: Introduction

First published in Richard O Havery (ed), History of the Middle Temple *(Hart Publishing, 2011).*

THE STORY OF the Middle Temple, like that of the Inner Temple, is vivid and remarkable. It is interleaved with the history of England and nations beyond the seas. Sir David Calcutt QC, Treasurer in 1998, to whose memory the book is affectionately dedicated, believed that a new history of the Middle Temple was long overdue. The result would, I believe, have gladdened him.

The land on which the Middle and Inner Temples are situated belonged to the Order of the Knights Templar from the twelfth century until the Order was cruelly suppressed in 1312. On the other side of what is now the Strand, on the site where the Royal Courts of Justice were built in the nineteenth century, the Knights indulged themselves in the remunerative but dangerous sport of jousting. At the same time they set about the creation of the wonderful Temple Church, which was consecrated by a rare visitor to England, the Patriarch Heraclius of Jerusalem, in 1185.

Parliaments were held in the Temple in 1272 and 1299, at a crucial stage in the development of Parliament after Simon de Montfort was slain at the battle of Evesham in 1265. Perhaps that provides the first indication of the link between lawyers and Parliament which has continued throughout our history. Certainly the researches by Sir John Baker have shown that lawyers moved in as tenants of the Knights Hospitaller, who succeeded to the land which formerly belonged to the Knights Templar, from about 1340, and the records demonstrate that the societies of the Inner Temple and Middle Temple, if not always distinct, were certainly so by 1388. At about the same time Watt Tyler and his rebels sacked the Temple, and not so very long afterwards, when Jack Cade and his rebels were wandering round London looking for something to do, they came upon the Temple, and Shakespeare created the memorable line, 'the first thing we do, let's kill all the lawyers'. By then, according to legend and Shakespeare, Richard of York had plucked a white rose and the Duke of Somerset a red rose, in a battle of words during an encounter in the Temple Gardens which culminated in the Wars of the Roses.

The Knights Hospitaller disappeared from England during the dissolution of the monasteries and the chantries. One Master of the Chapel was William Ermestede, who managed successfully to survive the changes to the religious establishment of the reigns of Henry VIII, Edward VI, Mary, and Elizabeth I herself. Presumably he was no theologian. Not long afterwards he was succeeded by Richard Hooker, author of *Of the Laws of Ecclesiastical Polity*, a true theologian, and a pillar of the Anglican faith. More recently, William Parry gave the tune for the great music in 'Jerusalem' to Walford Davis, the then Master of the Chapel, who secured the copyright not for the Temple Church or himself, but for Parry. Less fortunate was Ernest Lough, the treble in the Temple Church whose recording of 'O for the Wings of a Dove' was made into a record in 1927, but without any attempt to secure the royalties either for him or for the Temple Church. Lough stood with others and watched the church burning after bombs had been dropped in May 1941.

The *History* describes changes in the nature of the teaching of the law that has taken place in the Inn over the centuries. The earliest surviving Middle Temple reading contains a record of a debate from the 1430s between Chief Justice Newton (d 1448) and William Warbelton (d 1469). But the Middle Temple was not merely for the education of lawyers. It was reported that Henry VIII himself told a suitor 'he could not make him a gentleman, but bid him go to the Inns of Court, where an admission makes one a gentleman ...', and John Evelyn went to the Middle Temple from Oxford 'as gentlemen of the best quality did, tho' with no intention to study the Law as a profession'.

Our wonderful Hall, with its double hammer beam roof, was built under the auspices of the great Edmund Plowden between about 1562 and 1574. It was built on what was still Crown land, evidently in the confidence that the land would not revert to the Crown. The confidence proved justified when James I granted the Temple lands to the Inner and Middle Temples in 1608. Plowden was a Roman Catholic, but he remained as a Bencher of the Inn until his death in 1585, presumably because Elizabeth I herself had no wish to 'open windows into men's souls'. Unfortunately, but inevitably, during the national crisis of the Armada in 1588 eight members of the Inn were expelled for failing to take Holy Communion in the Temple Church.

From these times of turbulence and excitement, the Middle Temple is linked with some of the greatest names in our maritime history. They include Raleigh, Hakluyt, Gilbert, Frobisher, Amadas, Richard Grenville, John Hawkins, and Francis Drake himself, who in the present book is said to have had much in common with the great Denis Compton, 'a notorious partygoer and often to the wrong party'. He was, I believe, rather less modest than the great hero of so many of our youths, whose unassuming presence on a guest night will be an abiding memory.

The voyage of Bartholomew Gosnold, who discovered Cape Cod and Martha's Vineyard, along with Raleigh's settlement of Roanoake, were seminal moments in the history of what became the United States of America, and the first steps of the common law outside the shores of England. Edward Sandys negotiated the great Virginia Charter of 1618, which gave all the colonists in Virginia 'the liberties, franchises and immunities of English subjects' and recognised freedom of speech, equality before the law and trial by jury as principles for the colonies. Sandys was later described as the 'Father of American Constitutionalism'. Some 150 years later, the rebel colonists, influenced by charters in similar terms among most of the then colonies, included many Middle Templars. Five Middle Templars signed the Declaration of Independence, and seven signed the Constitution of 1789. The terms of the surrender of Lord Cornwallis were negotiated by another Middle Templar, John Laurens. When he was called to the Bench, the former President of the United States, then the Chief Justice, William Taft, said that he was 'strangely moved, finding myself sitting here in the home of Blackstone, in the very cradle of the common law of England and of America'. And the restoration of the Hall following bomb damage in World War II was financed in part by generous contributions from the American Bar Association and the Canadian Bar Association.

The Middle Temple is indeed linked with the development of the common law across the world. The links with Ireland are perhaps best embodied in Edmund Burke, who passionately defended the position taken by the colonists in North America, and encapsulated the principle of judicial independence when he spoke of disputes being submitted to the 'cold impartiality of the neutral judge'. John Dunning famously complained at the same time that 'the influence of the Crown has increased, is increasing and ought to be diminished'.

William Wentworth was one of the first to cross the Blue Mountains in Australia in 1813, and according to the Australian dictionary biography 'more than any other man he secured our fundamental liberties and nationhood'; Woomes Bonnerjee, a barrister in the High Court of Calcutta, was the first President of the Indian National Congress; Francis Bell was the first native-born person to become Prime Minister of New Zealand; and Jan Christian Smuts was a student member of the Inn from South Africa who fought against the British in the Boer War, but led South Africa to the side of the Allies in both World Wars. The Inn continues to maintain relationships based on respect and admiration with members of the Bar and the judiciary in many countries across the world.

The *History* highlights some of the Inn's literary connections, both among writers who were associated with or who were members of the Inn, and with literature, such as Shakespeare's *Henry VI*, in which the Temple forms an essential part of the story. Charles Dickens was 'entirely diverted from the pursuit of the law' when he became a 'writer of books'. Dickens was not the first—and we anticipate will not be the last—member of the Inn to identify contemporary failings in the administration of justice, and to seek improvement by using unequivocal language. We shall surely each have our favourites among the writers who have been associated with Middle Temple. I wonder whether John Webster, whose characters undergo bizarre experiences and extremes of suffering, may yet be accorded greater public recognition as the great dramatist he was. He might have had something to say about the proposal by Baron Auckland in 1799 that the law of adultery should be reformed so that those who 'engaged in an act of adultery could never marry each other'. And no writer could convey the way in which the spirit of the law can enter into a man's soul, as the dying words of Chief Justice Abbott witnessed: 'Gentlemen of the jury, you are discharged.'

The records of the disciplinary processes of the Inn date back to the earliest days of the sixteenth century. The variety of issues is remarkable, and in their way, these records tell us a great deal about the social history not merely of the profession but of the country as a whole. Thus, for example, in 1570 a member was suspended for three months for speaking English in a suit heard by the Chief Justice at the Guildhall in London. In 1722 it was ordered that no member of the Inn should eat in Hall unless wearing 'a decent and complete gown, whole and untorn'. In 1914 there was a remarkable debate about whether dishonesty or impropriety committed otherwise than in pursuit of the profession might constitute professional misconduct by a barrister. And we find that a member of the Bar refused to pay a penny a day extra rent for the installation of what was then a new water closet because he was fearful of an epidemic of ill health breaking out in consequence. In October 1952, when a Nigerian student was unable to obtain a recommendation for the purposes of membership 'owing to his suspected pro-communist activities', it was resolved by Parliament that 'it has not been the practice of this Inn to refuse an applicant otherwise qualified for admissions purely on grounds of his political views'.

It was not until the Sex Disqualification (Removal) Act 1919 that it became possible for women to join the Inns. The first woman to do so was Helena Normanton, who later took Silk. The first woman to be called to the Bar was Ivy Williams. The processes were slow. In January 1920 a newspaper asked the question 'are the Benchers of Middle Temple, after all, a little frightened of the women law students they have admitted?'. This year our Treasurer is Professor Dawn Oliver, and in 2007 one third of the 36 newly elected Benchers were women. Progress has been slow, but thank goodness that it has been persistent.

The Great Wars provided their own memorable moments. For example, In 1914 it was resolved that any permanent member of the staff should not suffer any loss of salary when serving in the forces, in effect so that the difference between his pay and his salary would be made up. It was also resolved that any members of the Belgian Bar present in England should become honorary members of the Inn with all the privileges of full membership. Special arrangements were made to allow exemptions from examinations following war service and injury. In 1921 Captain Bennett, who had been awarded both the Victoria Cross and the Military Cross, was given leave to omit the part 1 examinations and Airey Neave, the first British prisoner of war to return as an escapee from Colditz Castle, was granted exemption from his Bar Finals. The story of the saving of the east end of the Hall following bomb damage, when all the materials were collected together in some 200 sacks, tells of the devotion and commitment of those working in and for the Inns, no doubt defiantly replicated across London and the bombed cities of this country. The spirit was encapsulated in a letter following the damage to the Hall: '... it doesn't matter what we eat but it does matter that we should eat together.' When she was called to the Bench in 1944, Queen Elizabeth the Queen Mother wrote that it was 'most agreeable to be able to defy the Germans...'

For years there have been debates about the future of the profession. They represent something of a microcosm of the social history of this country. Perhaps of particular interest to today's generation of students is the debate that took place in the late 1970s and early 1980s between senior members of the Bench about the future of the Bar, and the differences of view between those who believed that the Bar should continue to remain a relatively small profession and those who believed that it should be significantly expanded. The consequences of the proposed changes to the arrangements for legal aid will bear very heavily on many members of the now much expanded profession.

History of the Middle Temple is a monumental work, crafted by a number of different writers, with consequent different styles of writing, based on careful research into the records of the Inn which now date back over 500 years. Between them, the contributors put the story of the Middle Temple into its context. It is a story of great fascination which will, I am sure, be of great interest not only to members of the Middle Temple itself, but to those in the wider community with an interest in one of this country's historic institutions.

Future of the Inn: The Middle Temple

This lecture was delivered at the Middle Temple in July 2014, in the middle of the year when I was the Treasurer.

My thesis this evening comes from Di Lampedusa: 'If we want things to stay as they are, things will have to change.'[1]

A few weeks ago that great legal historian, John Baker, found a record of an action in the Easter term of 1430 by a fishmonger against a man called Manciple for a debt of 40 shillings. The relevance of this story is that Manciple is recorded as being cook at the Middle Temple. Even more significant, it is the oldest record of any Inn employing a cook. Until now Lincoln's Inn held the record with a cook in the book in 1445.

So we beat Lincoln's Inn. At about that time, in 1444, the Leathersellers founded a livery company. The Haberdashers did so in 1448. The Armourers and Braziers followed them in 1453, the very year of Jack Cade's rebellion, and the burning of the Temple and the murder of lawyers who were already working there. We survived that blow and, as the links between the livery companies and their trades melted into history, we continued to thrive. There was one reason only. We remained relevant: relevant to the administration of justice and the profession of advocacy of which the Bar was, so far as the higher courts were concerned, the single source. Unless they were burnt down in the fire of London, or bombed by enemy action, the livery companies' great Halls remain or have been rebuilt, and many of them offer huge charitable support, often to education in a pleasant sociable environment, and I warmly welcome their continuing contribution to the life of the country. But their relevance to the selling of leather, or the making of armour or braziers, has broken.

That is the issue. Are we to become a charitable, but also happily sociable organisation, offering education and financial support for aspirant but uncalled barristers with remarkably impressive

---

[1] Giuseppe Tomasi di Lampedusa, *The Leopard* (London, 2007) (original Italian published 1958).

educational facilities for our members? For some, that is and will remain the main function of the Inn, and although limited, it is a fair vision. But perhaps the starting point is a little broader.

In my opinion the Inn must, so far as practicable, represent the interests of all its members, including those who have been called and are in practice. And I make no bones today about the particular area of membership I have in mind. We cater marvellously for the members who have not been called, and happily and warmly for those who are senior enough to become Benchers—many of whom, it is worth adding, work tirelessly for the Inn and its other members. But for the rest? Not so good.

Since I became Treasurer I have been alerted to the work of the Hall Committee. It is astonishingly fortunate that we have men and women of such quality on that Committee—astonishing because the turnout at election time is depressingly low. Yet the contribution by the Hall Committee is impressive. What we must now suggest to Parliament is that the Hall Committee representing the members of the Bar post-call and pre-Bench should be given a more enhanced role in the running and structures of the Inn. For now, however, I merely record how indebted I am personally, and how indebted all of you are, to those who make the time to serve the Inn on the Committee. For non-Benchers this is the crucial committee. We are taking steps to link a Bencher or Benchers on each circuit to the members of the Inn on the circuit, to act as a focus and information point to bring the Inn and the circuits closer together, and we are in the process of identifying members of the Inn in each chambers who might be persuaded to act as the focus, in relation to Inn matters, for the members of the Inn in the chambers. We must restore the connection between the Inn and its circuit members and the Inn and its non-Bencher members, but we need your help.

By the same token, although I am seeking to address every member of the Inn, the issues which have to be addressed, and today can only be a starting point—indeed the last of a series of starting points by earlier Treasurers—affect those of you here today who will be in practice at the Bar in 2030. Some, in 2040, some indeed in 2050. The future is long as well as short. We should not address the issues raised today as if they must be resolved for next year, or, say, 2018. My concern is not confined to the short-term future. And the younger members have a much longer stake in that future, and it is that future which must be paramount.

The independent Bar has for centuries been and must continue to be a national asset. It will continue to be what it has been for centuries, but only if it continues to attract and retain men and women of the highest quality to it. In the last couple of decades great emphasis has been placed, and rightly so, on attracting men and women who, for whatever reason, could not afford to consider joining the profession, but you do not have to live in a judicial ivory tower to realise that having joined the profession, many of them now need support if they are to survive in it.

I am not going to spend time in self-congratulatory mode, extolling the virtues of the Bar, nor shall I pretend that every barrister in independent practice is, by necessity, an advocate of sublime skill and power. There are, as there always have been, poor barrister advocates who have found a seat in chambers, and the harsh reality from my day, and long before it, and since, is that those who are not good enough have been driven out of independent practice. Indeed if the Bar is to retain its reputation as the repository of advocacy at its best, harsh as it is to say so, those who are not good enough should not survive. No one quite believes it when you say it, but it still remains true, that the Bar is a risky profession. Indeed at times it is cruel. I can look back at a number of careers that have faltered, sometimes because a talented practitioner has hit his or her optimum, and then for whatever reason failed to keep moving upwards; sometimes it is just ill-luck, sometimes a diminution in power, and sometimes youngsters come along who are better, and overtake. We spend much time talking about the risks at the outset, but you all know of those in practice 10 or 15 or even 20 years for whom the risks came home.

But we are where we are now. Today. Although how we have arrived here is of historic interest only, the steps on the way are relevant to a different question. As each change occurred, how, if at all, did the Inns and the Bar respond, and change their ways of doing things? One undoubted change is in education and training. I am not sure that the Inns themselves can claim all the credit, or whether credit is better given to a small number of inspired visionaries, but the educational facilities of each Inn, and the Middle Temple in particular, are remarkable. In his Review Sir Bill Jeffrey[2] was firm in his admiration for this aspect of our work. But let me just pinpoint one or two changes with which we have become familiar but which at the time were revolutionary. The admission of

---

[2] Sir Bill Jeffrey, *Independent Criminal Advocacy in England and Wales: A Review* (May 2014).

solicitors to advocacy rights in the higher courts; direct access by lay clients to the barrister; what, looking back on it, was the remarkable expansion of the number of men and women admitted to the Bar; the change in the relationship between the Inns and the Bar, with the Inns' disciplinary and ethical functions over the profession, first shared, but gradually diminished to extinction. As these changes have taken place, if the Inns ever had a form of trade union function, it has gone. One typical consequence is that in the greatest crisis which faced the publicly funded criminal Bar, although the Inns made representations on the subject, the Inns were not perceived by the Bar to represent a significant element in the argument. This exemplifies how the relationship has changed. The future of the Inns is ineluctably linked to the future of the Bar, but it is now clear that the way in which the relationship between the two must work requires that the Bar should decide its future, and how it will be structured, and how it should adapt and change to ensure the survival of the profession, and that the function of the Inns is to support the Bar and its endeavours to secure its future. But, I repeat, it is for the Bar, not the Inns, to have the vision and the will to negotiate and achieve the implementation of that vision. We can, if invited, offer suggestions and advice. This evening I shall be impertinent enough to offer some broad reflections.

With the vast majority of changes, the Inns and the Bar have been required to react. Sometimes, to general irritation, to react quickly to ill-considered proposals. But our structures themselves are poised to be reactive, rather than strategic. Four Inns of Court. Four Treasurers, each for one year. All the specialist Bar Associations with Presidents. All for one year. The Chairman of the Bar itself, one year. Although the successors are always known, the structures mean that the responsibility is carried for one year only, largely by men and women—always freely and voluntarily—who are at the same time trying to maintain a practice. Not always, of course. I do not have that burden. There is not much room for strategic thinking. Not much time for proactive thinking. I suggest that each of the four Inns should require the Treasurer, in our case the Deputy Treasurer, and the Deputy Treasurer elect to work together and act as a strategic body. In the Middle Temple that process has already started. Stephen Hockman and Christopher Clarke come to all my weekly meetings with the Under Treasurer, and virtually every other meeting as well. It is easy for me. I am retired. One of them is a busy practitioner, the other a burdened Lord Justice. But we are all three convinced that this is the only way forward. If the other Inns can be persuaded to adopt the same arrangement, the group of 12, together with the Under Treasurers, should meet from time to time and be available for discussions with the Bar on strategic issues when asked, where the arrangements for COIC (the Council of the Inns of Court) have not yet sufficiently developed for these purposes. The Chairman of the Bar, and his team, would thus have direct access to the Inns in a formalised structure rather than an arrangement which largely depends on accidental blessings of friendship. On any day he or she would be able to meet with those members of the strategic group who happen to be available.

When I said that we were looking at the situation we are in, today, what I was seeking to emphasise is that now is the time, with all the alarms of the last few years, for a strategic think about the future of the Bar, and its preservation. What are the changes which will have to be made to ensure the survival of the independent Bar? And they must be considered in the context, first, that not all the Inns are prosperous. So far as the Middle Temple is concerned, we have to make choices about where and how we spend our money. We cannot pay for everything. We cannot afford it. It is worth adding that the vast majority of our income is derived from renting out professional accommodation, some of which at least is in urgent need of refurbishment. We have wonderful loyal staff. Yet we have been forced to take steps which will diminish the arrangements for their pensions.

Simultaneously the Bar and the Inns must urgently contemplate the communications revolution, and create the strategies which will address the new world so vividly described by Richard Susskind in his recent lecture here in Hall.[3] Let me give a simple example. As I said a minute or two ago, our income is largely dependent on tenants using professional accommodation. It is not fanciful to imagine that by a process of evolution the demand for professional offices in the heart of London may reduce. Chambers would be unlikely to buck any such trend. At Middle Temple we have already put wheels in motion to change our statutes to permit the Inn to let professional accommodation outside and beyond the Bar. Obviously the requirements of the Bar come first, but if the Bar does not want the premises, we cannot leave them empty. That is a small example of the potential consequences of the communications revolution. It will—have no doubt about it—impinge hugely on the workings of

---

[3] Richard Susskind, 'IT and the Law—The Future', 17 February 2014.

the court system, and the way the profession will fulfil its responsibilities. Indeed I respectfully suggest that at every strategic meeting of the Bar, there should be an imaginary little notice with the words 'New Technology???' above the meeting. That applies to the Inn and to every set of chambers.

Where now? Of course the focus today must be the publicly funded criminal bar. But I want to make two points. First, I was in practice in the late 60s when the entire divorce law changed. What had been a financially prosperous section of the Bar was decimated. Good practices evaporated. Incomes dropped. People left the profession. The Divorce Bar became the Family Bar and gradually recovered. Children and money assumed much greater importance than proving a matrimonial offence. Second, no area of the Bar, however prosperous it may seem to be, is immune to potential threat. The effect of modern communications systems and globalisation is that the market for legal services is in a state of flux and changes can occur very rapidly. The pre-eminence of the Rolls Building in London cannot be taken for granted. A great deal of energy and determination are being put in to developments which would draw work away from London to, say, Singapore and Malaysia and Hong Kong. If there were any diminution in the quality of the judiciary sitting in the Commercial Court, much of its work would quickly evaporate. If this or anything like it were to happen, the Bar's relationship with the solicitors using the court would change. Just as one can see the attractions of the CPS to the Criminal Bar, one should recognise the attractions for senior barristers entering large firms of solicitors, enticed into partnership by wonderful packages, and briefed as in-house advocates. There will, of course, always remain a few, but it will be a significantly reduced number of shining stars. But the number of barristers in independent practice will diminish, and there will be less work for them. My single point is that no section of the Bar has ever been protected from change.

So, back to the Criminal Bar. I have read the Jeffrey Review from cover to cover, and in detail. There is more than one strand to it. One strand speaks of, and I agree with him, the Bar as the substantial national asset and the contribution it makes to the national interest. I do not diminish the importance of that finding, but that surely is not the end of the story, but rather the beginning. If it were otherwise, if the Bar were not a national asset, it would be difficult to justify its separate existence as a profession. I have also detected that in some quarters this first Jeffrey finding is seen to represent the end of the story. If I may say so, that is a narrow view. Surely it is only the beginning. Let us see what he also envisages. He foresees a smaller, more specialist criminal Bar. Well, being blunt, that means some will leave the profession. Perhaps more significant for the future of this area of work, he suggests an expectation, to be developed over time, that most of those seeking to become barristers would begin their advocacy as solicitors, that is, working in solicitors' firms or the CPS, and then moving to the Bar.

I have heard this same view expressed by others whose judgement I respect, and I concede at once that this may represent the future. But my emphasis is on 'may'. I do not see this as the inevitable process. It may be that more advocates would join the Bar from the solicitors' profession, but I do not believe that a virtually fused entry system into the legal profession should be conceded or countenanced in advance of it happening. This would provide a route to fusion, or at any rate, to the overwhelming majority of advocates in criminal courts being not barristers but solicitors. In a profession which depends on being 'briefed', why should more than a tiny handful of advocates move from security into uncertainty, particularly if the trend in the commercial and other specialist areas of the legal profession started to move in the opposite direction? None of this involves fusion of the two professions by regulatory diktat. Fusion can come as a reality which takes you unawares. Returning for a moment to the future of the Inns, once the reality is that there is a level of semi or practical fusion, or that the overwhelming number of criminal advocates are solicitors, you can envisage the demands by the Law Society, supported by those who are not enamoured of the Bar, and what they perceive as its privileges, demanding that the exclusive rights of the Inns to call barristers should be devolved into a much broader system for admitting advocates.

It is for the Bar to decide how the threat of backdoor fusion, assuming it is perceived to be a threat, should be addressed. Does the Bar go along with it? If so, nothing need be done. If not, it must take practical steps now, I mean now. And for the Inns, in the next decade, and perhaps longer, their main function would then be to offer sufficient support to the profession to ensure the survival of the Bar (whether publicly funded or not) as a truly independent profession, and to continue to attract bright, intelligent men and women to commit themselves to working in publicly funded areas.

It is a great disappointment that in my own contact with students over the last few years—both students at the Bar and those reading law at university—of those who wish to come to the Bar, and see it as their future, desperately few will touch criminal work. And yet, surely, whether a defendant is locked up for an offence he did not commit, and also, let us not overlook, whether an individual is acquitted of a serious crime of which he is guilty, matters hugely, and at the most serious level of cases requires highly qualified expertise from the advocates on both sides. Yet entry into criminal work is unattractive. Too many chambers which specialise in criminal work are not taking pupils. Lest anybody who reads this paper, and it will be published on our website, should misunderstand why this should be, this is not protectionism. It reflects the significant reduction in criminal work. The number of pupillages for this kind of work has declined dramatically, so that pupillages in criminal chambers have effectively dried up. Good established sets of criminal chambers have collapsed. Sir Bill Jeffrey notes that there are strong signs that the Criminal Bar is 'aging', with more advocates seeking to do crime than there is work for them to do, and with the inevitable process by which work comes down from above to those at the bottom, as the amount of work coming into chambers dries up, so those at the bottom tend to see less. Yet, simultaneously, the Criminal Bar is losing able men and women who can no longer afford to stay in practice. Why this has come about is the topic of constant discussion. But surely there is a much more important topic for discussion: how is the Bar going to address this combination of problems? Each has a bearing on the other.

When a group of barristers come together to form a set of chambers, each is independent of the others ... well ... not as independent as they like to think. There is an element of corporate structure. There is now, usually, a chambers manager. The chambers are funded by rent payment to a common fund, and although different chambers have different systems, many proceed on the basis of contributions based on gross earnings. Chambers are no longer known by the name of the Head of Chambers. Most have adopted some kind of corporate name. The idea of developing these basic structures into a more formal corporate entity may sound like an anathema. But I am asking that you should consider it. We have read about Alternative Business Structures (ABSs), now described as Legal Services Bodies. The Bar Standards Board is seeking amendments to provide for 'entity regulation'. I am not going to insult you, or alarm myself, by asking you to raise a hand if you have read the full paper containing these proposals. But if you have not, I respectfully suggest that you should.

I fully appreciate that a number of energetic sets of chambers have reflected on alternative business structures. Most are unconvinced.

Yet I cannot help noticing, as a result of conversations, that changes have taken place in some of the ways of practice of leading criminal sets. They are not the full ABS Monty, but they do represent more 'collective' arrangements. Obviously I am not going to break confidences. My urgent plea is that alternative business structures should not be dismissed out of hand. I am not for a moment suggesting that everything will be straightforward. But the choice is clear: unless there is to be a common system for entry into criminal advocacy, as reflected in Jeffrey, certainly so far as criminal work is concerned, the old-fashioned chambers structures must be reconsidered.

I am not advocating partnerships. I am not advocating that sets of chambers should, in effect, replicate firms of solicitors. Those chambers that did that would, in effect, become no more and no less than any other partnership of solicitor advocates. But it should surely not be beyond the wit of the finest legal minds to create systems which satisfy the regulatory bodies, and preserve the independent Bar, while increasing the level of communal interaction between members of chambers. Take one little example. Might it be possible to offer funding to young members of chambers after their funded pupillages are completed, by using them, at any rate initially, to go down to the police station at night and be present at interviews with the suspect? And for the trial work to come into chambers? Take another. Might it be possible to create an associate system, with an associate solicitor or group of solicitors, or even solicitors employed in the same way as the chambers manager? Even if these are all hare-brained schemes, if you address them, if you use your imaginations within the likely new regulatory structures, they may work to your advantage. As it seems to me, unless every possibility is addressed, and different chambers will have different ways of addressing the problem, the view that all criminal advocates will begin their careers as solicitors, with all the long-term consequences I have suggested, will prevail. One of our Benchers, Geoffrey Rivlin, is looking into these issues on behalf of the Bar. All I can urge you to do is, as I used to say to juries in the old days, to keep open minds.

I am perfectly well aware that a number of you here have given thought to these questions. My concern remains, however, that the profession as a whole has not, or that if it has, it has dismissed the ideas, without really reflecting closely on them. I grant you that like most other professions, the Bar is conservative in its approach. But surely within every conservative, we can find a radical fibre or two.

These decisions are, I emphasise, for the Bar. How can the Inns offer support to the Bar?

The Middle Temple spends a substantial proportion of its available income on scholarships. In any given recent year we have spent roughly £900,000 on supporting those who wish to come to the Bar. Of these sums, some £300,000 is based on trust obligations and the funds must be used in accordance with the terms of the deed. Let me now go back to my start at the Bar. I paid for my pupillage. The Inn generously gave me awards which paid for my entry into the Inn, and my call fees. It also gave me an award of £400 annually for three years after my call. £400 was a lot more money then than it is now. And so my first three years in practice, which in those days included a year of pupillage, were funded. I could afford to stay on and start and try to practice. And by the end of that time, if it had begun to appear that I was really not likely to attract much work, at least I would have been able to make a judgement about whether to continue or not. As the years went by, and the Bar prospered, at least in part to encourage an increased diversity in entry into the profession, it became a requirement that instead of the intending pupil paying his pupil master, chambers should provide a pupil with funds. Whether simultaneously or not, the process by which I was able to start at the Bar—that is, funding for the first three years in practice, eroded. One can see the logic. If you were any good your pupillage would see you set off on the golden road, and the road was gently downhill all the way. So, funding was diverted to the perceived need to support those who were trying for the Bar.

Today, in the publicly funded Bar, the road after call has become a steep upward and arduous climb. At the same time we are devoting huge sums of money, virtually our entire available income, to support those who have not yet been called. There is another problem, arising from the statutory arrangements which define the qualifications for entry into an Inn. These are not high. And its accomplishment, even at a higher level than required, is totally insufficient on its own to lead to a successful career. This, in a world in which, again in round figures, of every 2,000 men and women who join the Inns every year in order to be called, fewer than 400 will find a pupillage, let alone a tenancy, and of those 400, the available pupillages will rarely be in publicly funded sets. The end result is that a great deal of the Inn's money is spent on helping young men and women to go on expensive courses which will be unproductive of entrance to an area of the Bar which affects the public interest, and the area of the Bar which the majority of the most able ones will already have decided is not the place for them to go anyway. I fully recognise the needs of diversity, and the importance of encouraging men and women from disadvantaged backgrounds who are bright and wish to enter the profession, and the need for funds to be available for them before they are called. But my own belief, and I recognise and respect the contrary view, is that we should acknowledge the new world, and return to the days when some funding was made available for those who had been called, and in a tenancy, in order to support them. Because of our financial position, the only substantial source of such funds would have to be the awards we make before call. This, I think, is the huge debate for the Inns.

One method of support for those in practice may be to provide direct funding, in the way I was provided with it. Another, dealing with today's world, is to help increase the number of criminal pupillages, by the Inns—to a far greater extent than currently—subsidising additional pupillages within criminal chambers, to the same financial levels as the chambers themselves, in accordance with their obligations, fund a pupillage. So if No 71 set in the Heavenly Temple has one pupillage at £15,000 annually, the Inn should provide a second. I know that a start has been made on this process, and that not everyone is satisfied with the results. Perhaps with a concerted effort by all the Inns it might do better second time around. One problem, of course, is that the pupillage is not a tenancy, and that many criminal sets envisage a tenancy following a satisfactory pupillage. If there is no work for young tenants, then there is no point in offering the pupillage. But, if the junior members of chambers are expected to do any work open to a member of the legal profession, enough work may come in to enable them, if not to be made tenants at the end of pupillage, then to look forward to a tenancy after three or four years when they have proved their quality. Surely some of our funding should now go to those who have succeeded in obtaining tenancies, but for whom the struggle to make a living is marked.

We should recognise that the young man or woman of real talent under financial threat cannot survive at the Bar without further funding. The BBA (Barristers' Benevolent Association) provides funds for family and other disasters. The Inn should tidy over a disaster arising from the payment of late fees or whatever, to fund, if necessary on an interest free loan basis, the individual young man or woman. I recognise the difficulty of deciding between those who have no income because they have no great ability, and those whose income has, notwithstanding real ability, taken a tumble.

Enormous care and time are taken to ensure that so far as is humanly possible, current funding recognises talent as well as need. So in saying what I have, I do not imply criticism of the selection process. What I suggest is that we should consider reducing the amount that we spend on those who have not been called, and therefore raise the barrier against an award of funds to those already in practice.

Let us look at another use of our money. We have a remarkable library facility, with, if you choose to ask them, expert librarians who will hunt down virtually any reference you want. Many of you will have been indebted to the librarian and her team. However, in 2013 the library bill at the Middle Temple was close to £725,000. That is not just the cost of books; half went on staff. Thirty per cent went on the purchase of books and materials. Seven per cent on electronic and online subscriptions. Nine per cent on our specialist collections. The figures are much the same for 2012, and the figures for 2014 are consistent. This magnificent facility is but a few hundred yards from an equally magnificent facility at the Inner Temple. It is hardly a far horizon to Lincoln's Inn or even Gray's Inn, and I have no doubt that their expenditure, proportionate to their wealth, is much the same. We are all proud of our libraries. Efforts to rationalise the library arrangements between the four Inns have not been successful. But here, surely, the Inns must work together. We live in the digital age. In round figures four institutions, virtually within stone throwing distance of each other, are spending something around £4 million on library facilities for their members. Reconsideration by all the Inns together may be a way to release funds to assist those in practice.

The physical use of the library is not great. Walk in on any day at any time and many of the tables and chairs will be unoccupied. We need to reorganise our library facilities, and the huge amount of space in it. We must provide a system for 'hot-desking'. Members of the Inn, particularly those from outside London, should be provided with a small modern office, or business centre, with the necessary technology for them to use the office while they are in London, keeping in touch with their chambers and their clients and their cases. That facility should be regarded as part of the library system, within our Inn. The budget for this year should take account of the necessary expenditure for this purpose. It should also include the cost of making arrangements to provide safe storage facilities for members of the Inn to leave their overnight bag and papers, as necessary. Stephen Hockman and Christopher Clarke and I are addressing the conclusions to be drawn from my circuit visits with the relevant committees.

Reference to the library underlines the need for the four Inns to work together. Of course we do. There is mutual respect between each Treasurer for this year and no doubt the next and no doubt in years past. But we are all immensely proud of our own Inn, and the way we do things. Any suggestion for co-operation which might be seen as diminishing the contribution of the individual Inn to the profession tends to be viewed with suspicion. But it is not just the library. Is it really necessary, and a sensible use of resources, for each Inn to provide separate education facilities for those on circuit, and to do so when each circuit itself also provides for continuing education? Are these arrangements as co-ordinated as they could be, as they should be? I suspect that out on circuit, pleasant as it is to have the educational facilities offered by your own Inn, the more important consideration is that they should be offered, by someone. Each Inn could take it in turns to provide different circuits with a co-ordinated further education system, co-ordinated with what the circuit offers. This is all very sensitive, and I am aware of it. I particularly notice that in our Inn alone there are some 200 members who offer their time voluntarily and freely, and who do so under the umbrella of the Middle Temple. The trigger for what they do is loyalty to our Inn, and I have no doubt it is the same loyalty that draws the other volunteers in the other Inns to do the work. But, again, surely we can address this issue.

Logically, this leads me to the final consideration, at any rate for today if you are to go home. It would take a huge, undoubtedly revolutionary step for the Inns to co-operate together more in the way of Oxbridge Colleges, with the wealthier supporting the less prosperous. Wow. That is a revolutionary thought, and I immediately admit to my own reservations in having the nerve even to contemplate it for a moment. Nevertheless I have voiced the thought, and for this simple reason. If the function of the Inns is to support the Bar in the most practical and realistic way, then we, the Inns, may have to work together much more closely, not simply in a spirit of co-operation and mutual respect, but as a body. I know, I know. Igor Judge may have developed 'retireitous', one manifestation of which is an occasional daft idea. But, think 2040 and 2050. They are a long way off. But they will come and the Inns will have to address that world. The question which each Inn has to face is whether it can provide the necessary support for the Bar while they operate as four separate, independent Inns, or whether that support would be better provided at some future date by a form of reconstruction which would bring them much more closely together. If I abandon my last thought, then I might persuade you to go along with the idea that COIC may have to be given more muscle.

This has been a long lecture, and it could have been very much longer. I do not see 2014 as the end of the Bar as we know it. I came into this Hall in 1964 (that is, before the Divorce Bar was destroyed), newly called, to hear leaders of the profession tell me, a brand new boy, that the profession I had just had the privilege of joining had reached the end—the end of the Bar as we know it. There are always prophets of doom. It is unfair to call them Cassandras, because Cassandra's woeful prophesies were accurate, and well founded. What I am sure is inevitable is—and it is not Cassandra like to say it—that if nothing is done, or nothing very much is now done by the Bar and Inns, the Jeffrey prophesy in relation to the Criminal Bar will come to pass. The future of the Bar is in the hands of the Bar and, as I said at the very beginning, if you want things to stay as they are, things must change.

Why Read Law?

This is the basic text of a lecture given at different universities over the last few years. This particular lecture was given in April 2014 at King's College London where, following my retirement as Lord Chief Justice, I have been a Visiting Professor, privileged to talk to and listen to some fine young men and women among the undergraduate population and some men and women who have already achieved utmost distinction in their chosen subjects.

ADDRESSING AN AUDIENCE of law students and members of the Law Teaching Faculty, the question is ridiculous and the answer is obvious. So why has Lord Judge bothered to come and tell us what we know? The answer is that we are studying law in order to become lawyers, many of us to become members of the legal profession, hopefully to be successful, and possibly, if good enough, to be appointed as judges in due course.

That's that then. Perhaps the speaker should now go home and let us get on with our studies.

But is that really right?

Are law students the world over only interested in their own selfish professional careers and success, whether within or outside the law? If that is true, it is hardly any wonder that lawyers are so unpopular, selfishly earning a good living from other people's troubles. If true, it means that money and financial prosperity are the motivation.

I hope and trust that there is more to it than that. And indeed I know that for many of you there is more to it than that.

For a start there are many well-qualified lawyers who choose to work for organisations which do not pay them very well, but which are immensely rewarding in other ways. There are many lawyers in the charitable world. There are many outstandingly able men and women who teach rather than practise law, to the great advantage of students like you, and without the trappings of golden prosperity of some lawyers in private practice. Many successful lawyers take a significant reduction in their incomes when they accept judicial appointment.

So why are you, you, the individual man and woman at this university, studying law? More importantly, what should you get out of your years of study? It is surely much more than a good degree and a golden future. Notice my emphasis. What do *you* hope to get out of studying law at university?

The study of law will teach you about tort and trusts, contract and crime, property and intellectual property, and rights and remedies—yes, all that, but there is much more to it than that.

The study of law gives you huge additional opportunities to learn much more than the law. If you take advantage of them you will learn about your fellow human beings; you will think about your fellow human beings—the wonderful things they do, the dreadful things they do, the stupid things they do, the courageous things they do. If you are blind to the people whose cases will form part of your daily studies, blind to the stark fact that leading cases, however exciting for academic study, are or were about real people, who at the time of these cases, even if 100 years ago, will have felt that their whole life turned on what has now become a legal exercise for you; if you do not occasionally pause to think about them, you will when you qualify be a less sensitive, dry lawyer, and I respectfully suggest that you will be less in touch with the common humanity which we should all share.

How did the victim of the crime spend the rest of his or her life? What did the future hold for those little children who were separated from their parents? How did the doctor who was wrongly sued for medical negligence recover not only his practice, but the necessary confidence to continue to give robust, honest advice when the news for his patients would be bad?

I venture to suggest that at times when you are studying you should pause and think, even if for a moment, about the individual people whose lives and conduct you are studying. As you do so, your reaction to their individual situations will tell you something about the human being that you are. A lesson in self-knowledge is invaluable. But that is not the end of it.

The second opportunity that the study of law will give you is that it will test your attitudes to life. Your prejudices. Your preconceptions. The examples I am going to give you now are all real cases. Where do you stand on them? What does the law require the answer to be? What is the moral answer? Is there a conflict between the law and morality? It is the law student who has the opportunity to address these issues. I do not think that any other subject, except perhaps philosophy itself, offers so much food for thought—and philosophy is not as constantly grounded in the real world as the law, inevitably, is.

These examples are based on real cases. My first example is the heavily pregnant young woman who is suffering from very high and dangerous blood pressure.[1] She is strongly advised that unless she undergoes a Caesarean section, her baby may die. For reasons of personal belief she refuses such a birth, insisting that she will have her baby through natural labour and vaginal delivery. She is not mad or insane but she will not be persuaded. What is to be done? Which of two principles recognised by the law must come first? Her baby's right to a healthy life—indeed the very right to life itself (but is the baby in its mother's womb properly to be thought of as a human being?)—or the absolute autonomy of each and every sane adult to make choices about what may happen to his or her body? Should she be sectioned under the Mental Health Acts, thus enabling doctors to perform the Caesarean section without her consent? Or would that be a dangerous way of allowing the state to interfere with the genuine beliefs of its citizens which it just does not happen to share? A law student should be thinking deeply about these fascinating and important questions. Do you force her to undergo an operation? What is the position of the father in this situation? Does it matter? What about the doctors, with a sense of responsibility for both mother and baby? Upholding one right undoubtedly undermines the other. A law student needs to think.

Let us take another example. A man, but this could just as easily be a woman, is HIV-positive and knows it.[2] He begins a happy consensual sexual relationship with an always willing partner, but without ever telling her of his condition. For contraception she uses the pill. She is infected by him. If she had known she would never have had unprotected sex with him. Does it make any difference if it is clear that if she had known she would never have had sex with him at all? If so was it rape? If in this account it is the woman who was HIV-positive, did she rape him? But they both consented to intercourse. Was he guilty of causing her actual bodily harm? The criminal offence of assault? Does it make any difference if they are married, and that he contracted the infection as a result of extra-marital sex, but did not want to destroy the marriage and future happiness of the children? Change the facts, so that both the man and the woman, fully aware of the risks, had unprotected sex. Is it

[1] Based on *St George's Healthcare NHS Trust v S; R v Collins and Others, ex parte S* [1999] Fam 26.
[2] Based on *R v Dica* [2004] QB 1257; *R v Konzani* [2005] 2 Cr App R 198.

possible to consent to the risk of infection? Does such consent negative assault? Can you agree to risk life-threatening disease? What if
we are dealing with some other contagious disease, like tuberculo-
sis, which can be carried through kissing?

Take another example. A father of two young children, believed
to be a pillar of respectability and decency, is convicted of some
nasty indecency offences with children from another school.[3] The
moment his crimes become known, his own children will suffer
bullying and certainly be ostracised at their own school. Should the
press be prevented from reporting the case? On the one hand, there
are the interests of the children, always protected by the law, and
on the other, the interests of the public administration of justice in
open court, freely reported by a free press. Which should prevail?
In this situation which principle becomes paramount? Whatever
your view now, could you change your mind? Would your mind be
open enough to appreciate that there may be another point of view?
What of the position of the mother, already betrayed by their father,
desperate to protect her children: is her position relevant? And what
if a mother is convicted of serious offences? Should the sentencing
judge take account of the damage to the children of separation from
their mother? Would it make any difference if there were a father at
home who would care for them?

These are not academic exercises at all. There are many men
and women in the real world for whom events like these have happened. Whatever view you may have now, at this moment, the study
of the law will teach you to think logically, to think through principle, to identify the correct principle or principles which apply, and
then, having thought it through, to express your views in articulate,
coherent language.

The study of law will broaden your minds—not just about the
law, but about everything that bears on the lives that you young
men and women are going to live. You must be the thinkers. Disagree as much as you like with each other, but in learning the law,
learn to think for yourself, and learn to have open minds. Listen to
each other. Contradictory views must be respected. You will have
the opportunity to learn to think. Allow yourselves to be provoked
into thinking outside the box. You can never have a better subject
for the study of these big questions at university. If in due course

---

[3] Based on *Re Trinity Mirror plc* [2008] QB 770.

you become judges you will have the burdens and responsibility of giving the answer required by the law, which, it is perhaps worth noticing now, may not be the answer that left to yourself you would wish for.

The third area of opportunity provided by studying the law is that you are given the opportunity to contribute to civic life in our country.

You may wonder how, at this time of the day, there can be anything fresh to say about the rule of law. Probably there is nothing fresh to say, and almost certainly there is nothing that is utterly comprehensive that can be said. But you are studying law, and you should at the end of your time here have some pretty clear idea about the principles. We are not discussing some medieval problem like the number of angels that can dance on the head of a pin.

I want to discuss this issue with you because you are young men and women to whom these issues will matter for the whole of the rest of your lives, which will be longer than the rest of my life. But it does matter to us all, whether we are older or younger—and if I may say so, none of us should ever assume that the future of our institutions will take care of itself. What we know about the future is encapsulated in the simple little line of William Shakespeare: 'What's to come is still unsure'.

You all know many of his words—(Friends, Romans, Countrymen ... To be or not to be ... Once more unto the breach). But for us lawyers, the line of most significance is that what's to come is still unsure. In other words we should never take the future for granted. We also know something else—if you like, the other side of the same coin. The future is long, possibly very long, as well as short.

We are increasingly accustomed to immediate, indeed instantaneous reaction to news about every current event. And every immediate reaction is always narrow in perspective. The modern habit of immediacy tends to reduce the much more important focus on the long term and the strategic. Look at your television tonight or tomorrow night. Everyone will pile in and comment. Everyone will be a pundit. But who will come back to the television screen in three months' time, let alone 12 months, even if the punditry was wrong? To say so. And to be more humble next time.

As lawyers we should rapidly learn that we should never, ever take for granted the privilege of living in communities which respect the rule of law as fixed and settled. What's to come is still indeed unsure. Think long.

It is as true today as it was when John Curran said in 1790:

The condition upon which God hath given liberty to man is eternal vigilance which condition if he break, servitude is at once a consequence of his crime, and the punishment of his guilt.

Do we imagine that many people in Germany in 1930 would ever have appreciated how their democratic constitution could be subverted by Hitler? But it was. It was virtually impossible for them to do anything about it, without great risk to life, once the process of subversion was underway. That is why we have to be alert to the slightest infringement. In the result millions of people were arrested when there was no suspicion that they had committed a crime, and millions were incarcerated without trial, and millions died just because they happened to be Jews. Millions more died or were wounded in combat. Some of your grandfathers, or possibly great-grandfathers, were among those whose blood was shed in battle to extinguish the vile creed of Nazism. Some of your grandmothers, or great-grandmothers, lost husbands and sons, killed or maimed, in body or in spirit.

So these are important reflections for those of you who study law at this fine university. As I have said, you will learn all about tort and crime and contract and so on, and I can make the list exceptionally turgid, but apart from sometimes difficult, sometimes dull subjects, and apart from the excitement of working for a high-quality degree, what should those of you who study law at this university understand from your years of study, and what perhaps above all else should you carry with you into the wide world, into your professions, whether the law or not, and into your daily lives?

My answer is that you will understand the significance of the stories that I am about to tell you. Not everyone will: but you should. I hope you will get their significance now, before you have gained your degree.

The first story is well known and comes from Blackstone. We are in England in the reign of Queen Anne. In 1708 the Ambassador for Russia was arrested for non-payment of a debt of £50 incurred in London. He was of course very quickly released, but Peter the Great was the Czar of All the Russias, and he regarded what had happened as an insult to him personally. He therefore wrote to the Queen in England that the Sheriff of Middlesex and all others concerned in the arrest of the Ambassador should be punished, and punished instantly with death. Queen Anne no doubt took careful advice. A secretary was directed to inform Peter the Great that Her Majesty

> Could inflict no punishment upon any, the meanest of her subjects, unless warranted by the law of the land: and she therefore trusted that His Imperial Majesty would not insist upon impossibilities.

I am not sure that I should have wished to be the secretary in Russia who handed that message or translated it to Peter the Great.

The second story was brought to my attention by Sir Sydney Kentridge QC, one of the great advocates of the last decades, who made his home in England after leaving apartheid South Africa. In 1998 Nelson Mandela appointed a judicial commission to enquire into the administration of rugby, which, as you all know, is tantamount to a form of religion in South Africa. Those who then ran rugby in South Africa suggested that the President had not properly considered the matter himself in accordance with the statutory requirements; he had simply rubber-stamped the decision of the member of the Cabinet. President Mandela filed a detailed affidavit in which he deposed to the fact that the decision had been made by him personally after fully considering the facts. The judge in the case ordered President Mandela to appear in court to be cross-examined on his affidavit. The order caused considerable shock. And indeed it was a personal affront to a man whose stand on principle and whose integrity is one of the more heart-warming highlights of our world. But, as a matter of law, too, there was no precedent for making such an order against a Head of State, and indeed a very strong balance of judicial opinion over the centuries has been that it is not appropriate.

What did Nelson Mandela do? He did not move a higher court to set aside the subpoena. Nor did he claim executive privilege. He made it clear that he deprecated what he saw as an insult to his office as President (note: to his office, not to him personally), but asserted that an order of the court had to be obeyed by everyone, whatever their rank. So this great man went to court and he gave evidence, in the witness box in Pretoria, and was cross-examined for some hours, without veering from his customary dignity and courtesy. Here was a great man leading and teaching his newly enfranchised countrymen the practical meaning of the rule of law.

There are a number of different explanations or purported definitions of the rule of law. Let me offer you one from one of my predecessors, Lord Bingham of Cornhill:

> All persons and authorities within the State, whether public or private, should be bound by and entitled to the benefit of laws publicly made, taking effect (generally) in the future and publicly administered in the courts.

In this particular quotation he did not say, but it is clear from everything he did say, that to make the summary more complete he would add:

in which the judiciary is independent of the executive and legislature.

But Lord Bingham himself, rightly, described this as only a partial definition. For example, it does not address the *content* of 'laws' publicly made. Apartheid laws in South Africa before 1994 were laws publicly made in accordance with the constitution.

Let us look at the problem from another point of view: a play, with words attributed to Thomas More by Robert Bolt in *A Man for all Seasons*, chiding his son-in-law, young Roper:

This country is planted thick with laws from coast to coast—and if you cut them down—do you really think that you could stand upright in the wind that would blow then?

In history, Thomas More knew his man. When the king came to visit him in Chelsea, they walked up and down the garden together, and the king put his arm around him. After the king's departure, his son-in-law congratulated him. He was young and enthusiastic and thrilled. The king's Majesty had done Thomas More a great honour. But Thomas More knew his man. He responded that the king's Majesty

hath done me a great honour ... But if my head could wish him a castle in France it should not fail to go.

What, in the play, More was telling his son-in-law was that the rule of law protects us all—society, the community as a whole, and each individual in society—from anarchy, from the law of the jungle, from the triumph of the wildest and worst, from the rule of tyranny. It ensures equality before the law, which is the foundation of every single civil right. Unless everyone is equally entitled to a 'right', it is not a 'right' at all, it is merely an advantageous benefit handed down in some patronising way by those in power to those they think deserve it.

I emphasise that I am not talking about rule by judges, or lawyers, or administrators, or ministers, or governments. I am talking about the rule of law. Perhaps John Locke summed it all up in five words in his *Second Treatise of Civil Government* in 1690:

Wherever law ends, tyranny begins.

Tyranny of course is not only that of the dictator; there is tyranny of the mob, and the potential tyranny of populism. In his first inaugural address, Thomas Jefferson reminded us that 'the minority possess their equal rights, which equal law must protect, and to violate would be oppression'.

And of course, as I emphasis before you, judges too are governed by the rule of law. Judges have no dispensing or suspending power. Like it or not, we must apply the law as we honestly find it to be, in accordance with principle. We are all answerable for our own actions. And if throughout your lives you are blessed with success, and I hope that you will be, I offer you now, for reflection 40 years on from now, two salutary reminders. First: 'Be never so high, the law is above you', and second, the ending of Montaigne's great philosophy, reminding us all that, no matter how high the throne on which we sit, we are always sitting on our own backsides.

So what does this have to do with you, students of the law, here at King's? It is pretty obvious. But let me pause before we get there. The world does not love lawyers. Ever since the first person began arguing a case—and it was Adam who offered the first plea in mitigation in the Garden of Eden, and perhaps rather unwisely blamed his co-accused, the lawyer has been the subject of criticism. Some of it is justified, but not all of it. Those of you who know your Shakespeare will remember Henry VI Part II where, blood having been spilt on the battlefields of France, Jack Cade's rebellion enters London. In all that blood and gore there is one moment at which every audience I have ever been among laughs out loud. It is when the rebels are pondering where to begin, and Dick the butcher says 'Let's begin by killing all the lawyers'. And that indeed is what they did. The Temple, where the profession was already based, was invaded, and ransacked and burned. All this just a few yards up the road from where we are now sitting.

I wonder, I do indeed wonder when I hear the laughter, how many of those in the audience who laugh at Shakespeare's joke perceive that there is a link between the killing of the lawyers and a later breakdown of law and order and the civil war which follows, ending with the haunting, pitiful scenes of the son who has discovered that he has killed his father, and the father who discovers that he has killed his son, both of them then reflecting on the unknown woman who, although not on the stage, is a silent dominant figure in both scenes—the mother of one, and the wife of the other. These were not great nobles, fighting to establish a dynasty and destroying the rule of law by their ambitions, and dying in the process. These are the saddest scenes of all. These are the sadnesses of the common man and the common woman betrayed because the rule of law was not there to protect them. The rule of law is a bulwark against such dreadful disasters, and we should never take it for granted.

As a community you believe in it, as I do. We believe in it even if we do not know very much law. But for those leaving university having studied law, whether or not they practise the law, this is an opportunity which should not be missed, an essential lesson to grip hold of, because deep down in our history and our traditions as a nation we have an instinctive feel that the rule of law has served us well. It has not made, and it could not make, a perfect society. But without it our society would be catastrophically worse. You have to make sure that the rule of law does not vanish by mistake; that when it is threatened, you as intelligent, educated men and women will speak up for it.

So what's to come is indeed still unsure, but of this there is no doubt: the future is in your hands. You are the next generation. With success, influence and power will come to you; whether it does or not, those who study law must accept the burden of ensuring that the rule of law is safe and secure. In years to come the long-term safety of the rule of law must be the responsibility of those who are students of the law today. Guard it well.

And understand, from the very outset of your degree course, that there is indeed much more to studying law than studying the law.

Induction Seminar: Welcome

This is the basic text of a talk I have given over the years to close the Induction Seminars run by the Judicial Studies Board for newly appointed Recorders.

MY FIRST AND most pleasant duty is to congratulate you. I know that the road to Scarman House is very long, and tiring, and worrying. But here you are. You have got through the appointments system. Or maybe the appointments system has found you.

Having arrived here, I suspect that the intensity of this course will have left many of you exhausted. It is tiring. It is intense. It is not straightforward. And if nothing else, it will give you some idea of what judicial burdens can be like. When I was a new Recorder my clerk believed that I would get endless sets of papers done while I was sitting, and before I sat, so did I. I never did. Each day was tiring and effectively all-consuming. And so it will be for you.

But just as you are very tired now, one of the great things about this course is that you will make new friends. Your professional paths will never have crossed with people you have met on this course. Yet for years and years to come you will meet at JSB seminars when you are full-time judges, and smile together in recollection of the arduous journey which you have completed here together.

There was a time, you know, when there was no JSB. You were appointed and started to sit. You did your best, and you no doubt muddled through. I know of a man of great judicial distinction who was appointed as a High Court Judge before he had ever sat in any court. He asked for advice from the then Lord Chief Justice. He was told that the trial process was perfectly simple. The summing up had to deal with, and here was the list,

— Judge/Jury Function.
— Burden of proof/standard of proof.
— The ingredients of the offence—the defence.
— The facts—briefly.

It was all much simpler in those days than it is now.

Eventually the Judicial Studies Board was introduced. The early attitude was extraordinary. Looking back on it, virtually incomprehensible. But I went to seminars in the early 1980s as a member of the JSB, to be greeted time and time again by experienced judges telling us that we were interfering with their judicial independence. Of course we were not. Now, the vast majority of judges welcome the help that the JSB can give, and I suspect that you are all very grateful to have been here.

So what is this course about? We teach you something about the conduct of the trial and the sentencing regime which applies after convictions. At least you can know where to look. Your attention can be focused on amendments to the 2003 Criminal Justice Act, and the legislative amendments to the legislative amendments, and the legislative amendments to the legislative amendments to the legislative amendments of different legislative sections that have only just been brought into force, without any sound of trumpets. All this is immensely valuable, and the training will stand you in good stead.

What, however, this course cannot teach you are the essential judicial qualities. The course is not character improving nor character changing. We cannot teach you judicial patience, and fortitude, and determination, and courage—yes, courage—the courage to do what you believe to be right when you will know that there will be a clamour against you; and humility—yes, humility—to do what you believe to be right and simultaneously to recognise that as a human being you are bound to be fallible, but as a judge you are required to provide an answer rather than leave the parties in uncertainty.

This course cannot cure judicial dithering, nor, dare I say it, judicial idleness, or obstinacy, or weakness. Nor can we cure that dreadful judicial disease, 'judgitis'.

In very brief summary, judicial responsibility will test your character as a human being. No doubt you will all survive it, but the point which must never be forgotten is that you will indeed be tested. This is integral to exercising judicial responsibilities, and the effect will be intense.

I am speaking of these things because you are about to be entrusted with enormous power over your fellow human beings. People's lives will be in your hands. The power to order that a man or woman should be locked away, even only for 24 hours, or the power to deprive a parent of the joys of seeing his or her children when they want to do so, or limiting the hours of those joys to set times, exemplify the desperately important power that you are now being entrusted to exercise.

Assuming, as I do from the fact of your appointment, that you are indeed personally blessed with judicial quality, as the years go by do not for one moment assume that you can never lose it. You have to guard against the risk of looking in the mirror uncritically, because the truth is that even your very best friend cannot tell you that your judicial character is developing flaws.

This is all about you as individuals, but there is one more principle which from now until the end of your judicial careers you must not have so much firmly in mind, but should be part of your entire judicial fabric, that is, something that is the essential fibre of your judicial personality. That is an understanding of judicial independence and what it means, and a determination to protect and defend it. For me, it is all summarised in the response by Sir Edward Coke, Chief Justice of the King's Bench, to James I demanding to know what the judges would do if they had to decide a case in which the king himself was taking a particular interest. 'The judges will do what it is appropriate for the judges to do.' Not long afterwards, Coke was thrown out of office and into the Tower.

Our collective judicial independence is at the heart of the rule of law in this country. There is our own independence as individual judges, and the institutional independence of the judiciary, both extremely precious, and constantly and historically always under strain. Powerful governments, powerful executives, even in democratic states, by whatever process they may have come to power and whatever their political views, are not always totally enamoured with judicial independence. At best it can be an inconvenience, and at worst—well, I leave you to imagine how it must seem to a powerful executive when it is, from their point of view, at its worst.

When you are exercising your judicial responsibilities day by day, these issues will not be in the immediate forefront of your mind very often, but they will come into your mind from time to time. When they do, remember that you bear responsibility to the entire judicial family as a whole, to be independent and to think independently, but, even more important, that this is your responsibility to each and every citizen of this country. This is the ultimate burden of the judge, as a servant of the community.

Can we end by just remembering what judicial independence is not? Judicial independence is not a colourable excuse for being idle, for doing your own thing in your own way, for masking self-centredness behind eccentricity, or for showing off and disregarding the law, which binds you as it binds everyone else. You may have met judges like that, and you will not be numbered among them. But where you do your best, keep your judicial conscience spotless, administer justice tempered with humanity and are courageous without being loud about it, and humble without wringing your hands, you will find vast and deep levels of support for you from your brothers and sisters in the judicial family.

That support is vital to us all. All of us need it. I need it. I make no bones about that fact. And I have come here today to let you know personally that I am now offering you my support as I hope that you will offer me yours. And of course to wish you all good fortune in this exciting new stage of your professional lives.

Reginald Walter Michael Dias QC

I paid this tribute to Mickey Dias at Great St Mary's Church, Cambridge, on 13 March 2010. During my first two years at university, I read history, not law. When in 1959 I went up to Cambridge I sought to persuade my Director of Studies at Magdalene College, Ralph Bennett, that I should change from history to read law because I was determined to go to the Bar. He tested my determination, and having satisfied himself that I did indeed intend to make a career at the Bar, he advised me that as I was so certain, I would 'need a hobby for life' and then went on, 'why not read History?'. And so for two years I did. With this encouragement, my particular interests were constitutional history and the history of political thought. As my professional life became busier this advice became increasingly valuable, and as I suspect some of my lectures show, this 'hobby' has continued to influence my thinking and my perspective, as well as continuing to provide a constant source of relaxation. When I last saw Ralph Bennett I reminded him of the advice he had given me long before, and thanked him for it. The tribute paid at his memorial service to RWM Dias, otherwise known as Mickey Dias, is self-explanatory. He was the man responsible for teaching me law during my third year at Cambridge. His influence remained with me throughout my judicial career. I hope that it speaks of the warm affection and admiration in which he was held by so many of his students, not least me. I am unable to resist the opportunity to acknowledge my gratitude to both men.

I FIRST MET Mickey Dias almost exactly 50 years before his death. He taught me law for one year only, my third year. In that short time of, what, 24 weeks?, the impression he made on me was indelible, as it was with all of us who had the privilege of being taught by him. That it was a privilege was appreciated by me even as a callow youth, but as I have matured, my appreciation has deepened. It was an even greater privilege than I realised.

It is flattering for me to be asked to speak today on behalf of Mickey's former pupils. They have had some successes. Mickey's first Chief Justice was Michael Corbett, Chief Justice of South Africa during those exhilarating and tempestuous years when Nelson Mandela, another of the Fellows of our College, achieved his freedom. Whenever Mickey was congratulated on the distinction reached by his former pupils, he never failed to remind the speaker that his list of old pupils included a mass murderer. He never said whether he was a Magdalene man.

If Mickey was prepared to treat his old boys in this way, I shall maintain reticence, and not name any more of them. And you understand the man better if you remember that his first and foremost priority was to bring out the best in each and every one of his pupils, and that for him this was infinitely more desirable than basking in the reflected glory of those who had been blessed with good fortune. It is said that Mickey never forgot any of his pupils. Derek Oulton told me that he once made the mistake of asking Mickey whether he remembered a former pupil—now a man of some public distinction—who was visiting Magdalene that day. Mickey replied 'of course I remember him. He still owes me an essay'. He created the Lawyers' Dinner, to help ease some of the tensions that are inevitable at Tripos time. And then the Archie Leslie Prize was created: a combination of his mortification and remorse at leaving one of his pupils off the invitation list to the Lawyers' Dinner, and his lovely Nora's concern about the distress and bewilderment he must have caused. The undergraduate who had suffered most at Mickey's hands during the course of the year was awarded the Archie Leslie Prize, consisting of two meals. The adjudicator was Nora, and after her death, the Master's wife. I think, from all this, it is reasonable to say this great scholar was a devoted teacher.

My very first memory of Mickey Dias was the warmth with which those of my contemporaries who read law at the time when I was reading history spoke of him. Then I observed him for myself— when I was on my way to or returning from the Pickerel—meeting up with Nora, and I remember little children, being piled into an old van. I still remember the van. So I observed a family man before I knew him as a teacher. I do not remember any of the other Fellows from those long gone days who so publicly linked their families and their work. It was lovely. Mind you, his family, too, suffered from his devilish wit.

Julia tells me of an occasion when they were travelling in France, and visited a church where, as is the French custom, there was an ossuary. On the way out of the church Mickey found a postcard of the ossuary. He wrote a brief message and posted it to his mother-in-law. The message read, 'Wish you were here'.

Because of the warm affection in which we all hold him, we tend sometimes to forget that Mickey was born far, far away from these shores into a family of great distinction with a history of public service in the country we then called Ceylon, now Sri Lanka. Yet he came to make his life and his home among us. That was our privilege, but that was not how the script was intended to be read. It was 1939. Mickey's intellectual brilliance produced outstanding results. When he came down he served in the Home Guard while he read for the Bar. He was then supposed to go home. To our inestimable advantage, and not without having to withstand huge pressures, he defied the wishes of his family. He volunteered to join the Royal Air Force, in which he served from 1942 until the end of the war, as rear gunner—that lonely, dangerous cold spot, always staring out into blackness and possible (and, sad to say, very likely) death. Of course, like all that generation, he never spoke about it.

I have been shown a lecture he gave in Ceylon in 1949. He was asked to describe his 'experiences', and in the context of Neil Jones telling us about how his aeroplane bombed his own airfield, he said:

> The truth is that it was for non-achievement, or perhaps achievement in the wrong direction, that I gained any sort of notoriety. The medal for which I qualified was the Prune Medal … the Prune Medal was a paper decoration only for any piece of prize idiocy.

Even in the most desperate situation, he could not avoid a little humour. He described how

> anti-aircraft fire also had a charm of its own … bright reds, orange, yellow, green, blue and so forth and these winking specks of colour seemed to drift upwards towards and around you ever so gently … One does not believe for a moment that anything is going to hit you, that is, until one does.

He went on that it was

> a great mistake to glorify war … heroes deserve all the praise they can get … I venture to think that too much emphasis is laid on the glory of war and too little or none at all on the horrors of war.

Reading that lecture brought Mickey alive again, and reminded me of the clarity of his thinking and his mastery of the English language and his wisdom.

So perhaps I should just indulge myself a little longer by quoting something from the very end, this written at a time when the wounds of war were still gaping, and he had described some of his experiences in the aftermath of heavy bombing raids:

> It is in times of great distress that many good and many bad qualities appear in human beings. I am perfectly certain that it is human nature throughout the world, and not just a characteristic of this or that race.

The 'I am perfectly certain' is pure Mickey, and that observation, derived from his own direct experience of war, provides the counterpoint to the reading from *Dias on Jurisprudence* to which we have just listened.

And when the war was over, he stayed here. He was 24 years old. He had by now met Nora. He gave up all the manifold advantages which would have enured to him in Ceylon. A boy born with a silver spoon. And just to give us all a sense of perspective, it was an England which, despite its many, many virtues, was not only suffering the immediate after effects of the war, but it was an England in which Learie Constantine, the great West Indian cricketer, and their greatest all-rounder until Gary Sobers, was refused entry into an hotel because of the colour of his skin. Mickey would have suggested that you look it up at [1944] KB 693. The difference between Mickey and me is that he would have known that reference, and I had to look it up. But it is as well to remember that all his subsequent achievements and the legend he became depended on the young man who in England lacked any advantages at all. He was dependent on his own merit, nothing else—save of course for Nora.

And so, he started re-building his life, from 1947, with Nora at Aberystwyth. Aberystwyth can claim a few years of this illustrious career. His speciality was jurisprudence. I shall pass over the remarkably generous gesture of allowing a book to be published in joint names with the pupil who made use of the notes taken at Mickey's lectures. In the end the book was *Dias on Jurisprudence*. Some years later Zulfikar Ali Bhutto of Pakistan was being interviewed on the television. He was heard to observe that when one was faced with a group of rifle-waving Waziri tribesmen, it was no good quoting *Dias on Jurisprudence*. When he was told this story Mickey was heard to comment, 'and look what happened to Mr Bhutto'.

He came to Magdalene in 1955 as a Fellow, remaining here in Cambridge at Magdalene until his death. He was a college and university lecturer in law. The story is told that when he finished his last university lecture in 1982, the assembled undergraduates paid their respects to him with a standing ovation. In 1982 a standing ovation was much rarer than it is now.

When Michael Corbett retired in Cape Town, Mickey was sent an invitation to fly to a lunch to be held in Corbett's honour. When he arrived at the lunch he found that the table included a mass of his old pupils, judges, silks and distinguished lawyers. The lunch wasn't for Corbett at all, but for him. Those who organised it knew perfectly well that he would not have accepted the invitation if he had known the truth, that it was a lunch in his honour. But he was prepared to go for a lunch in honour of a pupil. When he was offered the full gamut of the many joys that South Africa can offer, his response was one that we all would recognise. He would love to, but he was afraid he couldn't. 'I've got a supervision to give.'

By now, tragedy had struck. We cannot avoid, and I suspect that he would have been heart-broken if we had not mentioned, Nora's tragic death in 1980. From a discussion with Julia it seems that although they had been married for over 30 years—this is my description not hers—the marriage was still a young marriage. He was desolate with grief. And the rest of his life was hollowed out—a victim of what Lamartine described when he wrote how the world could be depopulated when only one person was missing. Through all that and after it, and indeed suffering with it, the essential character and inner spirit that made him the man he was were undiminished.

Neil Jones has covered the wide extent of what Mickey taught. I would add simply that in each of these completely disparate and in many ways unconnected subjects Mickey Dias was an acknowledged master. Tennis was his game, but in cricketing terms he was a Test class batsman, bowler, wicket keeper, fielder, and umpire, brilliant at them all. The subject that most affected my career was the law of negligence, which, as he foresaw when he was talking to us, would expand rapidly through the second half of the twentieth century. It did. I used to understand it when Mickey taught it. Its expansion meant that over the latter half of the twentieth century the entire subject fell to be analysed and discussed in the House of Lords on at least 10 occasions. It is now much less clear than it was. I simply do not understand it as well as I did in 1962. If only Mickey were here to make it simple for me again. The award of the honorary rank of QC was a huge public accolade to this private man, an acknowledgement of the distinction of his scholarship and a mark of the high standing he enjoyed with those of us who practise the law.

His influence is with me still. To this day I look to my judgments to ask whether they pass the first MD test: 'Are you using precisely the right words to express precisely what you mean?' And to this day my judgments are drafted and re-drafted, until I hope my words are unambiguous and do not obfuscate my meaning. That, however, is just the language. If you like, the English. That is before you get anywhere near the law. For that came the shorter second test: 'What is the principle? What is the principle which applies to the facts of this case?' Every essay you wrote, and every tutorial you went to, required a search for the principle. And in those discussions an occasional eyebrow would be raised in surprise, and a series of questions would follow which, after you had answered a few, enabled you to recognise that you had been talking gibberish. So your thought processes re-started, enlightened by his tolerant patience of your stumbling footsteps, and, very very occasionally, stimulated by an inimitable wake up phrase.

Not so very long ago I recognised a Mickey Dias moment in the Court of Appeal when a Magdalene LJ was presiding. In those days, if the University will forgive me a moment of showing off, former pupils of Mickey's at Magdalene could have made up the entire constitution of a Court of Appeal. The case involved some very convoluted Chancery point, and the junior Lord Justice asked the question which suggested that he was way off the real point of the argument. The presiding Lord Justice showed that he had been a pupil of Mickey. He raised an eyebrow, and observed to Leading Counsel who had been asked the question:

Are you going to tell him? Or am I?

The search for principle leads to the answer to every judgment. But the search for principle is not confined to the law. Perhaps though, when Mickey was urging us to search for principle, and focusing on principle himself, he was unconsciously reflecting something of his own personality—his ethos, if you like, his life ethic. He was a man of principle. His life was governed by principle. Not physically a large man, the inner core was made of unbreakable steel, and it was simply not possible for him to waver from, let alone forsake, any principle in which he believed. I think, deep down, although at the time we would not necessarily have been able to articulate it, this was something all his pupils understood and admired.

So here we all are, a huge gathering of former pupils, colleagues from throughout the University, and friends, come from far and wide, some from abroad, some from here in Cambridge, but all of us together united to pay our respects to a great man and to salute his memory with warm affection. I am not, am I?, the only person here on whom Mickey Dias left an indelible influence.

David Thomas QC

This was my contribution published in Challenging Crime: A Portrait of
the Cambridge Institute of Criminology *(London, 2009).*

DAVID THOMAS IS the most improbable revolutionary you
could ever meet. Yet he has revolutionised the approach of
the courts in this country to sentencing. It has been a remarkable achievement—the product of an intensely inquiring mind,
close and meticulous analysis of impenetrable statutory language,
all accompanied by lively wit and warm good humour. That perhaps is why you will never find a judge who takes the slightest
umbrage at anything David says or writes. To the contrary, we want
to hear and read him.

A casual glance at the Criminal Appeal Reports of the early 1970s
will demonstrate that there was very little interest in appeals against
sentence, and even less access to them. It was possible to deduce
some desultory basic principles out of which David managed to
produce the appearance of consistency and coherence in his book,
Principles of Sentencing.[1] I still have my own copy, unfortunately of
the second edition. As I look at it, what strikes me is how slim a volume it is. Before that volume, and for some time afterwards, there
was nothing for practitioners. We all knew that the entitlement of
the state to impose punishment, and the true objectives of sentencing, and similar questions had provoked profound intellectual and
philosophical discussions. But for the sentencing decision itself,
we relied on judicial common sense and experience. There was no
structure; no real consistency of approach; no legislative interest.

David's life's work has been to illuminate the way in which the
sentencing process works in practice and, to the extent that the legislative torrent permits, to make it logical and coherent and consistent. Sentencing can never be a bureaucratic process, nor indeed can
it ever be scientific, if only because in the end every crime is specific
and the defendant is a human being with his own strengths and
weaknesses, which fall to be considered in the sentencing decision.

---

[1] DA Thomas, *Principles of Sentencing: The Sentencing Policy of the Court of Appeal
Criminal Division* (London, 1970).

In other words, in what seems to me to be the most difficult of all judicial responsibilities—the sentencing of a fellow human being—David has strived to ensure that justice should be done according to law, equally and fairly in the sentencing decisions up and down the country.

David was perhaps born with an inherent sense about the workings of most judicial minds and the art of influencing them. He has never attempted to tell us how we should perform our responsibilities, but he has supplied us with the information which enables us better to address them. What he has done is to enable all those individual judgments, and there are many tens of thousands of them annually, to be fully informed.

We have been, and we continue to be, immensely advantaged by publications for which David is responsible. He is the Editor of *Current Sentencing Practice*, the vast four-volume encyclopaedia which has replaced his single slim volume from the 1960s; *The Criminal Appeal Reports (Sentencing)*, two volumes annually, covering literally hundreds of pages; the Editor of the *Sentencing Cases* noted monthly in the *Criminal Law Review*; the Sentencing Editor of *Archbold*; author of the *Sentencing Referencer*; and a regular contributor to numerous other publications. It is why his studies of proposed legislative changes have entertained—and no less than entertained, alarmed—what can fairly be described now as generations of judges and recorders. It is why so much legislation, subjected to fair criticism by him before enactment, is so often amended because it is unworkable in precisely the way he forecast. It is why he commands the admiration, respect and affection of the judiciary and the legal professions and why the grant to him of the accolade of honorary Silk in 1996 was greeted with enthusiastic acclaim.

The legal establishment, supposedly so double-dyed conservative in its attitudes, was greeting the quiet revolutionary who had contributed so positively to the administration of justice, and applauding the overdue public recognition of that contribution.

Our Independent Judiciary

This (with the humorous beginning omitted) was my last speech as Lord Chief Justice, given at the Lord Mayor's Banquet on 3 July 2013. Readers who have got this far in the book will have read this message already, perhaps indeed more than once. Nevertheless I wish to end this selection of lectures and speeches by including my tribute to and acknowledgement of personal indebtedness to my judicial colleagues. Their daily contribution to the rule of law and the administration of justice is insufficiently appreciated and frequently underestimated.

LORD MAYOR, YOU have been very generous to me personally, and it has been an astounding privilege to have held this office. It is exactly 50 years since I was called to the Bar and in October it will be 25 years since I was appointed as a High Court Judge.

Rather than reminisce, may I offer just a few thoughts shortly before I leave the office.

The years have taught me that we have the priceless advantage of living in a country which respects the rule of law, and I believe equally respects its concomitant, the independence of the judiciary. I suspect that none of us can articulate it in quite the same way as John Locke—'where law ends, tyranny begins'—but as a community, right down to the very roots of our traditions as a nation, we have an instinctive feeling that respect for the rule of law has served us well. It has not made and it could never have made a perfect society. But without it our society would have been catastrophically worse.

I am not, of course, talking about rule by judges, or lawyers. Judges themselves are governed by the rule of law, which they are responsible for upholding without fear or favour. They cannot give judgments according to their personal whims, or prejudices, or preferences. They sometimes must give judgments contrary to their personal preferences, just because that is what the law requires. The difficulties they have to face are not always appreciated. They are easily criticised, and cannot answer back. That is what we are obliged to do. Such a responsibility cannot be fulfilled by craven judges, or pusillanimous judges, or by judges who lack fortitude, or indeed judges who fail to foresee or anticipate unintended consequences which may, however slightly, diminish their independence, without which the rule of law cannot be upheld. Vigilance therefore should be directed, not at events which in our country will not happen, but to small, even tiny little steps, which undermine these principles. That is where vigilance is needed.

It is inconceivable that in this country the army might threaten our elected government. It is inconceivable that a judge might lose office or be demoted because he or she gave judgment against the wishes of the government of the day. It is inconceivable that any minister might write to a judge, or get a secretary to telephone a judge, and let it be known that a particular result was expected. It is inconceivable that any judge, of whatever rank, would give a similar intimation to any other judge, however new, and however junior in the judicial hierarchy. None of these things have ever happened in my time. That should be a justified source of national pride. We can even say that it is most unlikely that they ever would.

But history is full of examples of the dangers of smugness, or indifference, or of taking things for granted. The future cannot be guaranteed. We never should guarantee it. Our world, the whole world, moves at breathtaking speed. We all puff and pant to keep up with it. We get caught up in the moment, and react, sometimes with little reflection, and in the haste we may fail to discern the small, tiny little steps, totally unintended tiny little steps, which might, long term, serve to undermine the principle of judicial independence upon which the rule of law depends.

Let me give one recent example. Less than 10 years ago, in 2005, and perhaps most important, although often overlooked, in 2007, spectacular changes to our constitutional arrangements were made. The independence of the individual judge in court was unaffected, but the consequences to the institutional independence of the judiciary as the third pillar of the constitution have not yet been settled. We must be cautious, meticulous in our scrutiny of any further proposals said to arise from these changes.

Let me give another example which affects everyone in this country, and indeed throughout the world. I do not think that the new world of communications and their impact on our lives has begun to be appreciated, not least because none of us has the slightest idea how they will develop in five, let alone in 10 or 20 years. Is it already beyond our ability to prevent some of the wicked suffering visited on children for the purpose of creating foul images for downloading and consumption? The speed with which information is disseminated is said to have been a crucial element in the Arab

Spring. But how do we avoid what at the moment may seem inevitable, that as this new world develops, centralisation and control will be accumulated by the authorities of the state? That would be unlikely to enhance our freedoms.

We simply have no idea where this will all end, so we must be watchfully alert. We must remain vigilant against the slightest encroachment on judicial independence, not because judicial independence represents some traditional flummery, some bauble, some meaningless superficiality, but because without an independent judiciary the rule of law would collapse. So the vigilance is needed, not for the sake of the judges, but for the security of their independence as a priceless asset to the community.

My Lord Mayor, in spite of all the difficulties, to be a judge is a great privilege, and it has been an astounding privilege for me to have held this office. From my brother and sister judges I have encountered nothing but kindness, loyalty and support, and, perhaps most important of all, true friendship, without which the responsibilities would have been crushing. I have had to ask many judges at all different levels of the judiciary if they would be prepared to take on additional burdens without additional remuneration or even much recognition, beyond my thanks. On all those myriads of occasions only twice has a judge asked to be excused, in each case revealing matters of personal disaster which had overtaken them or their families, which would have made it impossible. Without the willingness of the judges, and the toleration of their other halves of the consequent interference with their family lives, the administration of justice would collapse.

As well as thanking you and the City, my Lord Mayor, for this wonderful occasion and your generous speech, may I, through you, on behalf of both Judith and myself, express our profound gratitude to them all. The memories will keep us warm for as long as memory lasts. We shall miss you.